BUSINESSPAPER
PUBLISHING
PRACTICE

BUSINESSPAPER
PUBLISHING
PRACTICE

Edited by Julien Elfenbein

Editorial Director, Home Furnishing Group,
The Haire Publishing Company; Instructor
in Businesspaper and House Organ Journalism, New York University; Author of
Business Journalism

HARPER & BROTHERS, PUBLISHERS, NEW YORK

Library of Congress catalog card number: 52-5720

To

Jacob Kay Lasser

AUTHOR · EDITOR · TEACHER · MATHEMATICIAN

CONTENTS

Types of Businesspapers
Salaries
Definition of the Good Businesspaper
Functions of the Businesspaper

Introduction
How a Businesspaper Publishing House Is Organized,
   N. O. Wynkoop
Fundamentals in Businesspaper Accounting, *J. K.
   Lasser*

Circulation in an Expanding Economy
Businesspaper Circulation Fundamentals, *Floyd L.
   Hockenhull*
Determining Type, Quality, and Volume of Circula-
   tion, *Arthur H. Dix*
Building the Mailing List, *Gardiner Gibbs*
Twenty-five Do's and Don't's on Direct Mail, *Stanley
   R. Clague*
Reader Turnover, *R. O. Eastman*
What a Publisher Expects of His Circulation Mana-
   ger, *G. D. Crain, Jr.*

PREFACE

The American business press is advertised by one large publishing house as "the intercom system"[1] of private competitive enterprise. That is a neat way of saying it.

Our business press communicates to management the vital intelligence on which management makes operating and policy decisions; it also communicates the know-how for carrying out those decisions (equally important). This intercom system covers all the specialized work areas of industry. Industry with a capital "I" includes the professions, the sciences, and the trades—all human activity.[2]

Operating this vast business intercom system—collecting, processing, interpreting, and distributing technical know-how and intelligence in a way to profit not only the reader but the publisher as well—requires a certain kind of publishing know-how. This volume contains the publishing know-how. It was made possible by the generous unlocking of private storehouses of expert knowledge. It contains the know-how of businesspaper publishing and editorial practice as explained by leading practitioners: publishers, editors, and advertising, circulation, production, and promotion managers; and by authorities in the related practices of accountancy, advertising agency, the graphic arts, marketing, research, public relations, education, law, and government.

The book is in three parts: Administration, Editorial Department, and Public Responsibility.

Part One (Administration) defines the terms, the medium, and the field, and describes the administrative processes which function to produce and deliver periodically to management that compact package of know-how called the businesspaper.

Part Two (Editorial Department) is concerned with editors and their staffs, pressures under which they work, the highlights of their problems, among them being the changing attitudes and habits of their readers and the changing architecture of the magazine.

---

[1] Intercommunication system.
[2] See *Business Journalism*, Harper & Brothers, New York, 1945, Chapter II, p. 25, for new classification of industry.

Part Three (Public Responsibility) is concerned with the relation-ship that exists between editors and publishers and their several publics: the managers of private and public enterprises, utilities, institutions, departments and agencies of Government, and their own personnel. Those laws and regulations governing the conduct of the business press and the codified precepts laid down by the businesspaper publishing industry and its allies for their own behavior and moral guidance should be obtained by students (see Chapter 16) and studied in relation to these chapters.

"Agenda for the Future" contains some sharply analytical observa-tions by men selected for their constructive thinking. It is hoped these readings will not only stimulate the interest of the next generation of businesspaper editors and publishers but, in the meantime, cause present-day members of the business press to raise their sights to higher pro-fessional levels.

The businesspaper, or trade journal, or industrial magazine, or busi-ness newspaper as they call it in Canada, is above all else a continuous textbook of adult education. It is the textbook used by the Atomic Energy Commission, the Bureau of Mines, Rockefeller Hospital, R. H. Macy, the neighborhood store, General Motors, Merck Research Laboratories, Farmer Jones, the New York Stock Exchange, the man-agement of the Waldorf-Astoria, the A&P, The *New York Times,* the butcher, baker, and electric light bulb maker.

The businesspaper editor is a teacher—with this difference: he draws his text for tomorrow's lesson out of today's competitive struggle to make a living—a struggle going on all around him and of which he himself is a part, because every good businesspaper has one or more competitors.

There has been a growing demand among members of the working business press for a single, collected source of practical know-how about contemporary businesspaper publishing practice. Editors of internal and external house magazines have asked for it. Teachers and under-graduate students in schools of journalism have made repeated requests for a larger body of knowledge on the specialized business press.

Even more apparent has been the need for a book such as this among students and graduates of other professional schools: such as schools of business administration and management, finance and accounting, industrial relations, advertising, marketing, salesmanship, merchandising, retailing, engineering, agriculture, insurance, the sciences, medicine, law, and government.

The greatest drawback to the efficient and intelligent transmission of technical know-how in any field has been the absence or scarcity of professional skill and knowledge in the specific arts and sciences of *communication* itself. Paraphrasing an observation by Dr. Glenn Frank:[3]

The scholar is inspired by the passion to understand; the business journalist is inspired by the passion to be understood. Functioning in isolation each falls short of his maximum ministry to his time.

It is hoped that this volume will be helpful to the staffs of medical journals, law journals, agricultural, scientific, engineering, and other technical professional or industrial publications, as well as to those students in technical and professional schools and colleges who wish to prepare themselves for professional careers in technical journalism. The word professional is used consciously. The business press, because it requires better educated beginners and imposes a more scientific discipline, will eventually develop the standards for professionalism in journalism. The businessman himself, as Dr. Vannevar Bush told a group of engineers recently, is gradually becoming a professional man. In the past half century of college journalism instruction, teachers, textbook writers and others actively engaged in the practice have encouraged the concept that journalism is a profession. And, like schools of law and medicine, schools of journalism have become more concerned each succeeding decade with the need for (1) ethical standards of practice and procedure, (2) a better body of authoritative knowledge, (3) a training program under the supervision of professionals, (4) more attention to the specialisms of the profession, (5) and knowledge of the economics of publishing.

On reflection, education in the specialized fields of journalism seems to have made greater strides than in newspaper journalism. Today only about five per cent of our American colleges and universities have accredited schools of journalism after almost half a century of teaching newspaper journalism. We see more and more journalism schools which a few years back were devoted only to the newspaper editorial department now giving courses in magazine, businesspaper, and house organ

[3] Glenn Frank, *Thunder and Dawn*, New York, The Macmillan Co., 1932, p. 148.

journalism, and in many phases of publishing practice.[4] And the editors of house magazines and businesspapers hold clinics, seminars, and workshops with greater frequency than newspaper journalists.

In a world which depends so much on a free press, and in which the free press is under constant attack, the broad professional education of future publishers and/or owners of all means of mass communication is an important matter. In one of his periodic letters to the business press, Roy Eastman,[5] research consultant to numerous businesspaper publishing houses, wrote:

> The familiarity of the average publisher seems to run about in this order: he knows considerable about his competitors, including a lot of things that are not so. Then he knows almost as much about his own business. But he knows relatively little about the publishing business as a whole.

Which would indicate that there is more truth than poetry on the dedication page of A. J. Liebling's book on journalism,[6] where one finds this inscription:

> *"To the Foundation of a School for Publishers*
> *Failing Which,*
> *No School of Journalism Can Have Meaning."*

Rye, N. Y.   J.E.

---

[4] Joseph Pulitzer, in his will which endowed the Columbia University School of Journalism, forbade any courses on the "business" side of journalism.

[5] "The Isolation of the Publisher," New York, The Eastman Research Organization, January 22, 1945.

[6] *The Wayward Pressman*, Garden City, N. Y., Doubleday & Company, 1947.

ACKNOWLEDGMENTS

In the past decade two great universities situated in the principal publishing centers of the American business press began to take an active interest in business journalism.

Finally, in 1948, in cooperation with The Associated Business Publications, the Division of Adult Education of New York University and the Medill School of Journalism of Northwestern University (Chicago Campus) instituted lectures and seminars on businesspaper publishing practice.

Under the personal guidance of Dean Paul H. McGhee of New York University and Dean Kenneth E. Olson of Northwestern, leaders of the business press planned the courses, gave the lectures, and conducted the seminars.

A total of 1323 members of the working business press, from publishers and editors down to reception clerks and office boys, attended the first two-year courses. It was an extraordinary experiment in industry reorientation and objectivity. Many journalism students also attended these special courses in Chicago and New York City.

The generosity of C. Laury Botthof of Standard Rate & Data Service made possible the wire-recording of many of the Chicago lectures and several of the seminars. While most lectures at New York University were given from outlines, a few were written out. Several were recorded.

Some of the recorded lectures are included in the present volume. Other materials include papers written for the advertising and marketing businesspapers and some delivered as speeches before trade associations, publishers' groups, editorial societies, business organizations, and university classes. George Dusenbury graciously assented to my publishing the notes taken during his lectures to the business press.

Essentials and conclusions of several important research studies are incorporated in this volume: "Fundamentals in Businesspaper Accounting," by J. K. Lasser in the chapter on Accounting (Chapter 2); two privately printed studies made under the direction of Walter Botthof and C. Laury Botthof of Standard Rate & Data Service: "How Businesspaper Advertising Space Is Bought" (Chapter 4) and "Ways to Promote

More Businesspaper Advertising Space Sales" (Chapter 6); the procedures and conclusions of the "Continuing Study of Business Papers," by the Advertising Research Foundation (Chapter 5); and "A Survey of Public Relations Activities of Businesspapers" (Chapter 14). I am grateful for the privilege of presenting them.

My special thanks must be expressed to Edward Bernays who wrote an article especially for the final chapter, to Colonel Willard Chevalier for his special article on Personnel (Chapter 15), to D. B. Chase for his special article on Profit-Sharing Trusts (Chapter 15), to John R. Pearson for the specially prepared summary of Postal Laws and Regulations (Chapter 16), to Roy Quinlan for permission to use the material in Chapter 12.

I wish to express my appreciation to the editors and publishers, writers, authors, teachers, and other authorities who cooperated in the development of this volume. It is regretted that space limitation prevented the inclusion of many other valuable papers and materials.

Thanks are due the National Industrial Advertisers Association, Arch Crawford of The National Association of Magazine Publishers, A. W. Lehman of The Advertising Research Foundation, "Doc" Kynett of Audit Bureau of Circulation, and Adin L. Davis of Controlled Circulation Audit Bureau. My appreciation is extended to the publishers of the various advertising and marketing periodicals for permission to use materials.

I am deeply indebted to my own publisher, Andrew J. Haire, Sr., for great encouragement; to Arnold Friedman, chairman of the board, James G. Lyne, former chairman, William K. Beard, Jr., president, and to the members of Associated Business Publications for a grant; and to Irene Pearson and James Corke of the ABP staff. My thanks to Robert E. Harper and Russell L. Putman of National Business Publications; to Stanley Knisely, N. O. Wynkoop, Joseph Gerardi, Roy Eastman, Carroll B. Larrabee, Reginald Clough, Eldridge Peterson, Lyman Forbes, Angelo Venezian and James Blackburn; also to Robert S. Kenyon, Jr., R. A. Trenkmann, and J. K. Lasser of the Education Committee of ABP.

My indebtedness is large to my students at the College of the City of New York and New York University whose comment and criticism helped so much; to my own staff and my secretary, Marie Puglis.

J.E.

Part One

Administration

*"Education is the acquisition of the art
of the utilization of knowledge"*

ALFRED NORTH WHITEHEAD

CHAPTER 1

The Businesspaper as a
Career Opportunity*

One of the most rewarding of all careers in journalism is on the business press. Not monetary reward alone, although here men and women do find decent hours and good pay. They also find real opportunity to write, edit, teach and sell; to do product and market research; to specialize in advertising, sales promotion, sales training, production, copy-writing, the graphic arts, public relations, circulation, accountancy, personnel or library work.

To the creative mind competitive business enterprise is a great adventure. The business journalist finds action in the market place, among the producers and distributors of goods and services and all the creative people who help them make decisions, make ideas work. They make the real news, the big news that is changing the course of the world. The highest skill is required of those who cover business. But like all important careers in our industrial society the demand is not only for skills such as straight thinking and clear expression but also for moral qualities such as simplicity, candor, courage, and social responsibility and "the power of distinguishing what is first-rate from what is not."[1]

TYPES OF BUSINESSPAPERS

First let us be clear in our minds what is meant by a *businesspaper*[2] or *business magazine*. The businesspaper is not a house organ like *Dun's*

* Julien Elfenbein, *Journalism Quarterly*, Sept., 1948, Vol. 25, No. 3, p. 233. This material has been brought up to date and supplemented with new material.

[1] Sir Richard Livingstone, *Some Tasks for Education*, London, Oxford University Press, 1946, p. 49.

[2] There is no more reason to separate the word *businesspaper* into two words (although it is a frequent practice) than there is to separate the word *newspaper*

Review.[3] It is not a trade association bulletin like *NAM News.*[4] It is not a government publication like *Domestic Commerce.* It is not a catalogue or trade directory. The businesspaper is a specialized periodical

TABLE 1.   TYPES OF TECHNICAL PERIODICALS*
(Number, Circulation, and Receipts)

Periodicals	Number of periodicals published	Aggregate circulation per issue	Receipts (in thousands of dollars) Subscriptions and sales	Advertising
Agriculture and farm, general	95	16,514,389	$ 5,962	$ 32,098
Agriculture and farm, specialized	144	6,004,983	1,985	8,972
Business and finance	127	2,013,301	14,032	17,179
Educational	177	14,565,480	11,030	1,705
Labor	183	3,694,105	3,511	3,366
Legal	85	273,256	1,831	1,488
Medical and dental	143	1,893,790	4,668	6,724
Military and Naval	21	622,199	1,206	635
Religious	951	47,190,846	36,050	6,702
Science and technology	106	3,917,811	7,593	6,065
Trade: merchandising	472	5,310,482	7,655	54,693
Trade: professional, institutional, and service	298	3,099,216	6,114	25,032
Trade: industrial, engineering and technical	489	6,165,707	8,829	70,592
University, college, and school	17	64,160	106	312
Totals	3,308	111,329,725	$116,592	$238,653†

* U. S. Census of Manufactures: 1947, MC27A, p. 12, Table 6J (Published in 1949).
† See Tables 11 and 12.

of editorial opinion, technical know-how, and news information, independently owned and operated, like *Editor & Publisher* or *Iron Age.*

into two words. The veteran newspaperman, Carl Kesler, editor of the *Quill* of Sigma Delta Chi, concurred in this opinion in his March, 1948, editorial. Prof. Roland E. Wolseley favors the combination word "businessmagazine" (*The Magazine World*, Prentice-Hall, New York, 1951, p. 76).

[3] Published by Dun & Bradstreet.
[4] Official publication of the National Association of Manufacturers.

The term *magazine* is generic like the word *pot*. You have flower pots, tea pots, and the more or less obsolete type with two handles. You also have pressure cookers, electric coffee makers, double boilers, deep well cookers—all of the *genus* pot.

Businesspapers are published monthly in most instances, semimonthly, or weekly, and have one of these formats: 8×11, 9×12, or 11×11 inches (square), side-stitched, coated stock, attractive cover. A few are published daily in newspaper format, ranging from $11\frac{3}{4} \times 12\frac{1}{2}$ to $16\frac{1}{2} \times 22\frac{3}{4}$ inches. The standard editorial and advertising page is 7×10 inches. Advertising rates vary from $100 a page to several thousand dollars a page, depending on such factors as number and type of readers, their purchasing and influencing power, position of the advertising, size, frequency, use of color, publishing costs, tradition, etc.[5] Units of space sold are as little as an inch to 16- and 32-page sections. Deadlines vary with publications and publication dates. Usually two weeks to twenty days elapse between copy deadlines and publication delivery dates on monthly magazines.

That is where the similarity with any other type of magazine or newspaper ends.

Inside the businesspaper you find no circus make-up, no crime or sex stories, no "itchy, prurient journalism,"[6] no sin swathed in morality, no fiction, no gossip, no politics, no sports, no comics, no Hollywood or Broadway. On the staff of the businesspaper you find no multiple-minded master writers telling readers about Lana Turner's latest mate or the Kinsey report.

Before examining the career opportunities on the businesspaper, let us appraise some of the other types of business publications.

Published in the United States are 5741 internal and external house organs[7] and, of course, thousands of educational, religious, and labor association journals, Chamber of Commerce bulletins, government publications, trade directories, etc.

The internal and external house publication is subsidized by a single business organization, designed to discuss favorably a house's own prod-

---

[5] See Chapter 4 (Advertising) for additional information on rates and rate cards.
[6] Dale Kramer, "Don't Make 'Em Mad," *New Republic*, Dec. 1, 1947, p. 19. An analysis of the publishing formula of the Cowles Brothers, publishers of *Look*.
[7] *Printers' Ink Directory of House Organs*, New York, Printers' Ink Publishing Co., November, 1950. Listed 5552. A supplement listed 5741 (*Printers' Ink*, July 20, 1951).

ucts and services and to promote better employee, investor, customer, and public relations for that house.

Taken all together American house publications are an important "industrial press," but I have never seen a house organ publish unfavorable criticism of itself, its product, or its own house or disagree with its readers, and most of them shy away from controversy on "touchy" subjects. The same is true, naturally, of government publications.

The trade association bulletin is the official mouthpiece of a group of business units representing one particular segment of industry. Such bulletins are concerned with the economic welfare of their own membership. They never criticize their own membership or publish adverse criticism of their own activities; and seldom, if ever, do they subordinate the major objectives of their association to any outside interest when it may work a hardship on their own membership.

I do not impugn the editorial integrity of business magazines subsidized by trade associations, government bureaus, or private corporations, nor do I minimize the high value of their contribution to our industrial society. I simply state their limitations. Editorial policy can only be independent on a business publication that is independently owned and operated by men of high character.

The "general" magazine publishing industry reported 453 titles with an aggregate circulation of 117,174,235 per issue in 1947.[8] In terms of aggregate circulation per issue the largest single class of magazines is *comics*,[9] with nearly 89,478,359 readers per issue. Religious and fiction groups are runners-up in large circulation—especially the "pulps."

If we include as the business press such types as are arbitrarily established by the Census[10] the number of titles would be 3308, with an aggregate circulation of 111,329,725 readers. Most authorities eliminate the religious groups and give the business press about 1964 titles with a circulation of 28,989,867. This includes pass-along readership.

One type identified as "Trade, Merchandising, Professional and Industrial, Business and Finance," with 1386 titles and an aggregate circulation per issue of 16,588,706, comes closer to identifying the actual businesspaper field. Within this class are 658 audited businesspapers

---

[8] Fashion, fiction, home and garden, and "general interest." All figures have been revised to give the most recent tabulations. The U. S. Census of 1947 was published in 1949. See Table 1.

[9] The term "comics" is a misnomer. Many of these are crime and horror magazines which publish the know-how of crime and juvenile deliquency.

[10] See Table 1.

which offer, in my opinion, a great service opportunity to students who wish to make a professional career of journalism.[11]

The reason becomes obvious in an analysis of this readership: The 16 and a half million businesspaper readers are the technical and professional managers of human enterprise throughout our land. They make the decisions which affect the remaining 137 million ordinary people in America for tomorrow, or next month, or the next twenty years, whether or not many of those ordinary people even know how to read or how to reason.[12]

TABLE 2. READERS OF THE BUSINESS PRESS AND THEIR BUYING POWER*

Type of business	Owners, managers, and officials	Professional & semi-professional
Manufacturing	756,000	655,000
Construction	353,000	
Transportation, communication, & other public utilities	403,000	101,000
Wholesale & retail trade	3,024,000	151,000
Finance, insurance, & real estate	352,000	
Professional & related services	100,000	2,218,000
Government	302,000	252,000
All others	510,000	523,000
TOTALS	5,800,000	3,900,000

* From "Mechanizing Your Sales With Business Paper Advertising," a booklet published by McGraw-Hill, New York, 1948.
Conservative opinions set industrial purchases at 50 per cent of all buying in dollar value. The business and industrial market is well over one hundred million dollars.
Bureau of Census population figures total about 149,000,000, but of this total less than 59,000,000 are employed (labor force). Of the labor force there is a total of owners and managers numbering 5,800,000 and a total of professional and semi-professional people number 3,900,000. These two totals give you the 9 to 10 million described above as buying influences and they represent the type readership of the business press.

The businesspaper readers—only 11 per cent of the population—hold in trust the mass direction of men, materials, money, methods, and the media of communication—not only here but in vast areas of the world.

The chief responsibility for transmitting wider understanding to these

[11] Of the 1964 listings in the Business Paper Section of Standard Rate & Data Service (May 21, 1951 issue) 364 are ABC audited; 294, CCA audited; 1025, furnished sworn circulation reports on SRDS forms; 281, show no specific circulation figures (this includes annuals). The ABC and CCA businesspapers total 658.

[12] Total U. S. population including armed forces overseas, 153,900,000 (May 1, 1951).

decision-making managers, and through them to the rest of mankind, lies with the editors of these specialized independent technical periodicals.

What these businesspaper editors can do today to give wider understanding to their readers (the exceptional 11 per cent) will determine

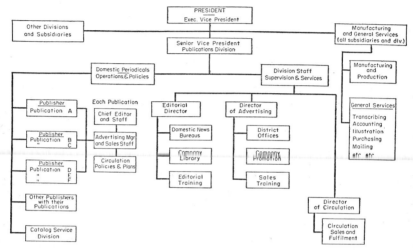

FIG. 1   Organization Chart of a multiple businesspaper publishing house. Under the heading of "Division, Staff, Supervisor and Services," the editorial director and the director of advertising have certain responsibilities which are included. They also have certain line responsibilities, as indicated. They serve as staff advisers and supervisors to assist the senior vice-president, in the operation of the publications through the several publishers. The "Manufacturing and Production" department was organized that its various units deal directly with the publishers and the publications so far as every-day operations are concerned, but the matter of contracts for the paper, printing, engraving and the other manufacturing operations is consolidated in the "Manufacturing and Staff Services" department for all the publications, books, international activities, etc. While the general services are under the one consolidated manager so far as their operations are concerned, the various service departments are so divided that specialized sections are available to serve the various operating divisions of the company.

the ultimate decision reached by the ordinary man about whether he wants private enterprise to keep on creating workable ideas for greater production and fuller employment; whether he wants our competitive system to keep on delivering a higher standard of living to more and more ordinary men; or whether he wants to scrap it all in favor of a big benevolent government or a big labor monopoly always battling a big business monopoly until both monopolies are gobbled up by a big police state which its propaganda journalists will describe as "the people's government."

SALARIES

On businesspapers the salaries vary according to the department, the job, the training, experience and the field. In highly technical and professional fields people are sought with specialized training and experience. See Chapter 15 on Personnel for a discussion of aptitude evaluation, screening, training, and incentive plans which, together with hours, vacations and other employe benefits are related to the question, "What is the salary?"

Compensation on businesspapers is good. Beginners are not started at high salaries but often receive more than general magazines or newspapers pay. On the country's leading businesspapers the chief editor's secretary receives a better salary than the average newspaper reporter. Businesspaper news editors receive better pay than the managers of press association bureaus which are outside the big cities.

J. K. Lasser in 1950 completed a special survey of the salary structures of 51 publishing firms which account for some 125 publications and about $130 million in annual revenue. Three-fourths of the magazines canvassed were businesspapers.

The Lasser study[13] covered all the major executive groups that go to make up the operating staffs of a publication: editorial staff, advertising and promotion heads, space salesmen, and circulation departments.

Salesmen's earnings vary in relation to the publication's annual billings. Larger companies have more salesmen in the higher earnings bracket. Where annual gross billings run over $2,500,000, an average of 15 per cent of the salesmen make over $15,000 a year. Only 5 per cent make over $15,000 where billings are from $500,000 to $1,000,000.

Although many companies still pay straight salaries for salesmen, the trend in recent years has run heavily toward salary plus commission on sales beyond individual quotas.

Where salesmen get straight commission plus expenses, the most common rate is 10 per cent. But on some magazines it is 8 per cent; on several others it is 11 to 12½ per cent; in one case, 13 per cent. Commission

[13] See *Tide*, March 10, 1950, pp. 46, 47.

percentages traditionally go down as the size per order increases. Straight commissions below 5 per cent are found at page rates above $4000. Where salesmen pay their own expenses they usually get from 12½ to 14 per cent. The standard commission to outside representatives is 20 per cent—sometimes 25 per cent where volume is small.

Where salesmen get salary plus commission, the commission percentage varies. Commissions of 7 to 8 per cent are given most often, but 5 and 10 per cent are common, as are sliding scales which run from 5 to 10 per cent.

Advertising directors of groups of publications average from $12,000 to $40,000 a year, depending on billings. The advertising director on a group of publications with annual billings of over $2,500,000 will get $31,900; where billings run under $500,000, the average diretcor's take is $12,700.

Advertising managers of individual publications get from $5500 to $32,000 a year. Advertising managers' average on publications over $2,500,000 is $25,400. Publications with annual billings under $250,-000 pay their advertising managers an average of $9000.

Paychecks for sales promotion managers ran from $5000 to $17,000. An average of $6300 went to those working for publications with annual billings from $500,000 to $1,000,000—those on publications billing over $2,500,000 averaged $12,500.

In the circulation department, salaries were geared to circulation. Since new or rapidly growing magazines often pay higher salaries than normal, there is no fixed ratio between salary and present circulation.

Circulation managers on business publications, where circulations are substantially smaller than consumer magazines, varied from $3000 to $11,000. Those under 25,000 paid an average of $4100; from 25,000 to 50,000, the average jumped to $8000; from 50,000 to 100,000 it reached $9600.

Where the field sales manager post exists, it usually rates a salary of 50 to 80 per cent of the circulation manager's in the same company. The average runs about 70 per cent as much. Field supervisors or assistant sales managers draw from $6000 to $16,000, up to 80 per cent of the earnings of the manager.

Barely a fourth of the companies covered in the survey had field selling forces of their own. Unlike advertising salesmen, subscription salesmen usually get a straight commission. Where circulation ran from 25,000 to 50,000, 56 per cent of the subscription salesmen made less than $3000 a year.

Considerable spread in editorial salaries shows up because of such factors as length of service, company policy, division of responsibility, etc. But the general level for any group seems to depend on the size of the publication. There is no consistent salary difference between consumer and business publications of similar size.

When an editorial director is responsible for several publications with a total annual revenue of over $2,500,000, he gets an average of $22,-600. Where annual revenue runs from $500,000 to $1,000,000, the average salary is $11,900. Lowest editorial director's salary was $10,-000; highest was $35,000.

Editors of single publications got from $3500 to $24,000. Where revenue was under $100,000, the salaries averaged $6400; from $500,-000 to $750,000, the average was $13,200; over $2,500,000, it hit $21,200.[14]

Assistant editors' salaries went from a low of $2700 to a high of $16,-000. The salary spread covers a wide range. For instance, on publications with an average revenue of over $2,500,000, the lowest assistant editor's salary was $4200, highest was $16,000. For publications with revenue under $500,000, the average salary ranged from $3300 to $4500.

Most publications apparently let the circulation manager handle direct mail. Where the post of direct-mail promotion manager existed, it usually carried a salary of $4500. The high was $7000.

In our own shop the hours are 9 to 5 Monday through Friday. Saturday is a holiday all year round. Two weeks vacation with full pay is allowed to all employees with the firm a year. Longer vacations are provided with longer service. We have group life, hospital, and surgical insurance, and a profit-sharing trust for every employee. Similar insurance, medical, pension, and profit-sharing plans exist in many publishing houses of the business press.[15] The editorial and sales staffs have liberal entertainment and traveling expense accounts. They travel extensively, usually by air, and are instructed to use the best accommodations. They are provided with everything they need in the way of clerical help, equipment, services, books, and magazines to increase their efficiency. Promotions take place within the organization in preference to seeking outsiders, whenever possible.

[14] Lasser calculates editorial salaries as "ten to twelve per cent of gross income." See Chapter 2 (Accounting).

[15] See Chapter 15.

The businesspaper needs men and women who are intellectually mature and intellectually curious. They must know how a contemporary society operates and what its problems are. The men and women we need must not only be educated in the specialisms of the communications industry but also in the liberal arts, the ethical and social sciences, and in citizenship as background for the privilege of operating or directing our type of communication lines.

My colleague, Philip Swain, chief editor of *Power* and *Operating Engineer,* who must hire graduate engineers on his staff, complains that many candidates for editorial posts are so occupied with their specialisms that they have failed to achieve a view of science as a whole, or an integrative point of view concerning our competitive society; and, sadly, they also have failed to learn how to communicate with crystal clearness what they do know, to others, or how to *listen* intelligently to ideas which others want to communicate to them.[16]

Each semester I give one lecture to my classes on the subject, "How to Think Effectively." College students in New York City are certainly among the most alert in the world. They ask a thousand and one questions of an instructor, but never in my experience has a student asked this question: "How does one think?"

In the report of the Harvard Committee,[17] communication is defined as the ability to express one's self so as to be understood by others. Obviously, this is inseparable from effective thinking.

"In most thinking," the report continues, "one is talking to one's self; and good speech and writing are the visible test and sign of good thinking . . . communication is not speaking only but listening as well; you cannot succeed in communicating your ideas unless the other person wishes to hear and knows how to listen."[18]

In vain I have searched among university bulletins and prejournalism courses or professional courses of schools of journalism for a course labeled "How to Think Effectively." Other subjects which suggest themselves are "How to Use Books," "How to Spell and Punctuate," "How to Talk" (to one person, a group of 12, or 1200), "How to Organize a Meeting, a Clinic, a Forum, a Dinner, or Preside Over a Committee."

---

[16] See Chapter 10.

[17] *General Education in a Free Society,* Cambridge, Mass., Harvard University Press, 1945, p. 67.

[18] *Ibid.,* p. 68.

Another would be: How to walk into an office, sit in a chair, what to do with one's hat, coat and brief case, how to make and *keep* a business appointment, how to telephone or write a letter soliciting an interview or a job—a course, in short, in "Business Manners."

Training is needed in practical methods of research, in the use and misuse of statistics and measurements, in the dangers of abstraction, the nature of proof, the pitfalls of language, the logic of definition, thought, conduct, the laws of organization, the techniques of pressure groups.

Smatterings and snippets of these subjects are now taught. I am suggesting them as subjects for *whole* courses.

In the first report of the President's Commission on Higher Education for American Democracy there appears this paragraph:

> It is essential today that education come decisively to grips with the world-wide crisis of mankind. This is no careless or uncritical use of words. No thinking person doubts that we are living in a decisive moment of human society.[19]

What better place for a career than on a publication devoted to the world's greatest need—adult education?

DEFINITION OF THE GOOD BUSINESSPAPER*

The good businesspaper is the continuous textbook of adult education for managers, both in its editorial and advertising columns. It is the up-to-the-minute, automatically self-correcting textbook in every technical and professional field. The good businesspaper does five specific things for American decision-makers. It provides:

1. Practical economics for advancing the status of every industry and profession.

2. The know-how for stimulating and preserving fair competition, for increasing production, improving methods and techniques, lowering costs, and elevating the working and living standards of employees.

3. The distribution technologies for delivering a higher standard of

[19] Excerpts from the first report of the President's Commission on Higher Education, *New York Times,* Dec. 16, 1947.

* Julien Elfenbein, from "The Challenge to America's Decision-Makers," a paper read before The Second Annual Magazine Forum, National Association of Magazine Publishers, Waldorf-Astoria, April 28, 1948; the definition was repeated in an address before the Cleveland Chapter, American Association of Advertising Agencies, on January, 1950, and published in the April, 1950, issue of *Advertising Agency.* Stanley Knisely, former executive v.p. of ABP first used the expression "continuous textbook."

living to more family units and a consequent higher purchasing power for goods and services.

4. The training, discipline, and inspiration for human leadership.

5. The impartial, documented, pragmatic editorial criticism which is the prophylaxis of the private competitive free enterprise system.

FUNCTIONS OF THE BUSINESSPAPER*

Nine basic functions performed by the businesspaper itself may be summarized as follows:

1. *Adult education function:* providing the technical "know-how": information on management, maintenance, materials handling, methodology, marketing, and merchandising.

2. *News function:* gathering, processing, and disseminating business news-intelligence: news of products and services, materials and methods, equipment and processes; news of people.

3. *Editorial function:* criticizing, guiding, crusading, and pioneering to advance the status of the individual and the industry, trade, or profession of which he is a part. Interpreting the meaning of news events and forecasting trends.

4. *Forum function:* Town Hall-in-print. A meeting place in the editorial columns for discussion and criticism by the readers of all phases of business and professional enterprise, including criticism of the businesspaper itself.

5. *Advertising function:* selling and merchandising goods and services in print and enlarging the "know how" of industry by means of paid advertising messages.

6. *Research function:* periodic engagement in and publication of market analyses, audience and readership surveys, product studies, and studies of buying, selling, and operating procedure and performance.

7. *Public relations function:* giving information to its various "publics": advertisers and potential advertisers, readers, advertising agencies, news associations, wire services, other media, trade associations, institutions, research groups, government, labor, its own employees, stockholders, investors, and the ultimate consumer.

8. *Public utility function:* the responsibility to give the reader all sides of important questions; to keep the columns open to statements from

---

* Julien Elfenbein, from a lecture, "The Use of Business and Trade Papers," before the Eleventh Annual Advertising Course sponsored by the Chicago Federated Advertising Club and the Women's Advertising Club of Chicago, Kimball Hall, Chicago, January 26, 1948.

the readers; the responsibility to provide continuous service at fair rates in return for the franchise from the public which guarantees freedom to the press to print the truth without fear or prejudice or revelation of sources.

9. *Industrial statesmanship function:* the performance of this function depends upon the attitudes of publishers as well as editors, an awareness of their social responsibilities, a sense of public trusteeship, a sense of identification with and appreciation of the interdependence of all human industry, of the relationship of the parts to the whole economic system, a devotion to what is known in law as the "public interest." To put the larger interest above any sectional, group, or private interest is to perform the function of statesmanship, whether you are a journalist or any other kind of public servant. A world loyalty is, of course, the best of all.

"You can help to show that greed, selfishness and arrogant power on the part of any group may lead to disaster in the nation," James B. Carey told businesspaper editors who had invited the youthful labor leader to address their body.

. . . There is a deep feeling in the ranks of labor, and I think the public generally [he said], that the business press is an obedient mouthpiece for the great corporations that dominate their industries. I know that is not an entirely true picture . . . you can prove it is not true by your independence in viewing our critical national issues and your willingness to give voice to points of view that the great corporations and their advertising executives might not like.[20]

A Secretary of Commerce, fifteen years earlier, Dan Roper, expressed his concept of the ninth function in these words:

There is no better forum for the expression of business ideals and for the creation of a spirit of cooperation and cohesiveness than the trade paper. Here, I believe, should start the enforcement of such agreements as are necessary and desirable for satisfactory business operation and for the service of the public, and which have behind them the sanction of honest and sincere business men.[21]

[20] James B. Carey, Secretary-Treasurer, CIO, from an address before the National Conference of Business Paper Editors, Hotel Plaza, New York, October 17, 1950.
[21] Daniel C. Roper, Secretary of Commerce of the United States in the Cabinet of Franklin D. Roosevelt, from a letter written January 8, 1935, to George S. Herrick, Universal Trade Press Syndicate, published in a pamphlet "The Future of the American Business Press," February, 1935.

Another Secretary of Commerce, Herbert Hoover, in a message to the business press in 1925, interpreted the ninth function this way:

The schools and colleges have an important place; the trade associations can do much in the fields of production and distribution; the Government bureaus that keep in contact with business can help promote sound leadership in industrial and economic thinking. All have an important place, but the business and technical journals are in the unique position . . . your great group of journals can not only recognize and support sound industrial leadership but you can also initiate it.

Secretary Hoover saw the business press as an important communication line between the State and industry. He began inviting businesspaper editors to his offices in Washington for informal conferences soon after his appointment by President Harding. These meetings resulted in the formation of the National Conference of Business Paper Editors. Mr. Hoover continued these intimate meetings with the business press when he became President of the United States, just as succeeding presidents have done.

In the three great crises of this century our country has called on administrators from large business corporations to head national defense. There was Baruch in World War I. There was Knudsen of General Motors and Nelson of Sears Roebuck in World War II, and Wilson of General Electric and Eric Johnston in the Korean war. Each of these administrators, as one of his first acts of office, called together businesspaper editors and proposed that the business press initiate leadership for industry in the national emergency.

"During the war days," said Charles Wilson, addressing editors and publishers in 1949, "if it had not been for the help of the business press I don't know what we would have done. The business press created miracles of production during the war years by their efforts. I will be ever grateful for the business press."[22]

Executives of individual businesses are not well situated to see the position of an industry as a whole [declared Dr. Neil H. Jacoby[23] at a session of

[22] Charles Edward Wilson, former President, General Electric Company; former Executive Vice Chairman, U. S. War Production Board, World War II (1942-1944); former Director, Office of Defense Mobilization; from an address before the Business Paper Advisory Committee of The Advertising Council in the University Club, New York.

[23] Neil H. Jacoby, Ph.D., Secretary of the University of Chicago and Professor of Finance; former Dean, School of Business Administration, University of California, from an address before the Chicago Business Paper Editors Association, Chicago, May 15, 1944.

Chicago Business Paper Editors] because they are daily engaged—as they should be—in the competitive struggle with other enterprises. Trade organizations likewise do not generally possess wide channels of information between the industry as a whole and its individual members. The business press sits squarely astride such channels. Consequently, the business press has an opportunity to step in and perform a function of industrial statesmanship that definitely needs to be discharged.

The business press should not limit its functions to that of a mere recorder of trade information. It should strive to become the statesman and leader of the industry it serves. The goal of the businesspaper should be no less than to foresee the changing relations of its industry to the whole economic system, and to point out to the members of that industry the broad lines of adjustment that they should make.

Finally, a businesspaper performs its highest function "by serving as the conscience of its industry," according to one leader of business. This is the way he put it:[24]

Every industry, and every company in it, is constantly tempted by the necessary pressure of the times to take the expedient course, to do the thing that it knows—deep down—it should not do. There is no one to remind it that it is going a bit too far this time; to suggest that it has overstepped the bounds of fair liberty, of better business, of government regulation, or even of good public relations. That is where the honest business publication should come into action, and by intelligent, constructive comment serve the best interests of all.

[24] Quoted by Reginald Clough, President and Editor of *Tide*, in an editorial, "The Functions of Business Papers," June 5, 1951, p. 14.

CHAPTER 2

Accounting

INTRODUCTION

An established and fair-sized businesspaper publishing organization is actually a group of separate organizations (called departments) under one roof, but when such an organization is young and small there may be no division. Two or three men will perform the functions of many men. The publisher may act as the editor or as the advertising sales manager, or both. One man may sell both advertising space and subscriptions. One man may prepare the editorial content and handle all details of editorial and advertising production himself.

Most business organizations that start small evolve much the same way. The administrators, the managers, and the workers in the beginning are the same people. As expansion takes place more people are added and more machines. The departments take on definite shape, the duties of department managers are more sharply defined, and overhead begins to be correctly allocated.

"A combination of human beings and machines" describes an organization, but not necessarily a successful one. "The administration," as Dr. Ordway Tead points out in his recent book,[1] "is the comprehensive effort to direct, guide and integrate human strivings which are focused toward some specific end or aims."

In other words the combination of necessary manpower, office equipment, and other tools and machines must be assembled in a "systematic and effective coordination" in order to accomplish certain desired and defined objectives. If the objectives are reasonable and worthy, in the public interest, and the effort intelligent the results should be profitable.

In one aspect a businesspaper has the social responsibilities of a profession where financial reward is incidental. The publisher and his

[1] Ordway Tead, *The Art of Administration,* New York, McGraw-Hill, 1951.

18

editors are concerned with the interpretation, criticism, and dissemination of current economic history; they are concerned with the welfare of business enterprise and the health of economic man. They are part of the free press.

From another aspect a businesspaper is a modern advertising agency, complete with art, copy, publicity, and research departments.

From a third aspect it is a manufacturing business like any other: it designs, produces, sells, and distributes a product—the businesspaper.

But the businesspaper differs from the usual manufacturing business in these respects:

1. It provides the customer with a brand new product every month, every week, or in some cases, every day.
2. It depends for its life on paper, printing, and engraving but seldom owns a paper, printing, or engraving plant.
3. It has two sets of customers and two distinct sales organizations:
   a. It sells the product to potential readers. The primary sales job is circulation sales.
   b. It sells the readership to agencies and business concerns. The secondary sales job is advertising space sales.
4. Its largest revenue (and in some cases practically its only revenue) comes as a result of the secondary selling function—advertising space sales.
5. It guarantees continuity in return for its privileges as a member of the fourth estate. A manufacturer whose product is not selling profitably, or for any other reason, may curtail, suspend, or postpone manufacture without going out of business. A businesspaper publisher's "inventory" is useless except for reference in a library or as wastepaper. He is obligated to publish at stated regular intervals and deliver to the same number of readers, whether advertising volume is good or bad. When he suspends manufacture he is out of business.
6. It criticizes the practices of its own customers openly for the public record.

As a rule, as we stated, businesspaper publishers do not own the mechanical departments of their business such as printing, engraving, and direct mail. But whether this equipment is owned or simply hired the operations must be controlled and directed by managers within the publishing organization. This department is operated like a modern manufacturing plant, from raw material to assembly line to distribution of finished product.

The managers of all departments within the organization—personnel, editorial, advertising, circulation, sales promotion, research, finance and accounting, production, printing, and distribution—are directly responsible to an administrative body and charged with carrying out its directives. Some of these department managers may actually compose the administrative body. Anyway they are logical candidates.

The administrators are the highest officers in a businesspaper publishing house: the owner or a corporation which legally serves as owner, a publisher employed by the owner, or the owner assuming the administrative role of publisher. Sometimes owners are listed on the masthead as editors. Sometimes editors become publishers and retain their titles as editors. Occasionally you see a masthead listing publishers, presidents and executive vice presidents but no editor. This is not good. There should be a chief editor whose chief responsibility is editorial service, not the business department; but he should be a primary administrative officer along with publisher, general manager, and advertising, circulation, production, promotion, and public relations managers.

Management is the agency which directs and guides the operations. Each manager performs a certain function (body of duties) explained in detail in the chapters that follow. In this chapter Mr. Lasser, who has spent many years examining and analyzing publishing organizations, reduces all businesspaper publishing activity to five major "essentials" and then divides the accounting practice into the same five groups:

1. Printing and distributing the publication
2. Soliciting, servicing and collecting advertising accounts
3. Preparing the textual matter of the publication
4. Soliciting, servicing and collecting subscription accounts
5. Generally administering and coordinating the activities of the business (overhead)

Lasser shows that the accounting for profit and loss on a businesspaper differs materially from accounting practice in other industries or even on general magazines or newspapers.

The publisher owes it to his staff, his advertisers, his readers, and his stockholders to operate a successful businesspaper. The margin between success and failure grows narrower every day.

HOW A BUSINESSPAPER PUBLISHING HOUSE IS ORGANIZED*

Before we put our new magazine together, let us take a quick look first at the dollar-and-cents picture of a businesspaper, because, after all, we are going into this thing to make money. What are the sources of income, where do the principal expenses come from, and what yields us a profit?

Our product is, of course, the magazine itself—made up of a combination of editorial pages and advertising pages. The editorial pages are the basic wares sold to your prospects, as a means for him to become better informed about his industry and his job. He will receive collateral information from the advertising pages, which will be valuable too.

For this service to the reader, he pays so many dollars per year as a subscription price. This income from subscriptions just about meets the cost of seeking out and obtaining the proper prospects to meet the publisher's circulation specifications.

In businesspapers, we are assembling individuals who represent large buying power. Such individuals might be the chief engineer of a textile mill, or the manager of a large hotel, or the buyer for a department store. In consumer magazines, you assemble only the buying power of the individual and his family. You will get more definition of this, of course, from succeeding chapters. Also, in later chapters, others will describe circulation methods in detail, and at that time you will learn of free-distribution papers as compared with the paid-circulation magazines I am mentioning. At any rate, the income from circulation on the customary businesspaper just about covers the cost of obtaining the subscription, of maintaining necessary records, preparing stencils, classifying the names according to business group, and so forth. Some publications lose a small percentage of their circulation income, others make a bit, none come near meeting the cost of printing, paper, and postage. Thus, subscription income, while it does produce a profit for the operation itself, does not contribute much towards paying for manufacturing the magazine.

The editorial department is obviously an expense. There are editors' salaries to meet, costs of drawings, engravings, typesetting, printing, and

* N. O. Wynkoop, publisher of *Power* since 1932; became a vice-president of the McGraw-Hill Publishing Company in 1937; since 1946 has served as controller of the firm. For many years he has headed up the Cost Accounting Committee of ABP. This paper, based on his lectures at New York University and Northwestern University, was published in *Magazine World*, March, 1947.

paper—with no offsetting income. However, it is the editorial section that is sold to the selected prospects and is the vehicle by which a reader market for advertising is created.

The source of income that makes business publishing possible comes from the advertising pages. This advertising is sold to manufacturers on the basis that their sales messages are placed in the hands of certain groups of men who are regular and interested readers of the magazine carrying these advertisements.

Putting all this together, here is what makes a businesspaper tick: good editorial, to the proper audience, with a large enough advertising volume—properly priced to support the service to the industry.

Now back to this new businesspaper we are going to create. We begin with the thesis that we are to serve an industrial or trade function not now being so assisted, or one which—in the originator's mind—is not being served effectively.

This originator, or creator, of a new businesspaper may be one who has editorial ability or sales ability. As a rule, he has the latter, so we will start with that assumption. So you pick out someone to work with you as editor, and with these two basic people—editor and publisher— you have the beginnings of a businesspaper.

Each of these two, in turn, chooses his own assistant, and your basic organization is ready to start producing a magazine with four people. The publisher selects an assistant or secretary with whom he has worked before and knows to have experience in publishing. Likewise, the editor has an assistant, qualified to answer letters of complaint, put together an article, style type, and do all the multitude of tasks inherent in setting up the editorial section of a magazine. In short, these assistants must have the ability to work hard and to turn out a considerable volume of work under the most pressing circumstances.

You, as publisher, will start out by doing certain basic things. First, you will define the market or field you intend to serve, in terms of business units (plants) and of individuals (readers). Either experience (previous employment) will give you this information, or you will attempt research on your own, generally doing so while on the payroll of your previous employer.

Now, with your market defined, your next step is to seek out ways of getting a *mailing list* that will be as near as possible to the coverage specifications of the trade or industrial group you have selected. This list will later be refined into a subscription list, and will be operated by a circulation department; but generally the list is bought from a mail-service outfit, whose business it is to assemble names and addresses of plants and men, indexed by industries and titles. These concerns then sell names as a monthly mailing service to manufacturers and publishers.

When the new publisher has thus determined his market and obtained a mailing list, he starts looking for a *printer,* not a very easy person to find under today's conditions. Usually, before the war, printers were as poorly paid and as overworked as the average farmer was in days past—and, as such, were an easy mark for taking on new publications. In this way, the publisher provides for his mechanical or manufacturing operation.

In the meantime, the editor is working—even though no editor ever figures on writing even a small fraction of his material. He starts by making friends with the specialists in the field who feel the urge to write, and from a large group obtains a small amount of printable material. The editor himself will write a page or two which might be called "The Voice of the Industry," which is usually a doctrine regarding his industry's problems.

The editor also is at work assembling various departments. In a merchandising paper, he would have such sections as Displays, Packaging, Sales Training, New Products, Inventory Control, and so forth. In an industrial paper, these departments would be Plant Operation, Maintenance, New Equipment, Questions and Answers, plus lead articles describing outstanding processes in the most modern plants.

Now, let us go back to the publisher, who has to provide for getting in some advertising. He can either intrigue some good salesman from another company, with a good following, to come into business with him, or he can put on his hat and start cultivating business.

A third method of obtaining advertising is to line up several publishers' representatives—who handle more than one paper normally and who have some knowledge of the field or market being developed. The publisher then engages them to take on the sale of his advertising space.

Finally, when all our advertisements and editorial material are assembled at our office, we have the problem of production, or putting it all together in magazine form. If you don't have an experienced man with you at the start, the printer usually winds up advising on typesetting, arrangement, layout, and so forth.

Let us look at what we have so far. There is the publisher, who has undertaken:

1. To asemble the organization.
2. To provide for its compensation.
3. To produce a list of names and addresses to be used as a basis for distributing the magazine. This later will be developed into a circulation department, but at the start the list is generally purchased or obtained from other sources. (His competitors will say he stole the list, which may or may not be true.)
4. To persuade a printer to undertake manufacture of the magazine.
5. To provide for the sale of advertising space, which function will later grow into the advertising sales department of our business paper.

Meanwhile, our editor has undertaken to provide source material from which service to the industry or group is created.

That is our basic organization.

Now, I would like to talk about a publishing house possessing a number of publications. These magazines have their own individual organizations as described previously—their publishers, editors, and so forth—but the staff above the publisher runs something like this:

First, there is the president, who has a board of directors as an outside group to advise him, and a general manager or executive vice-president as his inside coordinator. There will also be an editorial board, made up of chief editors of the various publications, and headed by a vice-president in charge of company editorial activities. This man is responsible for obtaining and maintaining individual editors and staffs of proper caliber and standing, and sees that they are serving their readers enthusiastically.

The editorial board will advise the president on large matters of editorial policy, and can undertake as a group the dissemination of certain basic subjects that all papers can treat regardless of specialized audience. Examples of wide-interest subjects would be (1) How to Reduce Unemployment, (2) Waste Salvage and Production Increase, (3) Labor Relations, and so forth.

The general manager will have any number of assistants he needs to keep an active check on other functions of the business, such as a vice-president in charge of advertising sales and district offices, another in charge of promotion and research, a controller, and so on.

Another important function in the multi-paper enterprise is that of the treasurer who looks after the moneys of the company, and who reports to the president through the general manager. Under the treasurer, as a rule, is a chief accountant and his staff which assembles items of income and expense and prepares operating statements. These are measures of progress or lack of progress in a property, but the treasurer has the further responsibility of taking care of these moneys and assets for the benefit of the proprietors or stockholders. From my experience as controller, I could spend an entire evening alone in telling you how important a well-operated accounting department is to the welfare of a publishing house, how many benefits a well-run department can bring, and how many liabilities a poorly operated department can deposit on your doorstep, but suffice it to say that, in a large publishing operation, the accounting function must receive the same careful care and management as the editorial and advertising phases of the business.

In a large company, the circulation department becomes a contract department serving each publication, and its operations are all performed inside the company, rather than outside, as in the case with our small, young magazine. Hence, it now becomes as good or bad as the company itself.

The printer of our early days has now become the mechanical and production department, which collects editorial and advertising material from the makeups, makes publishing schedules dovetail, and sees that the magazines are mailed on the set dates. This department is also responsible, of course, for quality of printing and for costs.

In a large publishing operation, certain services can be departmentalized for the common benefit of all publications. Such operations, which were performed by the part-time effort of individuals, or not performed at all, in the early days of our single magazine effort, are art and drafting, photographic, personnel, research and promotion, sales service, etc.

As an example of what is accomplished by company service departments for the individual publications, let us look at promotion. This division, as one of its responsibilities, creates and places advertising in newspapers calling the public's attention to certain major national industrial problems, and suggesting solutions. The good will, if this advertising is well done, gives the individual publication identified with this company standing above the run-of-mill publications, and makes easier the selling of advertising and subscriptions.

Finally, as an outcome or a by-product of the large publishing operation, there are book companies and directories which in some cases can be the tails that wag the dog. The editors of publications who are constantly contacting leaders in industry and persuading them to write articles are in a position to get these people to take on the writing of larger projects. And these editors themselves write books.

Let us sum up: From the smaller units, large, multi-paper organizations are created. If you want to study any industry or business, take first the small concern and look at its growth. You will find individuals blossoming into departments—and functions, which were once performed by one man's left hand on rainy Tuesdays, now being done by entire staffs.

But remember, all of the intricacy and size of the big house started with an editor and a publisher pushing nickels around in order to make a dollar or two. The only difference is that now somebody complains if not enough millions are made. Remember, too, that nowhere in industry are jobs and functions as interrelated as they are in publishing. The moral for the student is that he must learn his own relationship to the whole by studying the flow of material toward him, and away from him, as well as his own operation. If he does not he will be just another buoy in the channel of progress.

FUNDAMENTALS IN BUSINESSPAPER ACCOUNTING*

Accepted practice in the theory of accounting for profit or loss of a publication among businesspaper houses differs materially from that in use in other industries and even in some cases from that adopted by the general publisher or the newspaper. Behind each variance in operation is a distinct effort to align the mechanical recording of daily transactions into the most serviceable tool to management that can be secured. The principles involved may be very briefly stated to be:

1. The income and expense of each publication or service are separated as accurately as possible.

2. All expenses incurred in behalf of more than one publication (or more than one operating department of a publication) are distributed

* J. K. Lasser, C.P.A., privately published by the Cost Committee of the Associated Business Publications, Inc., New York, December, 1947. Mr. Lasser is Editor of the Handbook of Accounting Methods; Adjunct Professor of Taxation and Chairman, Institute on Federal Taxation, New York University; consultant to business press and book publishers; author of *Your Income Tax, How to Run a Small Business*, etc.

as completely and as equitably as possible to each publication and department concerned.

3. The income of a publication comes from three sources: advertising net billings; subscriptions; and net income from miscellaneous services such as reprints, cuts, art work, books, lists, etc., which arise as an incidental result of operating the publication.

4. The accounting for the expenses of a businesspaper is based upon the reasoning that the organization of a publication is composed of five essentials:

A. Print and distribute the magazine
B. Solicit, service, and collect the advertising accounts
C. Prepare the text matter of the publication
D. Solicit, service, and collect the subscription accounts
E. Generally administer and coordinate the activities of the business (the overhead)

We therefore divide expenses into the same five groups and then further analyze the groups according to the requirements of each company.

5. Such departments or functions as research, branch offices, art, service, make-up, stenographic, multigraphing, and file room, are separately accounted for and are prorated to the publications and departments which they serve.

6. Taxes or extraordinary items involved in financing (interest, etc.) are excluded from the operating statement to be later picked up in assembling net results of operations.

THE RESULTING STATEMENT OF INCOME AND EXPENSE

Based upon these fundamentals, an outline of an ideal operating statement for a publication listing the major items of income and expense would be as follows:

Income
Advertising, net of agency commissions and cash discounts

Expense
Mechanical and Distribution Costs
  Composition, presswork, binding, and mailing
  Paper
  Postage and delivery
  Wrappers, envelopes, etc.

Advertising Costs
  Salesmen's salaries and commissions
  Travel, entertaining, branch office costs
  Office salaries
  Promotion
  Other expenses

Editorial Costs
  Salaries
  Contributions
  Travel and entertaining
  Art work, photos and engravings
  Other expenses

Administrative Costs
  Salaries
  Rent, light, depreciation
  Other expenses

    Total publishing expense

Profit or (Loss) before Circulation

Circulation Income and Expense
  Income—Subscriptions

Expense
  Salaries
  Promotion
  Field salesmen's costs
  Fulfillment costs

Profit or (Loss) from Circulation
Service income, net of expense

Net Publishing Income Before Income Tax

Statistics

  Number of issues published in each period
  Paid advertising pages
  Editorial pages
  Filler pages
    Total pages

  Average number of copies printed per issue

Net Profit or Loss. The pages following will undoubtedly clarify the
fundamentals above set forth. They render first an explanation of the

three major sources of income (advertising, subscriptions, and services) and then a detailed review of the expenses within each of the five operating departments of the publication.

ADVERTISING INCOME

Advertising income means the amount derived from the billing of space for display pages, classified, color, or bleed pages, inserts, cover pages, and so on. It should be set upon the books and in all operating statements gross of agency commission and discounts. Short rate and rebate adjustments may be shown separately or included in the advertising billing figure.

Agency commission and cash discount are treated as a deduction from gross income in the preparation of operating statements.

House advertising for books, other publications, or for affiliated companies or directories is often included as paid space. The practice is hardly proper unless a separate account is set up to cover the income. Usually the billing rate is pure mechanical cost and inclusion of the element in ordinary billings distorts the statistical results.

CIRCULATION INCOME

The accounts to be set up should attempt to express circulation income according to its source so as to permit proper analysis of net income or loss from each type of activity. Thus the ideal expression would be accounts for net receipts from:

Sales by Mail Promotion
  New Business
  Renewal Business
Sales by Own Field Staff
  New Business
  Renewal Business
Newstand sales
All Other Sales (agencies, single copies, and business which is not
  definitely traceable to any one of the foregoing sources)

These are generally set upon the books at the net cash receipts for the month except in the case of newsstand sales. There it is reasonable to include as income for each month the amount billed to a news company less the provision for estimated returns if copies are returnable. In order to reflect the net income for each of the circulation classifications, it is sometimes advisable to set up separate accounts to cover refunds and the provisions for returnable copies.

The basis for including cash receipts only instead of the procedure in which income is prorated to the period in which service is rendered to the subscriber is so generally accepted among businesspaper publishers that no effort is made here to discuss it.

These four sources of income do not necessarily exist in each paper. The majority of publishers have no field organization or newsstand sales, their revenue coming from:

Mail promotion sales, through keyed efforts
Miscellaneous "float" receipts
Agencies—paid some percentage of the amount billed the subscriber
Single copy sales across the counter

Accounts for these would be created, dividing the mail promotion into new and renewal business and eliminating from it the net "float orders" which do not come in as a result of definite efforts. They and the single copy sales should comprise a miscellaneous classification. Group or bulk business is properly mail promotion if secured in that way or if secured by a field organization, credited to that source.

The "float order"—one that comes in without solicitation and as a result of the prestige of the paper—should not be included as a mail sale. To do so distorts comparisons. When the business cannot be identified with specific promotion, it should go into miscellaneous receipts.

SERVICE INCOME

Other income connected with the publication (sales of art work, copy service, cuts, reprints, books, etc.) should be so handled that the income on operating statements will show the net gain resulting from such activities. That is, the accounting records should credit all items billed and simultaneously charge therefor the cost of such services. This involves the setting up of income accounts for:

Sale of art and copy work
Sale of electros and engravings
Sale of reprints
Sale of books

Similar expense accounts will cover the cost of these services. Cost of such sales should be removed regularly from the mechanical or advertising costs in order that the latter may properly reflect conditions.

Sometimes there are many other sources of income within business-paper institutions that require separate costing. Some of these are:

Sale of space in a directory or catalog
Sale of directories
Sale of circulation lists
Sale of prospect lists
Addressing from stencils
Sale of special lists to the trade
Employment services
Brokerage services
Sale of research facilities
Sale of publicity
Sale of market service or other related special service

In principle no sources of income except the net revenue resulting from the sale of art and copy work, engravings, and reprints and books is permitted to affect the operating statement of a publication. All other revenues are regarded as extraneous to the normal operations.

Obviously this treatment is in a sense arbitrary. The principal defense for it lies in the almost universal practice of businesspaper houses to exclude all but the four named upon the theory that the others are separate operating departments which should be separately accounted for in order that reasonable control may be exercised over them.

Moreover, practice prevents the reduction of normal operating accounts to secure the cost of these so-called extraneous services upon the theory that the expense has been incurred as a cost of publishing. Thus sale of circulation lists should not serve to reduce subscription expenses unless the sale adds a new element, such as the expense of running off the list in which event that cost should be charged against list income. And book sales should not reduce office overhead unless the department increases overhead or uses space in the publication. In the latter case, it should bear the proper mechanical and mailing costs.

MECHANICAL AND DISTRIBUTION COSTS

Mechanical and distribution costs mean those elements involved in printing and mailing the paper. They may be defined as the cost of:

Composition, presswork, binding, and mailing
Paper
Addressing wrappers (or envelopes or pasters, whichever is involved)
Distributing the issues—including the postage and express

In many instances one or more of these costs is erroneously spread into one of the other four operating departments. Sometimes advertising or editorial heads are charged for the cost of printing their space, circulation is assessed for the press run, and so on. Accepted practice holds that true mechanical and distributing elements should be grouped into one department where the expense is incurred to facilitate control that is lost by spreading them all over the lot. Advertising expenses are specifically those involved with securing paid space; editorial, those necessary to prepare and illustrate the text pages; circulation cost is the expenditure required to secure and maintain a required list. None of these has anything to do with printing and mailing the publication nor is the price paid for that job within their control. Proper accounting for publishing expenses—particularly with any type of budgetary control—requires that these departments be charged only with the costs for which they are definitely responsible and can control.

In the vast majority of practices mechanical costs do not include the charge for engravings or art work—although they are admittedly an element in the make-up of the book. These are always deliberately assessed against one or other of the following:

The editorial department when it has ordered the material

The advertising department when it has inserted copy without the right to charge the advertiser for engravings and copy service

Income from sale of engravings or copy service when the advertiser pays for them

Otherwise, we would lift a controllable element out of its proper position. *Mechanical costs start where the printer takes over.*

Nor should the cost of make-up be included as an element of production expense. It is always treated as an advertising or editorial charge even where the work is centralized into one individual or department that handles the entire job. Then, of course, the cost is prorated to the advertising and editorial departments based upon the time devoted to the work of each.

Make-up functions are strictly advertising or editorial activities. They involve not only the pasting up of proofs into a dummy, but in practically every instance under our observation, the chasing of copy and cuts and a dozen other duties that are in no sense involved in the mechanical production of the book.

Sometimes, however, there is a direct salary charge to production. That arises when a specialist is stationed at the printing plant to insure proper quality and speed or when expert services are required in effecting economical distribution. Those are unusual elements that require distinct treatment.

Cost of reprints (paper, delivery, and printing) is not a proper mechanical expense. It should be lifted out of the printing bill and charged against the income resulting from the sale. Where there is no income, the charge should be made to the department responsible for the order (advertising, editorial, or circulation).

The accounts necessary to secure a proper analysis of printing and distributing costs are:

Composition—technically the hand or machine setting of copy, the proofreading, and the lock-up charges.

Press work—the charge for make-ready and running the entire issue, plus the cost of electrotypes used on rotary presses.

Binding and mailing—the bill for assembling, binding, and wrapping or inserting in envelopes of the issue.

Paper—the consumed portion of all paper stock used in each issue, including as a part of the cost freight and trucking charge for delivery of the paper.

Wrappers—the container used to deliver the issue, the envelope, "backbone," paster, box, etc.

Addressing wrappers—the cost of placing the subscriber's name, address, and delivery instructions upon the wrapper—a flat charge per thousand when the work is done out of the office and usually a proportion of the salary of the subscription department stencil operator or addressing clerk when it is done within the office.

Bulk postage—the cost of mailing the issue, second, third, or fourth class.

Freight and express in distribution—the cost of actual distribution or of sending the issue to some central point for mailing.

Sometimes this analysis is not attainable—particularly where the printing job has been let upon a contract rate of so much per page per thousand run. Then some abbreviation is reasonable. But just as often these eight accounts do not permit the full story to be told and it is necessary to supplement them with such guide posts as:

Author's corrections—an analysis (sometimes divided into the responsible departments, such as advertising and editorial) to indicate printers billings for changes after approved copy is submitted.

Killed matter—a record of charges for editorial matter which was set down by direction of editors and has never been used.

Extras—a detail of all unusual charges for service caused by delays of the advertising or editorial departments, such as holding presses, overtime, etc.

ADVERTISING COSTS

From the standpoint of administrative control it is highly desirable that expenses should be classified so as to indicate the responsibility for their incurrence. Admitting this, it follows that each of the operating departments of a publication should be charged with all of the expenses that are directly under the control of that department.

The function of the advertising department is the solicitation and servicing of collectible business. That involves these very definite portions of the organization of a publication:

The research, promotion, and publicity necessary to properly sell space.
The actual solicitation.
The servicing of accounts by marketing counsel, copy writing, art work, etc.
The make-up of the advertising pages.
The collection of the advertising accounts.

Some of these elements bring controversy. On the one hand there is the urge that the cost of collecting accounts is a financial expense to be included among those involving the receipt, custody, and disbursement of funds. Yet it must be admitted that in publishing, control of both the advertising and subscription departments requires that the disbursement to maintain their respective collections (together with any losses resulting) should be lodged in the department responsible and controlling the situation.

These and many other problems (including the charging of printing costs to the advertising department, allocating make-up charge to printing costs, and so on) will clear up if we can accept the reasoning that the organization of a publication is composed of the essentials necessary to:

Generally administer the business (the overhead).
Solicit, service, and collect the advertising accounts.
Solicit, service, and collect the subscription accounts.

Prepare the text pages of the publication.
Print and distribute the book.

In addition, we must concede that it is difficult to secure the measure of control necessary unless the advertising manager is properly charged with all expenses involved in his domain.

The basic accounts necessary to secure analysis of advertising costs may be set down as:

Salesmen's Cost

1. Salaries and commissions (the disbursement to the solicitors accounts being provided to accumulate the charge by territorial divisions).
2. Traveling and entertainment (the expense of salesmen with accounts —again to permit territorial accumulation).
3. Branch office cost (the proportionate cost of maintaining a branch office for the purpose of housing salesmen—editorial and possible subscription salesmen being accorded their proper allocation of the expenses—this account or a number of accounts to secure the territorial expense being intended to cover everything but the salesmen's salary and traveling expense, i.e., office salaries, rent, light, telephone, and telegraph, postage, supplies, depreciation, and miscellaneous disbursements).

Expense of Office Organization

1. Salaries (the advertising manager, his office staff, the make-up department chargeable to advertising).
2. Traveling and entertainment (the expenses of the business manager and his office assistants in the field).

Publicity and Promotion

1. Research cost (sometimes divided into salaries and expenses to express best the staff-members or outside cost of securing marketing data and the basis for furnishing solicitors with the technical knowledge necessary for them to properly counsel advertisers).
2. Mail promotion—the cost of circulars and publicity that go out of the office, sometimes divided so as to express:
   > Cost of preparing the publicity matter
   > Cost of printing
   > Cost of mailing and package

3. Advertising (the cost for insertion in other periodicals, including a fair charge—usually the mechanical and distribution cost—for use of space in other magazines published by the same house).
4. Conventions (the expense of exhibits; the cost of traveling and entertainment being charged elsewhere).
5. Dues (to organizations for which the advertising department is responsible, including the ABP and clubs frequented to secure business contacts).

SERVICE COSTS

1. Art work and copy (the cost of preparing copy and art work which is not sold to advertisers—either the cost of the employees and materials specially engaged or else the expense of purchasing the material from outsiders—this account being intended to cover the preparation of material for both prospects and active accounts).
2. Electros and engravings (those supplied to advertisers for use in their copy without charge).

Bad Debts and Cost of Collection

1. Write-offs of advertising accounts because of inability to collect, or a set-up to provide a reserve for possible bad debt losses.
2. Credit and collection expense (the salary and expenses of the collection department engaged upon advertising accounts).

Office Charges

1. Stationery and supplies (the actual supplies used by the advertising department where that is possible through a requisition procedure—but where it is not, then at least the material purchased for consumption by the advertising group).
2. Telephone and telegraph (the actual charge to the department where that is possible—but at least the toll charges).
3. Postage (the actual consumption of the department where that can be secured).

EDITORIAL COSTS

Editorial costs are those concerned with the preparation of the text pages of the publication. At the risk of being charged with redundancy, we repeat that good practice holds that they should not include the mechanical cost of the pages but that they should be strictly confined to the expenses which are directly under the control of the editorial function.

Salaries and Traveling Expenses

1. Salaries (the compensation paid to the editors and their staff including clerical expenses; sometimes divided up into editors, research staff, make-up men, clerical and stenographic assistants).
2. Traveling expenses (the traveling and entertainment expenses of the foregoing group).

Contributions

1. Contributions (the cost of manuscripts submitted by contributors other than the regular staff).
2. Exchanges and clippings (the cost of the periodicals received by the editorial staff and the special charges for services by the news and clipping bureaus).

Art Work, Photographs, and Engravings

1. Art work (the cost of preparing the art work—whether compensation to employees of the organization or the expenses of purchasing the material from outsiders).
2. Photographs (the disbursement for photographs except when they are submitted along with the contributions—in which event they are included in the contribution cost).
3. Electros and engravings (the charge for editorial electros and engravings).

Branch Office Expense

1. That proportion of the cost of maintaining branch offices which is properly chargeable to the editorial department, generally expressed here in one account, the detail being set up among the advertising expenses.

Office Charges

1. Stationery and supplies (the actual supplies used by the editorial department where that is possible through a requisition procedure, but where it is not, then at least the material purchased for consumption by it).
2. Telephone and telegraph (the actual charge to the editorial department for telegrams and telephone where that is possible; where it is not, at least the toll charges).

3. Postage (the actual consumption by the editorial department where that can be secured).

In practice, editorial expenses are readily ascertainable, the only difficulty which arises being that concerned with the propriety of inventorying manuscripts and cuts purchased for editorial consumption. That is often accomplished but it results in so much waste at the end of the period that we have invariably returned to the procedure in which the editorial department is charged for purchases in the month in which it issues its order.

CIRCULATION COSTS

The job of the circulation department is to solicit, service and collect subscriptions. For accounting purposes, these activities are divided into:

Cost of procuring new business by mail promotion.
Cost of procuring renewal business by mail promotion.
Cost of procuring new business by a field staff.
Cost of procuring renewal business by a field staff.
Cost of miscellaneous orders which do not come in from the above (float orders, agency business, single copy sales, etc.).
Cost of records of subscribers maintained.

This division of expenses represents the advanced thinking now adopted by businesspaper houses in order that they may procure proper costs of obtaining business from each source. It is a radical departure from previous costing of circulation elements but it is the natural result of the endeavor to determine the most profitable source of business in order that the maximum executive control of the department's activities may be secured. Hitherto we have been dealing with the net cost of procuring all subscription orders regardless of source, but present practice must seek to record sufficient data to permit the observation of trends within each type of activity.

Generally speaking, the fundamental divisions set forth above are fairly explanatory, provided it is understood that they treat controversial factors as follows:

1. The cost of collecting money due from subscribers (regardless as to whether it is upon a new or renewal order) is chargeable to the cost of securing that business and should, therefore, be included within the department involved (mail, field, etc.) whether or not collection costs are separately computed.

2. Such costs as those involved in maintaining records or lists (particularly analysis of subscribers by occupations, territories, etc.) for the use of the advertising or other departments, are not included within one of the four basic sources of the cost of revenues indicated above. Along with the expenditures involved in preparing stencils, ABC record, etc. they are placed into the cost of records.
3. The cost of running wrappers is not a circulation expense. It should be treated as a mechanical and distribution element.
4. Where an organization sells either prospect or actual subscription lists, the credit for the revenue involved from it should not serve to reduce the expense of establishing a list. The circulation department should bear the full cost of compilation. Any extra expenses incidental to the running off of the matter for revenue should be borne by that service itself.
5. Mail and field activities should not include the subscriptions resulting from agencies or float orders which come into an organization without solicitation. Mail business means purely the results of specific efforts. Of course, there is no such thing as an unsolicited or "float" renewal. Field activities are the results of direct contact by field men.

In order to effect a reasonable determination of the expenses of the five fundamental break-ups indicated above, the following accounts may be set up:

1. Cost of Procuring New Business by Mail:
   Salaries (all employees engaged in mail promotion work for new subscribers, including prospect list)
   Circulars (cost of all circulars used for soliciting new business)
   Postage (all postage used in mail promotion work)
   Premiums (cost of premiums given to new mail subscribers)
   Stationery and supplies (used by employees whose salaries are included above)
   Miscellaneous (all other expenses incidental to new mail solicitation)
2. Cost of Procuring Renewal Business by Mail:
   Salaries (employees devoting efforts to secure renewals by mail)
   Renewal notices (cost of notices requesting renewal of existing subscription)
   Postage (postage used on above renewal notices)
   Premiums (cost of premiums given to renewal subscribers)

Stationery and supplies (used by employees whose salaries are included above)

Miscellaneous (all other expenses incidental to renewal solicitation by mail)

3. Cost of Procuring New or Renewal Business by Field:
Salaries (of field salesmen and supervisors only)

4. Bonuses (bonuses or prizes given field salesmen)
Traveling expenses (expenses of field salesmen, supervisors, etc.)
Premiums (cost of all premiums given subscribers)
Commissions (paid field men for securing orders)
Salaries of office staff (all personnel engaged on field work who do not actually bring in subscriptions)
Postage (all postage used in this department)
Stationery and supplies (all stationery and supplies used by this division)
Telephone and telegraph (all charges incurred by office staff—those incurred by salesmen should go under traveling)
Miscellaneous (all other expenses incurred by this division)
When an organization does not have its own field force most of these costs will be eliminated.

5. Cost of Procuring Miscellaneous Orders:
Commissions to subscription agencies (all disbursements to subscription agencies)
Miscellaneous expenses (any other expense incidental to miscellaneous or "float" sources of revenue)

6. Cost of Servicing and Recording:
Salaries (salaries of employees preparing stencils, statistical or ABC records)
Stationery and supplies (cost of all supplies used by above employees)
Postage (all postage used in this work)
Miscellaneous (all other expenses incurred in this work)

ADMINISTRATIVE AND GENERAL (OVERHEAD) EXPENSES

The overhead expenses of a publication are those costs concerned with executive control that are beyond the direction of the four operating departments and are therefore accumulated into one group of costs.

They include a type of expense (rent, light, insurance, accounting, etc.) which is directly connected with the production, advertising, editorial, and subscription activities, and which, therefore, is sometimes included by prorations in those departments. Better practice sends such expenses to the overhead accounts upon the theory that the costs of administration should include all expenses incurred by the management to secure proper working conditions and proper control of the activities of the departments.

The possible accounts that may be provided to properly express the overhead are as follows:

Administrative and General Salaries

1. Salaries—all the salaries paid to those that are not members of the operating departments including the following separate accounts if that seems desirable:

   A. The executive staff
   B. The accounting department
   C. Purchasing department
   D. Telegraph and telephone operators
   E. Shipping and receiving clerks
   F. Stock room clerks
   G. Librarian, etc.
   H. Information clerks
   I. Maintenance or janitors

Rent, Light, and Depreciation, etc.

1. Rent (the amount paid for the use of the property recognized as the principal office but not including the rent of branch offices, these being specifically set up as advertising expenses, with proper prorations out of the latter to the editorial and subscription departments where they are concerned. Included in this is usually the electricity bills and janitor service, but separate accounts can be set up for the latter if that is desired. When interest, taxes, and maintenance costs are substituted for rent, they belong in this group of expenses).
2. Depreciation on equipment used (the annual provision required to recover the cost of equipment by the end of its useful life).
3. Insurance (the cost of insuring equipment, stock in office, and paper in the printers' offices). Expense of insuring officers is not generally treated as publishing expenses but is entered as one of the extraneous disbursements.
4. Repairs (the expense of keeping equipment in working order).

General Expenses

1. Traveling and entertainment (expenses of the executive staff and its assistants—see the group above which has been included under the overhead classification—the traveling expenses of these fit into this account).
2. Stationery and supplies (supplies used by the individuals who are charged as overhead, the balance of such expenses being included in the operating departments as previously explained).
3. Telephone and telegraph (the services to members of the organization who are charged as overhead).
4. Postage (the consumption by members of the organization who are charged as overhead).
5. Exchange on checks (the bank charge for collection of foreign checks and domestic drafts).
6. Professional services (the cost of legal and accounting services, except that the disbursement for collection expenses is included in its proper place as an advertising or circulation cost).
7. Dues (the dues paid in behalf of members of the organizations who are considered overhead, or assessments by those associations which are considered necessary for company policies).
8. Institutional publicity (the advertising or direct mail cost by the organization in behalf of all of its properties—as contrasted to specific advertising for one publication which is included as an advertising expense—this charge usually being a prorated portion of the total cost).
9. Charities (charitable contributions which do not represent true expenditures of the operating departments).
10. Ice, towels, and water (these, together with any other service features created for the benefit of employees are charged here or separate accounts created for them if it is deemed necessary).

Correct Allocation of Overhead

Proper handling of the overhead brings with it considerable difficulty due to varying conditions in different companies, such as the following—among a host of possible complications.

1. The one-paper house where the executive is also the advertising manager or editor, or both—here departmental costs will be incorrectly stated unless fair division is made of his compensation.
2. The large organizations where there is a manager in charge of a

paper (in addition to the advertising manager and editor) and also a group of officers supervising all papers whose compensation and expenses must be distributed over all papers.

3. The large organizations where the manager is also in direct charge of advertising for all publications.

Both the operating departments and the overhead costs should be stated as accurately as possible—particularly if worth-while comparisons to other publishers is hoped for. Accordingly, the following principles should be followed in all instances:

1. Executive salaries should be properly apportioned to the actual publications and departments served and not indiscriminately dumped into overhead. The latter should include only the compensation to those officers who devote their time to all departments and all papers.
2. In the small companies where the executive is also a department manager, that department should bear that part of his compensation which would be paid to replace him were he to devote his attention elsewhere.
3. In large companies, even where there is an executive staff that is in part chargeable to the paper, the manager whose activities are in part or in whole truly overhead should be charged thereto according to the time devoted.

One of the staunchest foes of uniformity in accounts is the head of the smaller company who actively replaces an advertising manager, for instance, and yet insists that his entire salary should go into overhead. Obviously, all unit costs and ratios are thereby distorted. On fewer occasions does the same disturbance arise in houses with more than one paper—where there is often present the insistence that there should be no expense in overhead other than the officers' and that all others should be prorated to departments.

The determination of the proper division of compensation is reasonably ascertainable in every instance we have ever seen, despite a number of occasions in which there was the previous insistence that it was not possible. In the interest of uniform costing, it should be conscientiously accomplished.

Division of compensation to managers brings up the question of distribution of other expenses which are in part direct charges to the paper and in part institutional disbursements. In the house with two or more papers, we must recognize that there are two types of overhead charges:

1. Those which are direct expenses of the paper (its manager, his staff, their traveling expenses, stationery, telephone, telegraph, postage, dues, etc.).
2. Those which are expenses of the house and should be prorated among all papers (the officers, their staff, and the same expenses, together with rent, light, depreciation, repairs, professional services, insurance, charities, publicity, etc.).

Sometimes two distinct divisions are set up to adequately distinguish between direct and institutional prorations, but more often they are merged into the one presentation of the administrative cost.

The question of an equitable basis for the distribution of the last group overhead is subject to much controversy. Many methods can be suggested, each probably as good as the other. We always leave the problem by expressing the adage that any process is safe provided it is consistently adhered to over a period of years.

The bases most used are:

1. Gross income
2. Direct expenses
3. A combination of the two

The latter has the decided preference and acceptance. In it the income and direct expenses of all of the papers owned constitute the denominator of a fraction, of which the income and direct expenses of each individual paper is the numerator. The fraction (for each paper) is then applied to the distributable overhead to secure the amount allocated to each. As an example, given an overhead of $100 to distribute, and the following facts:

	Publications				
	A	B	C	D	Total
Gross income	$100	$150	$200	$250	$700
All direct expenses	90	100	160	230	580
Net before overhead	$ 10	$ 50	$ 40	$ 20	$120

The overhead applicable to publication A is then

$$\frac{\text{Its income and direct expenses}}{\text{All income and direct expenses}} = \frac{190}{1280}$$

of the $100 overhead.

SUMMARY OF CONTROL RECORDS*

ADVERTISING EXPENSES   USE IN CONTROL

1. Detail of Prospect Lists (Card Files)

Name and address of prospect
Business
Products or lines
Financial rating
Name and title of person to see
Best time of day, week or month
    to see him
Next date to call or write
Competitive paper advertising
    volume
Potential volume obtainable
Complaints or reason for refusal
    to advertise

Direction of Salesmen's activities
through
  a. Routing
  b. Calls to be made weekly
  c. Arming him with sales argu-
    ment
  d. Budgeting his production
  e. Budgeting his traveling expense

2. Detail of Salesmen's Performance (Monthly Reports)

For each salesman:
  Sales by issue
  Sales by month
  Sales quota
  Compensation
  Travel expense

Measure of salesmen's worth by
  a. Comparison with quota or
    budget
  b. Comparison with previous
    record
  c. Comparison with competitive
    publications
  d. Relation of cost to income
  e. Study of the method of com-
    pensation
  f. Comparison with other pub-
    lishers

3. Detail of Salesmen's Expenses (Weekly Expense Reports and Record
    of Calls)

Itemize in minute detail:
  Cities visited
  Prospects called upon and
    sales made
  Railroad fare
  Hotel charges
  Meals
  Pullman

Justification of the expense through
  a. Elimination of backtracking
    and useless traveling
  b. Comparison with calls budgeted
  c. Relation of sales to calls
  d. Careful scrutiny of the reason-
    ableness of the expense item
  e. Comparison with budget

* Prepared by J. K. Lasser Co.

SUMMARY OF CONTROL RECORDS—*Continued*

ADVERTISING EXPENSES	USE IN CONTROL
Taxis Telephone and telegraph Valet and laundry, if allowed Entertainment, including person entertained and reason	f. Comparison of cost to income produced g. Comparison with other publishers

4. Detail of Promotion (Monthly Cost Reports)

Statement of costs by kind of promotion: Surveys of markets Advertising in other publications Industry analysis Salesmen's kits Presentations to advertisers Speculative copy Promotional mailings Salaries of employees	Maintenance of proper balance by a. Budgeting the expenditure b. Computing the cost per call or contact c. Comparison with previous record d. Relating sales to promotion where possible e. Obtaining prospect reaction f. Comparison with other publishers

5. Detail of Copy Service (Monthly Cost Reports)

Statement of costs by advertisers: Salaries on time basis Artwork and supplies Telephone calls or telegrams to secure late copy	Eliminate waste by a. Billing full cost where possible b. Reducing advertisers' abuses

6. Detail of Full Advertising Costs (Monthly Reports)

Salesmen's salaries and commissions Other salaries Social security taxes Traveling expense Telephone (toll calls) and telegraph Branch office expenses Promotion costs Misc.: Attending conventions; dues and subscriptions; stationery and supplies; postage; artwork, cuts, etc. not billed; bad debts	Hold these in line by a. Maintaining balance to income produced b. Comparison with budgets and previous experience c. Close scrutiny of each item of expense d. Comparison with other publishers

SUMMARY OF CONTROL RECORDS—*Continued*

CIRCULATION EXPENSES   USE IN CONTROL

1. Detail of Prospect Lists (Card File or Stencils)

Name and address of prospect   Direction of promotional activities
Business title of prospect   through
Former subscriber
Source of name
Date added to list

a. Testing list before adding to files

b. Check off of names found to be dead through salesmen's reports or mail returns

c. Preserving "dead" names to prevent their addition to list when new lists are purchased

d. Classification of list to facilitate rifle shot appeals, etc.

e. Budgeting orders to be secured

f. Budgeting expenses

2. Detail of Mail Promotion (Monthly Reports)

Number of pieces mailed
Copy appeal used
Keyed appeals
List or lists used
Direct costs of campaign
a. Paper
b. Processing
c. Mailing
d. Postage
e. Premiums
Results of campaign
a. Subscription secured (new and renewal); % to total pieces
b. Cost per subscription

Reduce costs and improve results of future campaigns by

a. Elimination of unsuccessful copy

b. Elimination of unsatisfactory names from active lists

c. Information as to success or failure of kinds of paper; methods of reproduction; cards *vs.* letters; stamps *vs.* meter machines; mailing dates; premiums

d. Analysis of costs to determine saturation points (diminishing returns)

e. Comparison with previous campaigns

f. Budgeting the expenditure

g. Comparison with other publishers

SUMMARY OF CONTROL RECORDS—*Continued*

CIRCULATION EXPENSES   USE IN CONTROL

3. Detail of Salesmen's Performance (Monthly Reports)

Number of subscriptions—new and renewal

Dollar volume—new and renewal

Quality of subscriptions secured:

a. Term of subscriptions
b. % from preferred list
c. % from miscellaneous sources

Compensation of salesmen

Expense of salesmen

Measure of salesmen's worth by

a. Comparison with quota or budget
b. Comparison with previous record
c. Relation of salesmen's cost to income
d. Comparison with cost of mail
e. Analysis of quality of subscriptions secured
f. Comparison with other publishers

4. Detail of Salesmen's Expense (Weekly Expense Reports and Report of Calls)

Itemize in minute detail:

Cities visited
Prospects called on and sales made
Railroad fare
Hotel charges
Meals
Pullman
Taxis
Telephone and telegraph

Justification of the expense through

a. Elimination of back tracking and useless traveling
b. Comparison with calls budgeted
c. Relation of sales to calls
d. Careful scrutiny of the reasonableness of the expense items
e. Comparison with budget
f. Comparison of cost with income produced
g. Comparison with other publishers

5. Detail of Full Circulation Costs (Monthly Reports)

Subscriptions sold by salesmen —new and renewal

Subscriptions secured by mail—new and renewal

Gross income per order

Cost per order (full cost)

New subscriptions

Cancellations

Total circulation income

Total circulation expense

Hold these costs in line by

a. Maintaining balance with income produced
b. Comparison with budget
c. Comparison with previous results
d. Comparison with other publishers
e. Comparison of costs of mail and field force efforts with re-

SUMMARY OF CONTROL RECORDS—*Continued*

CIRCULATION EXPENSES

Expenses separately for mail, field, and record keeping: Salaries and commissions; promotion; premiums; stationery and supplies; travel and entertainment; conventions; postage; telephone and telegraph

USE IN CONTROL

sults, taking long term renewal results into consideration

f. Comparison with other publishers

MECHANICAL COSTS

1. Detail of Composition Costs (Card File by Issues; Monthly Statistical Reports)

Advertising:
Number of advertisements segregated by sizes
Number of standing pages (including furnished plates)
Total advertising pages
Cost of corrections
Total composition costs
Average cost per page
Editorial
Number of pages by type sizes
Total editorial pages
Cost of corrections
Cost of killed matter
Total composition costs
Average cost per page

USE IN CONTROL

Reduction of costs by
a. Planning to reduce costly corrections
b. Elimination of frills
c. Intelligently budgeting future operations
d. Decrease in quantity of killed matter
e. Improvement in quality of copy submitted
f. Comparison of costs with those of other operators

2. Detail of Presswork (Card File by Issues; Monthly Statistical Reports)

Press run
Total pages
Size and number of forms
Regular
Extra Colors (number of color pages in each form)
Cost of regular forms
Cost of extra color forms

Economies may be obtained as a result of
a. Reduction in number of copies printed
b. Decrease in use of bleed and other costly form
c. Improved scheduling to eliminate overtime

33507

SUMMARY OF CONTROL RECORDS—*Continued*

MECHANICAL COSTS   USE IN CONTROL

Cost of covers
Cost of extras (in detail)
Total cost of presswork
Cost per M copies

d. Comparison of costs with other publishers
e. Decrease in acceptance of late material

3. Detail of Binding and Mailing (Card File by Issues; Monthly Statistical Reports)

Size and number of signatures
Number of copies mailed
Cost of extras
Total binding and mailing costs
Cost per M copies

Costs can be reduced by

a. Review of "special" costs in light of income collected
b. Binding in maximum size signatures
c. Change from envelopes to wrappers

4. Detail of Paper, Wrappers, Envelopes (Perpetual Inventories)

Kind of stock (size and weight)
Quantity purchased and received
From whom purchased
Price per pound
Quantity used and cost (by issues)
Quantity on hand and cost
Cost per M copies

Reduction of costs by

a. Switching from envelopes to wrappers
b. Larger purchases resulting from precise knowledge of requirements
c. Reduction in allowance for waste on part of printer
d. Change in texture or finish of paper
e. Decrease in sheet size for trim requirements

BUDGETING OBJECTIVES*

1. To provide in advance for all known factors and contingencies: that is, to insure considered planning before doing: to develop knowledge of the business: to replace "hindsight" with "foresight."

2. To provide a practical tool of management and accountability—a yardstick with which to check results against expectations and estimates.

3. To provide for the coordination of the various departments and activities of the business.

* J. K. Lasser, from a lecture before Medill School of Journalism, Northwestern University, Chicago Campus, February 17, 1948, on "Cost Control."

BALANCE SHEET FORM

ASSETS

CURRENT ASSETS

Cash .... $

Cash on hand ....

Notes receivable, less reserves ....

Advertisers' accounts, less reserves for bad debts, adjustments, and agency commissions payable ....

Newsstand receivables, less reserves ....

Inventories of paper and supplies .... ————

TOTAL CURRENT ASSETS .... $

OTHER ASSETS

Post office and miscellaneous deposits ......$

Advances to authors and employees, less reserves ....

Prepaid expenses ....

Deferred expenses upon future issues ...... ————

FIXED ASSETS, AT COST

Printing machinery and equipment ....

Furniture, fixtures, and miscellaneous equipment .... ————

$

Less: Reserves for depreciation .... ————

COST OF PUBLICATION—SUBSCRIPTION LISTS, TRADEMARKS, COPYRIGHTS, AND GOOD WILL ....

————

$————

CURRENT LIABILITIES

CURRENT LIABILITIES

Notes payable .... $

Accounts payable ....

Accrued taxes, interest, etc. .... ————

TOTAL CURRENT LIABILITIES ..... $

NEWSDEALER AND OTHER DEPOSITS ...

UNEARNED INCOME—ADVERTISING, SUBSCRIPTIONS, ETC. ....

FUNDED DEBT ....

CAPITAL STOCK ....

SURPLUS .... ————

$————

TABLE 3. RELATION OF COSTS TO INCOME
COMPARISON OF PROFITABLE MONTHLY BUSINESS PAPER OPERATING COSTS AND NET PROFITS

PUBLICATIONS WITH ANNUAL NET ADVERTISING INCOME OVER $500,000*

	1949 (%)	1950 (%)	Range in reporting figures (%)
Income			
Advertising, net of agency commissions and cash discounts	100.0	100.0	
Expense			
Mechanical and distribution costs			
Composition, presswork, binding and mailing	17.5	17.7	
Paper	8.2	8.0	
Postage and delivery	2.4	2.6	
Wrappers, envelopes, etc.	.9	.5	
	29.0	28.8	24–30
Advertising costs			
Salesmen's salaries and commissions	9.3	9.5	
Travel (branch office costs)	4.4	4.5	
Office salaries	6.2	6.2	
Promotion	4.4	5.1	
Other expenses	2.7	2.8	
	27.0	28.1	26–32
Editorial costs			
Salaries	7.7	8.2	
Contributions	.9	.8	
Travel and entertainment	1.1	1.1	
Art work, photographs, and engravings	2.5	2.7	
Other expenses	1.4	1.4	
	13.6	14.2	13–16
Administrative costs			
Salaries	4.1	4.5	
Rent, light, depreciation	1.4	1.5	
Other expenses	3.5	4.0	
	9.0	10.0	8–12
Publishing Expense	78.6	81.1	
Profit from Advertising (Before circulation)	21.4	18.9	
Circulation profit on income	1.1	6.0	
Net service income	.1	.1	
Net Publishing Profit on Gross Income (Before taxes)	19.7	17.6	

* Some of the publications in this group are monthlies and some weeklies.

4. Secure the following operating controls:

Due to the fact that money is spent for definite purposes, which have been carefully considered in advance by the executives of the company, waste is largely prevented.

Since all department heads participate directly in the preparation of budgets covering their activities, responsibility is definitely fixed.

Every budget which is prepared depends on other budgets. If all factors are properly considered, all departments must cooperate closely one with the other to obtain the best results. Consequently, the budget is an extremely practical and effective coordinating device.

The budget restrains unwise expansion. Before committing ourselves to new activities it must be definitely established that the undertaking is based on cold facts rather than an overenthusiasm.

The budget establishes a proper relationship between income and expense. It aids in the application of the principle of spending money in order to make money. It also acts as a definite check against the undue mortgaging of future income.

Estimated and actual results may be checked one against the other periodically. In this way, we keep in constant close touch with all activities and to investigate at once any situation which needs attention.

Budgeting planning is vital. It concerns such questions of policy as these:

Individuals who are to prepare the budgets.

Quantity of accounting data and statistical records to show past performances which will be necessary to aid the preparation of the estimates.

Type of executive control and approval which is to be exercised in approving the budgets.

Length of time to be budgeted.

CHAPTER 3

Circulation

CIRCULATION IN AN EXPANDING ECONOMY

The editorial and advertising departments exert all the efforts of men and machines toward bringing in news and technological information from the field. They then utilize production and mechanical departments to compress all this information into a readable form of presentation known as the businesspaper.

The circulation department on the other hand utilizes men and machines toward sending out this presentation, making it available to a specialized readership.

Upon the satisfactory performance of the circulation manager's multiple functions depends the success of the entire businesspaper publishing organization.

He has a four-way job according to Floyd Hockenhull, one of the contributors to this chapter: (1) He is the sales manager whose men sell the product (the businesspaper) to the logical readers. His salesmen are the publisher's only human contact with the mass of subscribers; (2) he is the delivery superintendent who sees that the package is received on schedule; (3) he is the office manager of a subscription department whose clerks and equipment must be as efficient as any in the organization; (4) he works closely with outside circulation auditors to furnish the publisher and advertising sales manager with continuous verification of the readership.

The circulation manager's position in importance parallels that of the editor's and the advertising manager's.

Like the editor he draws on the research department for information about the market and the audience reaction to editorial and advertising content.

Like the advertising sales manager he draws heavily on the promotion department to help him increase or maintain the readership.

Like both the editor and advertising manager he can only operate in line with basic policy laid down by his publisher and that may sometimes defeat his objectives and dampen his ardor.

The fortunes of a businesspaper expand or contract along with the industry it serves. For most businesspapers the industries they serve have expanded in number of units and volume of output. There will always be pressure from some advertisers to restrict the circulation to their particular type or quality of prospect or customer and thus keep the advertising rates low. The larger pressure comes from advertisers and agencies who want to increase the active circulation. These pressures pose a problem. Every publication has a point of diminishing returns. In order to keep their costs and advertising rates down many publishers are tempted to hold the circulation down. This may prove to be a penny-wise-pound-foolish practice for it may encourage a publishing competitor to come into the field with a stronger editorial setup, quickly build a larger circulation, and eventually take away the older publisher's best advertisers even while charging them higher rates.

The rate is always relative to the value you are giving.

In an expanding economy the demand for a publisher's particular brand of know-how is bound to increase. It is the natural impulse of a circulation manager to want to add these people to his list. Also, more advertisers and readers are becoming interested in foreign markets, and *vice versa*. As our country shows greater leadership in world political and economic affairs the American business press must assume a more influential position in world markets.

The publisher should rely on his circulation manager's studies made jointly with the advertising sales manager to indicate what refinements are necessary in circulation, if he is to get the most out of the publishing property, pace the industry, and maintain his competitive position. As he improves his service he is entitled to charge more for it.

This chapter on circulation falls into two parts. The first part is concerned with the operation of a circulation department, the functions of its managers, mailing list and field force, and a description of the independent bureaus that audit and verify circulation figures. The second part is concerned with the nature of the current controvery between publishers of paid circulation businesspapers and publishers of controlled (or free) circulation publications.

BUSINESSPAPER CIRCULATION FUNDAMENTALS*

Is the purpose of your circulation department to make a profit on the sale of your product as other manufacturers do?

* Floyd L. Hockenhull, Publisher, *Circulation Management* magazine; from a lecture before Medill School of Journalism, Northwestern University, April 20, 1948.

Or is the purpose of your circulation department primarily coverage of your field for your advertisers—without regard, or much regard, for securing revenue from circulation?

Most businesspaper. publishers use circulation as the base for advertising and do not expect to net any profits from subscribers.[1] Logically, the sale of the product to its readers should produce net revenue for the publisher. Theoretically, advertising is a byproduct. But in most cases the byproduct, advertising, produces the revenue. The tail wags the dog.

I believe circulation should yield a net profit and in most cases it can yield a net profit. You have to decide the purpose of your circulation for yourself.

CIRCULATION COVERAGE AND PENETRATION

You also will have to determine, as well as you can, the broad, over-all management policies relative to the degree of circulation coverage of your field, and to the degree of penetration into the field.

Circulation coverage is the degree of horizontal coverage of your field. To illustrate, if there are 3500 firms in the industry served by your businesspaper, you would have 100 per cent coverage with one subscription from each of the 3500 firms—a total of 3500 circulation on this basis.

Circulation penetration is the degree of vertical circulation coverage. To illustrate, if you have 5 subscribers in every firm, you penetrate the field vertically to that degree. In practice, it is virtually impossible to achieve 100 per cent coverage of a field of any sizable extent.

You also will have to decide not only your degree of circulation coverage of your field—whether 30 or 40 or 50 per cent and so on—but also you will have to decide in which stratum or level of your field you will strive for circulation coverage.

[1] *Editor's note:* An analysis of ABC reports of 100 ABP publications indicates that subscribers paid over $5 million (Canadian and foreign postage not included) for a million subscriptions. Of these subs, 78 per cent were received at full subscription price; 15 per cent in quantity sales; 3 per cent were Association subs; 3 per cent were direct reduced prices; combination sales, .007 per cent; group subs, .003 per cent. Channels of subscriptions were as follows: By mail, 65 per cent; publisher's own field force, 18 per cent; catalogue and other agencies, 10 per cent; associations, 3 per cent; miscellaneous, 5 per cent. Only 17 per cent of these subs were sold with premiums and these inducements were either trade directories or reprints of editorial content. The terms on which these subs were sold were: 63 per cent for one year; 22 per cent for three years; 12 per cent for two years; 3 per cent for six months (ABP Circulations Clinic, Chicago, June, 1950).

For the firms in all industries are in the form of a pyramid. The base of the pyramid is the small firms which buy small amounts of products and services. But 85 per cent of the buying power for your advertisers' products or services may be in only 35 per cent of the firms, the ones at the top of the pyramid.

Are you going to strive for circulation coverage of the 35 per cent of the firms with 85 per cent of the buying power—rather than for 100 per cent coverage of the field? You will have to decide.

You will have to decide, too, the degree of circulation penetration. Perhaps you will strive for horizontal coverage of the 35 per cent of firms with the greatest buying-power value for your advertisers, and also strive to get 4 or 5 top executives as subscribers in each of these firms.

Thus you would give your advertisers coverage of the firms with greatest buying power *plus* penetration to the degree of covering 4 or 5 top executives who control or influence the buying in each firm.

Degree of circulation coverage and degree of circulation penetration are two broad, over-all management policies in the business of publishing a businesspaper.

If you are the publisher or general manager, you will have to direct the careful analysis of your businesspaper's field. You will have to measure the buying power of the firms in your field by such measuring sticks as the number of people they employ; their financial ratings; their gross sales; their floor space; and the like.

HOW BIG A CIRCULATION

How big will your businesspaper's circulation be?

The size of your circulation depends upon many factors. Among the most important factors which affect size of circulation are: (1) The number of firms in your paper's industry and the degree of circulation coverage you want; (2) the number of executives who control or influence the buying of products and services and the degree of circulation penetration you want; (3) responsiveness of the field; (4) competition; (5) ability of your circulation department to sell; (6) subscription rate; (7) editorial merit of your businesspaper—but merit as seen by the subscribers themselves, and not necessarily as seen by your editorial department or even by yourself; (8) whether your policy is paid circulation or free circulation.

The circulation manager of a businesspaper, or any other publication, holds a four-way job. The circulation manager must perform four distinct functions.

1. He is the sales manager who sells the publisher's product to the readers, with all a sales manager's duties.

2. He is the delivery superintendent who sees that the readers get good, efficient service.

3. He is the office manager in charge of the department that is in direct contact with the subscribers and the nonsubscribers. The publisher should remember, by the way, that the only direct contact the mass of subscribers and nonsubscribers have with the publication is through the circulation department. The circulation manager must select and direct courteous men and women who have their hearts in their work.

4. The circulation manager is a key executive in the publishing house. While the circulation manager must be an expert in the routine and technical work of the circulation department, he is more and more valuable to the publisher as he gives executive attention to every factor in the over-all picture which may increase or slow down the publication's growth.

DETERMINING TYPE, QUALITY, AND VOLUME OF CIRCULATION*

Assume that you are about to become the publisher of a new businesspaper. You have picked out your field, planned your editorial content, estimated how much you will take in and what your costs will be. Now you are at the point of determining your circulation policy. You will have to decide on how much circulation, the nature, and the quality.

Let us consider quantity first: how big should the circulation of your publication be? Businesspaper circulations run all the way from 1000 to more than 50,000. The size of the field is, of course, an important factor, but this does not necessarily mean that the total number of bakeries, shoe stores, factories, quarries, or other kind of units that make up your field must be considered. In most fields the majority of units are too small to be worth covering.

Assume, for example, you are going to start a publication to serve women's garment manufacturers. You look at the trade statistics and find there are 20,200 plants in that field. You find a thousand of them

* Arthur H. Dix, Vice-President in charge of Research, Conover-Mast Publications; from a lecture at New York University, March 19, 1947.

are so small they have no employees at all. The whole plant consists of the boss, a sewing machine, and a spool of thread. Digging further, you find another 11,000 have less than 20 employees per plant. So you eliminate the 12,000 little plants; you drop 60 per cent of the field.

The remaining 8000 units employ 82 per cent of the labor, buy 80 per cent of all the materials and equipment. Employment is a very good gauge of a field's buying power. By limiting your field to the 8000 plants (only two-fifths of the total number of plants in the industry) you give your advertisers a coverage of four-fifths of the buying power. In this case you have used the number of employees as a gauge. There are a lot of other gauges. In some fields you might use financial rating. You get it in Dun and Bradstreet. Or you might use sales volume, floor space, or production capacity.

If you have any difficulty in deciding where you are going to set your limit, you can take it up with your prospective advertisers, because they have a very good idea of how big a plant should be to be worth putting on their own list. If a name is worth putting on their list, you can assume it is worth putting on yours.

So far you have size as a yardstick, but you need still another kind of a yardstick in determining circulation. You have to decide on the type of subscriber you want. Your publication may be aimed at designers or superintendents, sales managers, production executives, button-hole department foremen, or the brass hats. Perhaps you intend to serve all these types of executives. That means setting up circulation specifications. The success of your publication will depend to a great extent on how religiously you follow those specifications.

If you published a general magazine like *The Saturday Evening Post* or *True Romances*, it would not make much difference whom you got as readers, because everybody buys shoes, soap, cigarettes, etc. But your business publication is a specialized paper. You cannot aim your circulation shots all over your field. You have to fire those shots at the particular part of the field that you want to cover. The only kind of shots that are going to count for you are those that come within the particular field that you have decided to cover. Any copies of your publication that go to people outside that field weaken your paper.

It does not make any difference whether you send it to them free or whether they pay for it, because the subscriber only pays for a small part of the publisher's cost of supplying the publication to him regularly.

You have to make certain other decisions. You have decided on the type, quality, and quantity of your circulation. But you still have this question to answer: Are you going to charge readers for your publication or are you going to send it free of charge?

The relative merits of paid versus free or "controlled" circulation are widely discussed. There are many successful publications in each category. As a matter of fact, there are some very successful publishing organizations that use both types of circulation, and there are some successful publications with both types of circulation on the same publication.

First, let us decide what we mean by paid circulation and controlled circulation. It would be very easy if every publication had either a 100 per cent free or a 100 per cent paid circulation, but it does not work out that way. You find all kinds of averages in between. Some are 80 per cent one way and 20 per cent the other. Some are just the reverse.

So, somebody had to make a rule. The line is drawn exactly in the middle. The Audit Bureau of Circulations, the auditing organization of paid publications, says that if a publication has more than 50 per cent paid subscribers it is a paid publication. The organization in the free field, the Controlled Circulation Audit, formerly provided that if you have 50 per cent or more copies going to recipients without charge, you are a controlled circulation paper, but this proportion has recently been modified. [Editor's note: ABC minimum was raised to 70 per cent in 1951.]

Now, there is still a third type of circulation. It is used in fields in which a distributor or a wholesaler is an important factor. In these fields, the wholesaler or distributor furnishes the publisher with a list of his selected customers or prospects to which he wants the publication sent. The publisher receives payment from the distributor for those copies. Therefore, you can really call it a paid circulation, but it is not regarded as paid circulation in the true sense of the word because when you speak of paid circulation it means that the recipient or his employer actually pays for the paper. So this type of circulation is classed as "controlled."

Before the advent of independent circulation auditing, advertising claims were limited only by the conscience of advertising salesmen. On the same publication you might find circulation claims ranging from 100 per cent to 250 per cent above what the true circulation figure was. Things got so bad that the honest publishers, the conservative ones, said,

"We will not give out circulation figures." You cannot buy advertising properly without circulation figures, so advertising buyers often resorted to detective work to get it. One favorite device was for an advertising buyer to hire somebody in the print shop to watch the count on the printing press, and to tell them what the count was when the press run ended. When unscrupulous publishers discovered that, they started the count at a figure thousands above zero.

Now a word about circulation cost control. Cost control is the accountant's fancy term that gives one a pleasant sense of power. It sounds as if you can turn your costs on and off like a water tap but, of course, you cannot. Your power over many circulation costs is limited. If printing prices go up, you go up with them. Of course, you can control some of your costs by spending less money for promotion, but too much of that kind of control and you may "economize" yourself out of business.

The actual cost figures that the circulation manager watches like a hawk are his cost per subscription, per campaign, and per salesman. These are the yardsticks that measure his skill and his salesmen's skill.

The monthly expense statements the circulation manager gets from the accounting department are all right, but usually he spends a lot of money in one month and gets his subscriptions in the next month. There is a month's lag between cause and effect. So usually he pays more attention to the quarterly statement or the half-yearly or yearly statement.

Most people want to know whether paid publications actually make their money on circulation. J. K. Lasser keeps records of 105 business-papers and Ken Marks of that firm of auditors showed me that for 1946 the circulation profit on these 105 papers averaged 14.8 per cent. The circulation profit does not include any of the costs of printing the magazine or any of the editorial salaries or any part of the cost of mailing. It is just the cost of running the circulation department, circulation promotion, and so forth. It does not even include floor space or any of the brass hat salaries. This means that out of every $100 of circulation income, about $85 was spent, leaving a surplus of $15. Some papers save as much as 50 per cent of their circulation income. There are some that spend a little more in getting subscriptions than they take from subscribers. You cannot say: "I will save it by going free." Whether your circulation is paid or free you have the expense of maintaining circulation records, mailing lists, stencils, and so forth.

Oddly enough, the biggest factor of circulation cost is outside the circulation department itself. It lies in the editorial department. The circulation department is only the editorial sales department. Whether you are selling automobiles or girdles or businesspapers, the merit of the product is the biggest factor in your sales cost. Obviously, the more money you put into your product, the lower your sales cost; if you cheapen your product, the more you will have to spend in order to sell it. But even the most meritorious product must be *sold*.

Consequently, the businesspaper publisher, will have to decide how much money he is going to spend on his product and how much he is going to spend in selling it. Good selling will not move a poor product.

You may remember the story of Mark Twain's steamboat—the one that had such a big whistle that every time it blew, the boat could not get away from dock until it had worked up enough steam to run the engine again.

Editors of publications and the circulation departments have to work closely together. They have to work like Daisy and her boy friend on the famous bicycle built for two. If they both pedal in the same direction, the publication goes along at a pretty fast clip, but it is not uncommon to see an editorial department aiming at one class of reader and the circulation department trying to sell another class.

We all know that everybody loves editors. An editor is a good man to keep on the right side of. He can put your name in the paper. And you never saw anybody that did not like to get his name in the paper. So when an editor makes a field call, he is usually told, "You have a wonderful paper. I would not miss a word of it. I read every line of it," the editor comes back with his vest buttons bursting. He believes everybody in the field is waiting with bated breath for the next issue to come in. But the same man that made the editor's chest swell will tell the circulation salesman, "Look at that stack of magazines I haven't touched . . . and you are asking me to take another!"

It would be a very illuminating experience for an editor to conceal his identify, take a pad of subscription blanks, make some cold calls on the field, and try to sell subscriptions. It would make him aware of the terrific amount of competition for reading time that the editor of any publication faces. He would find he is competing not only with other businesspapers in his field, but also with a host of other publications he does not normally regard as competition—the growing number of letter services of the Kiplinger type, with organizations that supply abstracts

of businesspaper articles to relieve the user of the need of reading businesspapers, with daily business newspapers, sectional businesspapers,
the business sections of general newspapers, and weekly news magazines.

The editor would soon see that no one wants "just another businesspaper." He would find that the prospect, like the chorus girl, "already
has a book." The prospect does want an idea that will tell him how to
take the air bubbles out of his brass castings or put more air bubbles
into his sponge cake. Therefore, the circulation manager talks a great
deal about the ideas. After all, the publication is just the conveyor of
the ideas.

Circulation selling keeps you continually reminded of the fact that
the human mind is not eager to work. Businesspapers are not read for
fun or entertainment. They are adult school books, and most of us are
allergic to school books. That is the reason why you will find circulation
costs lowest on the publications whose editors present their material so
simply that it makes the learning process as easy and painless as possible.

Another big help in selling circulation is advertising volume. When
you are selling subscriptions, you find that if you have a big fat book
you can sell it easier than you can a skinny book. You cannot make an
editorial preference survey these days without having readers volunteer
the information, whether invited to or not, that they regard the advertising section equally as valuable as the editorial section.

When you start publishing your trade paper, you will wake up in
the middle of the night a couple of times a week wondering whether
your readers are actually getting any benefit from the brilliant gems your
editors are serving up to them. So you will begin thinking of some way
to stimulate reader interest outside of the publication itself. I suppose
that practically every businesspaper in the country at one time or another
has done something along this line; maybe it is only a postcard calling
attention to a series of articles that you are very proud of.

The odd part of it is that the circulation men are not as enthusiastic
as editors over this matter of reader-interest cultivation. This might be
due to laziness.

The critical time in the life of any subscription is the time it first
expires. It is on trial for the first year. Some may renew their subscriptions and some may not. You would think it would pay a publisher
to send some special letters prior to the initial expiration, but most
subscription men take a fatalistic attitude toward this matter. They feel
that the impression a reader got from the publication itself, from the

twelve copies or the twenty-four copies or fifty-two copies he received, outweighs anything the publisher can say about the paper. I recall a test that was made by a Chicago publication. They made an extensive investigation. They took their expirations for a six-month period and divided them into two parts. To one part they sent a long series of letters saying what a wonderful paper they had, calling attention to certain hotshot articles that had appeared in the publication and describing some fine articles to come. The other half got just the usual expiration letters.

When the dust cleared and they added up the results, they found they did not get any more renewals from the part that got all the fancy treatment than from the other part. But of course one test does not prove a great deal, and what works on one paper may not work on another. I understand that McGraw-Hill is embarking on a campaign—sending out a special series of letters to people whose subscriptions are expiring for the first time. Fortunately, this is something you do not have to guess about. You can split a list of expirations. You can give one special treatment and give the other ordinary treatment. You can find out whether it pays or not, and whether it is true, as most circulation men believe, that it is better to put the money into the paper rather than spend it in that way.

The idea in back of this, of course, is to increase your renewal percentage. That is what every publisher is striving for. It cuts down the cost of operating your circulation department. A high renewal percentage is a very nice thing for your advertising men to brag about. One of the most important things that I have to say concerns a new and excellent way to raise your renewal rate by taking your renewed and canceled subscriptions for a certain period and tracing them back to the source.

You might find, for example, if you did that research work, that a year ago you put in a lot of subscriptions based on a series of articles that were not followed up by your editors. You got people on your circulation list on the basis of certain articles, and your editors did not follow through. Consequently, they canceled their subscriptions or failed to renew.

Again, you might divide your expirations according to the various parts of your field. It might be divided into four or five different sections. You may find you have a high renewal section in one part of your field and a low renewal section in another. Obviously, the thing to do would be to give the low part of the field better attention or maybe cut it out altogether.

Again, you might divide your expirations geographically and find that you are doing well in the Middle Atlantic states or perhaps the Midwest and you might find you are losing a lot of subscriptions in the Pacific Coast or in the deep South, and obviously the thing to do would be to give them greater attention editorially.

If you employ subscription men, you might make another test to determine how they renewed. I recall one test of this kind that proved that the top salesman was actually the most expensive man on the staff, because he renewed only one-third of his subscriptions, whereas the average for the whole staff was fifty per cent.

It may have been safe at one time to use the circulation department as a training school, but it is pretty risky today. If you have an inexperienced circulation department these days, you can be pretty sure you will have a weak publication. For the circulation department is in charge of distribution, and if you look over the tombstones of the publishing graveyard, you will find most of them read "Died of bad circulation."

To repeat another important point: a mediocre mail-order campaign sent to an excellent list will be successful, but the most brilliant promotion campaign sent to a poor list will fall flat on its face.

It is the same with publications. No matter how ably your publication is edited, it will do you very little good unless you reach the right people. To sell them, you have to *reach* them first.

To maintain a potent circulation with a minimum of waste you have to have a good circulation department. It is no mere coincidence that the strong publications today are those with a strong circulation department. It is a good department to be in and it is a good department to grow in.

BUILDING THE MAILING LIST*

Whether your publication is paid or controlled, a good mailing list or prospect list is essential for sound circulation.

But good lists are not just wished into being. They require time to build and a lot of persistent and continued work to keep them effective. Experienced circulation men know that a good list will pay off even though you use mediocre sales letters, while a poor list will not produce enough orders even with the most brilliant promotion letter in the world.

Assuming you have a list at present but want to make it better, where do you start? Check your prospect list for these points:

* Gardiner Gibbs, Manager, Mail Circulation Sales, McGraw-Hill Publishing Company; from a lecture at New York University, March 19, 1947.

Does it cover the field of your paper? How old are the names in the present list? Where did they come from? How many new names were added in the last week, month, year? How many subscription orders from your last mailing? How many post office returns from your last mailing?

The answers you get to those questions will tell you whether you can use your present list successfully or whether it would be better to junk it and start a new one. If you decide to start a new list from scratch, sit down and map out what names your new list is to cover. Knowing the kinds of people that you want on your list, you are ready to go after their names.

Here is a partial list of possible sources for names that can be used in building a mailing list for almost any field. You can add others to fit the particular needs of your publication.

1. Standard directories such as Thomas', Dun's, Polks' or Moody's.
2. The classified sections of telephone books.
3. Reports from circulation salesmen in the field.
4. The membership lists of business or technical associations and societies in your field.
5. Public records such as business incorporations, automobile registrations, building permits, births, tax rolls, voters' lists, etc.
6. Registration records of technical expositions and conventions of leading men in your field.
7. Your former subscribers or expirations.
8. Questionnaires sent to present readers, asking for names of other people in your field.
9. Chambers of Commerce reports.
10. Alumni directories of technical colleges.
11. News items or personals in newspapers, magazines, and clipping services.
12. Inquiries from prospects for your publication.
13. The names on letterheads in your daily mail.
14. An exchange of mailing lists with your advertisers.
15. Buy the needed names from a recognized list house.

Having secured a start by tapping all or part of these sources of names for your new mailing list, you must next decide what filing method will be best for your needs. Your choice will be dictated by the various uses to be made of the list by the circulation and other departments in your company.

The standard filing methods for circulation mailing lists are:

1. Geographical, which means filing the names alphabetically by states, then alphabetically by cities in each state, then alphabetically by individual names within cities.

2. Alphabetical, which means filing all the names first by states and then alphabetically by individual names regardless of the cities in the state.

3. Chronological, which means filing by either of above methods but setting up a separate list for each new year, month, or period of time suitable for your use.

4. Population groups, which means filing by cities, counties, or rural or urban trading areas.

In addition there are several individual specifications or ratings that can influence the selection of the names you put in your list, according to the publication you are selling. For example, you would not want on your list the names of people earning $2000 a year as prospects for a $300-a-year financial service. You must tailor your list to your market.

Each filing method has its advantages and disadvantages. Geographical or alphabetical filing are generally used in circulation list work. Geographical filing makes it easy to sort your mail for mailing under third-class postage, but it permits a duplication of the same name, as you might pick up both the office address and the home address for the same individual. For example, you might have a person listed at his office with the Texas Company in New York City and also have the same person listed at his home address in Yonkers, N. Y. This would come to light with alphabetical filing. Alphabetical filing is also best for a list in a field where the individuals shift rapidly from one job to another. While alphabetical filing prevents duplication of names, it does make the sorting of mail to be sent under third-class, penny postage much slower. At McGraw-Hill we use both filing methods, according to the rate of turnover on various lists.

Most circulation mailing lists are not used frequently enough to justify the additional cost of cutting the names on stencil plates, so that a card list is sufficient. However, if your list is to be used two or three times a month, year around, you can gain some advantages and economies by putting the list on paper or metal stencils.

For the fastest delivery of your copies and promotion mail, be sure your mailing list includes the postal zone numbers required in cities of 100,000 population or more. The postmaster will give you a list of the cities requiring zone numbers and explain how the post offices throughout the country will put the zone numbers on your list—free of charge.

The same vigilance that goes into building your list originally must be constantly continued in its maintenance. If it is not, the present turnover of personnel in business, from 15 per cent to 40 per cent annually, will soon undermine and destroy the effectiveness of your list.

List work can be a boring chore or an interesting job. How your list clerks feel about it depends pretty much on how you present the work to them. Explain the job to them. Let them know how much their efforts influence the returns from your mailings. Tell them how much wasted letters cost. Keep your list people posted on the results obtained from the campaigns for circulation mailed over the lists on which they work. Show them the promotion pieces you use and tell them how many orders each one produced. If list clerks know and appreciate the importance of their work in the circulation operation, they will take real pride in doing a good job.

I hope you are now convinced that the mailing list is an important factor in the success of your circulation campaigns. There are no short-cuts, no easy ways of doing list building and list maintenance. Good lists take time and money to build. But good lists are worth money, and develope top-quality circulation with a high renewability.

So much for the list. Now, let us swing over to see how you are going to sell to that list.

We have determined the type and quality and number of our readers, and we have built a fine prospect or mailing list. If you have decided to develop your paper on a paid basis, we are ready to aggressively develop the circulation. There are two ways by which we can get the subscriptions. We can sell them by direct mail, or we can sell them by personal call through circulation salesmen in the field. We shall probably do as many publishers do—use a balanced combination of both methods to get the best coverage of our field at the lowest costs.

Let us first look at the mail-selling operation. There is nothing mysterious about it. It is a mail-order operation pure and simple. You send out letters selling the benefits of reading your businesspaper, and you get back subscriptions. How many sales letters you mail is generally determined by the number of subscriptions needed, the percentage of return from the mailings, and the cost of getting those orders. If the returns from your mail efforts is continuously too small and the orders too costly, you may decide to develop more of your circulation by field efforts than you originally planned.

One of the most gratifying features of selling circulation by mail is that your circulation manager knows at all times just where he stands, and that can be good or bad. There is no guesswork. There is an exact measure of the effectiveness and the cost of each individual letter sent out. So many letters or circulars are mailed. They cost so much. They brought in so many subscription orders and each subscription costs you so much. It is very simple.

Because he works with exact costs, your circulation manager has an opportunity to test ways and means of getting the greatest return for the money spent on each piece. It is in this testing of mail-order copy that you find one of the most interesting phases of circulation work. Testing alone could be the basis for a long discussion, but let me give you a few examples of what I mean by testing, and the surprising things you learn in circulation mail promotion work.

Your first basic test, of course, is to get your sales story told, in letter, folder, or circular form, so it produces a satisfactory result. Then, with a mailing piece that you know works, you can embark on a series of tests to run down the effectiveness of each of the many elements that make up your promotion piece.

For instance, take one small point—postage. Does first-class postage at 3 cents a letter produce more orders than third-class postage at 1 cent a letter? We mailed 2000 identical pieces at each rate in January and got 23 subscription orders from the ones mailed at first-class against 24 orders from those mailed at the third-class rate. This enabled us to save $20 a thousand on our follow-up campaign of 50,000 letters. (Ed. Note: Third class rate now 2 cents.)

Does a commemorative stamp help or hurt returns? Many tests have shown that a special commemorative stamp generally helps returns by getting added attention for your mailing piece. However, we ran into an interesting reaction when we tested a Roosevelt commemorative stamp against a regular 1-cent stamp. We tipped the stamp on a letter for the recipient to detach and use on an enclosed order card—the old "we pay the freight" idea. The 5000 letters using the Roosevelt stamp pulled 58 subscription orders while the 5000 letters using the conventional 1-cent green stamp brought in 112 orders, or nearly double the return of the Roosevelt commemorative. I don't know whether we should conclude that our list contains a preponderance of Democrats or a lot of stamp collectors. I do know we shall be very careful what commemorative stamps we use on future mailings.

Another interesting test is the old question: Does it pay to fill in the name of the individual on a mailing piece? Yes, by all means. Right after Christmas we tested an invitation type of circular. On 5000 the man's name was typed in the salutation while on another 5000 we used only a standard, running headline. The filled-in letters pulled 32 orders per thousand mailed while those without the personalized fill-in brought us only 21 orders per thousand. The extra cost of filling in the names paid for itself many times over in 11 more orders per thousand mailed.

We made many tests during the war, and several lately, to determine whether a two-page letter on two sheets was better than a two-page letter printed front and back on one sheet. We wanted the answer to this question because of the continued paper shortage. A test of 5000 letters prepared on two pages brought us 60 orders while the same letter printed front and back of the same sheet brought in 59 orders— only 1 order less. We use the one-page job and save our paper.

How much does asking for cash with the order hurt circulation returns? A test of 5000 letters demanding "cash-with-order" brought us 74 orders while 5000 of the same letter offering the customer a chance to "pay later when you get our bill" brought us 125 orders—10 more orders per thousand mailed. Since we collect 95 per cent of the credit subscriptions on this paper, it was much better for us to make the credit offer.

So much for testing. The possibilities are endless, and each test contributes to increasing the results of your mail-order efforts in circulation work. Let me warn you that you cannot make a test on any point and conclude you have established an irrevocable law for your guidance. Buying habits and conditions change. What worked for you last year may be a flop now. The value of any tests you make is in quickly following up what you have found effective, before the uncontrollable factors change—uncontrollable factors such as business conditions, strikes, floods, elections or war news, all of which affect mail-order returns.

It may interest you to know that periodically the New York businesspaper circulation managers pool their most successful, order-getting letters. These are published by the Associated Business Publications.

If you looked through this ABP book of successful circulation letters, you would find that many of them are two pages long. I know there are many people who feel that a letter should be short—never longer than one page. Believe me, circulation men would love to use short letters, but they wisely use the kind of letters that get the most orders, which in many cases is the longer letter. Perhaps the reason for long letters being successful is that in selling subscriptions each letter must be a complete sales story in itself. You cannot sell a prospect a little at a time, in a series of letters building up to a sale. You must tell the whole story and get the sale on that one solicitation. It is not the length of the letter but how interesting your sales message is to the prospect that determines the success of the letter. *Time* magazine uses three-page letters with good results.

Circulation men have one rule-of-thumb measure for pre-judging the possible success of a new letter. It is simply that if the editor or publisher likes it—watch out! That is no reflection on their judgment—it is simply that they feel the magazine should be sold "as a whole" which in mail-order selling is not the most productive approach.

Whether you sell subscriptions by mail or through field salesmen, the chances are that a good premium will reduce your subscription-getting costs. The word "premium" has an ugly sound. It suggests to many people slide rules, fountain pens, and safety razors. Such premiums are still frowned upon by publishers and by advertising buyers. But that attitude has changed regarding the premium usually offered by business publications today. Here the so-called "premium" is a collection or reprint of editorial material that has already appeared in past issues of the publication itself. Such a premium is simply the editorial content of the magazine in a little different package. Since the use of such premiums does not reduce the renewability of subscriptions, many business-papers use them successfully as an aid in getting new subscribers.

If you are a member of the Audit Bureau of Circulations, the value of what you can give away as a premium is limited by your subscription price. You cannot offer any reprint the cost of which exceeds 50 per cent of the basic one-year rate subscription price.

To prove that a premium pays for itself and is a good investment in mail-order selling, let me tell you about a mailing we made with and without a premium. A mailing of 5000 letters on *Electrical Merchandising*, with no premium, brought us 193 orders, or 3.9 per cent. Then we developed a small, paper-covered booklet on "Appliance Servicing," from editorial material in past issues. It cost us 12½ cents a copy. On a comparable mailing of 5000 letters, to the same list, offering this booklet, we got 296 orders, or 5.9 per cent—20 more orders per thousand letters mailed for an additional investment in the premium of $7.38. The orders without the premium cost us $1.03 while those with the premium cost us 80 cents each.

Now let us see how subscriptions are sold by salesmen making personal calls on our prospects.

Generally, field selling is more expensive than selling by mail, but there is not the wide fluctuation in costs that you will get in mail selling between good and bad business conditions. Since most circulation salesmen operate on a small salary and commission arrangement, the cost of subscriptions sold by field salesmen is more or less fixed. The publisher only pays for the orders sold.

There is no uniformity in the methods of operating circulation field salesmen. Some firms assign the salesmen to definite territories and credit the salesmen with business developed out of their territories. Other companies credit the salesman only with the sales he actually makes. In one case the salesmen can solicit renewals in advance of any mail effort; in another the salesmen must not start after renewals before mail does.

Field selling is most effective on those publications where the subscriptions can be sold in groups or where there is a large number of prospects in one company or plant and penetration to all levels of responsibility is desirable.

You may use subscription salesmen even though their selling costs may be higher than mail, for you may find that on your publication you cannot develop enough circulation of the kind you want by mail efforts alone.

The publisher of several magazines can use a field sales force to better advantage than the publisher of one paper. However, several single magazines find it very successful to employ one or two field salesmen on their papers. *Iron Age* is a good example. Another possibility for the publisher of only one magazine is to join with other, noncompeting, businesspapers and have the same circulation salesmen represent you as well as several other publications. This has been tried. It is not done extensively, but there is at least one field-selling organization that functions for a group of related merchandising businesspapers.

Some publications have had moderate success with free-lance salesmen in areas where prospects are fairly numerous—but this method is not used widely.

McGraw-Hill, I believe, operates the largest circulation sales force in the businesspaper field. At the present time we have 160 full-time circulation salesmen covering the United States, Canada, Mexico, Central and South America, England, Sweden, Norway, Belgium, Holland, South Africa, India, and Australia. Some of these men are specialists, concentrating on just one of our papers, but many of them sell subscriptions to all 26 papers.

Their activities are directed by a sales manager and three assistant sales managers. Fourteen district managers work with the men, training them and checking their efforts. They work hard and produce a good volume of high-quality subscriptions.

The average salesman selling subscriptions to business magazines is generally a pretty substantial citizen. I know in our own organization they are not "working their way through college." They have been through. Sixty-five per cent of our men are college graduates, averaging about forty-six years of age. I think they are typical of the men with other publishers.

There is no uniformity in the compensation arrangements for field circulation salesmen. A check with other publishers and J. K. Lasser's office indicates that their earnings gross from $2500 up to $16,000 a year. The average circulation salesman grosses from $5000 to $6000 annually.

TWENTY-FIVE DO'S AND DON'T'S ON DIRECT MAIL*

The following is based on what the circulation department experts say as a result of their direct-mail tests.

1. Never use a circular alone—always include a letter. Letter accounts for 65 to 75 per cent of orders; enclosure 15 to 25 per cent; card 5 to 10 per cent.
2. Color pays on cards, letterheads, in the letter itself.
3. Fill in letter or not; if you are willing to pay the extra cost to get certain select prospects, it pays. Hooven letters pay on prize prospects. Fill in your letter if you have your own addressograph plates.
4. Try fill-in in red.

* Stanley R. Clague, Secretary, The Modern Hospital Publishing Company, Chicago; from a lecture before Medill School of Journalism, Northwestern University, April, 1948. Mr. Clague is one of the founders of The Audit Bureau of Circulations.

5. Postage: 1¢ meter—printed (2 color) 1¢ indicia—stamps.
6. Two-page letters: use the back of the first page (although *Time* uses two and sometimes three sheets); one page seems best.
7. Order form separate; use card.
8. Require a signature on card when filled in (some doubt its need).
9. Get credit orders—additional subscriptions you get more than pay for losses and cost of collecting credit subscriptions.
10. Don't be fooled on a letter. Check credit losses. You may get big return but losses cut down the net gain.
11. Test, even on small lists.
12. Use same letter as often as every 90 days. Invitation has been used for twenty years.
13. Don't try to be funny. Stunts seldom pay. Don't preach. Be friendly. Be sincere. Be truthful. Don't oversell.
14. Because a piece of circulation promotion works on one publication does not mean it will pull on another in a different field.
15. Because *Time* or any other publication follows a certain form does not mean you can copy it and then sit back and wait for the orders to pour in. You may have a sad awakening.
16. If you make a test follow it immediately with your mailing. Do not wait. There may be a coal strike or something else may happen that will disturb the prospects. Your mailing may not reflect the test in results.
17. Keep in touch with the editorial department so that you will know when a red-hot article is coming or a series that you can use as selling bait. Series of articles help on renewals and help to collect on credit orders. If you sell on a single article in a single issue, the prospect will get the copy and you may never hear from him with reference to the amount due.
18. If the editor says your piece of promotion is good—look out! If another circulation manager says it's O.K.—toss it in the basket and start over again.
19. Watch your time of mailing. Some do not mail in summer months. Try it, you may be pleasantly surprised.
20. Test to see if there is any difference on returns between blue multigraphing and black. Majority use black with red.
21. Order card on colored stock gives two-color advantage.
22. If filled in, fold so that fill-in will show when envelope is opened.
23. Not necessary to clip enclosures to letter.

24. While return postage guarantee on envelope helps to clean your lists, it spoils appearance of mailing.
25. Watch your costs. Know what each order costs on each piece of promotion.

READER TURNOVER*

In a study we recently released to our businesspaper clients based on the composite data from our 1947 surveys for fourteen businesspapers, we wound up with a tabulation labeled "Reader Turnover."

It showed, for each client paper and for the composite of all fourteen, the length of time the readers had been reading the paper and, by inference at least, gave some indication of the rate of acquisition of new readers.

We frankly told our clients that our data were imperfect for this particular purpose, that so many factors entered into them as to cloud their significance, and that the only reason we included them in the report was that we thought they raised some interesting questions.

This illustrates a point we have made before, that the first purpose of all truly constructive research is not to get at answers but to get at questions.

The thing that impressed us the most about this tabulation was the wide range in the indicated rate of reader turnover—all the way from 3.1 per cent per year to 7.8 per cent. That would suggest a *complete* turnover in 33 years in the case of the first of these publications as against 13 years for the other. Of course it does not exactly work that way, but it does give us something mighty important to think about.[1]

This matter of reader turnover, its whys and wherefores, is one of the most important things in the life of a circulation man but it is one of the things most frequently overlooked by both editors and advertisers.

It is the rare editor and the rare advertiser who recognizes as he should that every issue he brings out or every issue in which he advertises brings him a brand new audience, small perhaps in numbers but important out of all proportion to its size. For it is these newcomers who must eventually and inevitably constitute your *entire* audience. The future life of

* Roy Eastman, president The Eastman Research Organization, from a monthly letter sent to clients, June 7, 1948.

[1] McGraw-Hill, in 1949, made 787,269 changes, additions, corrections, reclassifications, and deletions of a major or minor nature out of a total of 809,604 paid subscribers. The company stated in an advertisement in June, 1950: "3 out of 10 will vanish in the next 12 months."—Editor.

your publication or your business depends on how well you take them into camp.

But there is more to it than that—a lot more. The *rate* of reader turnover is something to ponder, again for both editors and advertisers. If you are an editor in a field where the obsolescence and consequent reader turnover is naturally high you have quite a different job from one where it is low. You have greater need to trot out the good old fundamentals and keep trotting them out. (And you would probably be surprised if you knew how much the old-timers like to be reminded too.)

If you are an advertiser this rate of reader turnover is one characteristic of publications and publication fields you should take into account but seldom do. Do not look for high renewal percentages in fields with naturally high reader turnover. Remember that when you have *low* reader turnover (often indicated by exceptionally high renewal performance) you have a much tougher job to make and keep your advertising interesting to those who have seen it year after year. While if you are advertising in a field that has a *high* reader turnover you have the same need as the editor to get down to basic fundamentals and not take anything for granted.

Never thought of that? Maybe it's time you did.

Then there is still another thing to think about. Reader turnover, in the publishing business, may be natural or artificial or some of both. It is not like customer turnover in the ordinary business. Most circulations are like hothouse plants, "forced" to provide marketable blooms. Circulations may be pushed up to meet a competitive threat or to justify a rate increase. Or they may be held down for similar reasons.

Hothouse circulations, like hothouse plants, are often short lived, not as hardy as those which grow naturally. Every circulation man knows that. These forced circulations need careful feeding and watering and that is the editor's job. It is not infrequently a part of *our* job to find out just what potential (for renewal or continued readership) the forced circulation represents, and what is needed, either in selling or in editorial service, to increase that potential. That is very practical, and often very profitable research.

It is natural, and perhaps healthy, for the space buyer to view any sudden circulation increase with suspicion. He is justified in inquiring into the reasons for it, the character of it, how good it is—that is, how well it has been sold—and how much of it is going to stick—or how well it is served.

To the publisher we can truly say, watch that reader turnover as if your life depended on it. For indeed it does.

WHAT A PUBLISHER EXPECTS OF HIS CIRCULATION MANAGER*

The circulation manager is an important part of a team made up of the editor, whose products he sells, and the advertising manager, who must merchandise the circulation he develops. Thus he is in a Tinker-to-Evers-to-Chance double-play combination at all times.

This means that the circulation manager should have the same complete understanding of the editorial objectives of the publication the editor has, and similar understanding of the market coverage needed by the advertising manager. In other words, the circulation manager should have the same over-all understanding of publishing problems and objectives possessed by the publisher himself.

He should understand publishing economics, with its emphasis on larger circulations and higher advertising rates. The trend toward bigger circulations in practically all trade and industrial fields is due partly because these fields have grown, but also because advertisers want and are willing to pay for more complete coverage of the important buying factors in each business or industry.

It used to be customary for publishers to think of coverage as represented by one subscription to each unit in the industry or trade field. But with buying power distributed among many factors, proper coverage today demands circulation which provides penetration of these key people and thus employs larger groups of subscriptions within a single unit. This is the kind of intensive coverage advertisers want and are willing to pay for. Because of the much higher costs of production and all other businesspaper operations, it is now necessary to think in bigger terms than formerly. The circulation manager should be able to contribute to the establishment of policies which will take into account methods of building the right kind of circulation to the right people at reasonable cost.

Publishers are highly budget conscious these days. Thus the circulation manager, whose operations may represent an important segment of publication expenditures, must be constantly testing improved methods

---

* G. D. Crain, Jr., Publisher, *Advertising Age* and *Industrial Marketing*, at the Circulation Clinic, Annual Meeting, The Associated Business Publications, Drake Hotel, Chicago, June, 1950.

and equipment for the purpose of producing and maintaining the desired volume of circulation at costs which are reasonable in the light of today's operating budgets. Study of new methods of building circulation may open the way to real economies, while the development of modern equipment for subscription handling may likewise provide definite opportunities in this direction.

The circulation manager who provides good teamwork has a right to expect similar cooperation from the editorial and advertising departments. Since his required knowledge of editorial programs is practically identical with that of the editor, the latter must keep him informed of editorial programs and the development of new features which can be successfully merchandised both to old and new subscribers.

I used to be a circulation manager myself, when I was publishing two monthly magazines with the aid of one girl. I have never forgotten the satisfaction with which I noted the response of new subscribers to a simple letter announcing the contents of a current issue. People want information on their businesses, and when the circulation manager knows what is going to appear in a forthcoming issue, he can tell them.

WHAT A CIRCULATION MANAGER EXPECTS OF HIS PUBLISHER*

The circulation manager should have full recognition from the publisher as one of the three equal parts of the triangle of successful publishing—editorial, advertising, and circulation. There should be no low man on the totem pole.

While the circulation manager should be entirely competent to plan markets, the publisher should lay down the official coverage desired, so that there will be perfect agreement by all three departments in objectives.

A circulation manager has the right to expect an attractive package to sell—interesting cover and enticing format—with editorial content strong in appeal to the markets wanted. He should be supplied with advance information on outstanding editorial features for advance publicity. He should have the authority to put pressure on the editorial department if sales resistance indicates lack of reader interest and renewal percentages are unsatisfactory.

For friendlier relations with subscribers, the circulation manager's

* William R. Hunter, Circulation Director, The Haire Publishing Company, Circulation Clinic, Drake Hotel, Chicago, June, 1950.

name should be listed on the masthead. Readers should know who to write to for personal attention about subscriptions.

The publishers should give circulation a reasonable amount of advertising space to devote to merchandising editorial content and for subscription solicitation.

The most modern fulfillment and record equipment and system available should be supplied for the efficient and economical operation of the department, which of course is to the financial advantage of the publisher.

The circulation department should be manned with an adequate staff to meet demands—for immediate fulfillment, for necessary records, for furnishing editorial, research, and advertising departments with all possible readership ammunition—without delay.

The circulation manager should have the authority to make special offers—extra copies, premiums, reduced prices or introductory offers, etc., for limited periods—when needed as the circulation tides rise and fall.

For variation the circulation manager should have the right to sign the editor's and even the publisher's names to subscription promotions. Courtesy naturally gives the editor or publisher the right to approve messages being mailed over their respective signatures.

The circulation manager should be invited to attend every editorial meeting and every advertising meeting so that he will constantly feel the pulse of the business vital for his guidance in performing a progressive job.

FIELD FORCE SELLING TODAY*

The average business publication salesman earns from $5000 to $15,000 a year.

When a publisher secures his full subscription requirements by mail, no field organization is necessary. When he doesn't, field salesmen become important. Of 291 ABC business publications checked, 126 have some salesmen of their own, 62 use outside field organizations, 22 use part-time salesmen, 81 use no salesmen.

A good subscription salesman will secure, in a week, the number of orders you can get in a month by mail from the same list of prospects.

If you use an outside field selling organization, check with the man-

* David A. Rabins, Circulation Director, *Chain Store Age;* ABP Circulation Clinic, Chicago, June, 1950.

agement and authorize only those salesmen best fitted on the basis of experience and background—and in the territories where you need business.

Check every field order by verification card or letter. This is a business insurance policy. Send bulletins frequently to field men. Feature special articles, unusual features, etc., to keep them interested and on their toes.

To build a field force of your own use newspaper advertising, check with subscribers, check your advertising department, place a classified ad right in your own publication.

Encourage salesmen to report on editorial comments. First-hand field reports (favorable or unfavorable) are vital and can help make your circulation job easier.

Permitting salesmen to take renewals is a distinct incentive to keep them rolling orders in. A quota assigned keeps the balance of new and renewals.

Rarely if ever is a business publication interested in increased circulation, unless it results in a higher advertising rate. Accordingly the problem for the circulation manager is—exactly the amount required—with every possible subscription, the quality desired.

SIMPLIFIED CIRCULATION RECORD KEEPING*

1. All incoming mail is handled by the bookkeeping department. They remove all checks and remittances and give each order a number, alongside of which they fill in the amount received from each subscriber. This eliminates the necessity for cash book or any other listing of subscriber names because the original order has all the payment information on it.

2. These original orders are then sent to the circulation department and are used to complete fulfillment operations. All instructions for making of addressograph stencils, sending of invoices, information for prospect department are all filled in on the original order. No extra forms are needed. With a series of keys and symbols all subscription orders are handled and understood by all departments.

3. The prospect file is handled with a series of colored cards. Each class of prospects has its own color. For example: executives, orange colored cards; store managers, white cards; clerks, green cards. When

* David A. Rabins, Circulation Director, *Chain Store Age;* ABP Circulation Clinic, Drake Hotel, Chicago, June, 1950. Mr. Rabins used many diagrams and exhibits. Only these highlights were recorded.

any of these prospects subscribe a yellow card replaces the one in the file. The yellow card is imprinted by the addressograph department from the new and renewal orders they receive daily.

4. *Chain Store Age* employs a functional system. Each clerk performs a specific operation for all of their nine publications.

5. A central filing system is used where all orders for all publications are filed alphabetically in one correspondence file. This file is broken up in one-year periods. Different color folders are used for each year so they can be easily identified. Three years of correspondence is saved. When the third year is completed the first year is taken as a unit and discarded. This eliminates the necessity of going through files to remove old correspondence.

FUNDAMENTALS IN SELLING SUBS BY MAIL*

In selling subscriptions—as with any product or service—there are certain fundamentals which have an important bearing on final results. It would be a mistake not to refer to them, at least briefly.

1. *The product.* Never before has there been so much competition for the attention of readers. Intensified efforts on the part of general magazines, television, heavy promotion of popular books—in a real sense they add to the competition of trade publications. Thus an important asset in selling subscriptions is a forward-looking publisher who will make the investments needed for a vital publication, well edited, with good make-up.

2. *The market.* Much has been said about the importance of up-to-date prospect lists; not enough about the selection of logical prospects. It is a poor investment to obtain good initial returns at the expense of low renewals. One publisher with whom I talked goes so far as to keep renewal records by lists and discards prospect lists that do poorly on renewals. Another makes regular tests to determine when returns from old prospect names fall to a point that is unprofitable.

3. *The price.* Price structure cannot be taken for granted on any product. If publications are using introductory rates, new tests should be made to determine the best offers. Reduced prices are generally even amounts in the trade paper field; are they better than odd amounts, as used by some general publications? And is the lowest introductory price necessarily the most effective in relation to renewal percentages?

* J. C. Chasin, Circulation Manager, *Printers' Ink;* ABP Circulation Clinic, Chicago, June, 1950.

4. *Techniques.* The lower levels of returns in many fields call for a change of pace. One publication I interviewed had been using mailings to its whole list. It was able to step up results considerably by subdividing the list into groups for a more specialized approach based upon appropriate articles. Another publication has started to use substantial quantities of automatically typed letters, first-class mail, with stamped reply envelopes. The costs are less per subscription than processed letters. More experimentation is essential to meet the challenge of new conditions.

Generally speaking, the publishers I interviewed reported that a reduced rate or premium book usually is best for getting the most subscriptions at the lowest cost. However, there are exceptions—three have recently discontinued the use of reduced rates or premiums because of competitive conditions in selling space.

It is interesting that none of the publications have been able to use sample copy mailings with enough success to warrant higher costs. Perhaps this is because a single copy is not representative.

THE AUDIT BUREAU OF CIRCULATIONS*

THE INTEREST OF THE ADVERTISER IN THE ABC

At the time ABC was organized, advertisers were closely identified with media selection and space buying. With the development of the agency business, however, more and more advertising functions were delegated to the agencies and the latter have taken on broader responsibility for the success of their clients' advertising. Today media selection is universally recognized as a major agency function. Instead of being handled in the advertising departments of national advertisers, the work of applying media to markets and the buying of space is now done almost entirely in the media departments of the agencies.

In spite of this transition of responsibility, however, the interest and the participation of advertisers in the work of the Audit Bureau has in no way lessened. With their annual bill for advertising in published media now over two and one half billion dollars,[2] advertisers recognize the need for maintaining their participation in the undertaking which provides constant protection for their expenditures. It would be con-

---

* Professor William H. Boyenton, Director of Advertising Division, School of Journalism, Rutgers University; from the booklet "Audit Bureau of Circulations," published by The Bureau in Chicago, 1949.

[2] See Table 4, U. S. Advertising Expenditures by Media.

jecture to say how much advertisers save through the operation of the Audit Bureau, but if it is even as low as ten per cent (which seems conservative), that would be approximately 250 million dollars a year.

Advertisers, through representation on the ABC board of directors, have a major voice in operating the Bureau and in establishing the standards that are so essential to the success of publication advertising. Advertiser membership is often referred to as a form of insurance for the protection of money invested in newspapers and periodicals. It is true of course that the information in ABC reports is available to all advertisers, regardless of their affiliation with the Bureau. Participation in the cost and sponsorship as well as the benefits of audited circulation, is made possible by means of advertiser membership.

The Bureau is widely recognized by business leaders as the outstanding example of successful self-government in industry. In the ABC they see a voluntary operation where unity between the buyers and sellers has resulted in standards of unquestioned integrity, the establishment and application of which have made the Bureau the greatest stabilizing force in the advertising and publishing industry. ABC membership therefore is not only an opportunity for advertisers to share in an activity that is indispensable to their most effective use of published media, it is also a means of endorsing the American principle of self-regulation in business.

THE INTEREST OF THE ADVERTISING AGENCY IN THE ABC

Agents Take Active Part in Organizing Bureau. It was an advertising agent, George P. Rowell, who took the initial step leading to verified circulation by bringing out the first issue of his American Newspaper Directory in 1869. Rowell's era marked the transition from the days of the "special agents" whose business it was to buy space from publishers and sell it to advertisers, to the period beginning with the turn of the century when their functions had increased to include the preparations of copy and art work and with their growing recognition as advertising and marketing consultants.

As a result of their leadership in the development of marketing and selling practices, the work of the agents became increasingly valuable to both publishers and advertisers. They introduced many new techniques and movements for improving advertising and increasing the effectiveness of advertising investments.

Economic Importance of Media Selection. The most frequently mentioned activities of advertising agencies are those in connection with plans, copy, and art work. Less well known but in fact the keystone upon which the success of these factors depend, is the selection of media. Of every dollar invested in publication advertising, by far the largest part goes to pay for advertising space. Therefore the allocation of the major portion of an advertiser's investment in published media becomes a problem of media selection.

Advertising requires the correct exposure if it is to produce the most profitable results. From the standpoint of copy writing, art work, and typography an advertisement may possess all of the elements necessary to a successful sales message. To attain its objective, however, it must be read by the right people in the right places. The important task of assuring profitable exposure falls to the advertising agency's media department.

ABC'S SERVICE TO AGENCY MEMBERS

Media circulations as well as markets are never static. The effective application of one to the other requires constant study and reference to the changing facts. With new publications starting, old ones expiring, and relative changes among those that continue, an agency's media department needs a working file of circulation data that is factual, complete, and up to date. Obtaining ABC reports through Bureau membership, instead of relying on hundreds of individual publications to furnish copies, is undoubtedly the safest and most convenient way to maintain an adequate source of media facts.

ABC Publisher's Statements and Audit Reports are mailed by the Bureau, as soon as available, to agency members. In addition the agencies receive the ABC Blue Books, bound copies of the Publisher's Statements for a six-month period. Bulletins announcing new publisher members and special notices covering resignations, cancellations, and suspensions are also included in the service to agency members.

P. L. Thomson, ABC President and for thirty-three years in charge of advertising for the Western Electric Company, once referred to agency membership in the Bureau as follows: "ABC reports are to the agency space buyer what a law library is to an attorney—indispensable for the efficient exercise of the agency's professional function. ABC membership obtains this material for advertising agencies and no agency can have complete space-buying equipment without it."

Affiliation with ABC, however, is more than a means of obtaining agency equipment that is essential to the most effective application of media to markets. It is endorsement of the principle that advertising investments should be made on the basis of facts and is visible evidence of an agency's recognition of this principle. It is also the client's assurance that his agency recognizes media selection as a major agency function and has a voice in the activity that provides constant protection for his publication advertising.

THE AGENCY MEDIA DIRECTOR AND ABC

In the successful advertising agency the media director is a student of markets as well as media. From information provided by government and business statistics he obtains factual knowledge regarding the potentialities that various markets offer for the products and services of his clients. He knows that the effective application of media to markets requires the use of all available factual data concerning the circulations of the publications in the fields to be covered.

The verified information in ABC reports regarding the quantity of circulation, how and where it is distributed, the prices that readers pay, and the many other facts reported provides a dependable basis for exercising judgements and making decisions.

Every media director receives thousands of pieces of publication promotion material and he himself is continually interviewing publication representatives. The quality of the promotion material and of the sales presentations varies widely. Some of these feature claims, independent surveys, and other research activities regarding the quality of the circulation. Such information is useful to the agency's media department providing only that it has factual and verified quantitative data as a base.

The status of media directors in agency operations has kept pace with the development of the agency business. Throughout the history of ABC they have cooperated actively in the Bureau's work. This is important because a knowledge of the rules that govern circulation standards is essential to the most effective use of ABC information.

ASPECTS OF PUBLISHER MEMBERSHIP IN THE ABC

Publishing Operations Aided. ABC membership is valuable to publishers not only in the sale of advertising, but also in connection with other publishing operations. The examination of a publication's circulation records by an outside, disinterested auditing organization gives the publisher a constantly up-to-date survey of his practices and progress. ABC reports visualize the activities in production, distribution, sales, and collections. This information is essential to an efficient operation and also aids the publisher in building and maintaining the volume, type, and distribution of circulation that is most salable to advertisers.

When a newspaper or periodical property is offered for sale, the volume of net paid circulation is an important factor in determining the selling price. Bureau membership makes it possible for the seller of a publishing property to provide unquestioned evidence of the publication's circulation in terms of industry standards. A study of current and past ABC reports gives the prospective buyer the complete and verified history and information that are essential to a sound business investment. This phase of the value of Bureau membership is widely recognized in the publishing industry.

The Analysis and Promotion of a Publication. A drawback to much publication research and promotion is its spasmodic use and lack of industry-wide coordination. By contrast, ABC measurement methods are standardized and coordinated, and reports of the measurements have been consistent. The consistency of the ABC's service should not lead to the error of taking ABC reports for granted. It should be observed that these reports are not static—quite the contrary. Although the *form* of the reports changes very little, the *facts* reported change constantly. To see the truth of this, one has merely to compare the reports of the same publication over a period of several years.

The reason for the existence of a business publication is its service to a special segment of society's whole field of employment—a profession, trade, or business, or a combination of them. This makes Paragraph 10 of the businesspaper Audit Report and Publisher's Statement, which supplies a breakdown of circulation by kind of business served, of particular significance in the businesspaper's effort to sell advertising space.

PUBLISHERS' DUES IN ABC

Annual dues, payable quarterly in advance, are based on total distribution as shown in the latest released regular publisher's statement. In the case of a new member dues are based on total distribution as shown in the initial audit. Dues are subject to change by action of the board.

BUSINESSPAPERS

Distribution bases	Annual dues Base rate and additional rate per 100 copies over base					
Under 2,000	$ 62.40	—				
2,000	62.40	plus	$1.44	per	100	over	2,000
3,000	76.80	plus	1.20	per	100	over	3,000
5,000	100.80	plus	.84	per	100	over	5,000
10,000	142.80	plus	.816	per	100	over	10,000
15,000	183.60	plus	.60	per	100	over	15,000
25,000	243.60	plus	.24	per	100	over	25,000
50,000	303.60	plus	.192	per	100	over	50,000
75,000	351.60	plus	.168	per	100	over	75,000
100,000	393.60	plus	.144	per	100	over	100,000

THE CONTROLLED CIRCULATION AUDIT*

Controlled Circulation Audit, Inc. is wholly and solely in existence for the purpose of auditing the circulation of its member publications—and to make available the results of such audits to advertisers and agencies. The promotion of the controlled circulation idea is not the function of CCA—that being something which, for the best interests of all concerned, should be left to others. My purpose is to give you a clearer picture and better understanding of exactly what is meant by controlled circulation—the only kind of circulation which is audited by CCA.

Before attempting to define controlled circulation we must first agree on the definition of a business publication, for this is the type of publication whose circulation can be controlled. Everyone knows what a business publication is, although no two might define it in the same words. Therefore, in order that we may be on a common ground of understanding on this point, let me quote the official CCA definition of a business publication:

A business publication is hereby defined to be one which is sent periodically and confined to a specific business, industry, trade, occupation, or profession, with clearly defined limits, recognized by the industry or group it serves, and rendering to that industry or group an editorial service.

* Adin L. Davis, Managing Director, Controlled Circulation Audit, Inc.; from a talk before The Technical Advertising Association (Boston Chapter of National Industrial Advertising Association), Boston, May 4, 1950. Mr. Davis was formerly advertising manager, Worthington Pump & Machinery Corporation; he is secretary-treasurer, National Industrial Advertisers Association.

While there is common understanding and agreement on the definition of a business publication, I am sorry to say that no such understanding seems to exist when it comes to a definition of controlled circulation. For a number of years I have been of the opinion that many of us, serving in important advertising jobs—jobs where the evaluation of media plays a very important part—have been sadly lacking when it comes to a genuine understanding of controlled circulation. I can make this statement without reservations, for during the past few months I have made it a point to ask advertising managers and agency media men to tell me just what the term "controlled circulation" meant to them. I can make this statement in relation to my own experience as an advertising manager—experience that covers better than twenty years in evaluating and buying business publication advertising space for Graton-Knight Company, in Worcester, for the Construction Equipment Division of Worthington Pump & Machinery Corporation, in Holyoke, and finally for the entire Worthington Corporation with its twenty-odd divisions and subsidiaries with headquarters in Harrison, New Jersey. In my own particular case it is only in very recent years that I arrived at what I now feel is a reasonably complete understanding of controlled circulation.

Considerably before 1930 a new theory of circulation had already been put into practice by quite a number of business publications. This theory was based on the premise that complete coverage of a limited, definable group, such as would naturally be the case of a business publication, could be achieved only as the publisher made his own decision to distribute his publication to that entire group. This could be done with complete free circulation, and be kept on that basis—a procedure which many publishers to this day adhere to in the strictest manner. Or it might include that portion of a publication's circulation which was being converted into paid, as long as that paid circulation measured up to the publisher's own definition of reader eligibility—in short, as long as the publisher elected to control it. Quite logically this new circulation philosophy became known as controlled circulation.

For the sake of further clarification let us take a simple, straightforward, although hypothetical example of just how controlled circulation works. Assume that you have decided to launch a publication which is to be directed editorially to widget manufacturers, and that you know from available statistics that there are approximately 10,000 widget manufacturers in the United States. Even though your publication may be of interest to many widget owners, widget operators, and others who are in one way or another connected with the widget business, you are establishing the fact that it is intended primarily for widget manufacturers and that you will control its circulation so that it will go to widget manufacturers only. Whether you decide to send your publication to the entire group of 10,000 widget manufacturers without cost to them, or whether you decide to accept and encourage paid subscriptions, has no bearing on whether or not your circulation is controlled. If you intend to keep it on the basis of free distribution it is obvious that you will be able to retain complete control. If you accept and encourage paid circulation there are two factors which you must consider. No matter how good your publication is editorially, human nature being what it is, you must face the fact that you will never be able to get 10,000 widget manufacturers to subscribe to it, and consequently will never achieve complete coverage of this particular group through paid circulation alone. Second, others associated with the widget business, although not actually manufacturers, will recognize the value of your publication and want to subscribe to it, and such circulation, although paid, cannot be classified as controlled, as it does not conform to your original definition of reader eligibility—widget manufacturers.

This is an extremely simple example of how controlled circulation works. In many cases the picture is much more complex, particularly where your definition of reader eligibility is far more than simply "widget manufacturers." In such a field as construction, for instance, where there are many kinds of builders and contractors, your definition of reader eligibility might be much more involved and difficult to settle upon. Whether simple or complicated, however, the principle remains the same.

With the above hypothetical example of how controlled circulation works in mind, let me give you the official CCA definition of controlled circulation:

Controlled circulation of a business publication is hereby defined as that wherein each issue is sent to recipients who conform to a pre-established Definition of Reader Eligibility, such definition having been submitted by the publisher and approved by the managing director.[3]

As a further interpretation and rounding out of the controlled circulation story I believe that a little CCA history may well be in order. By

[3] See "CCA 1951," a booklet issued in 1951 by Controlled Circulation Audit, Inc., explaining this definition in detail.

1931 it is my understanding that there were some 150 business publications in this country practicing controlled circulation. These publications were confining their distribution to limited, definable groups within an industry or profession. Most of them were doing this on a basis of free distribution, but some had a portion of paid circulation which could be classified as controlled and this was rounded out with controlled free circulation. At this time, 1931, there was no audit bureau in existence which would audit the circulation of publications if they were more than 50 per cent free. As most, if not all of the controlled publications in existence at that time were far more than 50 per cent free, they were ineligible for auditing by any existing bureau, and as a result had to remain unaudited or resort to what we today term "sworn statements of circulation." This meant that in spite of the integrity of the individual publisher of a controlled circulation magazine he was at a decided disadvantage in the eyes of the advertisers and agencies—either without an audit, or resorting to a sworn statement, which, then as now, did not carry the weight and prestige of an audit report issued by an accepted audit bureau. The result was that in October, 1931, 39 of these controlled circulation publications became the charter members of a new audit bureau—Controlled Circulation Audit, Inc. The two major requirements for a publication to become a member of CCA were (1) that its circulation must be controlled as defined by CCA, and (2) it could not have more than 30 per cent paid circulation. With a publication thus qualifying for CCA membership only the free controlled portion of its circulation was audited.

During the years since its founding, a number of changes have been made both in CCA rules of eligibility for publisher members and in actual auditing procedures. The ruling that no more than 30 per cent of a publication's circulation could be paid, if it were to qualify for CCA membership, presented no problem in those early days, as practically all controlled publications were largely, if not entirely, free circulation. However, as controlled circulation gained greater acceptance and wider use, this rule began to present a very definite problem. Certain CCA members were building up their paid circulation which, of course, was acceptable to CCA as long as it was controlled. This meant, however, that if as and when they reached the 30 per cent mark in paid, they would be disqualified automatically as CCA members—something which actually happened with a number of publications. As a result, in 1938 the percentage of paid circulation allowed a CCA member was raised from 30 to 50.

At this same time it was also decided that once a publication qualified for membership its entire circulation, free and paid, would be audited as long as it was controlled. No differentiation, however, would be made between the free and paid portions of that controlled circulation, as this was looked upon as a matter of individual publisher philosophy and economics—having no particular bearing on the three prime questions which a controlled circulation audit should answer: (1) Does the avowed recipient measure up to the publisher's definition of reader eligibility? (2) Is he actually in existence? (3) Does he actually receive the publication?

By 1947 it was recognized that further consideration would have to be given to the 50 per cent limit established for paid controlled circulation of CCA members, as a number had reached or were reaching that point and would become automatically disqualified for membership. Another factor demanding consideration was that many publications with more than 50 per cent paid circulation were supplementing it with free controlled circulation in order to obtain complete coverage for the particular group they wanted to reach. As no audit bureau existed which would audit the free circulation of publications with more than 50 per cent paid circulation, it meant that this often sizeable and valuable portion of such a publication's circulation could not be audited. Consequently, at that time, 1947, the CCA Board of Directors lifted the restriction that only publications with 50 per cent or more free circulation could qualify for membership, making it possible for any publication, regardless of its percentage of free or paid circulation, to qualify for membership. This was done so that (1) CCA members, whose paid portion of their controlled circulation was growing, would not be disqualified if they reached any particular percentage, and (2) publications with 50 per cent or more paid circulation might have the free controlled, as well as the paid portion of their circulations, audited.

So much for the history of CCA, which is part and parcel of the story of controlled circulation. The changes made in CCA rules and auditing procedure have been so done to keep pace with the steady progress of controlled circulation—a progress which is most tangibly evidenced in the growth of CCA itself, from 39 charter publication members in 1931 to its present total of 279.

I sincerely hope I have succeeded in giving you a clearer picture of controlled circulation, of what it is and how it works. Whether or not you believe it to be the best circulation philosophy for business publications, I am sure you will agree that it is a sincere, logical, and reasonable circulation philosophy, one that has been proved in actual practice and is very definitely here to stay. It may compete with, but it certainly does not criticise, other circulation philosophies. And this is good—for clean, healthy competition is the core of our American enterprise system.

I want to go on record, however, not only for myself but for CCA as well, as being ready and willing to cooperate wholeheartedly with any and all proponents of other circulation philosophies in promoting a cause that is close to the hearts of all of us—*that all businesspapers should be audited.* In this common cause there is most certainly a great overlapping of interests which should dwarf into insignificance the very normal, healthy differences that are bound to exist with competitive circulation philosophies.

These two additional definitions appear in a guide for members of CCA.[4]

READER ELIGIBILITY

The definition of reader eligibility shall be a description of the qualifications employed by the publisher in establishing his controlled list. All circulation classed as controlled circulation shall conform to the definition of reader eligibility.

VERIFIED CONTROLLED CIRCULATION

Verified controlled circulation is hereby defined as that portion of controlled circulation which has been positively verified by the publisher with respect to (a) accuracy of data shown on the mailing stencil, and (b) conformance to the publisher's definition of reader eligibility; such verification having been obtained not more than two years prior to the date of reporting.

PAID *VERSUS* FREE CONTROVERSY*

The questions most often asked by college students of journalism and advertising, in my experience, relate to the opposing philosophies of paid and controlled circulation practice, the soundness of one over the other, and the kind of auditing methods employed by both groups to prove their claims to advertising space buyers.

The free or controlled type of circulation is a phenomenon peculiar to the business press. The majority of publications in the newspaper and

---

[4] "CCA Members Guide," published in 1951 by Controlled Circulation Audit, Inc. Students may obtain sample forms used by publishers by writing the Controlled Circulation Audit and asking for the "Publisher's Statement."

* Editor's observations.

general consumer magazine field charge a subscription price although there are some free distribution newspapers and consumer magazines. External house magazines and trade association publications also usually have a free distribution to selected lists.

In businesspaper publishing enough important independent publishers are lined up on both sides of this paid *versus* free controversy to make it a matter of some gravity, not only to the business press but to advertisers, advertising agencies, and the Post Office Department.[5]

In 1911, there was one controlled circulation businesspaper, employing one editor, publishing about twenty pages of technical information a month, and serving one field: dentistry.

In 1949 it was reported that 300 controlled circulation business publications employed over 2008 editors and carried an average of 10,402 pages of editorial know-how monthly.

The pressure of the controlled circulation group on the government for parity of postal rates with paid circulation businesspapers, and their pressure on the Audit Bureau of Circulations to audit the free part of paid circulation papers served to widen the breach between these two groups in 1949.

The circulation schism is all the more serious today because it continues at a time when the business press should be concentrating all of its energies on getting a proportionately larger share of industry's advertising dollar in competition with consumer magazines, newspapers, radio–TV, catalogue, and direct mail. Instead, half of the business press spends much of its advertising and selling time and its dollars on the alleged weakness of the other half of the business press and thereby imperils the status and potential of the whole business press.

Some of those who take an objective view wish the issues to be resolved quickly but others believe the issues must be fought out at length before the business press can again assume a united front.

According to one publisher, "the split was logical and the controversy is healthy."

"With both fundamentals attempting to function in the same group (ABP) there was always confusion," he said. "The two groups were always at variance as to the policies to be pursued by the businesspaper publishing industry. . . . It brings the differences out in the open. The weaker businesspapers that were coasting along with little service and

---

[5] In May and June, 1949, about 24 publishing houses, mostly with part paid and part free circulations, resigned from ABP over the controversy.

no verification of readership except their own statements are now shown up."

The editors of *Printers' Ink* whose publication (paid ABC) has crusaded for many improvements in advertising and publishing practice assert that "whichever side they are on, publishers of good businesspapers should encourage every effort to introduce auditing methods that enable the advertiser to make sound judgments of the circulation of both paid and controlled papers."

"Certainly," say the editors of *Printers' Ink*, "no particular method of circulation automatically puts a publisher beyond criticism."[6]

"In the final analysis," said G. F. Johnson of the Eastman Kodak Company, "it matters not how a person receives a publication, but it is vitally important to know whether he reads it and whether by doing so he is materially aided in his field of endeavor. Service to the reader and the industry is the real yardstick by which a publication should be judged."[7]

In his statement Mr. Johnson had proposed a "revitalized" publishers' association encompassing "all businesspapers regardless of type of circulation." In a dramatic move two years later, in June, 1951, the National Business Publications, an association of controlled circulation businesspapers, announced that it had "opened its doors to both paid and free business publications."

To understand all the issues and reach any conclusions on the best methods of distributing businesspapers one must know something of the history of audited circulation. Dr. Boyenton's study, excerpted in this chapter, describes the half century struggle to expand and perfect the verified circulation technique.

To describe the opposing circulation philosophies, extracts are included in this chapter from the papers of Thomas B. Haire and Harvey Conover.

In the fight for postal rate parity the controlled circulation publishers describe the present postal law as an "antique" written for a period of American life that no longer exists. On top of this the general resistance of all publishers to postal rate increases adds fuel to the fire. The postal department is accused of "archaic" cost-accounting systems and "unrealistic" rate-making methods.[8]

All users of the mails, paid and controlled businesspapers, consumer

---

[6] *Printers' Ink*, June 10, 1949, p. 74.
[7] *Op. cit.* July 10, 1949, p. 48.
[8] Postal Law was enacted in 1879.

magazines and newspapers, catalogue houses and direct mail advertisers, have told the Senate and House, Post Office and Civil Service committees they want to pay their "fair share."[9]

"But what," asked the editor of *Tide*, "is their fair share? . . . What does it really cost the Post Office to deliver a million *Posts* or *Lifes*, or Sears catalogues, or direct mail pieces? What is the real deficit from 'free-in-county' circulation? What is the actual expense of the 'franking privilege' or of operating the RFD routes?

"Neither the Post Office nor anyone else knows the answers to those questions. It is tragic, and perhaps revealing, that the Post Office hasn't shown any great interest in wanting to find out those things. Neither have the Post Office's friends in Congress. Yet until you know those answers, you cannot determine the real price of postage."[10]

It has been suggested that a scientific study of postal rates and policies be begun to find out what type of publications are chiefly responsible for the huge annual Post Office deficit of over half a billion dollars. On the findings rate adjustments could be made to place the Post Office on a self-sustaining—or nearly so—basis.

In this chapter the Conover argument for postal rate parity and the Haire argument in opposition to free circulation will help the reader understand and recognize the obstacles that lay in the way of any swift or easy resolution of the current differences in businesspaper circulation practice.[11]

THE ARGUMENT FOR PAID CIRCULATION*

We should look at this current (paid *versus* free) situation not as a fight but as a difference of opinion—a difference in the philosophies of conducting a publishing business.

[9] In September, 1951, postal rate increases went into effect. Paid circulation businesspapers (which have second-class mailing privileges) received a 30 per cent increase extending over a three-year period (1952–1954) at the rate of 10 per cent of the base per year. The free or controlled circulation businesspapers (fourth-class mailing privilege) received no increase and failed in their efforts to get parity with paid circulation publications.

[10] From an editorial "Anybody Know the Price of Postage?" in May 4, 1951, *Tide*, p. 7, by Reginald Clough, president and editor.

[11] Students should study the history of verified circulation by reading "*Scientific Space Selection*," by O. C. Harn and "Audit Bureau of Circulations," by William H. Boyenton, published by the bureau in 1949.

* Thomas B. Haire, Vice-President, The Haire Publishing Co.; vice-president of the ABP; before the General Conference of The Associated Business Publications, Hotel Biltmore, New York, November 29, 1949.

The way *we* operate our business we have deliberately placed ourselves in the position of having to satisfy our readers and to publicly prove we are satisfying them in order to earn the support of advertisers. We have forced this upon ourselves by exposing our circulations to a strict, established public audit of certain data relating to how many readers we have been able to sell sufficiently well that they will buy our services for a specified contract period. We have made customers of our readers, and have thus obligated ourselves to them. On that basis we approach advertisers, telling them that while we may not ever be able to sell 100 per cent of their potential customers, we have been able to sell a substantial portion of them, and that they are very much worth reaching.

The fact that we have been able to sell a substantial portion of their potential buying influence, and make of them customers for our editorial service, enables us to offer advertisers a highly selective audience of readers, whose interest in our services has been predetermined, whose numbers have been accurately counted and publicly audited, not for our own protection but for the protection and guidance of advertisers.

Some publishers of controlled circulation papers tell advertisers that they give 100 per cent coverage, eliminate for them "nonbuyers" and that in so doing they eliminate waste; and between the greater coverage and this elimination of waste, that they give greater value.

We know from our own publishing experience that we cannot sell certain desirable individuals on the idea of subscribing to certain of our papers. Whether it is the fault of our circulation setups, whether the editor just is not doing the job for these certain individuals, or whether these individuals are just of a type who do not think they can learn anything more than they already know is not always easy to find out. We do know that it takes a lot of effort to sell the specialists in our industries a $2.00 or a $3.00 or a $5.00 service and it is an effort we would not be inclined to expend unless we thought it was worth while. We certainly do not think we would be offering advertisers as good values if we had free distribution. If we felt otherwise we would be fools to be putting out so much effort in the direction of building our magazine properties on a *paid* ABC basis.

The standards we are maintaining are standards set up by advertisers who want to know—and who now can know—the following about any ABC member publication:

How much paid circulation has it?

How much is unpaid?

What is the occupational or business breakdown of subscribers?

Where are they located?

How much do they pay to subscribers?

Were premiums used to get the subscriptions?

How many subscribers are in arrears?

What percentage of these subscribers renew?

They are the same standards which advertisers have accepted and are using in buying space in all other printed media—newspapers, magazines, and farm papers.

We all may have slightly different reasons for belonging to ABC. Some of us may feel vaguely that our position of leadership demands it. Others possibly feel that it is some sort of recognized symbol of quality that raises our paper a notch or two above some other unaudited papers, and that we therefore get more advertising space because of it. Still others may feel that since a good paper has nothing to hide, it is good business to subscribe to a circulation audit.

Historically, an audit of circulations was the conception of several men who believed that some verification of circulation claims of *all* printed media was necessary before advertising could emerge as an honest sales tool in which advertisers could safely invest.

From that day to this there has never been an ABP member who was not first a member of ABC.

That our organization did help to raise the standards of publishing among businesspapers and that it did contribute to increasing the stature of businesspapers in the eyes of advertisers, is a matter of record.

However, in the businesspaper field, while progress has been made, and publishing standards and ethics have been raised, the situation has not reached the point that has been reached in the newspaper, magazine, and farm paper fields: 1981 newspapers, 267 magazines and 69 farm papers are now members of ABC. Practically every worthwhile periodical in these categories is built upon the paid subscription, and the multiplication of paid subscriptions to constitute an audience—a market that is accurately measurable for the advertising buyer.

In the businesspaper field there are now roughly 350 members, out of approximately 1800, which is just slightly over 20 per cent—only ⅕th. A book could probably be written on possible reasons why advertisers, agencies, and publishers have allowed such a situation to exist, when other media have fallen so completely in line on the standard of the paid subscription as a measurement unit.[12]

The growth of the principle of controlled distribution of businesspapers arose out of the basic difficulty in selling subscriptions to relatively small groups of geographically scattered business specialists. The controlled principle was to give the magazine away if the publisher believed his list carried the names of buying influences, of people advertisers wanted to reach. Complete coverage of the market was the immediate promise.

Because 20 years or so ago (some 15 years after ABC was established) there were eso many unaudited, and irresponsible claims being made by publishers of more than 1000 unaudited businesspapers, advertisers balked at the wild claims, and the more principled adherents of controlled distribution set up an organization to raise their claims to the level of credibility. This organization was the CCA, which did count names on the publisher's list, check the count against print orders and postage charges. It was indeed a progressive step.

To be realistic, in the businesspaper field, the controlled distribution publishers have done a far better job of selling their type of distribution than we have done selling our type.

Bucking the precedent of almost complete membership in the ABC of every worthwhile newspaper, magazine, and farm paper, they have sold against these standards for measuring paid circulations as set up by the ABC and as accepted for all these other printed media. They have done so, necessarily, by belittling the significance of the paid subscriber as far as businesspapers go. They have partially convinced advertisers that businesspapers are different from all other printed media.

We have contributed toward what stature they now hold by not doing, all along, day in and day out, a sound job of constructively selling our own propositions—an important part of which is that our readers are entered on our books as our customers. They are readers because they want to be, not just because we, as publishers, figure they should be.

Essentially, we publishers of paid papers and the publishers of controlled papers disagree on fundamental publishing principles. We do not say we are right and they are wrong. All we say is that we are different. We are different in our thinking on one important point—the value of the paid subscription.

[12] 1951 figures show 1964 businesspapers with 364 in ABC, or about 19 per cent.

We know the weaknesses of lists, almost as well as the publishers who use them to distribute their magazines free, because we use lists, too. Our difference is that we cannot count names as subscribers or sell them as markets until we have, first, verified the names and, second, secured at least some determination of reader interest in the form of a subscription sale.

Early in school I was taught you cannot add an apple and an orange. Nor can you really compare them. Orange growers cannot sell apple eaters oranges by just saying oranges are better than apples. They are different.

We are different too, in our thinking, from the publishers who believe in controlled distribution. They believe controlled distribution is just as good—maybe even better than paid. We do not.

Free is free. Paid is paid. You cannot mix them together. You cannot add them together. You cannot average them out any more than you can mix, add, or average apples and oranges.

We have all had experience in trying to expand our market coverage in one direction or another. We call our staffs together and we decide that for a six-month or a year period we will give our prospective new readers the kind of editorial material our editor tells us they will want and they will buy. We give the circulation managers the green light. We then add, let us say, 1000 promotional copies to our run and the test is on. The editor gives the best he can. The circulation man sells the best he can. We all watch the results closely. If it clicks we have new readers, a new addition to our market, a new appeal to certain advertisers. If we have not been successful and cannot sell these new prospective readers, despite our best editorial and selling efforts, we have to come to the decision which it seems to me is the nub of this whole situation:

Will we give up our efforts to expand in this direction? Will we try a little harder for a little longer? Or will we leave these readers we have not been able to sell on our list as a controlled portion of our total circulation?

That, of course, is the decision that has to be made by the individual publisher—and naturally he is going to have to live with his decision.

We believe that during our trial selling period we should not dignify these sample copies to prospective readers by having them audited by the same organization which audits the copies we have been able to sell.

And we believe that, if it is our decision to keep on sending free copies to this 1000 who will not buy our service, we should not lower the values and standards we have built into our paid subscriptions. Our success in selling subscriptions should not be brought down to the level of our failures. The organization which for 35 years has been known as auditors of *paid* circulation, should not be allowed to put its stamp of quality on circulation we have failed to sell. That would diminish the importance of the circulation we have succeeded in selling.

It must be remembered that while the advertising fraternity has over-simplified this problem as a fight between Paid *vs.* Free, it is actually a "difference of opinion" within the ranks of ABC, in which every member is a "paid publisher."

To the degree that some ABC publishers want ABC to audit also the free part of their circulations, the difference of opinion is one of the relative values of the *paid* subscription versus the *free* copy.

Still, these publishers believe in paid circulation—or say they do—and at least half of their circulations must be on a paid basis in order to maintain their membership in ABC. That is what makes this problem so difficult to get at.

We who oppose the ABC's auditing of any free distribution believe there is a substantial difference between the controlled distribution of a publication and its paid circulation. We do not want advertisers to be confused. We do not want them to place the same importance on a *free* copy as they do on a *paid* copy. We do not want this to happen because we know there is a very great difference. One is a reader we have probably tried to sell and *could not*. The other is one whom we tried to sell and *did*.

Looking at some figures compiled last year, out of 327 businesspaper members of ABC at that time, 296 (or about 90 per cent of the total members) had more than 80 per cent of their circulations paid. When you consider office copies, sample and salesmen's copies, checking copies for advertisers and agencies, there does not seem to be much left worth auditing. Ninety-five per cent of all members had more than 70 per cent of their circulations on a paid basis. That leaves 5 per cent who have a problem of identifying to whom the unpaid portion of their circulation goes. It seems to me that these publishers deserve much credit for their membership in ABC and deserve credit also for their desire to identify and verify that part of their distribution which ABC cannot now audit because it is as yet unpaid.

But the solution is not, it seems to us, to soften ABC's standards as understood by advertisers and agencies, to accommodate the publishers in this situation. To do so would lessen in the eyes of advertisers the importance of not only the paid subscriptions on these businesspapers, but *all* paid subscriptions on *all* businesspapers.

Some few years ago there was a movement within ABP to broaden its base, to take in publications who were not members of ABC. This would have increased ABP's membership but would have, perhaps indirectly, rung the death knell of the paid subscription as a basis for accurate measurement of a magazine's audience. We thought then, and think now, that the paid subscription is too important to discard by admitting to membership publications which do not believe in it.

The reason for the interest in such a proposal was that while ABP has always had ABC as a requirement for membership, many member publishers also published controlled circulation magazines. While controlled circulation magazines had no vote in ABP's sessions, the member publishers who also published controlled circulation magazines were logically not inclined to vote on measures which would promote *paid* circulation.

That movement was defeated by majority vote. The "difference of opinion" again came to a head on the issue of ABC auditing the free part of paid circulations. It was the same issue more intensified. Again it was defeated.

In the final analysis, the space contract is the advertiser's answer to the question of "which publication best suits my needs right now?" That will always be the case and I seriously doubt whether any advertiser will place space because of the differences in the philosophies of publishers.

The advertiser will always look for the best buy and the decision will always be in his hands.

THE ARGUMENT FOR CONTROLLED CIRCULATION*

Our periodicals are unique in that they are wholly devoted to the dissemination of technical information of interest to small, highly specialized groups of individuals. They are, therefore, restricted in their circulation. They have no news stand distribution and are wholly dependent upon the Post Office Department for delivery to readers.[13]

* Harvey Conover, President, Conover-Mast Pub. Co., former Chairman of Legislative Committee, National Business Publications; from a statement before the Committee of Post Office and Civil Service, U. S. House of Representatives, Washington, D.C., April, 1949, pleading for parity of postal rates with paid circulation businesspapers.

[13] Members of the Controlled Circulation Audit, Inc.

Because of their limited fields, the circulation of the majority is less than 10,000 and the average circulation of all is below 18,000 per periodical. The aggregate tonnage of this segment of the periodical publishing business, as handled by the Postal Department, is so small as to be almost inconsequential. The combined circulation of all controlled circulation technical periodicals is less than that of *Life* magazine. When we consider the fact that the majority of our periodicals are monthlies and are therefore placed in the mails 12 instead of 52 times a year, it is apparent that even this comparison exaggerates their importance to the postal service.

If, moreover, we calculate the total tonnage of all classifications of mail handled by the Post Office Department, and compare it with the controlled circulation group, we find that our periodicals constitute less than $\frac{1}{10}$th of 1 per cent of the whole. The volume of controlled circulation periodicals is less than $\frac{1}{2}$ of 1 per cent that of second-class mail.

SMALL CIRCULATION VOLUME IS NO GAUGE OF IMPORTANCE

The importance of our publications to the national health, welfare, and military security of our country is, however, an entirely different matter. For the technical periodical is the principal instrument by which information regarding technological and scientific progress is disseminated to the industries, trades, sciences, and professions. Our publications are the clearing houses of information which give a Portland, Maine, pediatrician the know-how about a new rheumatic fever treatment technique developed in a Portland, Oregon, clinic—which tell a Los Angeles industrial safety engineer about a new punch press accident prevention method developed in a Farmingdale, L. I., aircraft factory—which explain to the Texas airport operator a new low visibility landing method that has cut accidents at a Michigan airfield.

Technical periodicals are the principal conveyors of information regarding the never-ending flow of scientific advances that are constantly expanding our great technical resources, referred to by President Truman in Point No. 4 of his inaugural address, and known during the war as "America's Secret Weapon."

New developments and better techniques are worthless until they are made available and are put to work by the specialists they affect. It is the function and responsibility of the controlled circulation technical press to see that these new methods and techniques are made available to those specialists in a total of 62 fields of professional and industrial endeavor.

A TWENTIETH-CENTURY DEVELOPMENT—GOVERNED BY A SEVENTY-YEAR-OLD LAW

Our periodicals have developed a new and improved technique in disseminating technical information—a method that was unknown when the postal law of 1879 was enacted. Because this law has never been modified to recognize this new method, we find ourselves in the position of having to pay postage rates 300 per cent greater than are paid by periodicals employing traditional circulation practices and performing identical services.

This postal law of seventy years ago under which we are now operating was, of course, designed to meet publishing conditions of that era. And it met those conditions well. In 1879 our industries were small. They were concentrated in a limited geographical area. Their methods were comparatively simple. The average amount of text material per issue was about 9 pages. This was adequate for the industries of that day.

But a glance at these technical periodicals reveals how radically the technical periodical business has been changed of necessity to meet and satisfy the highly complex needs of today's readers. The periodical of seventy years ago was so simple and inexpensive to produce that the publisher could show a profit on subscription sales alone. Circulation audit bureaus were unknown. The advertiser was forced to take the word of the publisher for the number of copies printed and the number of readers served. And advertising, although nice to have, was not essential to the profitable operation of the publication.

Contrast these technical periodicals of more than three generations ago with the modern controlled circulation technical periodicals you have before you. The reading matter carried has increased in volume from 9 to 79 and 100 or more pages per issue. This reading matter, moreover, has changed from general newsy stories of industrial activities to complex, highly technical material. Technical periodicals have developed into monthly textbooks for technicians who are expert in their specialized fields.

To keep pace with, or rather I should say in advance of, the growing needs of industry, the sciences, and professions, our technical periodicals have had constantly to expand and enlarge their editorial services. This steady expansion of editorial services has resulted in a sharply ascending cost per copy, for the field served by the average technical periodical is so small and compact that it is usually served adequately by a circulation of less than 20,000.

You can readily see that, being spread over such a small circulation, the editorial cost per copy is necessarily high contrasted with national magazines of general distribution which may divide their editorial cost over circulations of four or five million or more.

In the periodical publishing business the big part of the cost is editorial salaries, paying for contributions, engravings, type-setting, and other "first cost" elements. After you get your presses rolling the cost of additional copies is relatively slight.

As an illustration of the effect of circulation volume on unit cost let us consider these three modern controlled circulation technical periodicals, each serving a different field. An analysis shows that the cost of delivering 12 monthly copies of each of these periodicals to each reader is now $22, $34, and $66. Note how unit cost falls as circulation rises. The magazine with 40,000 circulation, which is very large for a technical periodical, has a unit cost one-third that of the magazine with 11,000 circulation.

In the face of these high unit costs, and they are not exceptional but are wholly representative, you can readily see that the payment of a token subscription fee of a few dollars, received from a portion of the field, is of little consequence compared with the all-important necessity of getting the valuable information in the technical periodical into the hands of every specialist who can benefit from its contents.

Today the subscription fee is merely a token payment.

NATIONWIDE GROWTH IS A PREDOMINATING FACTOR

But there is another equally important economic reason for the growth of controlled circulation technical periodicals. Let us go back to 1879, when the present postal law was enacted. We were still a pioneer nation, not a world power. Our industries, trades, professions, and sciences were in their infancy, depending on England and Germany for guidance.

Our commercial frontier was Pennsylvania.

When the law was enacted our industries, trades, professions, and sciences were mainly in a few Eastern states. Entire industries were confined to single communities.

Technical periodicals were few in number. The needs of their fields were elementary, and their readers were geographically concentrated.

Contrast that situation with what prevails today. Practically every trade, science, and profession is found in every one of the forty-eight states.

The nationwide dispersion of technical periodical readers is a major factor in the growth of the controlled circulation periodical press, as this method of distribution makes adequate service possible. The dispersion of technical periodical readers is also one of the reasons why the publisher relying on a paid subscription list finds himself in many cases paying more to get a subscriber than he actually receives in subscription income. The controlled circulation method of supplying technological information essential to the continued progress of the professions, industries, trades, and sciences has proved ideally adapted to the requirements of the twentieth century.

CHAPTER 4

Advertising

OBSTACLES TO SPACE SELLING

Throughout this volume the importance of editorial content is stressed, but there is no getting around the fact that the revenue from the sale of advertising space pays the piper. The money for publishers' and editors' salaries and other overhead costs—manufacturing, selling, rent, taxes, etc.—and the profits; all come chiefly from the sale of space in the advertising columns.

The realistic editor will concede that there is probably no more significant tribute to his efforts and those of his staff than the signed contract for advertising space brought in by the advertising sales department.

Whether a businesspaper is profitable is not only important to its publisher, advertising sales manager, and editor—it is important to the advertiser and the reader, too.

The advertiser is an "investor" in the publishing enterprise, like a man who has 100 shares of General Motors. His dividends depend on reader interest. The reader pays out time to read in exchange for something in the editorial and advertising columns which he hopes will benefit him. If the editorial service is second-rate the reader has thrown away his valuable time on the wrong publication and inevitably it will have fewer and fewer readers, followed by less and less advertisers.

Studies and audits by Lasser and others prove that the business press as a whole has become more valuable to readers because of generally improved editorial service, the result of buying higher priced skills and talents, and better advertising copy. It has become more valuable to advertisers because circulation has increased qualitatively and quantitatively and because the advertiser has learned more about using this precision tool.

The business press today serves as intercommunications system for a greatly expanded industrial market.[1] To pace that market it must render a first-rate service in both its editorial and advertising columns. But, while the publisher selects and pays talent to fill the editorial columns, he requires payment from those who wish to use his advertising columns and often has nothing to do with the talent employed in preparation of the advertising messages. This amusing couplet appeared in an issue of *Printers' Ink*:

TRADE AD

By Lew Owen

Selling to the industry
Is selling at the source.
Who writes these vital messages?
The copy cub, of course!

Too often the talent employed by the agency or advertising department of the advertiser to prepare businesspaper advertising is cheap talent because advertising space rates on businesspapers are cheap in comparison to rates charged by mass consumer media. The agency commissions are therefore small. Unfortunately, too many advertising agencies still look on *media* rather than *accounts* as their source of income. Agencies that think of income from the account rather than from the media assign their best brains to businesspaper copy. It is easier to "sell" a housewife than it is to "sell" an engineer, purchasing agent, merchandising executive, or some other technical specialist.

We have spoken of the high intelligence level of the readership of the business press and also of its great purchasing and influencing power. It is shortsighted for anyone to use second- or third-rate talent to prepare either editorial or advertising copy for this readership.

A prime weakness of the business press in the past half century has been its advertising rate structure. When most businesspapers started, the advertising rates were arbitrarily fixed to attract advertisers quickly. Sharp competition, tradition, and fear have kept them low—fear, because in specialized fields the number of potential advertisers is limited.

---

[1] The businesspaper advertiser taps a market potential eleven times greater than the consumer advertiser, per dollar invested. See *Industrial Marketing*, June, 1948; see also Table 2, "Readers of the Business Press and Their Buying Power," and Table 5, "Business Publication Advertising Volume by Publication Groups."

Today these rates, in most cases, are too low for the value of service rendered or the size and quality of the field covered. Rates do not reflect the cost of manufacturing and delivering the businesspaper to the reader today. According to Lasser it costs about 75 per cent more to operate a magazine today than it did before World War II.

Lasser suggested to businesspaper publishers at a convention in May, 1950, that they establish a minimum rate of $500 for a black and white page or $50 per thousand subscribers. On this basis the one-time black and white page rate for the *American Druggist* (circulation 58,457) would be $2900, or nearly four times the present rate of $790. *Fortune Magazine*, with a circulation of 249,343, instead of asking $3190 a page would ask $12,450 a page. On the other hand, *Linens & Domestics* magazine, with a circulation of 3158, and a page rate of $300, is getting $100 per thousand readers, but is still $200 below Lasser's minimum.[2]

"Rate per page per thousand readers" is the way mass circulation media are compared. In the businesspaper field such a basis of comparison has no meaning in itself. This point is better understood by the business press than it is by the advertising profession.

Six obstacles to successful space selling confront the businesspaper advertising executive, Lasser told businesspaper publishers:

1. Agency preference for consumer media because the low rate structure of businesspapers rebates them so little in agency commissions (15 per cent). They say they lose money on businesspaper accounts. Lasser suggested that a need might exist for improving the cost accounting method in many agencies. Businesspapers should not bear all the costs that agencies now insist on charging businesspaper accounts.

2. Dissipation of advertising funds into other media: general, women's, and home magazines; metropolitan newspapers (particularly Sunday editions); radio and television.

3. Over-competitive selling—"running down one another"—generally dramatizing the weakness of the entire business press, besides aggravating clients and their agents with this kind of argument.

4. "Writing down" to space buyers while "writing up" to people above them. More intelligent advertising to business and advertising executives in "executive language" is needed.

5. Selling on a "me-too" basis. Little effort to create ideas for advertising campaigns is found in much of the "selling."

6. Failure to "think big, act big, look big." Analyses show decreases

---

[2] Advertising rates quoted are from *Standard Rate & Data Service*, August 21, 1951 (Business Publications Section).

in the promotional budgets of businesspaper publishers even while they are urging their own advertisers to spend more advertising and sales promotion dollars.[3]

Three additional obstacles might be added to Lasser's list:

7. Inadequate circulation—the failure of many businesspaper publishers to deliver a large enough market to mass producers in their own fields. Many publishers are reluctant to spend money to get and serve a larger readership because it would mean increased production and mailing costs. As the manufacturing units of an industry increase and the output increases the circulation of any magazine claiming to be spokesman for that industry should increase in like ratio, if its editorial content and its physical presentation are good. This point brings us to the last two obstacles:

8. Poor architecture, bad physical appearance, poor design, faulty techniques in presenting news and know how.[4]

9. Editorial anemia.[5] Poor performance by second-rate editors. Evidence of editorial performance will always be the most important ammunition in a businesspaper space salesman's war bag. But you cannot buy first-rate editors and editorial assistants if your advertising volume is small. While a businesspaper publisher must be aware of prevailing competition, his rates for space should be set on the basis of the values he delivers plus the cost of efficiently performing the services he is called on to give his readers and advertisers.

This chapter is concerned with the functions involved in selling those values and services and describes the functions involved in buying businesspaper space, from the preparation of the budget to the placing of the space contract.

FUNCTIONS OF THE ADVERTISING SALES DEPARTMENT*

The advertising department of a businesspaper is a very important part of the whole operation, because about 90 per cent of most publications' income comes from advertising and the balance from circulation or services. The advertising department, the sales department, that is, pays the bills for all the other departments.

[3] J. K. Lasser, C.P.A., "My Look at Your Business," a paper read before the ABP annual conference in Chicago, May 3–5, 1950.
[4] See Dusenbury, Chapter 11.
[5] See Marsteller, Chapter 17.
* Robert E. Kenyon, Jr., advertising sales manager, *Printers' Ink*, from a lecture at New York University, February 26, 1947.

CLOSE RELATIONSHIP OF EDITORIAL AND ADVERTISING PAGES

Advertising pages and editorial pages are really twin brothers. The editorial pages tell readers how to perform a certain manufacturing operation. The advertising pages tell the reader with what specific brand of equipment he can perform that manufacturing operation. Business-papers are editorial clearing houses of technical information, or "know how," plus news about industries, trades and professions. Business papers tell about new processes, methods of manufacturing or selling, give helpful ideas on operating a factory or a store at lower cost and higher profit, and tell the news of people and activities in the business, industry, or profession served.

The success of the editorial job depends primarily on how helpful the publication is to its readers. The advertising pages can be equally helpful and informative, because, after all, readers want to know about specific products. They read the advertising pages just as they read the editorial pages: to get information about products or processes that will help them in their business. Consequently, the success of advertising pages largely depends on the degree of helpful information they give to readers.

ADVERTISER'S RESPONSIBILITY TO READERS

For this reason, advertisers have a definite responsibility to readers. An advertiser should write advertisements that are helpful to readers, keyed to their specific interests, and these advertisements should be as informative as possible about his product. If an advertiser writes in this manner, his advertisements will produce results for him in sales, in inquiries, or, at the very least, in favorable impacts upon readers.

To write such advertisements, an advertiser must first find out what his customers think about his product, how they use it, what they like or do not like about it, improvements that might be made in it, operating instructions that ought to be given so that the product can be properly used. Personal interviews are the best way to get this information. If an advertiser cannot do this, he should hire a qualified research organization to dig up this very important information.

An advertiser, moreover, should be familiar with the various publications he uses, because the editors know intimately their readers' problems and can supply the answers. An advertiser, by watching the editorial content of a publication, will know what his customers are thinking about, and this will enable him to write copy that will be helpful and important to readers, his customers.

ADVERTISING MANAGER'S RESPONSIBILITIES

This is the background against which the advertising department sells space in its publication. The advertising manager, as he is sometimes called, or the advertising director, who is really a sales manager, is responsible for the entire sales activity of the publication. He usually reports directly to the publisher and does such things as the following: develops the sources of business; determines sales strategy; plans sales material; supervises promotion and research activity; hires, trains, and supervises salesmen; assigns accounts to the various salesmen; allocates territories; sets quotas; sets up sales records and controls and analyzes information in them; supervises the make-up of the advertising pages in the publication; and maintains good customer and public relations.

The advertising manager will, of course, have a group of salesmen and representatives working under him. He will also have assistants responsible for sales promotion and record keeping.

A businesspaper has a natural list of advertising prospects, made up of companies making products or supplying services bought by the publication's readers. The advertising manager must be sure that all the worth-while companies in these classifications are adequately covered by salesmen and by promotion.

PUBLICATION'S RESPONSIBILITY TO ADVERTISERS

A businesspaper has a direct responsibility to its advertisers to help them advertise effectively to its readers. Some advertisers sell in many different markets or have too-limited facilities to find out for themselves the way to advertise effectively to each one of these markets. They therefore depend to a large extent on publishers for information about markets and about advertising effectively to prospective customers in those markets.

Because the cost of renewal business is usually less than the cost of new business, the advertising department can help keep its costs low and the publication's profits high if it renews a high percentage of its business. Business, of course, will renew more readily if advertisers are definitely getting their money's worth. Therefore, the advertising department has an excellent reason for making sure that advertising is helping advertisers sell more products.

SALES STRATEGY

The businesspaper advertising department has three things to sell. In its sales strategy it has to emphasize one or more of them depending on the particular circumstances.

1. It must sell the publication. Advertisers want to know about the publication's editorial content; its readership; readers' problems; circulation; rates; its importance and influence in its field; and how it helps the advertiser sell his product.

2. It may have to sell the market served by the publication. Very often a prospective advertiser does not realize the increased sales volume he might get from a market through an advertising program. A publication knows the facts about its market better than anyone else; therefore, it is in a strategic position to tell an advertiser or a prospective advertiser how to develop his sales volume in that market. The Federal Government and newspapers very often look to businesspapers for market facts and trends.

3. The advertising department occasionally has to sell advertising. Some prospective advertisers have to be shown what publication advertising can do for them. Therefore, the advertising department must give such prospects fundamental information on how and why the publication should be used. Other advertisers have to be given copy ideas because they do not know how properly to use the white space they buy in the publication. To give advertisers copy ideas a publication should interview its readers to find out what they want to know about the products advertised in the publication and what they expect from the advertising of these products.

A publication can make all this material available through the personal contact of its salesmen, through direct mail, and through its own advertising in newspapers and magazines.

Advertisers should realize that business publications can help them and should therefore make the fullest possible use of this assistance in order to reach a specific and specialized audience as effectively as possible.

There are times when a publication can go so far as to help new advertisers set up complete sales and advertising programs.

The sales material used by a publication salesman includes such things as the circulation statement, rate card, readership studies, exhibits of editorial content, evidence of reader interest, circulation and linage comparisons with competing publications, lists of advertisers, success stories, market studies, copy ideas.

WHAT THE SALESMAN DOES

You can see that the salesman is a pretty important part of the selling operation. A good salesman has enthusiasm, intelligence, an agreeable personality, a willingness to learn, and an ambition to grow in his vocation. These qualities, plus experience with people, may actually be more important in a new salesman than specific space-selling experience.

A salesman sells advertising to accounts which have been assigned him by territory or by type of account. He works out of the home office or a branch office of the publication. He is a full-time employee and is paid by salary or commission, or sometimes by a combination of both.

A good salesman must educate his prospects and not just peddle space. He must interpret his highly specialized publication and market to his advertisers and prospective advertisers. He has to fit his publication to their specific needs and sales problems. Sometimes he may have to sell the idea of advertising or his market before he can sell his own publication.

Idea selling is the best selling, and should be the primary strategy. A salesman should give advertisers ideas on how to use his publication and how to sell in his market. This kind of selling is geared to the selfish interest of the buyer and not the seller, which is important psychology: you are always more interested in you and your problems than you are in the other fellow's. In order to do idea selling, the salesman must constantly study his market, its problems, and ways in which advertisers can effectively advertise and sell to it. He must thoroughly know his publication, its readership, editorial content, objectives, and achievements. He should contact readers in order to have first-hand knowledge of their problems. A salesman who can say to a prospect that he has just had a talk with John Jones (who presumably is an important customer for the prospective advertiser) and that Jones told him such and such, makes a lasting impression upon his prospect.

Does this kind of selling pay off? It certainly does. For instance, at the January, 1947, convention of the National Publishers Association, James W. Young, Chairman of the Advertising Council, gave a handsome tribute to space salesmen. He said that the better salesmen of his acquaintance had helped him immeasurably by bringing him new ideas and by keeping him in touch with the best thoughts of the advertising business.

Then there is a well-known agency head who was accused by his associates of seeing too many people. He brushed off these objections by saying that the time wasted on unprofitable calls was more than paid for by ideas given him by salesmen who respected his willingness to listen and learn.

Factual selling is secondary strategy. An advertiser must, of course, know about the circulation, rates, and editorial content of a publication, but these should be directly related to his specific objectives.

The relative cost of using competing publications is important but not primary. After all, the cost of advertising in any businesspaper is low when compared with the purchasing power of its readers.

Too much emphasis on circulation figures ignores the quality and extent of readership, It also ignores the fact that readers are a homogeneous, fraternal group not confined by state borders.

PUBLISHERS' REPRESENTATIVES

Most of the selling is done by full-time salesmen working out of a home or branch office. However, many publications also use the services of publishers' representatives who are likewise salesmen but who are on their own, representing a group of publications in territories where the volume of business for any one publication is not large enough to support a branch office. Publishers' representatives receive a straight commission, running somewhere between 15 and 25 per cent of net billing. In all other ways, they follow the same procedure as a publication's own salesman.

PRODUCTION MANAGER

The production manager's responsibility is to follow advertisers and agencies for copy and plates to make up the advertising pages of each issue, to see that the plates and copy are delivered to the printer and that advertisements to be set are approved by the advertiser, to keep records on contracts and schedules, to send out bills for space used.

SALES CONTROLS

The advertising manager must have certain records and controls in order to know in detail whether or not his sales efforts are bearing the right kind of fruit. Among the facts and figures the advertising department must have are the following: Names of and principal facts about all advertisers and prospects; data on contracts, insertion dates, expiration dates; weekly or monthly sales volume; breakdowns by salesmen, territory, classification; quarterly or monthly forecasts; sales of competitors; earnings and expenses of salesmen; number and quality of calls they make, and accounts where they are spending too much or too little time; points of sales resistance and effectiveness of sales material; analysis of sales costs by salesmen, territory, classification, size of account, unit of space; the proper relationship between total sales and total expenses; the amount to be spent for promotion and research. The advertising manager must have a budget in order to keep expenses in line with anticipated income from advertising. The budget would include such items as salesmen's salary and expenses, administrative and office expenses, sales material and promotion expenses.

RELATIONSHIP WITH AGENCIES

Advertising agencies are important to a businesspaper, though not as important as they are to a consumer publication. After all, agencies do have a considerable influence on the buying of advertising, even though the advertiser usually has the final decision. More advertisers today rely on agencies' specialized services than in the early days of businesspapers. In addition, most agencies now realize the value of businesspaper advertising to their clients, because of its growth and because of Associated Business Publications educational programs. Publications once had to provide copy service for advertisers, but agencies or the advertisers now handle it, with few exceptions. Publications, of course, can still pass along copy ideas.

PROMOTION AND RESEARCH

An important part of the advertising department's responsibility has to do with promotion research, so these activities are very often under the jurisdiction of the advertising manager. However, each of them will be discussed in separate sections of this chapter.

QUALIFICATIONS OF A GOOD SPACE SALESMAN*

I. Does he really know industrial advertising?
A. Has he a basic understanding of the fundamental principles of industrial advertising as a sales tool?

* The Industrial Advertising Association of New York used the above questionnaire as a guide to its active members in evaluating their candidate for the Annual Award to "The Space Salesman of the Year."

B. Does he have some concept of the arithmetic of advertising in terms of doing faster, cheaper, and more frequently some of the sales jobs that otherwise must be done at higher cost by salesmen alone?

C. In short, can he talk on even terms with those of his customers and prospects who do understand and practice good advertising—and can he guide and help educate those who are floundering?

II. Does he endeavor, before selling, to learn something about the prospect's business?

A. Does he try to find out what the advertiser's sales and advertising objectives are?

B. Does he try to find out what product features are of particular interest to his reader group?

C. Does he try to get hold of the prospect's rated list of products or services—rated list of markets—rated list of functional groups influencing purchases?

D. Does he explore the advertiser's methods of distribution; learn to what extent sales contacts are made direct by salesmen, through dealers, through wholesalers, etc.?

III. Does he really know his own product?

Has he essential knowledge of such matters as:

A. The market his publication serves and the volume of the advertiser's product it accounts for?

B. The relative importance of various functional groups within that market in terms of their buying influence or direct buying power?

C. How his particular publication serves, editorially, the job interests and needs of some particular functional group or combination of groups within the market, and how well it covers them numerically?

D. How his circulation is built and how it penetrates and covers the market his publication purports to serve?

E. To what extent the physical characteristics of his publication, such as format, constitute a promotional advantage?

F. Full information on the organization behind his publication?

IV. Does he organize and present his story well?

A. Once he knows something about the advertiser's aims and the uses of his product in his field, does he talk specifically about the advantages to be derived by the prospect through proper use of his publication?

B. Does he spend too much time comparing his magazine with competitors' papers? (In other words, does he do a positive or negative selling job?)

C. On the positive side—does he make suggestions on things his readers might want to know about the product in question, as a clue to the most profitable use of the space that might be bought?

D. Does he occasionally call on readers to learn about their interests, needs, and confusions in relation to various types of products?

E. Does he frequently bring from his editors information regarding trends in his market and possibly suggestions about things to be said about the products?

V. Is his frequency and timing of calls satisfactory?

A. Does he call only when he has something of real interest concerning his paper, his market, or to offer some constructive suggestions regarding your advertising or sales program?

B. Does he avoid calling during the periods usually set aside for opening the day's mail and signing outgoing mail?

C. Is he punctual when appointments have been arranged?

VI. Does he have a pleasant personality?

A. Is he courteous, friendly, and helpful?

B. Does he follow through on promises made?

C. Does he work intelligently, tactfully, and considerately with both agency and advertiser?

D. Can he take a turn-down gracefully, with the attitude that, after all, right or wrong, the advertiser is trying to do the best he can with the money at hand?

VII. Does he appear to rely too much on entertainment as a sales tool?

TEN OBJECTIVES OF CREATIVE ADVERTISING SALES EFFORT*

Pre-war, post-war, anytime, and all the time, the businesspaper has two things to sell:

* William K. Beard, Jr., President, Associated Business Publications, Inc.; former Vice President and Manager of Promotion and Research, McGraw-Hill Pub. Co.; from a lecture at New York University, November 20, 1947.

First, it has a selective audience of people concerned with one industry, or one function in industry. In other words, a specific audience in a specific market.

And second, it has an editorial service geared to the specific needs and interests of that market and audience. Put another way—a pre-conditioned advertising target.

To sell advertising in our specialized medium we have today, like we have always had, three kinds of tools.

First, *the tools of research*, which give us factual information on our markets, on our publication, on its audience, and on advertising performance.

Second, *the tools of promotion*, which—taking our own medicine—means to spread the story of our paper and its market to the fraternity of people who should be advertising with us. Promotion is doing for us, as salesmen, what we say it does for the salesmen of our advertising accounts.

Third, *the tools of selling*, which is our inbred and cultivated sales ability plus the "props" an accommodating and alert home office has put into our brains and our brief cases.

Here are ten objectives or directions creative advertising sales effort can reach for. They are *my* ten points. Another man could give you his list and it could be much different—without being necessarily a better or worse list than mine. Make up your own. I had to think a lot to get this group of sales purposes organized and it was wholesome mental exercise. I commend it to you.

1. Sell expanded industry:
   a. To raise sights of the advertising job;
   b. To demonstrate the need for larger circulation and higher rates.
2. Sell the economic function of advertising *today*:
   a. To help maintain stable economy by
   b. Keeping the reservoir of demand well stocked and
   c. Reducing the costs of selling.
3. Sell advertising application to problems of today:
   a. Productivity;
   b. Service and deliveries;
   c. Labor relations;
   d. Battling higher costs.

4. Sell good copy:
   a. Research on reader interests;
   b. Copy testing.
5. Sell adequate scheduling and dominant space.
6. Sell against competition:
   a. General media;
   b. Direct mail, films, etc.;
   c. Competing businesspapers.
7. Sell turnover in jobs:
   a. Emphasis on young men;
   b. Unique value of paid circulation.
8. Sell advertising versus inquiries.
9. Sell higher advertising costs.
10. Sell new accounts, developing small and young advertisers.

GETTING MORE BUSINESS THROUGH BETTER SUPERVISION AND TRAINING*

Here is a checklist that sales managers of businesspaper advertising can profitably use to help them prepare for hard selling. It is just a working yardstick, not an exhaustive treatise, on a subject that is usually mastered only through trial and error.

1. ARE YOUR SALES OBJECTIVES GENERAL OR SPECIFIC?

Are you, for instance, working for an over-all increase in units and dollars? Or are you just trying to hold your own in a declining market? Or are you trying to increase your percentage of your field? Do you want to get new accounts or get more business from your present accounts? Your specific objectives will shape the course of your selling.

2. DO YOU HAVE A HIRING POLICY?

Do you have a clear idea, based on your experience, of the kind of man who best sells your market and publication? What kind of ability, background, and experience gives you the best results? Do you know, or do you just grab the last known applicant? Do you use sales aptitude or I. Q. tests? Media sales managers who do use them say they are a big help in selecting salesmen.

---

* Robert E. Kenyon, Jr., Advertising Sales Manager, *Printers' Ink;* from an address before the Associated Business Publications, at their annual meeting, Hot Springs, Va., May, 1949.

3. DO YOU THOROUGHLY TRAIN YOUR NEW SALESMEN?

Or do you just rush them once around the office, hand them a rate card, a circulation statement, pat them on the back, and send them forth? *Selling is not just doing what comes naturally.* Many more salesmen are made than are born with a signed order in their mouths. Of course there are a few exceptions, very few, and they soon gain management status. This checklist is not for them (or for you); it is for the 90 per cent that are not self-starters. Not every publishing house is set up to give a formal training course to its new salesmen, but even small houses can have a new salesman spend time with each department, or actually work in it, as well as have conferences with the publisher on general policy and with the sales manager. The information he gains in this way will make him a more intelligent salesman when he is calling on your prospects.

4. DO YOU HAVE CONTINUOUS TRAINING FOR ALL YOUR SALESMEN?

This is even more important than preliminary training for new salesmen. It may be trite to say that knowledge is power, but it is eternally true. If you want your men to be salesmen of advertising, and not peddlers of space, you must continually increase their know-how. Since adequate and continuous training is a most important phase of competent supervision, let us break it down into its four aspects.

5. DO YOU CONTINUOUSLY TRAIN YOUR SALESMEN IN ADVERTISING?

Because they are, we hope, selling advertising, it is rather important that they know enough about its principles and practice so they can intelligently discuss with your prospects the ways in which it helps them sell more goods. Bill Marsteller[6] commented on how poorly qualified are most businesspaper salesmen to discuss advertising with the men they call on, even salesmen of ABP members who otherwise are the cream of the crop. Your salesmen should understand the power of advertising well enough so they can resell the advertiser who wants to dump the budget when his sales slump and the one who considers advertising an expense rather than an investment. They must be particularly well informed on businesspapers because, as a speaker pointed out in his discussion of the problems of the merchandising group, too many people are not sold on businesspapers. Finally, they should know something

[6] See Chapter 17, for paper by Marsteller.

about other media and direct mail so they can properly integrate your publication into the prospect's whole program for advertising.

6. DO YOU CONTINUOUSLY TRAIN YOUR SALESMEN ON YOUR MARKET?

Your salesmen should be experts on your market. Your customers and prospects are looking for facts and an understanding of the market they reach when they use you. And your salesmen have to provide them. Do they? They should know the latest figures and statistics and be able to tell how to sell to your market.

7. DO YOU CONTINUOUSLY TRAIN YOUR SALESMEN ON YOUR PUBLICATION?

Do you give them comprehensive, detailed interpretations of your editorial objectives, methods, and achievements; your circulation and methods of increasing it; your reader influence or loyalty; your advertising volume in total and by classifications? Do you tell them of effective ways for advertisers to use you? Do you give them plenty of case histories and success stories? The answer to all these questions would probably be "Yes" if your salesmen, and you, could put the basic sales story for your market and publication into fifty words.

8. DO YOU CONTINUOUSLY TRAIN YOUR SALESMEN IN SELLING?

Remember selling is not playing by ear, but following the established scales and chords—following, that is, the tested rules and techniques. Take AIDA, for instance. Maybe some salesmen think of it only in operatic terms. They should know that well-known formula so well they follow it without knowing it. That rare bird, the self-starter, knows how to get *a*ttention, arouse *i*nterest, create *d*esire, and get *a*ction; but how about the other 90 per cent? Are you sure they do?

Do they plan what they are going to say to the prospect before they see him, or do they just hope for inspiration when they walk through his door?

Do they talk about his problems and how you can help solve them? Bill Marsteller said most of those calling on him "have no idea how we sell, what we sell, to whom we sell, or what our plans for the future will be."

Do they give him useful information and helpful ideas from your publication, market information, or research?

Do they study his sales promotion and advertising and talk to his salesmen so they get a clear picture of his objectives and plans? The advertising manager of the Rockwell Manufacturing Company asked the salesmen of the eleven publications he uses what they thought of his last advertisement. Eight of them had not the vaguest idea of the content of his most recent advertisement, or what it was trying to accomplish or how well it was keyed to the magazine's audience.

Are they detectives on problem accounts so they can ferret out the real reasons for not getting the business and not simply coast along on the inevitable alibis and buck-passing? Do they find out who is primarily responsible so they can work on the real source of your trouble?

Do they cover all bases regularly and see everyone who has an influence on the buying decisions?

Do they always ask for the order?

Do they make more service and social calls on customers than sales calls on prospects?

Do they write plenty of letters: after important calls so the prospect has it in black and white for his files; between calls; personal notes to important people at important customers and prospects; letters promoting your editorial activity? To quote Bill Marsteller just once more, he has been asking salesmen to put their stories in letters so he could really digest them and file them for future use. "Not more than 50 per cent ever write me, and of those I have received, only two said anything that made sense to me as a buyer of advertising space."

Do they have good bedside manners, or are they like that last fumbling salesman who called on you—for the last time?

Do they plan their work and work their plan?

All these questions about selling techniques are particularly important just now because your younger and newer men are experiencing their first buyers' market and your older men may be rusty and stale.

9. HOW DO YOU TRAIN CONTINUOUSLY?

Do you have enough personal conferences so you know what each salesman is doing, saying, and thinking? Such conferences are excellent opportunities to coach your men and keep their spark plugs clean. Do you use sales meetings to give group training on advertising, on your market, on your publication, and on selling? Or do you have merely routine meetings complete with needles for the drop in sales last week of your latest pet idea? Do you use outside talent occasionally, qualified speakers on advertising, on your market or on selling? Continuous training is the essence of your supervision, so don't get lost in the daily bustle and forget your long-range objectives.

10. DOES YOUR SALES PROMOTION REALLY HELP YOUR SALESMEN SELL?

If done right, it will pre-sell your prospects and give your salesmen sharp tools to work with. If not, give the money to charity; it will be more useful. Here is what Al Hauptli, publisher of McGraw-Hill's *American Machinist* and *Product Engineering*, said about promotion at the Sales Managers Clinic:

I feel that sales promotion and advertising are among the most important jobs the businesspaper has facing it today. In my publications we believe in advertising. We practice what we preach. We do a real publication advertising job on a continuous basis. We merchandise this advertising, and we do it not by just sending a reprint, but we take our publication advertising and convert it into sales literature, each piece of which stands on its own feet. It has been very successful. I think promotion is so important it deserves the attention of the publisher of a magazine and every other top executive. . . . A good promotion job helps your salesmen. It helps unify your sales story. The publication which is doing a well-planned and outstanding job in businesspapers, following it up by direct mail, and using all the other good promotion tools will find that its salesmen are tying in and telling the same story, instead of having these salesmen tell one story in one territory and another story in another territory. Good promotion has been very effective for us in channeling and developing a sales story which the entire staff is telling, and telling at the same time.

Is your promotion dramatic and graphic?

Is it constructive or merely competitive?

Does it give your prospects a vivid picture of your market and publication or is it overworked with clichés?

Do you have a basic presentation on your market and how to sell to it, your publication and how to advertise through it? A presentation for group meetings as well as for individual use? It is important to have your complete story packaged in either an easel flip-flop or a slide film so your customers and prospects will get a thorough indoctrination at least once every two years.

Do you have special presentations for important customers and prospects or for certain groups? It could be based on the basic presentation with elaborations for the particular people you are trying to sell.

11. DOES YOUR COMPENSATION PLAN FOR SALESMEN OFFER AN INCENTIVE?

The task of supervising salesmen can be lightened considerably if they have a minimum security salary plus an incentive commission or bonus. Getting the right plan is no easy job. In getting ready for the Sales Managers' Clinic, John Whelan asked thirty businesspaper publishers about their compensation plans. Twenty-eight of them had forty-one different plans. A third were dissatisfied with their present plan. That is some indication of the difficulties in setting up a good plan. But it can be done, and should.

12. DO YOU CHECK THE RESULTS OF YOUR SUPERVISION?

Of course you have records and reports of sales by salesmen, territory, and classifications; of competitors' sales; of sales costs for each salesman and territory; call reports and carbons of letters. But these are quantitative only. You want a qualitative measure of what you have done. So, do you review accounts periodically with each salesman, particularly problem accounts, to discover how well those things have been done that should have been done? Do you make frequent calls yourself, other than to put out competitive bonfires, with and without the salesman, on his regular contacts and on higher echelons to get a first-hand feel of your customer relations? Do you sometimes make cold calls to see for yourself what your men are up against, how well your promotion has penetrated, what your points of resistance are? Have you ever had a survey made for you by a qualified research firm among your customers to find out what they really think of you?

A soul-searching self-examination along the lines of these questions and many others that have occurred to you as you read will quickly suggest ways in which you can vastly improve the supervision and training you give your salesmen. With even a slight improvement in this direction you should find your salesmen are selling harder and therefore selling more businesspaper advertising.

A SUGGESTED PROGRAM

No one sales program is right for all publishers, but here is one that is based on the twelve-point checklist and may be helpful in drawing up your own.

1. Your basic sales story on market and publication should be told

to every buying influence at every advertiser and important prospect. That story should be simple and dramatic; and should be visualized in an easel or slide film presentation.

2. Every prospect (and suspect) in each territory should be seen by October 1, or reassigned.

3. Every buying influence at every advertiser and important prospect should be seen at least twice from now to December 31, or the account reassigned.

4. Salesmen should make at least four sales calls a day and turn in call reports at the end of the day. A sales call means a specific sales talk that asks for the order; follow-up and service calls do not count.

5. Salesmen should write at least four letters a day, with carbon copies turned in daily; these should include letters following up an important sales call to summarize the main points covered, letters promoting your editorial content, and letters to people they have not seen recently.

6. Salesman should list by Friday afternoon the names of 25 people he intends to make sales calls on the following week.

7. Salesmen should plan their calls before walking into the prospects' office; they should base their calls on useful information and helpful ideas from the editorial pages of your publication and from your market information or research.

8. Remind your salesmen, in meetings and personally, that one sure way to get attention and arouse interest (the first two steps in the AIDA formula) is to talk about their prospects' objectives, methods, results, and problems. To do that your salesmen should first study their prospect's advertising and sales promotion and talk with several of his salesmen to find out what they are up against in selling; secondly, your salesmen should call on a dozen or more of their prospects' customers and prospects to find out more about their sales problems. Then your salesmen can make a specific proposal based on facts that should guarantee their arousing desire and getting action (steps 3 and 4 of AIDA). This is creative selling at its best.

9. Review once a month with each salesman his accounts and particularly his problem accounts so you can be sure he is doing everything he can to get an order.

10. Arrange monthly sales meetings at which you have qualified speakers on advertising, or businesspapers, on your market and on selling as well as members of your own organization to interpret editorial and circulation activity.

"COMBAT TIME" IN SELLING SPACE*

What is a prospect?

A very intelligent advertising space salesman was working on an account that made a large line of handling equipment exclusively for the automobile trade. The salesman was putting in important time with this manufacturer trying to convert him to making the type of equipment that would fit in one of our fields, so that we could have a chance to sell him. Now this might be all right if you have run out of prospects, but there were still a lot of prospects we had not sold that were making things that were applicable in our field. That is not recognizing a prospect. A prospect, to be a prospect, has to first of all have a product that he is manufacturing, that is applicable to the field you serve. Next he has got to have some money. Thirdly (that which makes him even a better prospect) he has got to have a real predisposition to advertise. You should not have to sell him the basic idea in advertising. If you get those three characteristics you have got a prospect.

Now, you will find some exceptions to those rules. Occasionally you will find somebody that is, for instance, trying to sell some stock and they want to enhance the value of it and will make a splash in your field temporarily. That is not a real prospect for the long haul.

Where do you find prospects? You find them, sometimes, by just chasing smokestacks. You find them by looking in the places where they would be spending dollars if they were interested in the field. One good way of finding prospects is to get one of the logical buyers of things in one of your fields to save for you the mailing pieces usually thrown in the wastebasket. Look over the stuff that is thrown in the wastebasket and you will see who is trying to sell him something. You will get a pretty good index as to who is active in that field.

And of course your competitor's businesspapers are always good places to look for prospects. If they are spending money with your competitor, they have a predisposition to advertise in your field, to say the least.

How are you going to plan your time? You have only got a certain

* Russell L. Putman, President, National Business Publications; president, Putman Publishing Company and founder of the Putman Awards in Industrial Advertising; from a lecture before the Medill School of Journalism, Northwestern University, Chicago Campus, May, 1949. The use of the term "combat time" by Mr. Putnam may be explained in the fact that he was a pursuit pilot in France in World War I and a Lt. Colonel in the U. S. Air Corps in World War II.

number of hours in which you can actually go out and see people and talk about business. You have got more hours than most salesmen like to admit because there are some people who get to their offices at eight o'clock in the morning. They are easier to talk to at that time than they are at any time in the day.

I have also known men whom I never called on until about a quarter to six. I could not get past the girl at any time before five o'clock. But after five o'clock you could go in and they would have their feet up on the desk. You would have a nice talk with them.

So, you have got to accommodate your time to your knowledge of your territory and of your prospect's habits—and then you have got to plan your time for writing letters, keeping records and making out reports, so that it does not steal away from your "combat time."

And when you are in talking to the prospect, what do you say? Like the doctor, you ask questions—you try to *diagnose* why this man is not buying the space and the amount of space that you would like to have him buy. When you find that out then you can start working intelligently.

Now, if we can diagnose as a doctor diagnoses; if we can find out what the specific trouble is, then we can begin to give the treatment, in terms of our story, that fits best for his case. In medicine, and it is true in advertising as well, the man that makes money is the man that is the best diagnostician. The doctor cannot treat you properly until after he finds out what is really wrong. We believe you have got to sell the account as well as the agency. You cannot expect to sell the agency and leave it to him to go out and do your work. Only in certain cases is this possible—where the account is already so well sold that they will take any recommendation about your publication from the agency and accept it. You should not expect an agency man to go out and sell an account for you. The agency's main job is to get along with his client. If you think he is going to stick his neck out and contradict the client or try and force something down the client's throat, just to get your publication on, you are more of an optimist than you are a realist.

HOW BUSINESSPAPER ADVERTISING SPACE IS BOUGHT*

The purchasing of businesspaper space cannot be considered a stereo-typed operation. The functions involved in the buying process are all recognized and executed, but the manner of approach, the habit patterns

* C. Laury Botthof; from "A Survey of Advertiser and Agency Buying Practices and Patterns for Businesspapers" published by Standard Rate & Data Service, Chicago, 1948 (second printing, 1949).

evidenced, are varied and diversified. Few advertisers and agencies approach each of the functions involved (establishing a budget, selecting a market, preparing the preliminary list or approving the final list) in a comparable manner or delegate responsibility to comparable titles.

It is also fairly obvious that the title of an individual within the advertiser or agency organization sheds little light on that individual's responsibility within the steps involved that lead to the placing of a businesspaper contract. This is universally true regardless of the amount of space placed by the organization in question. The advertising manager, the sales manager, the account executive, the media director, primarily, individually, and collectively exercise varying degrees of responsibility within the buying process. Their relative responsibilities within each of the functions are discussed below.

PREPARING THE BUDGET

The preparation of the budget is a cooperative affair requiring the dual efforts of the advertiser and agency representatives. Primarily, the advertising manager, the general sales manager, the account executive, and the media director are most often called upon to render opinions.

Titular Responsibility. The amount of space placed by the organization will affect the relationship of the titular responsibility to the budget.

The advertising manager's relative influence increases as the amount of space placed by the advertiser increases.

Conversely, the president's participation decreases as he obviously relieves himself of a duty which can be delegated.

The general sales manager's participation in budget problems exhibits no variance in relative influence, but could very well swell with importance if the departmental or regional sales managers are added to the total score.

Agency participation increases in direct relation to the amount of space placed, thus exhibiting indirectly the advertiser's recognition of the need for specialization and outside counsel on budget problems.

However, as with the advertiser, there exists no clearly established titular responsibility among agency representation. Generally, the account executive will be present at such discussions and more often than not, the media director will either share this responsibility or substitute for him, particularly among agencies placing over 2000 pages of space a year.

The agency principal is reported to exercise the greatest amount of influence in the medium-size agency.

The agency planning group serves as the agency representative when such a unit is active within the agency organization. Agencies report increasing participation for this title in direct relation to increases in amount of space placed. Other independent research had previously established that the larger the agency, the more apt it was to include an operating plans group.

Few organizations, either among advertisers or agencies, tend to adopt and pursue comparable procedures, thus making it difficult to generalize. Client and account executive collaborated most often among agencies buying less than 2000 pages of space, and the media director was called upon to participate with these titles in the large agencies.

Number of Titles Participating. Budgetary problems, as pointed out, require the attention of at least two, if not more titles, within the advertiser and the agency organization. The number of titles called upon to confer will increase proportionately to the amount of space placed. It would be safe to assume that groups of three titles is the average minimum number of titles participating in advertiser and agency conferences dealing with budgetary problems.

SELECTING THE BUSINESSPAPER MARKET

The advertising manager exercises the greatest amount of decision in the selection of the markets in which the businesspaper advertising campaign is to be conducted. This responsibility for decision is performed after consulting with the sales managers and the agency account executive. In the larger agencies, the media director will either share responsibility with or substitute for the account executive.

Although the line of responsibility for decision appears to be clearly defined, a wide variation is indicated in the manner in which the titles participate as consultants. Few advertisers or agencies approach the market problem in the same way.

The size of the respondent appears to have little or no effect upon the exercise of decision. But in the matter of influence, it is clearly established that the research director and agency planning group play an increasingly important (though still minor) role in direct relation to the amount of space placed by the agency.

Who Decides. It is the advertising manager who is empowered with the right of decision. This responsibility exists regardless of size of the advertiser. The general sales manager is a factor, but he usually shares this responsibility with the advertising manager or the president. Occasionally, the account executive shares the power of decision with the advertising manager.

Analysis by Size of Advertiser. The size of the advertiser organization does not appear to affect, in any way, the relative importance of either the advertising manager or the sales manager. Among advertisers, the sole influence of size appears among the small advertiser where the presidents' influence is much stronger. Among agencies, the sole exception appears among the larger agencies where the media director gains in influence by substituting for or sharing with the account executive his minor role as a decider.

How Is the Decision Problem Approached? Decisions regarding the selection of businesspaper markets is described as an advertiser responsibility. Primarily, the advertising manager alone will execute this function. In those instances where two titles share the responsibility of decision we will generally find that the advertising manager will be working with either the sales manager or the account executive.

Who Influences the Selection of Businesspaper Markets? The advertising agency and the advertiser's sales department play important behind the scene roles in this matter of selecting markets. Almost any title may be called upon to represent the agency in market conferences. In addition, members of the sales department are also called upon to offer opinions, make suggestions, and serve in an all-around consulting capacity.

The general sales manager is the key advertiser representative.

Titular responsibility   who exercises influence? The exercise of influence among advertisers is clearly defined as the responsibility of the sales department and the degree of influence (or participation) in market conference will increase as the amount of space placed by the advertiser increases.

Agency participation, also, will increase with the amount of space placed. However, there are variations evidenced among all titles elected to represent the agency. While the relative importance of the account executive as a factor participating in the selection of markets remains fairly constant, the relative importance of the agency planning group and the research director increases as the size of the agency increases.

The agency principal and the media director fluctuate in relative importance, primarily in the medium agency where the media director is reported to play a less important role and the agency principal increases his participation in market selection problems.

Within the agencies, the account executive ranks as a primary influence.

The media director plays a major role in the small and large agency, whereas the agency principal confers with the client in the medium agency.

As the amount of advertising to be placed increases, more agency titles are called into conference or asked to examine markets. The account executive, working alone, will most frequently represent the small and medium agencies.

The major participants in the function of selecting the markets in which the businesspaper advertising campaign is to be conducted are (in order of importance): The advertising manager, account executive, sales manager, media director.

PREPARING THE PRELIMINARY LIST

Who Prepares Initial List of Specific Businesspapers to be Used? There does not appear to be any one standard agency-advertiser relationship for selecting media. The function may be executed in one of several ways by any of several titles. Generally, the advertising agency will prepare the list, during which process the advertiser may or may not be consulted.

The agency representatives sharing the responsibility for the preparation of the initial list may be the agency principal, account executive and/or the media director. Their relative degree of responsibility will vary according to the degree of specialization permitted by reason of the amount of space placed by the agency and according to the individual peculiarities of organization present within the agency. It is quite evident that title is not respected in the exercise of the functional responsibility for selecting businesspapers, although size may have some influence. Any title or even many titles may be involved in different combination.

The agency representative(s) will share responsibility with or consult with the advertiser's advertising manager. The following are the procedures for preparing preliminary businesspaper lists:

1. The agency with sole responsibility prepares the list and submits it to the advertiser in final form.
2. The agency prepares the initial list, reviews it with the advertiser and then revises the list before resubmitting.
3. The agency prepares appraisals of media serving particular markets

in comparative form, which is then submitted, with recommendations, to the advertiser who makes the selection.

4. The agency and advertiser together confer on media and collaborate on selection.

Advertiser Response. The advertising manager is the sole advertiser representative exercising responsibilities for the preparation of preliminary lists. This responsibility may be absolute, or shared with the agencies. The advertising manager may also serve as liaison within these organizations who delegate complete responsibility for preliminary lists to the advertising agency.

The amount of space placed by the advertiser does not appear to influence the nature of the responsibility exercised by the advertising manager.

Agency Response. The account executive, the media director, and the agency principal all exercise major responsibilities in the selection of businesspapers for the preliminary list.

However, the degree of responsibility exercised by each of the above titles will be dependent upon the volume of space placed by the agency. In those agencies placing less than 2000 pages of space annually, the account executive and agency principal are most active.

In the over-2000 class, the media director is acknowledged as being responsible. The media director (working alone) was described most often as the habit pattern pursued. This characteristic, however, is true only for the larger agencies. The medium-sized agency mentions the account executive (working alone) most often, while considerable mention is also afforded the agency principal. The small agency, for the most part, apparently prefers to have the account executive and the media director work together.

MARKET DATA WANTED BY MEDIA BUYERS

1. What is the market served by the publication?
   a. What is the market potential?
   b. How large is the market?
   c. What are the market characteristics?
   d. How important is the market?
2. Is the businesspaper reachning a well-defined group of readers?
   a. Who are the readers?
   b. What are their job responsibilities and why are they important to the advertisers?

c. What is the field or working interest covered?

d. What evidence is available to indicate acceptance and readership among these readers who comprise the well-defined field?

e. Has this well-defined group of readers been recognized by others?

f. How and why do the readers comprise a clearly defined group to which advertising of specific products can be directed advantageously?

    a. As a check on readers by desiring evidence that the publication is read by the *right* persons.

    b. As a check on editorial by desiring evidence that the quality of editorial adequately matched the reader common interest.

3. Is the editorial matched to the interests of the reader group?

    a. Nature of editorial content.

    b. Editorial policy expressed in terms of how it matches the interests of the readers.

    c. Publication itself.

    d. Data on readership—evidence of acceptance of editorial quality.

    e. Qualifications of editorial staff.

4. Is circulation offered in quantity and quality to match the characteristics of the market?

    a. The number of people there are of the type for whom the business-paper is edited.

    b. Where they are (geographically and/or by industry).

    c. Whether the total circulation includes a satisfactory percentage of these people to represent coverage.

    d. Renewal percentages as an instrument of measure of the quality of circulation.

    e. The methods by which circulation is obtained may help in evaluating its quality.

5. Is the format clear and practical?

    a. Information regarding format desired by the advertisers and agencies:

    "Advertising front and back."

    "Advertising opposite editorial."

    "Appearance."

    "Position information—visibility."

    "Volume of advertising *vs.* editorial content."

    "Color information."

    "Size of space units."

b. Mechanical requirements:
Page size
Plate requirements.
"Color reproduction qualities."
"Data included in a typical SRDS listing."
Miscellaneous
The following kinds of information are sometimes regarded:
"Details on all special issues."
"Merchandising services available."
"Information services available."
"Guarantees."
"Issuance data—(monthly or weekly).

The question of rates is not included because information regarding rates is considered an obvious requirement. Also, it was considered that rates are primarily an instrument of measurement employed by the media buyer within the process that leads to the recognition and acceptance of publication values.

SOURCES OF MEDIA INFORMATION

From what source is media information (for the preparation of preliminary lists) presently obtained? These are rated by both advertisers and agencies in the following order of importance:

1. Past experience (businesspapers previously used successfully).
2. Standard Rate and Data Service.
3. Media salesmen.
4. Media promotion.
5. Media trade press advertising.

Other sources of media information included:
Brad-Vern[7] for study of competitive programs.
Experiences and opinions of other advertisers.
Own observation and analysis.
Impartial surveys.
Reading habit studies.
Personal and mail surveys.
Specific questions to media.
Industrial Marketing Data Book[8] as primary source.

[7] Published by *Printers' Ink*, New York.
[8] Published by Advertising Publications, Inc., Chicago.

Own sales staff.

Company readership studies.

Surveys among sales offices, distributors and customers.

Own survey among customers and prospects.

APPROVING THE FINAL LIST

The Responsibility for Approving the Final List. Responsibility for approving the final list is an advertiser function. Top management will approve the budget dollars and leave the selection of media to the judgment of the advertising manager. The agency account executive may be called upon to serve as a consultant.

How Is Approval of the Media Selected Approached? For the most part, the advertising manager will be the final authority over the choice of media. However, the general sales manager may share this responnibility with the advertising managor cither actively or as a matter of routine. The exact relationship of the general sales manager toward the responsibility of approving lists is not clearly defined though it appears to be fairly obvious that in principle he is expected to exercise more influence than is indicated.

How Is the Agency Responsibility Toward Approval of the Final List Approached? The agency responsibility, if any exists, is to offer counsel and to explain why (if questions arise) certain selections or recommendations were made. The agency representative in these instances is usually the account executive, and, in the case of larger agencies, also the media director.

RESPONSIBILITY FOR PLACING CONTRACTS

This was regarded as an agency function. However, approximately 8 per cent of the advertisers reported that they, themselves, placed the businesspaper contracts.

PLANNING AND PLACING CONTRACTS

In What Months Are Businesspaper Advertising Campaigns Generally Planned and Contracts Generally Placed? The planning of businesspaper advertising campaigns and the placing of businesspaper contracts require attention for a considerable portion of the year. Activity and interest in businesspaper advertising, while experiencing a peak in the September–January period, does not appear to be restricted to any one or a series of months. It is a year-around activity.

Advertisers report that an average of 4.7 months are devoted to this activity and agencies estimate that 7.7 months are required. (It is considered that this average is understated rather than overstated. Many respondents to this question merely indicated their peak months—others while indicating peak months implied that other months were employed as well. In either instance, the implications, though fairly positive in character, were not included.)

Advertiser Response. The August–December period in any one year is reported to experience the heaviest *media buying and planning activity,* but there are no months that are ignored. May, with the lowest relative rank, was mentioned in 13.6 per cent of the replies. November was most often mentioned.

The average number of months employed for this media buying and planning activity is reported to be 4.7.

All months are mentioned as being used for *placing businesspaper contracts,* but the months mentioned most frequently are December, November, January, and October, in that order. An average of 1.9 months is utilized.

Indications are that the smaller the advertiser, the more apt he is to start placing his contracts early and to devote more time to this activity.

All months are reported to be employed by the advertiser respondent for *planning businesspaper advertising campaigns.* The peak months are designated as October, September, November, August, December, and July, in that order. An average of 3.2 months are utilized.

Again it appears that the smaller advertiser begins his media planning activity earlier, although the average amount of time devoted to this activity is comparable for all three groups.

Agency response. The *buying and planning activity* is reported to be a year round activity. Although the peak season is reported by agencies to be from August to January, no single month can be regarded as unimportant. June, the month mentioned least frequently, still was mentioned in 44.2 per cent of the total response.

In addition, it was reported that an average of 7.7 months were utilized by agency respondents for this activity. It might be mentioned that 36.5 per cent of the respondents (the highest for any period) reported that all 12 months were devoted to this activity.

All months are reported to be employed by agencies for the *placing of businesspaper contracts.* The peak months are November, December, and January. The slowest months reported were July and August, but even these were mentioned by 30 per cent of the respondents.

An average of 5.8 months was reported for this activity. It is also interesting to note that the larger the agency, the more time is devoted to the placing of businesspaper contracts.

All months are reported as being employed by agencies for the *planning of businesspaper contracts*. The peak months reported are August through January, inclusive. The slowest months, February and June, were each mentioned by 37.5 per cent of the respondents.

An average of 6.4 months were used for planning businesspaper campaigns, with more time and an earlier start being devoted to the activity in direct relation to the amount of space being placed.

BE CAREFUL WHEN JUDGING BUSINESSPAPER ADVERTISING BY INQUIRIES*

Never in the history of businesspaper advertising have there been so many who, to paraphrase the Apostle Thomas, say "Except I shall see direct returns from my advertising, I will not believe." What has aptly been termed "the passion for inquiries" has become epidemic.

This passion has been heightened by the growth in the number of product-inquiry type of businesspapers, by a healthy urge to take advertising less on faith and more on measurement, and by a natural reaction from that lush wartime interlude when the deluge of advertising permitted publications the luxury of rationing their space.

But whatever the reason, the simple fact is that today substantial manufacturers of established products (sold through salesmen) are judging their businesspaper advertising by the inquiries they produce. The worth of individual advertisements that are designed to aid the salesmen is weighed on inquiries. We see Agency A losing an account to Agency B, because Agency B says it can write copy that will produce a flock of leads the client's salesmen can follow up and turn into fat orders.

Is this hunger for inquiries good, or is it bad?

The hunger itself is eternal and universal. It has always been and always will be, as long as our system of free enterprise prevails. Every manufacturer's mouth waters at the sight of a stack of top-quality inquiries. But what may happen when the inquiry yardstick is used indiscriminately to measure advertising values?

First let us consider what the advertising is designed to accomplish. If the product advertised is sold wholly through the mails, if its manu-

* Arthur H. Dix, Vice-President in charge of Research, Conover-Mast Publications; from an article in *Printers' Ink*, January 20, 1950.

facturer has no sales force and no distributor organization and plans to have none, then the value of the advertising is properly measured wholly by direct inquiries and orders. The advertiser is in the mail-order business, and his advertising is properly of the mail-order type. His cost per inquiry (or rather cost per dollar of sales resulting from inquiries) is the sole determinant of the value of his advertising. But the mail-order advertiser is the exception in the industrial, merchandising and other fields served by businesspapers. In the great majority of these cases, the product is sold by direct salesmen (or manufacturers' representatives) or by distributor salesmen.

The normal channel through which an order goes from buyer to seller is *through the salesman*. The normal function of the advertising is not to *compete* with the salesman but to *aid* the salesman in getting a customer or holding one. The advertising is a sales lubricant. Regarded as an element of total selling expense, advertising in fields served by businesspapers averages about 10 per cent of the entire sales budget. Advertising is the tail. The dog is salesmen's salaries, the sales manager's salary and other elements of direct selling cost. In mail-order selling, advertising is, of course, the entire dog.

Now, if advertising can perform adequately its prime function of aiding the salesman and at the same time produce quantities of worthwhile inquiries with a high sales-conversion rate, isn't that all to the good? Why, certainly! This happens not infrequently in the case of manufacturers with inadequate sales representation. It may happen to any manufacturer with *adequate* sales representation during that period when a new product or established product of new design is in process of getting known to its field. Advertising can make the new development known to the entire field at once, whereas it takes even a large sales force some time to spread the news by personal call.

But new products and revolutionary new designs are the pie à la mode exceptions. The everyday, corn beef and cabbage jobs consist of selling a known product in competition with other known products.

HOW ADVERTISING HELPS SALES

The main job of businesspaper advertising is to make it easier for John H. Stumpf down there in St. Louis to sell our particular make of traveling cranes, or show cases, or cutting oil, or turret lathes. The going is hard for John. In sales volume he runs second to George H. Tree, who handles our chief competitor's line and has been in the St.

Louis territory much longer than John and has better connections. So what we have to do is to help John by reducing the number of cases where John has to start from scratch with prospects who have never even *heard* of our company, let alone know that our product has a manganese steel gazookus which practically never wears out, whereas it's common gossip that the one George H. Tree sells has to be laid up for repairs at least every eighteen months, tying up the whole plant.

We feature our gazookus in our advertising, so that John has a running start when he makes his calls, and if we hear that he finally landed the business of the Southwestern Steel Co., which had hitherto been cozy with George H. Tree, we feel maybe the advertising helped. We would be certain if we had known, as even John did not, that the reason he got Southwestern Steel was that the vice-president in charge of production and the purchasing agent had seen our advertising of the gazookus, and that was what swung the business in our or John's favor. John never knew what got the business for him, so he never told his boss, the sales manager. But even if he had known, he might not have passed the word along, because selling is so hard that it is the rare salesman who admits that he got an order by anything other than his own unaided efforts.

Let us get back to the advertising that helped John land the big Southwestern Steel account. The copy was based on the chief selling point of our product. Headline—YOUR TRAVELING CRANE IS PRACTICALLY NEVER SHUT DOWN FOR REPAIRS IF EQUIPPED WITH THIS MANGANESE STEEL GAZOOKUS. That is a good eye-catcher. Trade papers are scanned for ideas that will cut costs and increase profits. It would be nice if the vice-president in charge of production had clipped the coupon in the advertisement: "Send us your booklet telling us all about the Gazookus." But he didn't. Why didn't he?

Important buyers in the specialized fields served by businesspapers are called on by salesmen. That is the way business is done. Salesmen are a primary source of information regarding products and services these important buyers employ. The normal channel through which interest created by advertising flows is through the salesman.

Now, if instead of employing a headline based on the product's major selling point, you write advertisement selling the booklet: FREE—GET THIS VALUABLE KNOW-HOW MANUAL, you should increase your inquiries, but at the expense of doing a selling job in the advertising that will help John H. Stumpf on his daily rounds.

This mail-order technique for producing inquiries usually involves long copy. The audience is deliberately restricted to those who will endure the full treatment, and you get your inquiries from a portion of those. To attain *depth* of impression you have sacrificed *breadth* of audience.

Will the value of the inquiries so obtained compensate for the loss in broad selling power of the advertisement? Mostly, "No." Sometimes, "Yes." If John is holing up with a redhead in East St. Louis instead of making his calls, then you are making the advertising serve to turn up leads that John ought to be unearthing in his daily calls. If John is covering his territory adequately, then you are in a sense competing with John.

If John has a bigger territory than he can handle properly, and more prospects than he can call on, then some bird-dogging might justifiably be done for him by means of mail order type of advertising in publications or in direct mail, in order to flush out inquiries.

But that is an uncommon and usually temporary situation, because on the whole the fields served by businesspapers are well covered by salesmen. As the fields are specialized, the prospects are limited in number, and it is rarely possible to garner substantial numbers of high-octane leads over an extended period by using mail-order advertising. The reason for this is that the salesman gathers these leads in the course of his daily rounds. Usually he has had his eye on them before they were even amoebae.

In digging up worthwhile inquiries it is ordinarily difficult for advertising to compete with salesmen. The cost of advertising-induced inquiries usually mounts sharply as lists are exhausted; and if the management judges the value of the advertising solely on inquiry production, the advertising manager or agency is impelled to strain for replies. This in turn dilutes inquiry value. Salesmen squawk when obliged to waste time running down dud inquiries, and the advertising is damned.

"But," says the advertising manager, "I have to show direct return to keep the management sold on advertising." That's too bad. The boss has been reading Cadillac ads in the *Post* or *Fortune* or the *Christian Science Monitor*. Last week he bought a Cadillac. He never clipped a coupon.

COUPONS DO NOT MEASURE RESPONSE

The fact is that apart from exceptional instances it is dangerous to weigh the worth of a businesspaper advertisement on the number of inquiries it has produced. The most wasteful advertisement may produce the most inquiries. It is axiomatic in practically every field that the men important enough to be called on by salesmen—the men the salesmen have to sell to get an order—are the least likely to send a direct inquiry as the result of an advertisement. This is not due to an innate lack of responsiveness. The same man who will clip and mail a trout lure coupon in *Field & Stream* will pass by a coupon in his trade paper, because trout lure salesmen do not call on him, but the salesmen who sell the products he uses in his business *do*. If anything important to him in his business is developed, he knows he will be informed of it.

The desire to measure the results of advertising is laudable, but like trying to unscrew the inscrutable, a wrong answer is worse than none. Take two publications, A and B, serving the same field. A pulls twice as many inquiries as B. Is A a better publication than B? First the quality of the inquiries must be examined. If B has a higher quality of readers than A, the type of readers important enough to be called on by salesmen, then the chances are that B will not pull as well as A. The reason is that the less important a reader is, the less likely he is to be on the salesman's call list and on the manufacturer's direct-mail list. Therefore, he will have to make direct inquiries to get product information he wants.

So publication A will have produced more direct inquiries at the expense of influencing the type of men the advertising is aimed at—the men the salesman has found have the most buying influence.

A publication may enhance its inquiry-producing power by rotating its circulation. As is well known to mail-order men, new lists outpull old lists by at least 4 to 1. If publication B is regularly mailed to the important stratum of a field, the stratum with maximum buying power, which is that regularly called on by salesmen, and if publication A rotates among all strata, then publication A will produce more direct returns. This may be all to the good if the advertiser is in the mail-order business, or if the function of the advertising is to provide the salesmen with leads. But it is *not* good if the advertising's aim is to aid the salesmen in selling the major market.

None of the foregoing is intended to disparage methods of weighing the relative merits of different copy appeals or different publications. It is simply a warning against using inquiries as a gauge without careful consideration of all factors involved.

If the advertising manager or agency handling an account that sells through salesmen is always obliged to justify the advertising by producing direct inquiries, the situation is usually unfortunate for all concerned. The primary function of the advertising is usually to promote sales *through the normal channel.* If an astigmatic management forces the use of mail-order tactics, the sales staff finds itself bucking a tough competitive market without the armor of sound advertising. That is a good way to ruin a business.

HOW BUSINESSPAPERS REGARD SMALLER AGENCIES*

There is still a lot of educational work to be done by publishers of legitimately established trade publications to offset the bad impressions made in the past by racketeering businesspaper publishers. The Associated Business Publications, Inc. has led the way to higher standards of businesspaper publishing and advertising practices. All ABP member publishers subscribe to its standards and support its efforts to build a greater appreciation of good businesspapers. They also support its efforts to help advertisers and agencies get the most for the money they spend in these papers.

I wrote to 25 well-known businesspaper publishers, situated in all parts of the country, and asked them several pertinent questions. The first was: *"What are the favorable factors in dealing with the* smaller *type of advertising agency?"* The answers were summed up as follows:

1. It is easy to make contact with principals and get quicker action and decisions.
2. Most smaller agencies appear to be willing to do a more solid trade promotion job.
3. Such agencies usually specialize in certain fields, thus making for efficiency.
4. They are willing to accept clients with small or limited appropriations, and from the client's point, often do a more conscientious and intelligent job.
5. They always welcome and show their appreciation for any help afforded by the publisher. Most big agencies usually work on their own.
6. They generally charge lower production costs because of lower overhead as compared with bigger agencies.

* John J. Whelan, General Manager, The Haire Publishing Co.; former Chairman, Merchandising Division, Associated Business Publications; former Chairman, Dotted Line Club, N. Y.; *Advertising & Selling*, May, 1948, p. 41.

One publisher said in regard to this question: "Many advertisers, particularly in businesspapers, get better and closer attention from a medium-size or small agency than from the larger kind because they deal with principals rather than young assistants hired to help the account manager."

The second question I asked was: *"Outside of credit, what are the unfavorable factors?"* I eliminated the credit question because that is a basic one. However, as a problem it recently has become more acute, partly because a large number of new advertising agencies went into business in recent years, especially during the war. Many have become credit problems for businesspaper publishers.

Other unfavorable factors in dealing with the smaller advertising agency as seen through the eyes of businesspaper publishers are:

1. Insufficient resources, including limited facilities and personnel.
2. Tendency at times to take on more accounts than it can properly handle
3. Lack of flexibility in being able to perform in a first-class manner all types of services that an account needs.
4. Many have an inferiority complex, hesitate to fight for their convictions, and bow too easily to clients' whims.
5. Many have a tendency to hang on to unprofitable accounts.

SMALL AGENCY WEAKNESSES

The third question was: *"What do you feel are the principal weaknesses in the set-ups of smaller agencies?"* Actually, this question is so closely tied up with the preceding one that there was some repetition in the answers I received from publishers. Most of them mentioned credit. Aside from comments on the credit angle, publishers remarked that:

Too many small agencies still go to advertisers and say, "We can handle your businesspaper advertising for nothing" on the dangerous and fallacious assumption that they can live on the publisher's 15 per cent. . . . The principal weakness, we feel, is that expressed by an account of ours who just the other day turned down a small agency we had recommended because they did not think they would receive enough attention from the principal of the firm. They were afraid that, because his limited-size agency had so many accounts, their particular account would be handled by assistants rather than the principal.

The next question was: *"What factors do you consider important in recommending an advertising agency to an advertiser?"* These are some of the important factors—not, however, in the order of their importance:

1. The agency's past experience and history and—very important— the ability and experience of the particular individual assigned to handle the account.
2. Facilities which will enable them properly to service the prospective advertiser.
3. Experience in the advertiser's problems.
4. Financial stability and moral character.
5. An agency that will honestly advise, stand on its recommendations, and not be "pushed around."
6. An agency that is not selfishly "consumer-paper minded," but which recognizes that consumer advertising, while important, does not supplant trade paper space and is but one element in the bigger promotion picture.

FEES AND SERVICE CHARGES

The next query was: *"Should the smaller advertising agency ask a fee or a special service charge for handling businesspaper space?"* Publishers were greatly in the majority in agreeing that special fees or special service charges should be made in order to give the agency some guarantee that it will profit from handling the account. They also indicated that this would tend to make the agency's recommendations much more independent and not tinged with the desire to build commissions on fat appropriations.

The comment was also made a number of times that the fee basis should be for the entire operation and not on businesspapers alone. On the other hand, a few publishers said that smaller agencies should work on a fee basis only in connection with businesspaper space. This theory may give rise to argument on the grounds that it penalizes the business-paper publisher to some extent in the eyes of the advertiser.

This matter of charging a fee is entirely up to individual advertising agencies, but there is a desire expressed throughout publishers' comments to see that the agency is in a position to make money—which in turn wil help them to do a more enthusiastic and all-around, better job for the account.

The next question was: *"What other plus factors do you find in doing business with smaller agencies?"* Responses can be summed up along general lines. Publishers said they would normally prefer to do business with the smaller agency because the latter is not so conscious of the 15 per cent that comes from the higher rates in consumer publication advertising. Comments indicated that the smaller agency normally is a better friend of businesspapers than is the bigger agency.

The next question asked for *specific examples of teamwork between publisher and advertising agency that helped to do a better job for the advertiser.* Many examples were given, some with names of advertisers and agencies mentioned. There was every indication given that the cooperation between advertising agencies and businesspaper publishers is very close and that they are teaming up constantly to do a better job for the client.

PROPER RELATIONS OF TRADE AND CONSUMER MEDIA*

There seem to be two major fallacies in the current thinking among some consumer goods manufacturers and their advertising advisers as to the function of consumer media as opposed to trade media.

The first fallacy is that distribution of a product can be achieved through national consumer advertising alone, by creating enough consumer demand to force the wholesaler and/or the retailer to stock the product. The second fallacy is that the advertiser is reaching the dealer, himself, most effectively at the same time that he is addressing the consumer—and through the same media.

In most cases, consumer advertising is *essential* after trade distribution, *helpful* during trade distribution, *wasteful* before trade distribution, and *impractical* as the means of achieving trade distribution.

Trade advertising has often effected distribution without benefit of consumer advertising; but only in freak cases has consumer advertising brought about distribution without specific advertising, promotion, or selling effort to the trade. In introducing a new product, a big splash in national consumer media can't be expected to flood every retailer with consumer demand—regardless of how good your advertising may be.

It is a matter of simple arithmetic. Estimate the number of people who, during the first ninety days of your national advertising, will actually march into retail establishments and flatly demand your product by brand name. Divide this figure by the number of outlets that could logically carry your product. And you have the power of that consumer demand in the average outlet, over a three-month period.

* Ben Sackheim, President, Ben Sackheim, Inc.; from an address before The Haire Publishing Company's Graphic Arts Course, January, 1946. Mr. Sackheim has served advertisers and agencies in many capacities, from copy cub to account executive, from researcher to marketing director.

Is it enough to make Joseph Retailer locate your company and place an order? If you are a realist, the answer is "No"—or at best, "Maybe" —whether your product is jewelry or jam, bedsheets or brass, carpeting or cosmetics, flour or floor wax, pots and pans or pens and pencils— or what have you?

When you put all your advertising money on national consumer advertising to win trade distribution, you're playing a long shot. Unless there has been strong pre-selling to Joseph Retailer or his sales clerks, ten or fifteen "consumer demanders" coming into his store over a three-month period would scarcely be felt.

In the meantime, consumer demand and advertising dollars are being wasted. It is self-evident that the consumer can't buy it, if the dealer has not got it. The consumer who asks for it where it isn't sold will in most cases walk out of the store with a substitute. And it is a rare product that has no substitute. That's why it is good business to contact the trade first, forcefully, directly, and consistently—through salesmen and through trade advertising.

One dealer is worth a thousand consumers. That is an understatement. The dealer stocks and sells a raft of products that are not nationally advertised at all. In almost every case, the sale of such products would be accelerated through national advertising. But, even without that, the dealer apparently moves those products—through his own local advertising or through sales effort across the counter. Somebody sells the dealer and the dealer sells the products.

Obviously, in introducing a new product or reintroducing an old one, the sound, efficient procedure is to sell the dealer first—win his good will and retain his good will. Then he will join his forces with yours in going to work with John and Jenny Public.

When you reach the dealer through national consumer advertising, you reach him indirectly and ineffectively. You address him as a consumer, not as a businessman. You are attempting to sell him a bill of goods while he is eating his breakfast or listening to a sports broadcast or to his favorite radio comic. You are trying to talk business when he is trying to forget business.

You can reach the trade directly and effectively through salesmen, trade papers and direct mail. They all talk to the dealer about business when he is business-minded, and they talk to him as a businessman.

When you approach a retailer while he is reading his trade paper, he is most susceptible to your sales message.

As a rule, wholesalers' salesmen are too busy chalking up orders to talk up products. Few manufacturers can afford to have their own salesmen call on all present or potential outlets often enough.

This leaves trade papers and direct mail as the most logical means of giving your products and company full and frequent trade coverage. The comparative efficiency of these media depends on many factors peculiar to the manufacture's specific problem. The most successful manufacturers use both trade papers and direct mail.

Trade paper advertising, however, has certain obvious advantages of its own. It is economical. The publication does the printing, binds a number of "direct-mail pieces" of various companies together in one package, and handles the distribution. In this way, the cost of printing and mailing of the advertising literature is divided up among the participating advertisers.

But the biggest advantage is that the recipient does not regard his trade paper as advertising matter. It is his newspaper. It is his business counsel. It tells him what is taking place in his industry. It points up merchandising trends. It is a conference room. It is a market place. It is a buyer's reference book. It is a prospect list. It is a sales promotion calendar. It is an advertising guide. It is a field survey. It is a sales training course for clerks. It is a suggestion box and memorandum sheet.

In allowing certain trade advertising as an admissible cost on Government contracts, the United States War Department and Navy Department recognized the value of the trade paper to the industry. The official statement reads: "Certain kinds of advertising of an industrial or institutional character, placed in trade or technical journals . . . essentially for the purpose of offering financial support to such trade or technical journals, because they are of value for the dissemination of trade and technical information for the industry are . . . an operating expense incurred as a matter of policy for the benefit of the business and the industry."

RATE-CARD TERMINOLOGY AND PRACTICE*

The advantages of certain uniform practices with relation to advertising rate cards has been apparent for a long time within the ranks of the

* From a 73-page report, "Analysis of Variation in Terms & Policies Appearing in the August, 1950, Business Paper Section, Standard Rate & Data," made by Robert Marshall of *Architectural Record,* Chairman of the ABP Sales Management Committee, and A. R. Venezian of McGraw-Hill; published in May, 1951, by Associated Business Publications, Inc., New York.

business press. In May, 1951, the variations in terminology and practice were examined. Below are listed 25 areas in which there are wide variations. No recommendations were made as these practices require further study and analysis.

RATES

1. *Short rates and rebates:* Some publishers prohibit overlapping of contracts in arriving at short rates or rebates, others allow overlapping.
2. *Frequency versus bulk rates:* Some publishers establish their rates on the number of times the publication is used. Others establish rates on the amount of space used within a given period. Still others have a combination of both. The majority base their rates on frequency
3. *Bleed rates:* Many publications do not show costs on bleed. In some cases rates quoted are on a percentage basis, others on a flat charge basis. Rates from "10 per cent to 25 per cent" were shown by 186 publications; 172 show rates from "$5 to $90."
4. *Inserts:* Rates quoted often do not state such details as trimming charge (if any), binding charge (if any), etc. Back-up charges, if reported, are sometimes based on cost per thousand and sometimes on a flat cost basis.
5. *Color rates:*[9] Rates sometimes do not indicate standard colors; cost for matched colors frequently is not stated. Rates from $25 to $200 were shown by 44 publications.
6. *Cover rates:* Sometimes quoted on a flat basis, sometimes on a

---

[9] The use of a second color in advertisements to identify a company's product or get better visibility is steadily increasing. The American Association of Advertising Agencies jointly with the Associated Business Publications and the National Business Publications, in July, 1951, recommended a program for standardization of second colors. A study was made of 692 second colors submitted by 229 business publications. The most popular colors were:

Red	217	publishers
Blue	150	publishers
Green	130	publishers
Yellow	111	publishers
Orange	84	publishers

The 4A's have issued a booklet showing swatches of five standard colors with scientific identification available to all ink manufacturers. *Recommended Standard Second Colors for Business Publications.*

The publishers' representatives on the joint committee for standard second colors affirm that such standardization will result in savings to individual publishers and make a contribution to the needs of advertisers.

percentage basis. Sometimes frequency is specified. Other times, publishers state "rates on request." Often the publisher does not sell the front cover but this fact is not stated. Rates from $55 to $1250 were shown by 84 publications.

7. *Special position rates:* Rates range from a flat to a percentage basis. Some publishers do not include information on special positions. At other times, mention is made that rates will be quoted on request.
8. *Spread rates:* Costs sometimes based on flat rate, other times on percentage basis. Some publishers indicate positions acceptable for spreads, others do not.
9. *Fractional page rates:* Sometimes rates are quoted on a frequency basis, at other times on a bulk basis. Often publishers do not provide any information on fractional space rates.
10. *Small production charges:* Information is often lacking. Details on screen not included. Type of plates preferred not shown. Frequently publishers do not state that costs necessitated by production plates or repair of worn or damaged plates will be passed on to the advertiser.

SPECIFICATIONS

11. *Imprinting of proof sheets:* Some publishers identify their proof sheets, others do not. Details of identification vary. Advertisers and agencies are confused because they do not know source of proofs received.
12. *Use of plastic plates and plastic molds:* Advertisers and agencies question publishers as to their policy on the acceptability and use of plastic plates and molds.
13. *Column widths:* Some publications make up two columns, others three columns, and still others both two and three. In addition, the widths of both the two and three columns vary between publications.
14. *Paper stock:* Weight and finish of stock frequently is not stated for run-of-book or for inserts.
15. *Receiving and returning of plates:* Details on the length of time plates will be kept by the publisher vary. Arrangements as to forwarding of plates also vary.

UNIFORMITY

16. *Contract copy requirements:* Publications do not employ uniform statements in describing regulations on acceptability of copy.
17. *Invoicing:* Invoices vary widely, embracing such items as color,

special position, space, issue used, page number, agency commission, and other factors.

18. *Rate protection clauses:* Length of protection varies between publications; 13 weeks, 90 days, 6 months, a year. Some publications do not include a protection clause in their specifications or rate cards.

19. *Procedure in announcing rate changes:* Application of rate changes varies tremendously between publications. Some apply the new rate immediately on both old and new advertisers. Others protect advertisers for a stated period. Still others protect advertisers to the expiration of the contract year.

20. *Date of rate change:* Some publishers indicate effective date of rate change, others not. Some rate cards are numbered, others not. Rate changes are sometimes made effective with an issue, other times effective with a month of the year.

21. *Advertisers' index:* Publishers vary their listing on advertisers' index. Some show the name of the agency; others include all advertisers who have used the publication within a stated period; some prohibit the listing of subsidiaries and affiliated companies. Frequently policy on this is not stated.

22. *Agency commission:* Arrangements for paying agency commission vary in terms of the number of days allowed, commission permitted, etc. Some publications do not indicate whether or not they pay agency commission. The majority pay 15 per cent, with no time limit.

23. *Cash discount:* A large variation exists on number of days permitted, whether or not date applies to mailing of invoice, issue date, date of invoice, or receipt of invoice. The majority grant 2 per cent, 10 days.

24. *Closing dates:* Lack of information on final closing for black and white, color, inserts, and special positions.

25. *Split runs:* There is a lack of information on acceptability of split runs.

TABLE 4. U. S. ADVERTISING EXPENDITURES BY MEDIA*

Medium	1949 Million dollars	1949 Percentage of total	1950 Million dollars	1950 Percentage of total	Percentage increase, 1950 over 1949
Businesspapers	248.1	4.8	251.1	4.4	+1.2
Farmpapers	20.5	.4	21.2	.4	+3.4
Newspapers					
Total	1905.0	36.6	2063.2	36.3	+8.3
Natl.	465.0	8.9	521.0	9.2	+12.0
Local	1440.0	27.7	1542.2	27.1	+7.1
Magazines					
Total	492.5	9.5	514.9	9.0	+4.5
Weeklies	245.4	4.7	261.1	4.6	+6.4
Women's	128.6	2.5	129.4	2.3	+0.6
General	83.6	1.6	87.5	1.5	+4.7
Farm	34.9	.7	36.9	.6	+5.7
Radio					
Total	628.0	12.1	667.1	11.7	+6.2
Natl.	383.0	7.4	390.6	6.9	+2.0
Local	245.0	4.7	276.5	4.8	+12.9
Television					
Total	68.4	1.3	185.0	3.3	+170.5
Natl.	49.2	.9	131.1	2.3	+166.5
Local	19.2	.4	53.9	1.0	+180.7
Direct mail	755.6	14.5	803.2	14.1	+6.3
Outdoor					
Total	131.0	2.5	142.5	2.5	+8.8
Natl.	88.4	1.7	96.2	1.7	+8.8
Local	42.6	.8	46.3	.8	+8.7
Miscellaneous					
Total	953.1	18.3	1043.1	18.3	+9.4
Natl.	483.3	9.3	527.4	9.3	+9.1
Local	469.8	9.0	515.7	9.0	+9.8
TOTAL					
Natl.	2965.1	57.0	3235.5	56.9	9.1
Local	2237.1	43.0	2455.8	43.1	9.8
GRAND TOTAL	5202.2	100.0	5691.3	100.0	9.4

* *Printers' Ink*, Aug. 10, 1951, p. 29.

TABLE 5. BUSINESS PUBLICATION ADVERTISING VOLUME BY PUBLICATION GROUPS (1950)*

Publications grouped by fields	Advertising volume (Thousands of dollars)	Percentage of total
Manufacturing	103,367	45.9
Construction and architecture	20,718	9.2
Mining, petroleum, and lumbering	13,062	5.8
Power and public utilities	4,729	2.1
All other industrials	3,828	1.7
SUBTOTAL, INDUSTRIAL PUBLICATIONS	145,704	64.7
Retail outlets	25,898	11.5
Personal services	4,954	2.2
Hotels, clubs, restaurants, theatres, etc.	7,206	3.2
Medical, dental and similar professions	12,611	5.6
Transportation and transportation services	5,180	2.3
Finance, banking and insurance	3,603	1.6
Government and education	6,306	2.8
Export and import	6,531	2.9
Miscellaneous trades	7,207	3.2
GRAND TOTAL	225,200	100.0

* From an article "Business Publication Volume for 1950 Analyzed," by A. R. Venezian of McGraw-Hill Publishing Co., in *Industrial Marketing*, September, 1951. The figures represent 1680 professional, technical, industrial, and trade publications as listed in *Industrial Marketing*'s "Market Data Book." See Table 1 in Chapter 1.

TABLE 6. HOW THE INDUSTRIAL ADVERTISING DOLLAR IS INVESTED*

Budget Item	Millions	Percentage of total†
1. Business publications	$225.2	36
2. Company catalogs	93.8	15
3. Direct mail	50.0	8
4. Exhibits	25.0	4
5. Point of sales	6.7	1
6. Reprints and preprints	6.7	1
7. Visual sales presentations	6.7	1
8. Publicity and public relations	25.0	4
9. General and farm magazines and newspapers	62.7	10
10. Billboards, radio and television	6.7	1
11. Production	43.8	7
12. Administration	50.0	8
13. All others	24.7	4
TOTAL	$627.0	100

* A. R. Venezian, "Business Publication Volume for 1950 Analyzed," *Industrial Marketing*, September, 1951.
† Percentages used to project Industrial Advertising Volume are from a 1941 NIAA Budget Study.

CHAPTER 5

Research

"Research is not a thing you do in a laboratory. It is a state of mind. Research is an organized method of trying to find out what you are going to do after you can't keep on doing what you are doing now."
—Dr. C. F. Kettering, "Research Looks to New Horizons"

THE SCIENTIFIC METHOD

All departments of an alert businesspaper publishing house engage in research because each manager is trying to uncover new facts which will tell him "what to do after you can't keep on doing what you are doing now." Businesspaper publishing practice involves six kinds of research activity, usually conducted simultaneously and continuously:

1. *Editorial research*, to increase the effectiveness of the editorial service; to find out how, what, and why people read; the degree of reader interest in the various departments and feature articles; "pass-along" reading; home reading; etc.

2. *Advertising research*, to increase the effectiveness of the advertising messages; to determine what readers want to know and need to know; campaign continuity; use of coupons; etc.

3. *Circulation research*, to determine the needs, responsibilities, and power of the readers; to determine how readers operate, buy, and sell; the size and type of the business firms they work for; reasons for non-renewals; etc.

4. *Media research*, to determine the relative standing of the publication and its competitors; to determine coverage of specific groups by job interest, by fields; etc.

5. *Mechanical research*, to improve production, reproduction, and presentation techniques; to learn the value of double spreads, inserts, color, special positions, bleeds, etc.

6. *Selling research*, to improve the methods of selling space, sub-

153

scriptions, services, etc.; to determine if printed promotion helps the salesmen; what kind of information advertisers and agencies want, etc.

Users of publication space are beginning to demand that agencies and publishers employ a more scientific method in arriving at facts and conclusions about audiences and markets. The success of research in science has proved the validity of the scientific method.

What is the scientific method? In essence, it is this:

1. *Thoroughness:* finding all the facts. Uncovering new facts.

2. *Responsibility:* checking and evaluating every step in the study. Confirming facts. Challenging unsupported statements. Eliminating wishful thinking, exaggeration, prejudice.

3. *Collaboration:* research is not a one-man or one-department operation. It requires the coordinated effort of many people with many types of specialized knowledge.

4. *Continuity:* serious research must be a continuous operation to measure trends and to get consistent maximum results.

5. *Integrity:* you cannot cover up, distort, or dissemble. You must lay it on the table, face up, for all to see. If there is error you welcome the error. "The whole point of science," declares the famous physicist Dr. J. Robert Oppenheimer, "is to invite the detection of error and welcome it."

6. *Communication:* semantic discipline in use of language which will convey exact meaning about your experiment and your findings.

Many people think of science and scientific method as the same thing but they are not. Science is a generic term for the large body of knowledge (technologic data) that scientists have collected down the ages: laws, principles, constructs, formulas, hypotheses, theories, etc.

Scientific method is the *procedure*—the *modus operandi*—by which most of the knowledge was discovered or deduced, then verified, then expanded, then partially discarded, then improved, reinterpreted, and finally verified again and accurately communicated so that other qualified scientists in other times or places could concur with one another in regard to it.[1]

The scientific method is beginning to be used with greater sincerity in all the social sciences, and in the communications industry particularly.

[1] See schema of scientific method, outlined in "The Nervous System and General Semantics," a paper read before The Society for General Semantics, by Russell Meyers, M.D., Associate Professor of Surgery, College of Medicine, State University of Iowa; Chairman, Division of Neurosurgery, University of Iowa Hospitals. *Etc.*, Vol. 5, No. 4, p. 231, Summer, 1948.

To describe any study as "scientific" except to the degree that it employs a scientific method is simply to practice a fraud. Unfortunately, for many years advertisers have been so inundated with "statistics" based on incompetent and half-baked "research" that most buyers of space have come to regard audience studies and market surveys with justifiable suspicion. Only confidence in the sponsors of a study and full knowledge of the methods used to get the facts and arrive at the conclusions will allay such suspicions today.

"Sound research," wrote C. B. Larrabee, publisher of *Printers' Ink* "is in danger of being nullified by the unsound work of a few igno-ramuses or charlatans."[2]

Another point: Those who buy space or anything else as a result of research should insist that researchers use uniform standards. Some dis-cussion occurs in this chapter on the subject of improving the standards for research. Although never adopted, the "Proposed Code of Profes-sional Market Research" and "Standards of Practice in Reporting Survey Results" discussed in Chapter 16 on Laws, Codes, and Regula-tions, seems a step in the right direction. It should be studied in con-nection with this chapter.

Finally, research is not something you can turn off and on to get results. Effort must be continuous—even after first results.

World War II interrupted experimental work for the "Continuing Study of Business Papers," begun by ABP in 1939 in cooperation with the Advertising Research Foundation. In 1945 this activity was revived and in the autumn of 1948 the research program for the industry began in earnest.

An administrative committee to supervise this "Continuing Study" composed of men from ANA, AAAA, NIAA, and ABP was set up.[3]

The publications selected by the administrative committee for pilot studies were *Foundry* and *Chemical Engineering*. Two years were spent on this work. For the first time in the long history of businesspaper publishing there had been worked out an industry research program to be based on scientific method.[4]

---

[2] May 16, 1947, *Printers' Ink;* see also "Advertising Needs Science Clearing House," *op. cit.,* August 10, 1951, p. 5.

[3] See Appendix 1 for Alphabet of The Businesspaper Publishing Industry.

[4] "The first complete study, made on *Automotive Industries,* was released by the ARF in April, 1949. Since then four more studies have been made: *American Builder, American Machinist, Chemical Engineering, Business Week*; as of March, 1951, ABP and its members have invested more than $137,000 in the Continuing Study of Businesspapers.

I am happy to be able to include the techniques of the "Continuing Study" in this chapter. Attention is directed to other valuable research studies summarized in Chapter 4 and in Chapter 6.

RESEARCH IN BUSINESSPAPER PUBLISHING*

Research, in simplest terms, means finding out facts. Take a quick look at the research activities of a great railroad like the New York Central. Defined by law as a "common carrier," the railroad's business is to move people and goods from one place to another on a schedule and at a price. Its research is of three main kinds.

Through consumer research it finds out what kind of rail accommodations people want when traveling. It measures physical contours of all kinds of people to design seating, lounging, reclining, and sleeping. It asks travelers all kinds of questions—then proceeds to design coaches, sleepers, diners and club cars intended to so please the public as to draw patronage and to satisfy its customers.

Through market or sales research it seeks facts to induce more people to travel by New York Central; more freight to move by New York Central.

Through research in engineering it seeks: (1) economy in its operations—better conversion of fuel to power, less deadweight, faster speeds, most effective use of expensive manpower; and (2) safety in its operation.

That is research for a great railroad whose competition is other railroads, trucks, buses, airplanes, pipe lines, boats and automobiles.

Businesspaper publishing is very like the business of railroads. We move ideas or information in a train of pages, from a point of origin to many destinations. Unlike the New York Central, however, our destinations are never fixed terminals. Our destinations are the minds of men, our goal is motivation of the quick-changing minds of those men.

In businesspaper publishing our competition is complex: other businesspapers, consumer magazines, newspapers, news letters, radio, television, cinema, to name but a part of this competition.

In this business of ours, we find the same kinds of research activity as in the New York Central. One kind is aimed squarely at product improvement. The second is aimed squarely at procuring more effective

* Judd Payne, F. W. Dodge Corp.; from a lecture at New York University, March 12, 1947. Mr. Payne was formerly Executive Director of Associated Business Publications.

selling ammunition for marketing the publication as a product. The third is aimed at the development of methods and controls likely to insure adherence to a planned publishing program with maximum economy. These three basic types of research may overlap to some extent, yet when carefully organized need never fight one another.

Because of the nature of this businesspaper publishing business, every one of us is like a man in a small boat on the open ocean, so far as our research horizons are concerned. That horizon line completely encircles us. Whether we look toward the editorial, circulation, promotion, advertising, production, or accounting problems of our business we find challenging opportunities for effective research.

Why is this? Because the basic equations with which we deal are changing constantly. Some of these factors are economic, having to do with the shapes and kinds of markets we serve. Some are technical, such as the processes or methods employed for the production or distribution of certain capital or consumer goods. Some have to do with the means at our disposal for the design and production of our publications. Some are psychological, such as the shifts in reading habits that are created by new competition, be it from the introduction of microfilm reference libraries or from television or from news letters, or from socio-economic conditions in general.

Charles Kettering, head of General Motors research has said: "A problem clearly understood is generally fairly simple." Surely, if we were to lay down guides to research activity of any kind in this business we should start by defining our problem; then making a plan; then providing for execution; finally, for interpretation of our findings.

And we must bear in mind that while some research can be exact, as for instance the making of motion studies in the performance of a printing operation, much research logically deals with human behavior, which goes beyond the area of precision measurements and into the realms of psychology and psychiatry. The fact that this is true, makes the latter type of research all the more challenging.

Most publications have an audit of circulation. Actually it was the formation of the Audit Bureau of Circulations in 1914, in response to the demand of advertisers and agencies, that established the first real research cornerstone in businesspaper publishing. The later establishment of the Controlled Circulations Audit was a further basic move toward encouragement of greater research among businesspapers.

It is recognized that the number of copies of a publication mailed constitutes one possible measurement of the worth of that publication at any given time. Likewise, it is known that the amount of purchasing power of people on the receiving end is important. Clearly, the kind of coverage is sought that represents the logical reader target for the kind of a publication being edited.

Many of us go to great expense to procure and to present attractive editorial matter which we believe to be of outstanding and timely merit. Actually, however, the delivery of a plausible package to a logical audience is not businesspaper publishing. It can even be a racket. One example of this is the puff sheet, selling editorial content and distribution at fancy prices to publicity seekers.

The product represented by a legitimate businesspaper is the amount and kind of reading and reader action it receives from its recipients. The worth of the product, in the last analysis, must be judged by its number of actual readers, by kind and character, in terms of the service it is presumed and expected to render its readers.

Product research in business publishing must therefore be aimed at procuring facts on the amount and kind of reading we are generating as the end-product of our total operation. This type of audience and readership research, to be good insurance, needs to be continuous. It can be done by editors, subscription people, and by advertising representatives, although anyone actually identified with the staff of a particular publication faces two difficulties. The first is that it is often difficult, particularly for editors, to procure objective testimony, and the second is that timely standards against which to measure testimony may not be available except after years of experience. For these reasons many publications rely heavily on outside organizations for this type of research.

In general, where publications have used data procured by staff members, on so-called "total audience" or "readership" to promote advertising sales, advertisers and agencies have been unwilling to take such findings seriously. There has been a widespread conviction among buyers of advertising that no satisfactory technique exists for exact measurement, either of the full extent of a business publication's audience, or for the extent and care of actual readership.

During 1946 and 1947 the Advertising Research Foundation, working on a grant from the Associated Business Papers, Inc., has been actively at work on the development of a technique that may become standard for audience and readership evaluation in the businesspaper field. For its pilot study, an issue of the magazine *Foundry* was checked. It is now reasonably clear that a technique is likely to grow out of this pilot study which will be satisfactory to the American Association of Advertising Agencies, the Association of National Advertisers, the National Industrial Advertisers Association—to businesspaper publishers.

The day may come, (as is beginning to happen in the newspaper business) when many businesspaper publishers will use authentic, continuing readership studies, along with their circulation audit statements, as standard, universally accepted, sales tools.

R. O. Eastman, who has probably done more work than any other man in businesspaper editorial research, designed primarily to make possible product improvement, agrees that the following suggestions, loose as they are, are about as specific as any that can be made, if one is interested in going ahead with product research under his own steam:

1. For interviews, select a very small but representative group of known recipients of your publication.

2. Time your interviews sufficiently after the issue under study has been received, that the reader has had full opportunity to read the issue.

3. Frame questions aimed to establish care and extent of reading of each page in the issue under study.

4. Relate reading to the function and current activities of the reader.

5. Repeat procedure with all individuals who may have received and read the particular copy of the particular issue under study.

6. Make continuing studies, selecting each sample on same basis.

7. Record your findings so that over a period of time you may establish trends and have a basis for relating results to new procedures established on the facts substantiated by your study.

If you are an editor and set out to do this kind of a job, you are likely to come up with some brand new ideas as to the editorial material you should be presenting and be quite willing to eliminate certain kinds of content that you have previously held to be important. You may become convinced that less tonnage of words, simpler language, shorter stories, more and bigger illustrations, stronger action headlines, point the path to greater and more productive readership.

If you are a circulation manager, you may find that advertising content is more salable than editorial content and that your most salable editorial content is product news often buried in the back of your book.

If you are an advertising representative, you may find that a half dozen interviews a week with your readers, not your advertising prospects, in terms of their current problems and the kinds of information they are finding in your publication that is helping them, will be worth tons of statistics in your briefcase in explaining how big your market really is and what your subscribers are currently buying in that market.

Many business publications have found it possible to procure a good deal of useful qualitative information from subscribers by the device of mailing a detailed reader interview to a cross-section of subscribers each month. In some cases, such questionnaires yield returns as high as 20 and 30 per cent and when mailed to a cross-section of subscribers, whose subscriptions are up for renewal in the near future, they find that the use of this device not only yields information helpful in improving the publication but also increases renewal percentages. The known weakness in this mail procedure is that it fails to procure returns from unresponsive readers whose real reactions are also vitally important to the editor.

Used to only a small extent in publishing so far, the so called panel technique can prove highly useful in readership research. This calls for the setting up of a cross-section group of individuals, sometimes called editorial advisors, who are paid for regular reports on specific content of specific issues. This flow of information again is useful, primarily in a qualitative measurement of reading, rather than a quantitative measurement.

But a word of warning. Tabulating the conscious reaction of a selected group, expert though they may be, is always risky business. Your test covers necessarily only a few of almost an infinite number of reader preferences. It is warped by the self consciousness of the persons being tested. They are not bona fide readers in the mood to read. There is no such thing as a completely representative group. One might say that the difference between what such persons think they want to read and what they actually will read is about as great as between the economic conditions this country wants and what it seems to be getting. By all means do this type of research, but be sure to check your findings against other means at your disposal.

Out of all product development research, consistently pursued, come benefits like these:

1. Understanding of the actual rather than the theoretical reading habits of subscribers.

2. Understanding of the effects of one kind of a story presentation against another kind.

3. Understanding of the relationship of advertising reading to editorial reading.

4. Gradual accumulation of data on which to edit and circulate a publication, with maximum precision, so far as generating greatest possible readership is concerned.

Research, intended to make selling more effective, is a constant function of every well-organized sales department. Such research is mainly designed to procure facts intended to:

1. Relate the audit figures of a publication to the market it serves in terms of coverage of purchasing power in that market.

2. Clarify how purchasing or product selection takes place in the market served.

3. Define the size of market for a specific type, kind, or family of products and services in the market served.

4. Establish duplication of coverage within a market of competing publications or media.

5. Establish reader preference among media serving a specific group of individuals within a market.

6. Ascertain the kinds of information that readers want about products they buy or specify.

7. Ascertain pass-along or secondary readership of copies distributed on a paid or controlled basis.

8. Evaluate types of copy through reader interviews as a means for helping advertisers use space more effectively.

9. Refine data on specific functions of readers to make possible detailed studies of coverage of markets within the total market served by the publication.

10. Develop case studies of sales successes based in whole or in part on a specific advertising campaign.

11. Analyze and close out inquiries generated by coupon offers or by other means.

This list of eleven typical kinds of market, media, and copy research is not complete, but rather is intended to be representative of the kinds of studies that are going forward in most publishing shops.

Sometimes, as in the case of *Baker's Weekly*, technical laboratory product and equipment testing facilities are involved. Or, in the case of *Architectural Record*, the field services of 750 market fact reporters are employed.

Bear in mind that any study is going to pay off in proportion to its integrity and timeliness. Presentation of half-truths as fact will not in the long run sell advertising. Generalizations, based on very little evidence, will prove a boomerang more often than not. We all remember the case of the packaged candy manufacturer who hastily withdrew the slogan, "The Candy Bar with the Hole in It," when he found his competitor saying, "All Candy—No Hole." Make sure your claims are based on fundamentally superior talking points—otherwise they will boomerang.

Publisher-sponsored studies of duplication or reader preference may be very good for the ego of the sponsoring publisher but few such studies find enough gullible buyers to pay their freight.

The best research for selling purposes puts an understanding of the marketing problems of advertisers and prospects first; backs that understanding with constructive, objective study; yields a kind of information that actually helps the buyer buy businesspaper space intelligently and use businesspaper space intelligently. If one checks the research studies that have been published by the businesspapers that are acknowledged leaders in their fields, one will find that these comments almost invariably hold true.

Few businesspaper publishers conduct systematic and continuing research aimed primarily at development of new publications or new operations logically related to mainline businesspaper publishing. However, a direct by-product of sound sales research may be the development of such opportunities.

Beyond opportunities for new publications as such, many publishers have found it possible out of research to develop profit from operations such as the following:

1. Book publishing, perhaps involving the re-use of editorial originally published as magazine content.
2. Sale of books of other publishers.
3. Reference annuals, sometimes containing market statistics.
4. Prefiled catalog files.
5. Special news letters.
6. Sales of lists, perhaps including subscription lists.
7. Sale of market research facilities or studies.
8. Sale of market, price, or cost data.

Businesspaper publishing is fundamentally an idea business—idea generation, idea extraction, and idea transmission. The major expense in any such business is the cost of manpower, made up of salary outlays. More and more publishers, realizing this, are going in for job analysis and are applying aptitude tests to candidates for jobs ranging from accounting to selling. This kind of research is almost certain to be applied inceasingly, for it has been demonstrated that it does definitely reduce turnover and increase efficiency.

Next to the cost of manpower, production is our most costly item. Larger publishers, more or less controlling their printing establishments, are far advanced in the introduction of equipment and methods that point to maximum economy in the face of high and increasing hourly wage rates.

Because most publishers are dependent on outside printers and engravers and because many such printers and engravers have not in the past been notably progressive in their drive for better methods or new techniques holding promise of quality improvement and lower unit costs, it is clear that increasingly, both publishers and production men must make it their own business to research possibilities for improvement in this area. Time spent on this research front, particularly by production people who have an over-all understanding of operations, can usually lead to highly worthwhile results.

OUTLINE OF RESEARCH PROCEDURE*

1. Select one group of customers, prospects, or men influencing the purchase of the product. This may be an industry group—coal mine operators, textile superintendents—or a functional group—design, production, management, etc.

2. Make sure you know in general what you want to find out from your calls.

3. Decide on a product or on a group of two or three related products in which you are interested.

4. Pick out a dozen companies close to home for a start. Get the names of the men you want to see. Make sure that those men represent the industry or functional group you have decided to call on. Do not call on the wrong men.

5. Tell your prospective interviewee exactly who you are and why you want to call on him. You will have no trouble getting in if you explain your purpose and ask his help.

6. Put aside your own knowledge of the product and the company.

* Summary of points from the Professional Development Committee, National Industrial Advertisers Association, published in 1948 in a booklet "The Why and How of Business Paper Advertising," by Stephen Goerl of Stephen Goerl Associates, New York.

Let the user tell you what "he" thinks about your product and your competitor's product.

7. Have a mental list of three or four main questions, or subjects to be covered.

8. Keep the interview "informal." You are just out visiting with users of your products.

9. Swap information. The best way to get information is to give information. After a few calls, you will be able to report problems or experiences of others called on in your interview. John Smith is always interested to learn about Joe Bloke who is doing the same kind of work at another plant.

10. Find out what the man reads—businesspapers, manufacturers' house organs, etc. What information does he get from these of greatest value to him? What kinds of articles? On what subjects? This gives a good clue to his interests and to the kind of information he wants.

11. Remember that you are looking for information. You are not selling. If your man tears your company apart, or criticizes your product or services, just listen and ask questions to get the whole story. Never defend, never attempt to justify anything. But be sure to find out WHY he feels the way he does.

12. Start with a discussion of his job, his job problems. Find out when and where he uses products like yours. What brands he uses, which companies he usually deals with on these products. Why? Keep forever on the job of asking "Why?" If you know how he thinks, what he thinks and if you know "why" he thinks that way—then you know what to do about it in your advertising and promotion.

13. When you have made a dozen calls, analyze what you have found out in terms of its value to you. You will find that you have failed to get some information; that you have collected some irrelevant material. Study this, revise your approach, refine your method of procedure, then go out again, and you will come back with some powerfully useful material.

14. Field interviewing demands constant practice. The only way to learn the knack of field research is to get out and try it, get out and keep at it. The more calls you make, the better you will get. It is a lot of fun and very enlightening.

15. There are several supplementary sources for gathering information on the job interests and job problems of customers and prospects, and on the information they want:

a. Field engineering reports, which reveal the specific needs of users of your products.
b. Call reports of salesmen, which reveal the questions about your product and services asked by your customers and prospects.
c. Complaint files—which suggest opinions, prejudices of customers and prospects, and often their need for information to insure proper use of their products.

The results of a properly conducted market survey are of great value to any company, whether it sells locomotives, printing papers, or artificial flowers. These results are the safest guide in keying advertising messages and conveying to readers the information in which they are most interested. *To convey such information is the basic principle of effective advertising.* It is the surest method of inducing readers to read a particular sales message.

HOW TO PRESENT MARKET RESEARCH MATERIAL*

Here are some of the basic factors usually considered by business-papers and agency men in passing along market research information:

ELEMENTS

In most instances the elements which make up the market presentation generally follow this outline:

Letter of transmission
Title
Objective
Summary of findings
Recommendation (if any)

Method employed in gathering data
Tabulation of data
Charts and sources

We find this order satisfactory because the majority of market research reports are aimed at management or department heads. By presenting the objectives, summary and recommendations at the beginning, the reader will get the feel of the project quickly. The details on the procedure used in gathering the market data, the charts, and sources are supplied for those interested in the details. Often, a copy of any questionnaire used in digging up market information is also included.

* Walter Painter, from a seminar on Market Research, Businesspaper Publishing Course, Northwestern University, Chicago Campus, May 13, 1948. Mr. Painter showed specimen folders, easels, and a slide film.

FORMAT

Most businesspaper publishers use one of the following arrangements for channeling market research information to advertisers, advertising prospects, and agency men:

Letter or memo	Easel display
Booklet	Slides or slide film
File folder	Motion picture

The type of presentation (also whether we should use color and visual illustrations such as pie charts, bar charts, graphs, etc.) will depend on the nature of our research project and kind of audience we have in mind.

If the project is an "all inclusive" study, we will want to make the presentation more complete and show more visual elements than in a "one problem" answer.

Then, too, the size of the advertising potential will need to be taken into account in planning the scope and format of a market presentation. Obviously, we could not afford to spend $10,000 for a research project on a marginal product.

SOME PRESENTATION DO'S AND DON'T'S

Much of the effectiveness of a market presentation depends on the objectivity and clarity of the material shown. Here are some practical production tips from experienced market study men:

Keep presentation as simple as possible.

Slant it directly to your audience—not over or around them.

Do not pack too much copy on one page or slide—drive home one fact at a time.

Beware of "stoop and squint" jobs; make sure that all figures, charts, and data are large enough to be seen at a distance.

If more than two or three persons are to be present you will want to arrange for supplemental lighting for exhibits.

Most advertising and sales managers and agency folks say they want to see the date on market studies.

Steer clear of biased statements. They lessen value of market studies as instruments of helpful information.

If any data are supplied by Bureau of Census or other outside agency, be sure to give them credit.

Many advertisers and agency men say they like to know the make-up of any sample used in research work.

Indicate if your publication or an outside organization gathered and digested the market information.

Use charts and graphs wherever they will help deliver your market data more quickly and clearly.

Strive to get a fresh slant in your illustrations. Too many pie charts may tire the reader. Mix in rows of machines, piles of dollars, lines of people to vary the appeal.

Avoid use of publication "sell" or material not relevant to a particular research project.

Show actual numbers along with percentages. It may help in comparing your report with others in same field.

DON'T'S FOR MANAGEMENT ON READERSHIP REPORTS*

Research is not a substitute for judgment. It is an aid to judgment—and a mighty potent aid. Readership surveys are simply one form of research. They are not intended to serve up decisions on any kind of platter, silver or otherwise. Their purpose is to aid in formulating sound decisions.

Unfortunately, in management circles, Starch[5] findings are apt to become the basis for sweeping decisions lasting into perpetuity. That is understandable—if not excusable. It is understandable because advertising remains one of the few functions in business that continues to defy efforts to reduce it to an *exact* science. Most assuredly, modern research techniques have taken a sizable chunk of the gamble out of advertising. But the most fanatic research expert willingly admits that until the study of the human mind, both individually and in the mass, becomes a true science (today it can scarcely be classed even as an art) advertising will entail certain risks.

Naturally, management executives—who control advertising purse-strings but who are all-too-seldom advertising experts—are wide open for any procedure or program that seems to promise the elimination of guesswork in advertising. That is why, when a presumably "foolproof" advertising formula or testing program is announced, it is promptly

---

* From *Grey Matter*, August 1, 1950, a semi-monthly publication of The Grey Advertising Agency, New York. This particular issue was devoted to the subject: "Taking the Starch out of Starch Reports."

[5] Daniel Starch, Inc., a research organization.

greeted with loud huzzas by management. Some years ago, for example, when a presumably sure-fire testing program was publicized, it was greeted dubiously by the advertising fraternity but welcomed by some management executives. Time seems to have proved that the advertising fraternity's evaluation of that particular program was not far off the beam!

However, sure as sunrise, there will continue to appear on the horizon new procedures, new techniques, new programs that *"guarantee"* to take *all* of the gamble out of advertising. And, in between their appearances, management executives will fall back on readership reports to sustain them.

SEVEN DON'T'S

1. Don't accept readership reports as gospel. They are nothing of the sort.

2. Don't assume that readership reports automatically spell out final decisions. They do nothing of the sort.

3. Don't take the position that a readership report on one ad lays down a formula for a continuing program of advertising. Readership reports are of statistical value only when analyzed over a considerable period of time, on a cumulative basis, and including a considerable number and variety of advertisements. A readership report on a single ad, or even on a half dozen ads, run in just one or a few publications, is as much of a guide to advertising as a week's weather report is a guide to annual weather conditions!

4. Don't try to read readership reports yourself. You do not try to read the laboratory reports of your chemists or your engineers. You have these technical papers briefed and interpreted for you. A readership report is a technical paper—as technical as any report prepared by, or submitted to, your technicians. Have it briefed and interpreted by your advertising manager.

5. Don't judge your advertising manager—or your advertising agency —on the basis of readership reports. As we have already made plain, readership reports are merely guideposts to decisions; they cannot make decisions. And remember they are merely *one* of a number of research tools needed in evaluating advertising.

6. Don't put your advertising manager—or your advertising agency— in the position of producing high readership ratings "or else." That leaves them no choice but to produce high readership ratings—and

that's such an elementary trick that any neophyte could turn up ratings that would tickle the heart of a management executive.

7. Don't judge advertising media on the basis of meager readership reports. Readership reports aid no more—and no less—in media selection than in the choice of advertising appeals, art, layout, etc.

TRENDS IN THE RESEARCH OF READERSHIP*

There are two types of information available about media. One type is circulation figures. These are purely quantitative. They are developed by the simple process of counting and keeping records. The validation of this procedure deals with figures instead of people. This validation is carried on by the Audit Bureau of Circulations. The facts and figures released by them are so basic, so important in both the buying and selling of advertising space that the ABC has become the cornerstone of all factfinding in advertising and it is going to continue to be that no matter what developments take place in either readership or audience studies.

The other set of data consists of findings which are based on sampling —on the law of probability. These measurements deal with people. Since the primary purpose of advertising and publishing is to inform, educate, and influence the people, the necessity of finding out more about them, what goes on in their minds, how and when and why they respond to contents of various media and advertisements is fundamental.

Three methods are used currently to measure the reactions of people to advertising: (1) opinion studies of publications or advertisements; (2) data, which for the want of a better name, we have elected to call "audience," and, (3) readership studies of advertisements and editorial material item by item.

Opinion studies of publications do not by any stretch of the imagination come under the classification of readership studies, nor should there be any confusion in distinguishing them from readership or audience reports.

The distinction between audience and readership data is not as clear. The reason for this lies primarily in the fact that there has been and can continue to be some overlapping between the two. At one time or

* A. W. Lehman, Managing Director, The Advertising Research Foundation. This excerpt from a paper originally read before The National Publishers Association, January 16, 1947, in the Waldorf-Astoria, was revised and brought up to date by the author in May, 1951. No basic changes have been made in the methodology since 1947.

another nearly everyone in national advertising circles has been completely confused. The buyers and builders of advertising seek a monetary standard with which to measure and compare results. So they have taken various readership figures and listenership figures too, which have *not* been designed to permit the determination of cost per reader or listener, and projected them to the number of readers or listeners and in turn, to the cost per reader or listener. Efforts of conscientious researchers to prevent this misuse have not availed.

While advertisers and agencies have been projecting unprojectible readership figures, various publishers have issued audience figures which, broadly speaking, are projectible and which the publishers have projected. That is, they have published the results of surveys in the terms of number of thousands or millions of people who looked into or claimed to have read something in a given publication. Readership ratings on individual items were either not obtained or not published. It has been most difficult for the lay mind to understand why certain readership data, which is so similar to audience data, cannot be handled in the same manner as the results of audience studies. I shall try to explain: In all the readership studies of which I am aware, except the continuing studies transportation advertising, businesspapers and farm publications, all published by the Advertising Research Foundation, the interviewers are permitted to hunt for, in fact, are encouraged to find, people who admit reading the issue being surveyed. Obviously, such a system of interviewing cannot develop either a true cross-section of the population or of the circulation. Only true cross-sections can be projected to circulation and population.

On the other hand, conscientious efforts have been made by the underwriters and the researchers of audience studies to obtain a true cross-section of the population. I refer to studies like the *Life*, *Look*, and *Good Housekeeping* surveys, and the study of the Magazine Advertising Bureau.

To eliminate the confusion which exists between the straight audience studies and straight readership studies, it is necessary to set forth some definitions.

AUDIENCE STUDY

An audience study is a study which reveals the total number of people over a given age which has looked into a given issue of a publication. It does not reveal information on the readership of advertisements or on items of reader text.

READERSHIP STUDY

A readership study is a study which reports the percentage or number of people reading either the various editorial items or advertisements or both. It is an item-by-item measurement, not a measurement of the book as a whole. Now, just to complicate things a little let me add that the two can be combined.

THREE TRENDS

Trends in the research of readership can be broken up into three parts: (1) trends in the quantity of data; (2) trends in the development of readership techniques; and (3) trends in the use of readership reports.

1. *Trends in Quantity of Studies.* The number of public or syndicated readership studies, current and planned, can be counted on one hand. They are the Starch Reports (started in 1932), Continuing Study of Newspaper Reading, Continuing Study of Transportation Advertising (1944), Continuing Study of Farm Publications (1946), and the Continuing Study of Business Papers (1948). Until the Advertising Research Foundation, with the cooperation of the Bureau of Advertising of the American Newspaper Publishers Association, launched the Continuing Study of Newspaper Reading in 1939, Starch was the sole source of readership data. Let me add that there was a period during which another syndicated advertising readership service was available.

2. *Trends in Techniques.* Chronologically, the Starch service comes first. However, there has not been any significant change in the techniques used by Starch for measuring reading, so there is no trend to comment on.

To those of you who are impatient and wish to dismiss all studies because they have not reached the precision of two plus two equals four, I want to say this: During the next decade the economic forces which will prevail will challenge the effectiveness of all advertising. The need for improvement in advertising will be so great that you cannot afford to wait for technical perfection or anything near it.

If our ancient mathematicians had given up on the problem of measuring the area of the circle because of technical shortcomings, the great mechanical age we live in would be in the future. Let me remind you that the Babylonians used three as π, and the great Archimedes didn't have the correct answer either. In fact, it wasn't until 1700 that Metius, a relatively unknown mathematician, got the answer.

3. *Trends in Use.* Every important advertising agency, and many

manufacturers and publishers, subscribe to the Starch reports. They make great use of them. The evidence is the statement made by Starch that during the last 18 years the readership of advertisements measured by him has greatly increased. Even if you grant that copy and layout would have improved anyway, and credit the readership reports with only a half or a third of the increment, the result when applied against the dollar involved is tremendous.

Many agencies have special departments or individuals assigned to the job of analyzing and interpreting readership studies. Some of these agencies make an important feature of the knowledge which they possess of readership data in their own presentations to potential clients.

There will never be mathematical formulas which will take the place of *thinking* in the publishing or advertising business. I do not propose for one instant to advance the theory that readership studies can take the place of judgment and skill. Rather, they set up guideposts which help advertisers and media make finer and better judgment which, in turn, increase the effectiveness of advertising and improve its value as a sales tool. With a full complement of readership studies in every medium more, not less, initiative and creative skill will be needed.

TECHNIQUES OF THE CONTINUING STUDY OF BUSINESS PAPERS*

1. GENERAL SURVEY METHOD

The first of the objectives of the Business Papers Study is to determine how many people read a typical issue of a particular businesspaper. It is necessary to determine how readers obtain the paper, and to classify them according to business functions and buying power.

The second major objective is to measure the exposure and reading of advertising, as indicated by evidence from advertisements and from editorial page traffic. The influence of such factors as position, size, and color are to be determined when a sufficient sample is accumulated.

Businesspapers have several characteristics which complicate the process of attaining these objectives. Most businesspapers have a comparatively small circulation extended over an extremely broad area. Some of the books are comparatively thick. While businesspapers are mailed to both business and home addresses, it is believed that they are

* From the Appendix of Study No. 4, *Chemical Engineering,* p. 189, published by Advertising Research Foundation, Inc., N. Y., March, 1950, as part of the ARF's Continuing Study of Business Papers.

read by more people at the place of business where they may be circulated around a more or less formal route-list. To complicate the situation further, businesspapers vary enormously in make-up and classes reached.

Because of the difficulty of obtaining accurate information from individuals about all of the business publications they read, the procedure of interviewing only on a single publication at a time was adopted. A "qualifying kit" is used to determine who is a reader of the measured issue of the publication. The widely-accepted recognition method is then followed throughout the book in order to discover just what has been seen or read by each reader.

2. SELECTION OF THE SAMPLE

The natural impulse in attempting to discover the total audience of a publication is to select a sample of copies in circulation and attempt to ferret out the readers. Since printed circulation is known, the solution lies in the determination of the average number of readers per copy. This approach has been thwarted in audience surveys of other types of magazines, because of unidentified newsstand buyers and other problems in tracing the life-history of specific copies.

The Business Papers Study is probably the first published research in which the total audience is presented on the basis of the number of readers discovered by tracing the itinerary of a representative sample of copies. The explanation lies in the fact that many copies go to known addresses in places of business, and that a majority of all readers probably see the publication in a place of business. Many copies are circulated regularly along formal route-lists. If it is feasible to interview readers at their place of business, then it is also feasible to determine the audience of plant copies by following these routes.

Prior to the first regular study of a businesspaper, a considerable amount of effort and money was expended to determine whether people could be interviewed successfully at their places of business and whether route-lists could be followed. The question is not merely whether readily available people can be interviewed in the plant, but whether the readers of mandatorily selected copies can be approached and interviewed successfully. The exploratory studies showed that this could be done with a sampling success of probably above 70% for industrial papers. Such a modest level of success can only be accomplished at considerable expense and with repeated callbacks. Because of the danger of obtaining very misleading information if short-cut methods were used, it was recommended and approved by the Technical Committee that a rigid sampling procedure be followed.

3. SPECIAL SAMPLING CONSIDERATIONS

An adequate sample for a businesspaper must include a sufficient number of copies as well as a sufficient number of total readers. This sample must be correctly distributed according to circulation in plants and in homes. It is necessary to have a sample which is adequate for measuring item-by-item reading through the book as well as adequate for measuring the total number of readers.

Since there must be an adequate number of copies in the sample, and since there may be several readers per copy, it is not always necessary to interview every reader. However, such readers as are interviewed must be selected on a systematic basis, with little regard for what may be convenient for the interviewer.

An arbitrary minimum of 150 copies of a publication has been specified as the lower limit. Another controlling factor is the specification that there must be a minimum of 200 successful interviews through-the-book with qualified magazine readers.

The problem of the sample design is to select a large enough sample to circulated copies, in excess of 150, to produce a minimum of 200 successful interviews through-the-book with qualified readers. This means that enough copies must be selected to represent a large enough group of potential readers to produce a minimum of 200 qualified-reader-interviews. Stated another way, this means that enough copies must be selected to represent enough potential readers, to produce enough claimed readers of the particular issue to produce, in turn, enough qualified readers who will then cooperate in developing 200 interviews.

It should be noted that some copies of businesspapers go to company addresses without designating a person. Other copies go to persons who are not themselves potential readers, but who merely pass the copy to the intended readers. For these reasons it is not practical, so far as audience figures are concerned, to distinguish the audience originally receiving the publication from others who eventually read it.

The involved factors described above do not add greatly to the complications of sample design, but merely make it necessary to select several sample sizes in advance in order to ensure the prescribed minimum of successful interviews through-the-book.

4. STEPS IN DESIGNING THE SAMPLE

The sample used in this survey is based upon the "area probability" design. In this design a sample of interviewing areas (called primary areas or units) is first sampled on a probability basis. Then within each of the selected primary units a probability sample of subscriber names is designated for interview. Thus, the final sample is arrived at after two stages of sampling.

The first step in actual design of the operating sample is to define the geographic scope of the survey. Since most business publications have a small number of copies going into extremely remote areas, it is usually possible to delimit the area to be sampled in such a way that a large geographical area is ignored without the loss of more than a very small percentage of total subscriptions.

The second step is to decide upon the basis for stratification of the primary units within the total area to be sampled, prior to the drawing of the interviewing areas in the sample. Stratification takes into account such characteristics of all primary units as the amount of circulation or degree of penetration, the density of population, characteristics of the particular industry and other factors which may be peculiar to the publication or to the industry which it serves. The basis for stratification must be studied and decided upon for each publication individually.

The third step is the division of the total area into regions in which the various strata are properly distributed. It has been specified for the Continuing Study of Business Papers that there should be at least 10 separate interviewing areas in each survey. Thus, there may be a division into 10 regions with 1 interviewing area in each, or 5 regions with 2 areas in each, or some other combination which will accomplish the purpose.

The fourth step is the selection of an interviewing area or areas in each region on a known probability basis. This step presupposes that each region has been subdivided into primary sampling units, stratified as indicated above. The primary sampling units may be made up of geographic units such as counties, post offices, or combinations of post offices.

The fifth step is the drawing of subscriber names from the complete list in each selected locality, this drawing to be done on a purely random basis. The subscriptions are stratified, before names are drawn, in order to ensure the right representation of such factors as home and plant subscriptions, individual and group subscriptions, etc.

The sixth step, which goes beyond the actual sampling operation, is the addressing of questionnaires to a number of the selected subscriber names for the purpose of obtaining advance information about route lists. Replies to these questionnaires are intended to provide a clue as to the number of potential readers per copy, and thus aid in determining how many subscription copies must be followed up in the overall sample. It may then be possible to reduce the selected sample of subscribers on a random basis and still achieve the minimum specified sample of potential readers.

The names on the returned route lists are not accepted as being necessarily accurate or complete. These lists, even though incomplete, are a rough guide to the interviewer in planning his approach. Also, being equipped with the names of some persons regularly receiving a copy from a particular subscriber, the interviewer has a psychological advantage in gaining access along the pass-along route. Much initial resistance can be eliminated in pursuing the subsequent receivers of copies for which route lists are available in advance.

THE INTERVIEWING METHOD

The basic interviewing method in the Business Papers Study is known as the recognition method. It is called the recognition method because typical readers are asked to recognize or identify issues and items which they have seen prior to the interview. The strength of this method lies in the fact that readers receive and look through publications in the normal manner and are completely unaware that they will later be asked questions about their reading experience. Every factor which contributes to the reader response is permitted to develop in a perfectly normal and spontaneous manner.

The objectives of the Business PapersS tudy require the measurement of both the total size of the reading audience and readership through the book. These are, in fact, two separate objectives requiring two separate interviewing operations. The purpose of the first operation is to determine who, among all of the potential readers, has actually read or looked through the measured issue. The second operation is concerned only with those who have read the issue, and is designed to find out what they looked at and what they read.

When surveying monthly publications, interviews are conducted six to eight weeks after the publication date or receipt of issue by the sub-scriber. However, interviewing may continue up to the time subscribers receive the second succeeding issue of the publication. In the case of semi-monthly publications, interviews are made from four to six weeks after publication date or receipt of issue by the subscriber, but may con-tinue until subscribers receive the third succeeding issue of the pub-lication.

Determining Who Is a Qualified Reader. The definition of a reader, as stated in the objectives, includes those persons who give evidence of having seen or read at least one item in the measured issue. In order to provide an objective measuring device, for qualifying genuine readers, a kit of editorial matter was designed.[6]

The qualifying kit for most publications is made up of 10 selected editorial items intended to represent the entire issue in a general way. A similar selection is made of items which have not yet been published. The unpublished items are mixed in systematically with the published ones. At the proper time in the interview, the claimed readers are asked to pick out the items which they remember having seen.

In order to provide a proper introduction for the qualifying kit, a series of covers of the publication is shown to the respondent earlier in the interview. This gives the respondent an opportunity to designate which issues he has read, or thinks he may have read. If the respondent designates the cover of the measured issue, he is then asked to go through the qualifying kit based on that issue.

As the respondent approaches the qualifying kit, he is advised that it contains items which are not yet published, as well as those from the specified issue. He is encouraged to use all possible discrimination in identifying only those items which he positively remembers having seen or read. All items which he is in doubt about, or which he thinks he has not seen, are counted in the negative.

Later on, in the tabulating process, identification of items in the qualifying kit is checked. Those claimed readers who succeed in identi-fying more of the current editorial items than of the unpublished items are considered to be qualified readers. However, this tabulation is not attempted during the interview, so that all respondents continue in the interview just as though they are qualified readers.

[6] Lucas, D. B., "The Controlled Techniques for Magazine Audience Measure-ment," *Advertising & Selling,* Vol. 35, No. 11, Pp. 16, 17, and 114-120, Novem-ber, 1942.

Recognition of Individual Items. The measurement of reading and noting of individual items, both editorial and advertising, follows the well-known recognition procedure. In essence, those who claim to have read the particular issue are asked to go through it and point out the items which they remember having seen and read. This is a process of self-reporting with regard to reading done prior to the appearance of the interviewer.

The details of the recognition interview are made very specific, in order to make the surveys both adequate and consistent. The business paper is always handled by the interviewer, who turns the pages and directs the questions. When a page is turned, the interviewer does not point or call attention to any specific item nor does he name it. He merely asks the respondent whether he has seen anything on the particular page or spread before him. This is the entire basis for determining which items the respondent has actually seen.

Once the reader signifies that he has previously seen that item, the interviewer is permitted to designate various parts of the item and ask about them. If the item is an advertisement he will ask about illustrations, headlines or reading matter and will inquire as to which elements were seen and how much was read.

Only the specific identification of any item or part of it is accepted as evidence of previous reading. No record whatsoever is made of general remarks such as the comment that "I always read so-and-so." Instead, the interviewer pursues the specific question as to whether the respondent happened to see or to read the particular item to which he is referring. Only positive answers are interpreted as evidence of reading or noting.

The record of item-by-item reading and noting is made with a crayon on a fresh copy of the issue prepared for readership interview. The crayon is applied directly on the items, and marks are made in such a way that the reader readily understands their meaning. This serves as a double check on accuracy, since the record is made on the copy in front of the respondent and since the respondent himself can indicate corrections.

Despite every precaution in applying the regular recognition method, it is known that inflation occurs on certain types of material. While such inflation represents an inaccuracy in the responses of readers, it is assumed to be caused primarily by the similarity of editorial items or advertisements, especially when run as a series. Deliberate distortions are believed to be eliminated to a large extent by the use of the qualifying kit. The kit makes it possible to eliminate those persons who are unable to give any objective evidence of having read the issue at all, and whose item-by-item claims would be meaningless. Only those persons who have qualified themselves as genuine members of the audience are included in the tabulations of readership through-the-book.

Practical Length of the Readership Interview. Information available on the optimum length of the readership interview points to a maximum of approximately 200 pages. Although a large percentage of readers can be persuaded to carry on with an interview covering slightly more than 200 pages or items, cooperation and discrimination gradually decrease as the interview grows longer. It should also be noted that the decision as to the length of the interview is not entirely a technical question. It is also a question of judgment as to the importance of obtaining a maximum of detailed information on readership.

To reduce field costs and at the same time increase interviewing efficiency, a maximum of 160 pages has been specified for the through-the-book readership interview. The pages to be included are selected in an entirely objective manner. For example, if the surveyed issue ran 320 pages, the basic plan would be to show the respondent, and record his readership of, every other two pages through the publication. Certain deviations from the basic plan may become necessary in order to avoid such situations as interviewing on only one-half of an advertising or editorial feature spread. Finally, some slight modification of the basic plan may be required to ensure that the scaled down interviewing copy is representative of the contents of the book as a whole in respect to large *vs.* fractional advertisements, etc.

After the pages have been selected for interviewing, copies of the survey issue are unbound, certain pages eliminated and the copies restapled. In this way, the interviewing copy presents a familiar appearance to the claimed reader of the issue.

Sequence of Pages. It is believed that interviews following the regular page sequence may favor or work against items in certain page locations, especially in thick books. In order to reduce this inequity so far as possible in the recognition method, the interviewing sequence in thick books is varied.

The method of varying the sequence is to start the interview in different parts of the book. The book is, in effect, divided into several sections. These sections are gone through, with different respondents, in a rotating series of prescribed sequences. In this way, the last part of the book is sometimes covered first while both the interviewer and respondent are comparatively fresh. While it is not believed possible to eliminate all effects of boredom or fatigue, this procedure should help to equalize their influence on items in different page locations.

Obtaining Background Information. Following the interview through the publication, a number of questions are asked to describe and classify the respondent. These questions have to do with his importance to editors and advertisers. They cover such points as the position of the individual in his firm and his buying influence, either direct or indirect.

Other questions help to provide a check on the representativeness of the sample.

SUPERVISION OF INTERVIEWERS

Interviewers are trained by the research operator in or near the region in which they will work. Training is a detailed process requiring the development of considerable skill as well as an understanding of the field procedure. The chief supervisor must work individually with every interviewer to ensure competence as well as uniformity.

The work of each new interviewer is observed during calls and his records are studied afterward to ensure that they are satisfactory. This is especially important in the recording of responses to the qualfying kit and to the item-by-item procedure through the book. None of the interviews is accepted from any field worker until he has proved his skill and dependability to the satisfaction of the supervisor.

Emphasis in the Business Papers Study can best be understood when it is realized that interviewers using the recognition method have traditionally "hunted" for readers. Furthermore, there have been very few restrictions on the kinds of people going into the sample. The business-paper procedure does not, and cannot, permit the interviewer to hunt for readers as such. Instead, he is assigned the tracing of potential readers of specific issues. Whether they have actually read the issue is no concern, whatever, of the interviewer except that he must determine whether or not they are readers.

As further assurance that the interviewer will place emphasis where it is desired, he is not compensated on the basis of readers or calls or any other unit of accomplishment. He is paid on the basis of the time put into his assignment, and his speed and efficiency are left entirely to his conscience and judgment. The interviewer must always understand that his compensation will be the same, regardless of the extent or type of reading information he turns up.

READERSHIP FIGURES

The total reader audience of the measured issue is found by first obtaining the number of claimed readers in the sample who demonstrated their familiarity with the contents of that issue. These are persons who identified more published items then unpublished items in the qualifying kit test. These qualified readers are then computed as a percentage of the total sample interviewed. Finally, this percentage is projected to the total circulation.

Scores on Individual Items. The reading or observing of individual items within the publication is computed as percentages of the qualified readers who saw or read each item.

Advertisements. The readership score for an advertisement is the percentage of qualified readers of the measured issue who remembered reading or seeing any part of that advertisement—the headlines, illustration, or copy. For advertisement of quarter-page size or larger, scores also are given for readership of the advertisement's major elements.

Editorial Items. The readership score for an editorial item is the percentage of qualified readers of the measured issue who remembered reading some of that item. Excluded from the item score are those who read only the headline or those persons who looked at the accompanying picture but did not read the article. The percentage who observed the illustration(s) is given separately.

Features. The scores for "read some" and "read most" on editorial features represent those qualified readers of the publication who have actually read some running text material on the page or on the "spread" where the feature begins. Persons who indicate reading only in the continuing columns of a feature, beyond the initial page or spread, are not included in the score recorded for the feature. Persons who have only seen pictures or only read captions or cut-lines are not included in the scoring of the feature—except for features which are composed solely of pictures and cut-lines. In such cases, the score is based on the readership of the cut-lines.

Departments. The scoring for departments, which are repeated in similar form from issue to issue, is different. All readers of any segment of a department (not including pictures or cut-lines) are included in the over-all score for the department—providing the contents or format clearly identifies the item as a special unit of the department. Therefore, the "This Department" score is cumulative, and includes all persons who have read any part of the text in the department.

It is clear that this method of scoring editorial departments produces high ratings for the department as a whole. Any individual item in the department may contribute to the score for "This Department." By way of contrast, the "read some" and "read most" scores for editorial feature articles may appear conservative, since these ratings are limited to readers of running text on the first page or opening spread of each article. However, an editorial feature article must be looked upon as one, unified item. It is more meaningful to omit tabulation of casual reading done by those who see only the carry-over columns, than to include this reading as a part of the total rating of the article.

The scoring on advertisements is slightly different from editorial matter. It will be seen that an advertising headline receives a score, since the headline is often an effective advertising unit in itself. Also, the reading of headlines is included in the scoring of "Any This Ad" in advertisements.

A caution should be used in interpreting these item-by-item scores. They are percentages of persons who were qualified as readers and who have seen or read the items. Since these readership claims for individual items are subject to whatever factors produce inaccuracies in such claims, it is not recommended that they be projected actually to total numbers of observers or readers of individual items.

In general, such projected totals may not be greatly at variance with the facts but their use is discouraged because such a practice might impute greater accuracy to percentages that is believed to exist. This statement is based upon the assumption that inaccurate scores on individual items are likely to vary according to the nature and content of the item.

This caution does not interfere with the maximum use of data in evaluating the reader appeal of individual editorial items or advertisements. Percentages may be compared with each other, providing that a degree of judgment is exercised in estimating how accurate such percentages can be expected to be. Major features or items which are highly distinctive may be assumed to be rated with a considerable degree of accuracy. However, when comparisons are made with items that are not distinctive from issue to issue, one should make allowance for possible inflation due to the familiarity of appearance of the items.

Every precaution has been taken to produce the most accurate ratings possible. As previously stated, claimed readers who do not pass the qualifying kit test are deleted in arriving at the base for computing item percentages. Thus, their reading claims on individual items are omitted. In addition, it should be remembered that the survey samples for the Continuing Study of Business Papers are designed to represent all persons who had had an opportunity to read the issue by the time they were interviewed.

These features are important advancements in readership research and increase the usefulness of the study to advertisers, agencies, and publishers alike.

CHAPTER 6

Sales Promotion

TAKING THE MEDICINE YOU PRESCRIBE

In its sales promotion department a good businesspaper takes its own medicine.

Much of the know-how prescribed by the business press for trade and industry is in the form of ideas and methods for promoting the sale and resale of goods and services.

The businesspaper is unexcelled in preaching what others should practice but its own sales promotion practice sometimes leaves much to be desired.

As pointed out in the introduction to Chapter 2, the businesspaper has two sales organizations, circulation sales and advertising sales. The promotion department of a businesspaper is concerned with mass selling to the two audiences: (1) the advertisers and potential advertisers; (2) the readers and potential readers.

To the people who buy advertising space the sales promotion manager may talk about his editors and the editorial service, his publication's collateral services, the audience or the market the businesspaper reaches; or, he may talk about the successes of other advertisers. To the people who read the businesspaper he may talk about the advertisers' messages or the editorial messages in terms of the benefit to the reader.

The promotion manager's media are letters, broadsides, booklets, house advertisements in his own publication, house organs, the advertising, marketing and selling and buyers service publications, the daily newspapers and the "Warbags"[1] of his salesmen.

In military terms the promotion manager may be said to lay down the artillery barrage for the advancing foot soldiers—advertising and

---

[1] The salesman's briefcase contains market and readership studies, editorial surveys, case histories of successful advertising campaigns, photostats of Letters to the Editor, etc., etc.

subscription salesmen. He softens up the target. Facts are his ammunition.

Where does he get his facts? He gets them everywhere but chiefly from the research department. If he is alert he will make calls with advertising and subscription salesmen to find out for himself what readers and customers need and want. He will enlist the counsel of advertising agency media men and account executives, for these men are in a way salesmen for his publication.

The promotion manager should serve his publisher the way a managing editor serves an editor. He should sit in on all policy-forming conferences relating to advertising and circulation, help plan and help execute the plans.

He should plan promotion over the long pull as well as for the expediency of the day.

In Chapter 4 on Advertising the reader was given the results of an inquiry into the space-buying habits, needs, viewpoints, purposes, patterns and practices of advertising agencies who employ business-paper advertising space in their plans to promote and sell the goods and services of their clients.[2] These findings are converted, on the pages that follow, into ways and means to help sales promotion men put that know-how to work to sell *more* space more economically on business-papers.

For overy thirty years *Standard Rate & Data Service* of Chicago, who made this study, have been publishing a basic monthly service for publishers, advertising managers, and space buyers containing complete, timely information about media, in four sections: Businesspapers, Newspapers, General Magazines, Radio-TV. The staff of S.R.D.S. make it their business to learn who buys and who influences the buying of all media; why they buy; what they buy; how they buy. In the process, they also learn how businesspaper publishers can make their space selling and promotion plans fit more exactly into contemporary space-buying patterns.

Two research methods were used by S.R.D.S. to develop this study for the business press:

1. Questionnaires were sent by mail to a large group of business-paper advertisers; to all advertising agencies reporting the placing of a

---

[2] "A survey of Advertiser and Agency Buyer Practices and Patterns for Businesspapers," published by S.R.D.S., Chicago, 1948.

thousand or more pages of businesspaper advertising; and to a random sample of agencies placing from 500 to 1000 pages in businesspapers.

2. A continuing series of direct field interviews were held with sales and advertising executives in companies using businesspaper space and with the principals, account executives, media directors, and space buyers of their advertising agencies.

The findings of the direct field interviews, originally published by S.R.D.S. in 1948 as the *Business Paper Promotion Handbook,* are summarized with permission of the publishers.

In the chapter on Research we learned about the "Continuing Study of Business Papers" now being conducted by the Advertising Research Foundation under sponsorship of the Associated Business Publications. This is a mechanism for industry-wide promotion of the business press. It also provides member publishers with an opportunity to use the same accurate, thorough, and reliable research techniques of the ARF for their own publications and then to employ the results in their own promotions.

WAYS TO PROMOTE MORE BUSINESSPAPER ADVERTISING SPACE SALES AND REDUCE UNIT SALES COSTS*

Space selling is the art of persuading the right people to select and use the right publications for their advertising.

The purpose of this study is to consider some of the ways you can sell more businesspaper space and at the same time reduce unit sales cost.

The major premise is that you can increase sales volume by helping prospects understand how your publication matches their needs.

The minor premise is that you can reduce the unit cost of selling space by dividing the necessary sales work appropriately among the several commonly used sales-producing tools.

The major premise demands that you probe, first, into the question of who is instrumental in the selection of businesspapers and, second, into what those people want to know about a publication before they can intelligently buy and use space in it.

You have much to gain, obviously, from concentrating the major part of your sales effort on those people whose influence on space buying

* From "Business Paper Promotion Handbook," published by Standard Rate & Data Service, Chicago, 1948. See "How Businesspaper Advertising Space Is Bought," Chapter 4.

is the result of their regular job responsibilities, such as sales and advertising managers, agency principals, account executives, and space buyers. Of course, such concentration may by-pass certain possible influences, subtle or artless, such as the board chairman's wife who champions some publisher friend's interests, but it applies your effort, nevertheless, where it is most likely to bear fruit.

The Space Selling Job. What does the publisher have to do to convince advertisers and their agencies that their use of his paper will serve their purpose and serve it economically?

The job varies in degree and intensity, of course. Some prospects are tougher than others. Some publication values are more difficult to demonstrate than others. Numerous variations affect the degree and completeness of effort required to convince different prospects. But the underlying principles involved hold through all the variations of their application and are subject to analysis.

In general, these are some of the steps involved in selling space:

You must locate worthwhile prospects.

You must remind these prospects constantly of:

—your publication

—its market

—its kind of readers

—its coverage of the market

—its editorial scope

—its format

You must sell and re-sell each prospect on:

— how your paper fits his need

—how to use your paper most profitably

The degree of efficiency with which those steps are performed reflects in sales volume and in space selling costs, of course. It is increased or decreased by the manner in which you use the space selling tools at your command—space salesmen, direct mail promotion, and space advertising.

Consequently, our consideration of the advantages and disadvantages inherent in the major space selling tools bears considerably on the basic arithmetic of selling more space at lower unit sales cost.

Such sales operations as are listed above obviously should be performed by the lowest-cost combination of sales tools that can do the job most efficiently.

The Space Salesman. The space salesman is the Number One space selling tool. The good space salesman can and sometimes does execute every step in the process of producing an order, from the time he discovers a new prospect until that prospect becomes an effective user of space in his paper.

In such instances, the salesman is to the production of orders what the handcraftsman of old was to the production of goods. The workmanship of both might be of the highest quality. But the amount of work they can do is definitely limited and each job is highly expensive.

Assuming, for the moment, that the good space salesman can sell the men he sees (and certainly it is difficult for any space salesman to sell men he cannot see), it is obvious that the more men he sees, the more space he sells. The limiting factor is time. Anything that increases the salesman's selling time increases his capacity for turning in business.

If you relieve your salesman of any of those steps, or of any combination or part of any of them, you increase his chance of seeing more people, hence, selling more space.

The Printed Word—the Salesman's Helper. Appropriate use of the printed word in its various forms, such as direct mail promotion and publication advertising, is the means you can use to aid and abet the salesman's work, save him time, relieve him of the load of communicating information that can be handled as economically or more economically in print.

The printed word makes it possible for you to mechanize many parts of the sales producing job, just as machine tools mechanize many motions the old-fashioned craftsmen did by hand.

As the machine tool speeds up production and lowers unit production costs, so the printed word speeds up selling and reduces unit selling costs by performing some parts of the sales producing operation faster and more frequently that can be done "by hand" alone.

The most effective division of labor between salesmen and the printed word may vary in some degree for every publication. But the governing principle is this:

The printed word is the more economical tool for making constantly available *to the bulk of your prospects* all the information about your paper that helps them understand its basic values as an advertising medium for them.

The space salesman is the more economical tool for closing individual sales by showing *each interested prospect* how your paper fits his particular plans and needs. The less time he has to spend doing what

the printed word can do as well or better, the more time he will have
for closing sales.

The effectiveness of your use of these sales producing tools depends on:

What you say when you talk to prospects,

How many prospects you say it to, and

How often you say it to them.

Who Selects Businesspapers? Space in businesspapers is a means to
an end. The interest of its buyers and users is primarily in the *end* and
not in the *means*.

Advertisers want to sell their products, their services, or their ideas.
How can they reach the largest number of potential buyers at the lowest
cost per reach? How can they create and maintain buying interest in
the product at the lowest possible cost? Who is clothed with the responsibility of finding the answers to such questions?

According to the advertisers who cooperated in our inquiry into the
practical, everyday processes of space buying, numerous people have
fingers in the space buying pie—in the selection of what publications to
use for the advertising of their products.

Top management, up to and including the board of directors, is interested. But their interest centers in *how much it costs*—and what do we
get for our money?

Their primarily "profit" interest, however, frequently leads to more
detailed interests in specific markets and specific media, although usually
the sales manager and his advertising manager are clothed with the
responsibility of selecting the markets for concentrated cultivation and
the means best suited to developing them.

The Sales Manager. The man most interested in practical answers
to all manner of sales problems is, obviously, the man who is responsible
for activating the sales function. For the sake of simplicity, let us call
him the sales manager, regardless of what other title or titles may adorn
his escutcheon due to the different lines of organization different companies follow.

The sales manager's job depends: (1) on the volume of sales he produces, not necessarily today nor tomorrow, but year by year; and (2)
on how much he spends to produce that volume, year by year. His principal interest is markets and how to develop them.

His primary sales tool is direct selling through his own salesmen, his
jobbers, distributors, dealers. His secondary sales tool is the printed

word in whatever forms may be necessary to implement, supplement, and multiply the effect of his direct selling efforts.

The Advertising Manager. The sales managers of most companies that are big enough to be of interest to you have advertising managers and/or advertising agencies to counsel them on the use of the printed word; to prepare copy, select media, and handle the multiplicity of details involved in the use of the printed word.

Frequently the advertising manager is a key man in the building of the advertising budget. Often he is vested with complete authority over its use. Almost always one of his chief concerns is media selection.

Although the advertising manager may be subject to the influence of the president and other top policy executives, as well as to the decisions of the sales manager, these men have primary interests other than advertising, while he is chiefly concerned with nothing but the use of the printed word as a sales and promotional tool. Copy, media selection, and the multiplicity of details involved in the advertising arm of selling are his daily chores. And in most companies, his right bower is an advertising agency.

Agency Organization. Although advertising agencies, as well as companies that advertise, exhibit a considerable range of variations in organization responsibility and authority, the function of media selection is common to all of them.

Agency principals, account executives, media directors, and space buyers are the usual agency participants in media selection. In some agencies, the media director or space buyer is a highly qualified specialist, who sits in on plans board and client conferences and carries the principal responsibility for media selection. In other agencies, he is most concerned with the gathering of data under the direction of the account executive or agency principal.

In many agencies, the selection of what publications to use is a conference matter with influence more or less evenly divided among principals, account executives, and media men. These interrelations of media selecting responsibility vary, not only as between different agencies of varying size, but also as between different accounts in the same agency.

Media Selection a Well-Organized Function. Since a large proportion of most advertising budgets goes into space, no wonder we find media selection so important and so well organized a function with so many people participating in it.

Our field research has brought out a large volume of information on this subject. Whatever *titles* those people have, from the president of the advertiser organization to the space buyer in the agency, whatever their major responsibilities may be, when they are concerned with the selection of advertising media, they are participating in the media buying function. They are all media buyers. And they are in need of information that helps them form intelligent judgments and make intelligent choices.

Let us repeat that, with emphasis: *They're in Need of Information.* Every man who participates in the selection of businesspapers wants to *know* before he decides.

Here is how one of them put it: "We are interested in the publication's editorial, and in the functions of this editorial; in its circulation—free, paid, whatever; in its advertising volume. It is a difficult job trying to remember stories after you have listened to eight or nine men make their pitch. Common sense, therefore, is an important factor. Evaluation of media is a personal choice. Rate per thousand has no meaning in the businesspaper field. We have to assume the selectivity of readers. What we need is factual information. True, this factual information is dry, but it is the basic ingredient of what comes later on."

What Sort of Information Helps Media Buyers? Advertisers and agencies want to buy *space* in the same sense that a manufacturer wants to buy a *machine*—not because they want the space (or the machine), but because they want to do something that the space (or the machine) can help them do better or faster or more economically.

Since the use of space involves an expenditure of money for which the advertiser desires to get full value, the selection of what publications to use for any given purpose demands that advertisers and agencies be well informed about the various publications that are possibilities.

Difference Between Publisher and Advertiser Viewpoints. Our field investigation among advertisers and agencies clearly defines what *sort* of information helps media buyers make intelligent decisions. It is interesting to note how far apart publishers and advertisers frequently are in what they consider important about publications.

Publishers are seldom at a loss for glowing superlatives with which to extoll the virtues of their publications. Here are a few headlines of recent publication ads:

"Editorial Leadership" . . . "FIRST in advertising volume" . . . "FIRST in number of agency users" . . . "FIRST in number of exclusive advertisers" . . . "The IDEAL advertising medium" . . . "Leads all others in the field" . . . "Far Ahead" . . . "100% Coverage" . . . "Oldest

in the field" . . . "Dominates its industry" . . . "Largest Circulation in
Its Field" . . . "First Choice" . . . "Your Best Bet" . . . "Maximum
Coverage of Buyers" . . . "The KEY to Your Market" . . . "Oldest and
Biggest" . . . "No. 1" . . . "Highest and Fastest Growing Circulation"
. . . "The Favorite of Advertising Agencies" . . . "Most Widely Read"
. . . "The Best Value for Your Advertising Dollar" . . . "A MUST for
your profits" . . . "Six Times a Winner" . . . "Most Effective Medium"
. . . "Strongest Coverage" . . . "Outstanding" . . . "Way Out in Front."

Picture the advertiser or agency wallowing through such a sea of daz-
zling claims? Yet spend a day with the mail that goes over a media
buyer's desk, or flip through the pages of any publication in the advertising field, and there it is!

All that advertisers and agencies want are the simple, quiet, informative facts, the unobtrusive truth that helps them distinguish one publication from another, that helps them recognize each publication for
what it really is and select those that reach not just the largest number
of people, but the largest number of people *who are most likely to buy
their specific products.*

Advertisers and agencies are not infallible. When they are thoroughly
and constantly informed of a publication's service, as reported by an
authoritative source, their regard for that publication runs high. Their
ability to appraise its specific values is increased.

Agencies need reliable information for use in reselling clients, or
keeping them sold on a publication. And such information should be
readily and immediately available in regular sources of reference and
use.

An account executive in a large midwest agency summed up the
space buyer's viewpoint neatly when he said that a publication's promotion should be "filled with sales points rather than competitive, boast-
ful, bragging blurbs."

*What Is the Nature of the Information That Helps Advertisers and
Agencies Make Fair Decisions?* If you could listen in when agencies
and advertisers talk shop among themselves, you would quickly find out
the kind of information that interests and influences them. Their minds
run along pretty well defined channels.

Perhaps every individual would tell his troubles in different words;
but when you came to digest what you had heard, you would find it
falling into a pattern that is as sure a guide to effective publication promotion as you can ask for.

Our field interviewers have actually done some "listening in" for you.

What they report are not our ideas, but your advertisers' and prospects' and their agencies'. Here is the gist of what these people point out as the values that guide them in their judgment of businesspapers.

Four Points of Major Interest. Almost to a man, media buyers disclosed the following four common interests. Consider them carefully. This is the sort of information *they want.* The value of your promotion can be increased by the manner and detail in which it covers these four buying interests:

1. *Market:* What are the characteristics of the publication's market that make it worthwhile for my product?
2. *Readers:* a. *Who* are they? *What* do they do? *How many* are there?
   b. What plants or businesses, and how many, do they represent?
   c. *Where* are they?
3. *Editorial:* How does the publication's editorial content match the interests of those readers?
4. *Format:* Is the publication's format attractive to readers and practical for advertisers? Has it any distinguishing values?

Let's expand each of these major interests with a few observations and a few direct quotes from the interviews themselves, which exemplify commonly held opinions and thinking.

It may help to remember that advertisers' and agencies' regard for publications is purely selfish: They are looking for means of selling their products most economically; and that is all. They want the publications that are read by the largest number of people who are most likely to buy, or influence the buying of, their products. *Their thinking always begins with their product.*

1. MARKET

What Are the Characteristics of Your Market That Make It Worthwhile for the Advertiser's Product? What information about your market will contribute to the advertiser's (and his agency's) understanding of how to approach it more effectively? Or what will help him relate that market properly to his sales and advertising objectives?

Market statistics are useful, of course; *but a clear picture of the up-to-date conditions that are peculiar to your market is even more helpful.*

The emphasis is on the *characteristics* of your publication's market. Why is it a fertile field for your prospect's sales cultivation?

To Illustrate the Point. In textile manufacturing, statistics on spindleage by fibers, fiber consumption, number of employees, looms, motors, pour from the research departments of the textile publications and other organizations.

But such figures have meaning for the advertiser only if he sees them in terms of sales opportunities for his product. What do they mean in terms of new looms, new bleaching processes, new printing machinery, new motors, air conditioning?

Your market changes constantly. Many of its changes mean unanticipated opportunities for advertisers. Your *editors* keep your *readers* abreast of such changes. But what are you doing to keep *advertisers* and *agencies* informed on those trends in terms of sales opportunities?

One well-known media buyer puts it this way: "Market information should include indications of the field's constant shuffling and changing activities. Whether it is moving in or out, up or down. What new product applications are possible; what new market possibilities are opening."

2. READERS

Are Your Readers People Whose Buying Influence Is Important to the Advertiser? Now we are close to the core of advertisers' and agencies' principal interest in businesspapers. Once the broad market in which a publication serves is identified with the advertiser's interests, the next considerations are:

1. *Who* are your readers? What do they do? What are their job-interests and responsibilities? How many people are there of the kind your readers are? What percentage of this total do you reach? Does this represent adequate coverage?

2. How many and what plants in what industries are represented by your readers? What is the total number of plants in those industries? Does the percentage you reach represent adequate coverage?

3. Where are the plants represented by your readers located geographically?

All three of these considerations are separate and distinct phases of what is commonly referred to as "circulation."

The loose use of the term "circulation," however, tends to obscure the basic interests advertisers and agencies have in mind when comparing publication values.

Let us see if we can clarify this subject in terms of those basic advertiser and agency interests. After all, readers of the right kind and number, and properly located, are mainly what the advertiser buys when he contracts for space in a businesspaper.

The first of these considerations—who—is on the human or *qualitative* side of the advertiser's interest. It demands a sufficiently clear definition of the functions your readers perform to enable media buyers to gauge their importance as buying influences for specific products.

The second and third considerations—how many plants are covered and where are they—are *quantitative*. The desired answers to them will show how your publication's coverage and penetration matches the market potential.

Who Are Your Readers? In spite of audited circulations, buyers of advertising space still find it difficult to get clear definitions of publication audiences *in terms of who their readers are* and *what those readers do* that makes them important to the advertiser.

Advertisers and agencies alike, regardless of size and regardless of how they are organized, complain—sometimes bitterly—about *too much* defensive space selling, *too much* competitive selling, *too much* of the "who-do-you-want-to-reach-we-got-'em" type of selling; *too little effort to define reader interests clearly and to interpret those interests in terms of the advertised product.*

These advertising men also suggest the basic weakness of the "numbers racket" among businesspapers—the weakness of such publisher claims as "Biggest Circulation in the field."

Parallel to Personal Selling. We find advertisers and agencies in general thinking more and more in terms of the same sort of specific coverage for their advertising as for their personal selling. (What sales manager permits his *salesmen* to call on Tom, Dick, and Harry, when only Tom is a prospect?)

They want to know *who* your readers are, *how many* of them there are, and *where* they are, by industry and geographical location.

Numbers of readers, *per se*, don't count with any buyer who *thinks*. (And don't kid yourself—most of them *do* think.) Yet we find many publishers still trying to sell space chiefly on the basis of numbers, with only an occasional passing nod to the idea of specific coverage of specific functions in specific industries or groups of industries.

Anything your advertising, your promotion, your selling does to define clearly your publication's group of readers, and the common interests that form them into a valuable market for the advertiser, will earn the attention—yes, the gratitude—of the people who select businesspapers for their advertising.

Let's put it down again: The advertiser's prime interest is in reaching the largest possible number of the people for whom his message is intended, and *no others*. His interest is indelibly cast in terms of *his product*. Who have you got that might influence the purchase of *his product*? How many? Where? That's all.

3. EDITORIAL

How Does Your Editorial Content Match the Work Interests of Your Readers? Does it concentrate on the full range of common job interests that characterize your market? Does it provide essential news? How does it gather its news and its information? Do its readers regard it as a practical source of working information?

Circulation figures are no guarantee of readership. Only the contents of the publication, developing subjects that match the real job interests of the men it claims to serve, can secure the sort of attention that builds advertising value.

What are the editorial objectives of your publication? Is it a vertical paper, serving a single industry; or is it a horizontal paper, serving some function that is common to several or all industries?

Scope and Quality of Service. Demonstration of how your editors are fulfilling the requirements of your readers, both in the *scope* of the interests your paper serves and in the *quality* of the service it renders, can help advertisers see more clearly where your publication fits into their plans and how to use it properly.

Almost every man who is doing a conscientious job of publication selection regards editorial content as a most important guide to advertising value. Yet how to appraise editorial content justly remains a discouraging problem without enlightened help from the publications themselves.

How do your editors cover the job interests, functions, and responsibilities of your readers? What are the subjects they are giving major attention and how are those subjects related to the interests of the various types of readers you reach, if you reach more than one type?

Is your paper strong on How-to-do-it articles; on news; on economics; on prices; or what are its main subjects?

What evidence of its influence on readers can you demonstrate?

Such questions illustrate "the kind of editorial job a book is doing," and they help advertisers and agencies to get a clear picture of the kind of people your readers are.

4. FORMAT

Format is the form, size, type face, margins, general style, and arrangement of a publication, when printed and bound.

As most publishers know, format sometimes carries important weight for or against the choice of a businesspaper as an advertising medium.

Complete Agreement. The field interviews with advertisers and agencies found remarkably complete agreement on the four values we have just considered. Four values that suggest a reliable pattern for the selling, promotion, and advertising of business papers.

You can find a dozen ways to activate the presentation of any one or any combination of those values, and each will be effective so long as it imparts clearly and reliably *the features that distinguish your publication from all others.*

Give advertisers and agencies a clear, qualitative portrayal of your publication in terms of those four basic values—market, type of readers, editorial service, and format—and you can be sure your selling and promotion are doing an efficient and effective job.

Collateral Interests of Advertisers and Agencies. Certain collateral interests, which are not inherent in publications themselves, came up for discussion during the course of our field interviews with advertisers and agencies. A wide difference of opinion seems to exist on the relative importance of these interests; but, other things being on a par, any one of them might influence a buying decision. Here are five of these collateral interests:

1. *Market research:* What can you offer advertisers and agencies about your publication's market for their specific products?
2. *Copy preparation:* How can you help advertisers improve their use of space in your paper?
3. *Photo services:* Are your editorial photo files of possible interest to advertisers? Or do you have a field set-up that can help them get illustrations for their advertising?
4. *Mailing lists:* Can you offer mailing lists and mailing service to advertisers who supplement their use of your publication with direct mail?
5. *Buyers' guides:* Are they a regular feature of your paper—to help the readers find the advertising of any specific classifications of products they are interested in? Or do you publish a special annual buyers' guide issue?

Uniformity Wanted. One more matter that media buyers give important weight is their desire for uniform information—information organized in a way that enables them to compare fairly publications in the same fields or serving similar functional groups.

HOW TO REACH PEOPLE WHO INFLUENCE THE SPACE BUYING

The most constructive things you can do promotion-wise to increase space sales and to reduce sales cost are:

1. Create and keep fresh a clear impression of your publication, its field, and its purpose.
2. Multiply your contacts with advertisers, prospective advertisers, and their agencies.
3. Inform advertisers and agencies as completely as possible about the features of your publication that are important to them.
4. Be sure such information is available at the time media buyers are most likely to consider it—when they are deciding what papers to use.

Sales and advertising plans and programs are being considered constantly. The market potentials for established products expand or contract; new distribution factors come into play; competition takes unexpected turns; new products make their appearance; a variety of forces, some unpredictable, some carefully planned, keep the over-all market for businesspaper space in a state of flux.

And repeatedly these whirling market gyrations bring together the elements that make a prospect for space in *your* publication. Some manufacturer decides that he wants to reach the kind of people your readers are. *That is the time when it is most important that he understand and appreciate what your publication can do for him.*

That is the time when the advertiser and the agency *want to know.* And that is the time—neither sooner nor later—that the impressions built up by your salesman, your direct mail, your publication advertising can bear fruit.

A very large part of your space selling cost is wrapped up in your effort to have your publication recognized for what it is at the time advertisers decide that is what they want.

Let us have a look at the well-known tools you can use to implement these two factors—pertinent information and proper timing—that contribute constructively to selling space:

The space salesman
Direct mail
Advertising, marketing, and selling publications
a. Editorial type
b. Buyers' service type

Let us take these up one at a time. Each has a particular job that it can do best and most economically in any well-integrated sales program.

THE SPACE SALESMAN

The space salesman is (or should be) by all odds the No. 1 space selling tool. His forte is *closing sales*: interpreting the publication in terms of each prospect's specific advertising problem and interests; getting names on the dotted line.

But, because the *final* steps in closing a sale usually require personal work, and therefore clothe the salesman with a degree of indispensability, for reasons of economy he should not be required to carry the whole load of selling. Side by side with his indispensability goes cost. The salesman is the most costly of your sales tools. But his relative cost goes down as the volume of space he sells goes up.

The less time the salesman has to spend digging up new prospects, or doing the informational parts of the selling job that can be done for him by some form of the printed word, the more time he will have for the part of the job he can do best—*closing sales*. The more space he will sell and the lower his sales cost will be per unit of space.

The Salesman as Interpreter. Field interviews clarify the space salesman's importance as an interpreter of the values of his publication in terms of individual advertisers' specific needs. He can get in his best licks filling in the gaps in the information the advertiser and agency have been able and prefer to obtain in other ways. He can spend his time most profitably working with prospects who want to do a job that space in his paper can help them do.

This is not to suggest a counsel of perfection. No space salesman can spend all, or perhaps even the largest portion of his time servicing prospects who are at the point of building their publication lists; becoming familiar with their advertising problems; studying their needs; presenting his story in the light of those needs.

Yet the more time the salesman *can* spend in that manner and, after the sale is made, helping the advertiser get the most out of the use of his space, the more effective calls he will make and the more business he will produce and hold.

So we find among the publishers a wide recognition of the No. 1 *sales-closing* function of space salesmen. At the same time we find them in a quandary as to what to do to help the salesmen exercise that function more frequently. It is the same quandary that many manufacturers of industrial products find themselves in, until they understand how to use the printed word in promotion and advertising, not merely as a means of "keeping their names before the public," but as *a means of saving their salesmen's time and energy for the work the salesmen can do best*—closing sales.

Relatively Few Chances to Close. The space salesman who has to handle his space selling job all by himself has relatively few chances of closing sales. He has too much else to do and too little time for doing it.

He has to dig up new prospects; he has to begin at the beginning with them; he has to supply, more or less continuously, a large amount of information to new and old prospects and to his advertisers; he has to keep his advertisers happy; he has to see, or *try* to see, everybody.

Yet the space salesman's most profitable function, as with the salesmen for the products advertised in his publication, is *closing sales*—interpreting his paper in terms of the personal work interests of each prospect.

Every time the publisher uses the printed word to unearth a new prospect, it gives the salesman more time for closing an old one. Every bit of information advertisers and agencies get through printed data readily at hand saves the salesman's time and makes it easier for him to close sales. Every routine contact made in print keeps your paper fresh in the minds of your prospects and advertisers and relieves the salesman for more urgent calls.

So, effective, economical space selling teams up the space salesman and the printed word. It is a matter of getting the information that helps people buy space to the right people, at the right time, and by the right means—by space salesmen, by direct mail, by advertising in the publications that advertisers and agencies read, and by running supplementary information in the buyers' reference books they use.

DIRECT MAIL

Many publishers spend the bulk of their promotion money for direct mail—processed letters, folders, brochures, booklets. Certainly this use of the printed word can perform certain parts of the sales job more economically than they can be performed in any other way.

For example, direct mail permits close control and timing of announcements that may be intended for very specific groups of people or that require precise timing.

Direct mail is indicated for such material as market survey results or other detailed reports that require more or less elaborate presentation and considerable space.

Direct mail is also useful for making conveniently available for filing any desired information of a more or less permanent, data-folder nature.

In general, direct mail offers attractive economies when it is used to follow up and qualify inquiries before they are turned over to the salesman; to sharpshoot specific functions or prospect classifications; to get voluminous information more quickly into the hands of more prospects than can be done as effectively or economically by other means.

Direct Mail Runs Risks. But there are great risks in direct mail. The competition is ferocious. The old "circular file" is rapacious. Only the fittest pieces survive. And the fittest pieces are those that carry information wanted by the recipients—information that contributes to the major interests.

Advertisers and prospects put great emphasis on information that helps them form their own judgments about a market's value or a publication's value in terms of their immediate advertising problem.

They like a piece of direct mail, or they don't like it—they use or file it for future use, or they discard it—according to their quick appraisal of its contents.

And they discard most of it because most of it either contributes no useful information or what it contributes is out of date by the time they need it. (The plea for "dated" mail pieces was frequent and urgent. The media buyer is constantly fearful of using information that no longer applies.)

They are busy men, swamped with all sorts of demands on their time and attention. At the same time, they are experienced men and much concerned with their own immediate interests. Only direct mail that contributes to those interests and that carries information not easily obtainable from their accustomed reference sources stands a chance of living long enough to do the job you want it to do.

THE ADVERTISING, MARKETING, AND SELLING PUBLICATIONS

Your salesmen and your direct mail can reach the men you *know,* or whose names you can get. They may constitute the great majority of all the people who have any influence in selecting your publication for their advertising and still leave unreached some people whose weight on the scale of buying influence is important or even decisive. Most of these unsuspected prospects are reachable through publications they read and use.

There are two broad types of advertising, marketing, and selling publications: the editorial type, such as *Printers' Ink, Industrial Marketing, Tide, Advertising Age, Sales Management, Advertising Agency and Advertising & Selling, Western Advertising, Southern Advertising and Publishing, Markets of America,* and *The Advertiser*; and the buyers' service type, such as *Standard Rate & Data Service* and *Annual Market Data and Directory Number.*

The reasons for *reading the editorial* type publications and for *using the buyers' service* type publications are so different that the two actually present different kinds of promotion opportunities.

The Editorial Publications. One of the principal parts of the space selling job your use of such publications can perform is to reach the unknown or hidden buying influences your salesmen and your direct mail cannot reach.

Another function your trade paper advertising can perform economically is to tie your publication into the selective news and how-to-do-it interests of the advertising and selling professions—to keep forever reminding people, those you know, as well as those you do not know, that there is such a publication as yours, who its readers are, and what values it offers any advertiser who desires to communicate with those readers.

In addition to the broad differences in readership and usage between the editorial type and the buyers' service type of advertising, marketing, and selling publications, there are characteristic differences between the several publications within the editorial type group itself. No two are alike editorially, hence no two attract quite the same reader following or are read for the same reasons.

For example, the advertising man or sales executive who is interested in the general how-to-do-it experiences of other advertising and sales people will follow a paper like *Printers' Ink* or *Advertising Agency.*

The advertising man who has a primary interest in industrial advertising experience turns first to a publication like *Industrial Marketing.*

The sales executive who is looking for ideas and who wishes to keep informed about the progress and trends in management techniques looks to a magazine like *Sales Management.*

The man who must keep up to date on the goings and comings and transient doings in all branches of advertising activity takes a news-item paper like *Advertising Age*, or a news-article magazine like *Tide*.

The Buyers' Service Publications. We have just seen how successful use of businesspaper advertising in the editorial type of advertising, marketing, and selling publications must be predicated on the fact that, here, *the seller must seek the buyer.*

Just the reverse of that is true in the buyers' service type of publication. Here *the buyer seeks the seller.* You do not have to strain to get users' attention. You are not competing with editorial matter. You are contributing to their purpose in using the book—to get buying information. And that is the key to the successful promotional use of the buyers' service type of publication.

These are not news publications, nor how-to-do-it publications, but direct usership publications—sources of basic publication and market information that are in constant demand by the people who select businesspapers and buy space in them.

Besides *Standard Rate & Data Service,* there is another buyers' service publication in the businesspaper field: *Market Data Book,* which is a special issue of *Industrial Marketing* and published annually. It carries editorial material contributed by members of various businesspaper staffs, along with brief reference material that is brought up to date once a year.

CONCLUSION

Advertisers and agencies—your customers and prospects—have told us who participates in media selection: who has to be sold.

Advertisers and agencies have told us what sort of information influences their space buying decisions: what you have to demonstrate and prove.

Advertisers and agencies have told us how they normally get such information: how you can make sure of reaching them.

And what they have told us can be summed up in these two statements:

1. You can increase sales volume by helping prospects understand clearly how your publication matches their needs.
2. You can reduce the unit cost of selling space by dividing the sales work appropriately among space salesmen, direct mail, and advertising in the "editorial" and "buyers' service" publications.

PUBLISHERS' SALES PRESENTATION OUTLINE*

A presentation, as outlined here, will provide publishers' representatives, advertising agencies, and advertisers with qualitative and quantitative information on markets covered, type of readers, circulation, editorial policies, and other needed data to enable them accurately to compare any publication with others in the same field.

The form should only be used as a guide upon which to base your presentation.

In addition to statistical data, put in your presentation all market information, charts, and selling information needed to give a space buyer an opportunity to justify his selection of your paper.

On items that do not apply to your type of circulation put only the notation, "*Not pertinent.*"

WHO ARE YOU—HISTORY AND BACKGROUND?

1. Name of publication?
2. Date of presentation?
3. Name and address of publisher? (If a charity or political organization, fill out completely the supplementary form for the purpose.)
4. Date of first issue?
5. Frequency of publication?
6. Is circulation audited by Audit Bureau of Circulations?
   a. Is circulation audited by Controlled Circulation Audit?
   b. If not, what form of proof of circulation will you furnish?
7. Is publication the official organ of any association?
   a. What association?
   b. Do association membership dues include subscription price?

WHAT MARKET DO YOU SERVE?

8. Class, industry, or field served?
9. Subdivision of class, industry, or field or type of individual to which publication particularly appeals?

WHAT IS YOUR CIRCULATION HISTORY?

10. Average circulation per-issue-per-year and advertising rate, for the preceding ten years?

* Prepared and recommended by The National Industrial Advertisers Association, Chicago, to businesspaper publishers. The information is kept on file for N.I.A.A. members.

11. Total (paid and not paid) circulation per issue for the six months' period ending ————, and date each issue's mailing was begun and completed?
12. Average total distribution for period stated in Item 11?
    a. Subscriptions—addressed to individuals or attention of individuals?
    b. Subscriptions—addressed to firms?
    c. All other paid circulation (such as net single copy sales, and single issue sale in bulk)?
    d. Total average number of copies mailed regularly without charge to individuals or firms for whom publication is edited?
        I. Copies addressed to individuals or attention of individuals?
        II. Copies addressed to firms?
        III. If rotational method is used for part or all of list, append a comprehensive statement, showing number of names rotated and state period of rotation; if not periodic, append explanation of rotational system used?
    e. Advertisers?
    f. Miscellaneous circulation of no direct benefit to advertisers, such as correspondents, advertising agencies, exchanges, complimentary, subscription salesmen, samples, employees of publisher, etc.?

WHAT ARE YOUR CIRCULATION POLICIES?

13. Qualifications, if any, determining eligibility to receive publication regularly—include only circulation under a, b, and d, Item 12?
    a. Functional or occupational qualifications?
    b. Financial or business-volume qualifications?
14. Information regarding section d, of Item 12?
    Give a comprehensive statement as to source of supply of names?
    a. What is your policy in placing names on your circulation list?
    b. How do you determine the number of copies mailed to a large or small company?
    c. Number of names removed from and added to circulation list during period covered by this report?
15. Authorized prices for sale of this publication during period stated in paragraph 11?
    a. Regular prices: Single copy, Regular issue? Special issue?
       Subscription, 1 yr.? 2 yr.? 3 yr.? 5 yr.?

b. Special subscription offers, all prices for various periods, including renewal and extension offers (not in combinations)?

c. Combination sale prices for clubs including this with other publications?

d. Group organizers' price for this publication alone?

16. Annual subscription expirations, renewals, and percentage of renewals, for the preceding five calendar years?

17. Analysis of subscription sales for the preceding five calendar years?

18. Period (for period stated in Item 11)?

Less than one year?

One year or more but less than two years?

Two years or more?

19. Combination subscription sales for period stated in Item 11?

a. Known combination sales?

b. Known not to be in combination?

3. Subscriptions received from intermediary unable to determine whether sold in combination or not?

Total subscription sales, combination and others?

20. Premiums (for period stated in Item 11)? In sales listed below as subscriptions sold with premiums, the premiums were offered by publisher or with his knowledge.

a. Subscriptions sold with premium?

b. Subscriptions sold without premium?

Total subscriptions sold in period?

21. Average number and percent of subscription-in-arrears, up to three months, per issue for preceding five calendar years.

WHERE IS YOUR CIRCULATION?

22. Breakdown of circulation into states and counties: Canada; individual territorial possessions; and individual foreign countries. Circulation in any county amounting to less than 1 per cent of total for state may be grouped with circulation in other such counties under head "Other Counties"? (If a county breakdown would not adequately represent your particular type of audience, please give breakdown by size of towns within state, such as under 10,000, over 10,000, or give whatever type of breakdown is needed to show coverage of buying influences throughout each individual state and explain your reasons.)

23. Breakdown of circulation by industrial classifications (publications concentrating in one or more major classifications, such as food industries or process industries, should subdivide such major classifications)?

WHAT TYPE OF READERS DO YOU HAVE?

24. Breakdown of circulation by occupational functions (job interests) —covering total circulation under classifications a, b, and d only in paragraph 12?

WHAT IS YOUR EDITORIAL HISTORY—WHAT ARE YOUR POLICIES?

25. Average number of pages of editorial matter per issue during the last five years?
26. Average number of pages of paid for advertising per issue during the last five years (not including advertising by publishers, donated space, space paid for with due bills, space paid for with merchandise, and advertising exchanged with other publications)?
27. What percentage of your advertisers have been with you for more than one year? What percentage of your advertising volume does this represent?
28. Who comprise the editorial staff and what special fitness have they for addressing your particular field?
29. What percentage of your editorial space was used during past 12 months for:
    a. Original staff articles?
    b. Original contributed articles, paid for?
    c. Original contributed articles, not paid for?
    d. Organization proceedings?
    e. Material reprinted from other publications?
    f. Syndicated material (news releases, etc.)?
    g. News items?
    h. Miscellaneous (new equipment data, catalog listings, personal notes, obituaries, etc.)?
30. Do you maintain a buyer's directory?
    In each issue?
    In a special issue?
31. What are the rules governing the number of listings given each advertiser?

WHAT SPECIAL SERVICES DO YOU PROVIDE?

32. Do you maintain a copy or photograph service for advertisers?
33. What charge, if any, is made for this service?
34. Give complete information on rates.

RATE CARD INFORMATION

35. Agency commission?
36. Cash discount and general terms of payment?
37. Is any allowance made for complete plates, involving no typographical expenses on the part of the publisher?
38. Do you guarantee uniform rates to all advertisers using the same amount and kind of space? Do you make any concessions from regular advertised rates listed in Item 34? If so, explain?
39. Publication and mailing dates?
40. Forms close, with proofs   without proofs   ?
41. Will you accept unblocked electros of full plated advertisements?
42. Columns per page: Advertisements?   Editorial?
43. Page sizes: (Show only dimensions on space units regularly sold)
    a. Colors: What are Standard Colors? Cost of Standard Colors? Cost of Special Colors?
    b. What are your specifications for inserts, weights, size, etc.?
    c. What size should bleed plates be?
44. If this periodical is not of a size accommodating a 7 x 10 advertisement on one page, what is the reason for the odd size?
45. Halftone screen requirements; regulations regarding solid backgrounds, Ben Day screens, electrotypes, etc.
46. Is publication as sent to readers printed on same type and weight of stock as samples sent to advertisers and agencies? If not, explain?
    a. Are color pages and black and white pages printed on same type and weight of stock?   If not, explain?
47. If publication is a member of ABC give date of Audit statement from which information given in items 5, 8, 10, 11, 12, 15, 16, 17, 18, 19, 20, 21, 22, 23 and 24 is taken or based?
    a. If publication is a member of CCA give date of Audit statement from which information given in items 5, 8, 10, 11, 12, 14, 22, 23, 24 and 46 is taken or based?
48. Miscellaneous rules and regulations of the publisher, if any?

(Signature) . . . . Notary . . . . Title . . . .

CHAPTER 7

Production

PARTNERSHIP OF PUBLISHER AND PRINTER

Efforts of editors and the advertising men are weakened and sometimes wasted if the business publication does not reach its readers when it is supposed to reach them. But even where the time schedule is rigidly observed, if the product delivered is a poor physical presentation of the editorial and advertising content the loss is just as serious. Moreover, all the efficiencies and economies achieved in other departments of the publishing organization are cancelled out if the production costs are out of line.

This chapter is as much concerned with the type of man at the controls as it is with the methods used to operate a production department.

In the introduction to Chapter 2, it was pointed out that very few businesspaper publishers own their printing plants. The direction and supervision of this operation is a high administrative function. Production Manager is the title of the administrator in a businesspaper publishing organization who is responsible for the printing.

The operator of the print shop also must be looked upon as an executive officer of the businesspaper publishing house. In other words, as Edward McSweeney points out in this chapter, the publisher and printer must form a "mental partnership."

In many multiple publishing houses editorial make-up and editorial production are invested in the editorial department, performed by a special group of editorial art directors and layout men working with the managing editors and production men.

Editorial production know-how is discussed in Chapter 12.

In this chapter no attempt has been made to reproduce sample records or forms. There is no standard practice in systems and methods used in production. Any businesspaper publishing house will furnish a portfolio of its forms to students on request. These are known as insertion orders, advertising contract memos, work sheets, layout pages, copy follow-up cards, printing and engraving purchase orders, shipping orders, etc.

A complete bibliography on production is published by the New York Employing Printers Association.

The Joint Committee on Advertising Reproduction of the American Association of Advertising Agencies and the National Association of Magazine Publishers has published several reports on "Improving the Physical Presentation of Advertising in Magazines." Report No. 3 contains a summary of the recommended standard specifications for advertising reproduction material in magazine letter-press wet printing.

MANUFACTURING THE BUSINESSPAPER*

Let us leave the world of publishing for the time being and go into the world of paper and printing—generally referred to as "the Graphic Arts." It is a world so full of tradition that, at first glance, the outsider gets the impression it enjoys living in the past; a world full of arts and crafts that are marvels of precision, and complicated machinery that only a very skilled mechanic can understand and operate; a world that only recently has begun to feel the impact of applied sciences; a world that has had so long to develop a jargon of its own that it sounds like double-talk.

In twenty-five years in and around printing, I have never found anyone who knows the meaning of all the words. It is a world dominated by unions who have carried forward many of the traditions of the "craft guild" into the atomic age; a world where you will hear a lot of talk about "standard" hour rates and unit costs; but you will soon discover they are constantly adjusted up or down to fit an immediate situation. A world where every owner or manager is his own director of labor relations. A world that has yet to understand the full meaning of public relations. A world so fascinating that many of the people who have been inoculated with printer's ink look upon their jobs more as avocations than vocations, usually at a financial sacrifice.

To give you a better understanding of a printing plant, try to think of it as a number of different types of business under one roof. Start off by segregating the preparatory functions. A publisher does some prepara-

* Edward McSweeney, consultant to publishers, printers, paper makers, ink manufacturers; associated formerly with Butterick Pub. Co., Condé Nast, Street & Smith; from a lecture at New York University, April 7, 1947.

tory work, but we are concerned chiefly with manufacturing in a printing plant.

These functions in the printing plant, with the material the publisher has furnished, are comparable to the design, blueprint, and die-making departments of an average manufacturer. Just like any other business, these functions are the hardest to control from an expense standpoint. Because the publisher's "preparatory" functions are repetitive, they should receive constant scrutiny. In the manufacturing of short-run businesspapers, that is the place (and right now about the only place) where material progress can be made in reducing costs.

Think of the pressroom as a "Conversion" operation where raw paper is converted into a semi-finished product.[1]

The bindery can be classified as "Completion" operations and in a businesspaper printing plant, it is relatively simple except when special issues raise problems that require special handlings.

The mailing department in a large plant is a combination shipping department and post office.

Printing plants that handle all of these operations under one roof are referred to as "integrated" plants. Many of the smaller printers, particularly in the larger cities, subcontract their preparatory and completion work to trade compositors and trade binders.

Morris Goldman gave an excellent talk on rising costs at an ABP Cost Clinic. In addition to being a good statement of the problem as it affects both the publisher and the printer, he presented a list of over fifty points for the publisher to check against his own operation.[2] I have gone over Mr. Goldman's list carefully and can make only a few additional suggestions:

1. The best way to start solving your manufacturing problem is to go into a "mental partnership" with your printer. Try to learn his point of view and his problems, and even offer to help him with his labor relations.

2. Another important point, often neglected, is that the publisher should keep careful records. Be sure, too, that they are identical with the records kept by the printer.

3. Concentrate on better pre-manufacturing planning, both within your own organization and with the printer's representative, and furnish

[1] See Fig. 10 in Chapter 12.
[2] Morris Goldman, J. K. Lasser Co. "Checklist To Aid Control of Businesspaper Publishing Costs" is published by ABP for its members.

the printer with a dummy that eliminates as much guesswork as possible.

4. Check your production schedule with your printer and see if a change or adjustment in your present schedule might ease his problem.

5. Discuss with your printer the possibility of his subcontracting part of your color requirements if they are exceptionally heavy. This practice is followed in the general magazine field.

6. Review your printing contract to determine if higher base rates might result in fewer extras and lower over-all costs.

7. Study the possibility of working with your printer on a cost-plus basis.

From personal observation, I really believe that most publishers have done a very thorough job of exploring every possible way to hold their printing and paper costs in line, and that few, if any, will find the final answer to their cost problems in that direction.

The only other direction to look is towards the publisher, but that is much more difficult because it is always a lot easier to blame the printer and the unions than it is to take a good strong dose of self-appraisal.

Perhaps the best way to start is to go back to the fundamental that cost ratios are important only after something has been "sold." In other words, the publisher should never for a moment forget the importance of the selling function in his operation and that his package must always come first.

Another important point is that no one has ever devised a method of forecasting the influence of competition on costs.

If it is true that during periods of relative prosperity publishers are inclined to over-do "after the fact" research, then it is also true that as costs continue to rise, the emphasis must go over to more "before the fact" research.

IMPORTANCE OF COORDINATED PRODUCTION CONTROL*

Production in a businesspaper publishing organization is *manufacturing*. Production takes the editorial material prepared by the editors and the advertisements sold by the advertising men and turns it over to the printer to make the finished magazine.

The accomplishment of this manufacturing procedure requires a multitude of detailed operations. We call all these varied jobs that go into the manufacturing of a magazine "Production."

* Charles H. Hashagen, Treasurer and Business Manager, Lebhar-Friedman Publications, Inc., publishers of *Chain Store Age*; from a lecture at New York University, November 6, 1947.

These production activities are varied. They extend through or touch practically every other department in a publishing concern.

Some of these production functions are done in the advertising department. Some are done in the editorial department. Some may be done by the purchasing department, and some may be done in the business office. But no matter in what department they are performed, if they relate to the actual manufacture of the magazine, they are a part of production and of interest to us here.

To get a picture of all the operations that go into the manufacturing of a business magazine, let us list them:

FUNCTIONS IN MANUFACTURING A BUSINESSPAPER

1. Securing appropriate facilities for the printing, binding, and mailing of the magazines
2. Purchasing necessary paper stock for the magazine
3. Processing the editorial manuscript that the editors write, sending it to the printer, checking on galley proofs, making up dummies, and okeying page and stone proofs
4. Preparing the editorial layouts, ordering art, photos, and cuts
5. Collecting the advertising copy, sending to printer, sending out proofs, correcting ads, keeping cut records, and watching position and color
6. Making up the book; laying out the pages of the book in proper order to take care of advertising and editorial material
7. Instructing the printer for the most economical handling of printing
8. Checking printer for quality and delivery
9. Checking bills, paper consumption, and waste
10. Preparing wrappers or envelopes for the prompt dispatch of the issue
11. And last—but by no means least in importance—scheduling all operations so they will synchronize and be done on time

These jobs cover a lot of territory. All of them are a part of every publisher's manufacturing process, from the smallest paper to the largest organization.

Who should perform each of these tasks, who should be responsible, is the first point to be considered.

If we were to check a dozen business publications, we would probably find that in each one these jobs are performed by different individuals in various departments. There is no "standard" method of organization.

Each publisher assigns these jobs differently. But among the publishers who have an efficient production procedure, one condition is common to all—such companies have a coordinated control of all production activities.

The experience of successful publishers has shown that no matter who performs the various production jobs, no matter what department handles them, all production functions must be coordinated through central supervision and responsibility. And this is true in a small company as well as a large organization.

It does not matter whether the job is given to a vice-president in a large company, a business manager, production manager, managing editor, or make-up editor; no matter what you call him, one man should be responsible for all production so as to give "coordinated control." And, this is the most important point: The production manager given this job must have the authority equal to the task of coordinating all parts of the manufacturing process.

Without coordinated control a publishing company cannot manufacture efficiently to mail on time.

Without coordinated control, a company cannot produce its magazine most economically.

Let us go over these various production activities one by one to see how coordinated control helps, and the lack of it hinders, efficient production operation.

1. *Procuring Printing and Mailing Facilities.* Engaging a printer is, naturally, a very important step. The contract is usually signed by the principals of the publisher and the printer. But the first step toward coordinated control begins here. The production manager who is to be given the job and responsibility of getting out the books should be present at all discussions and negotiations with the printer. If he is not present at such meetings he is considered of only secondary importance by the printer and cannot, therefore, be effective in his day-to-day contacts with the printer after the deal is made.

Thus, the first link in coordinated control is building up the production manager as your representative in all matters that affect printing of your magazine at his plant.

As an example of the importance of this, I can remember my own experience many years ago when I first started in this business. I took over a replacement job as production man on an established trade paper.

The arrangements for printing had been made between the publisher and the owner of the print shop a long time before. They were on very friendly terms. In my brushes with the printer on getting out ad proofs, getting galleys back in a hurry, having forms put on promptly, getting delivery on time, it was quite difficult for me because I was just a new-comer without much standing.

The printer and his superintendent paid little heed to my complaints, and it was only when I could bring my boss, the owner, into a particular situation that I was able to get what I wanted. This, of course, was a difficult position for me as well as an inefficient one for the company. I had a devil of a time getting the job done as I knew it should be handled. It was not until some time later when I was able, through my own efforts, to effect a change to a new printer that I was able to do a more efficient job. The new printer had some respect for my authority, and I was then able to relieve my superior of the petty annoyances of day-to-day contacts with the printer. I accomplished a better production job for my company.

Recently a young man with the title of production manager had been instructed by his publisher that he was not to go into the printer's plant. Apparently this request emanated from the printer. I cannot undertsand why the printer did not want any representative of a publishing customer in his composing or press room unless he had something to hide. And, if there was anything the printer was trying to hide it was to the pub-lisher's interest to have his man on the job.

If the publisher had built up his man in importance the question of entering his plant would never have come up. There is no question that the production manager should have the right to go into any part of the printing plant at the time his work is being done.

If you make a clerk or office boy out of your production man, his efforts when dealing with the printer will be ineffectual.

Having the production manager active in contract relations, either on a new contract or renewal, can save a publisher money too. Who but an active production man knows of the little things that can save money on a job? Often a publisher is approached for a 15 or 20 per cent increase on going rates by his printer. This should open up the opportunity to review costs of certain detailed operations. A production man who knows his job should be able to spot leaks in a contract. Give him an oppor-tunity when your contract is up for renewal. Maybe your printer's charge for split rollers is way off from current practices. Maybe his rate on bleed pages is way out of line. Maybe the charge for extra proofs is unreasonable. Maybe the paper waste scale is too liberal. Or maybe your contract does not provide for any set waste scale, which it surely should.

These are some of the loopholes an experienced production man can detect. He can help a publisher if he is given an opportunity to get into the situation before the contract is signed.

To do his job properly, a production man must at all times work closely with the printer so as to be aware of his problems, and should be in a position to help him whenever he can. A production manager should interpret the needs of his company to the printer and at the same time should get the cooperation from his own organization in doing what the printer requires.

2. *Purchasing Paper Stock.* The man responsible for production, in addition to having a very definite voice in the selection of the plant that does his work, should have a very definite say in the materials that go into the production. While the editor's, publisher's, and advertising man's opinions as to the kind of stock best suited to the needs of their field must be regarded, it should be left entirely to the production manager to secure it. Given the need, who is in a better position than a competent production manager to keep informed as to what paper is currently available and what quantities he should buy? Who but the production manager should be responsible for checking the records on the receipt of the paper, the consumption for each issue, the amount of waste charged against each issue, checking the paper bills, and checking the physical inventory periodically at the plant? These are all vital parts of production, and they must be governed by one individual. The responsibility of having the stock on hand when it is needed, in the proper size should not be divided.

Yet I know of a case where the paper records on a trade paper published here in New York are being kept by a bookkeeper as a confidential record. Before this concern's production manager can print the issue he has to inquire as to whether there is enough paper on hand. Why this is done I cannot imagine unless the publisher does not want the production man to know what he is paying for paper. It should be obvious that such a situation is just ridiculous.

In securing paper, the production manager should be left to scout out the sources, if not actually sign contracts, and he should be given the full responsibility for maintaining adequate paper supply, checking paper records, paper waste, and other details that enter into it.

I talked with a production man the other day about paper waste. I asked him how much he allowed his printer. He said they had no set rate. The contract was made by the publisher. Having no set waste scale these days is like doing a job cost-plus. You are very vulnerable. Paper is part of the production manager's job and he should have a hand in it from the beginning: check on the use of every last sheet if you want to save money on paper. If you divide this responsibility, your production operation just cannot be completely successful.

3. *Processing Editorial Manuscript*. I suppose that in most publishing organizations, the decision as to what type face to use, type style, etc., is usually considered one of the editor's prerogatives, but here, too, such decisions should only be made with the advice of the production manager.

I remember a case in our office some years ago where an editor had a special box to set. The job was given to a new man to specify. He had a wonderful time with the printer's type specimen book picking out certain faces of just the right style, etc. He did not realize that what he ordered was monotype which took longer to set and cost much more. After days of delay, he finally got his proof and at the end of the month we got the extra bill. It did not take us long to educate this new man into "checking production" thereafter on any new ideas.

The production manager who is abreast of his job knows all the type that is available at his printer's shop, the matrixes that are available in the largest supply, the possibility of getting new type faces, and the other technical considerations that enter into the final decision. Of course, mechanical factors are not the only considerations entering into a decision, but if editors make decisions on type styles that require hand insets, monotype composition, hand composition, etc., without checking with the production manager, you are likely to have extra cost and require extra time in the setting of editorial material.

In devising the routine of handling manuscripts, the question of whether to make corrections on the galleys or page proofs, the method of handling dummies, okeying pages and stone proofs, etc., should be left to the production manager's judgment. If he is equal to his job, he most surely will know the peculiarities of the print shop he is using so that, in supplying copy, your system will be in keeping with the printer's method, assuring a prompt and better handling of all copy.

The production manager's position in this may seem obvious to us, yet I remember a case where a production manager of my acquaintance just was not allowed to handle the editor's copy. In this case the editor was so afraid to have anyone else handle his manuscript that he insisted on sending it directly to the printer without the production manager having the opportunity to look at it. I hope this situation does not prevail in any of the companies you are connected with, because it stands to reason that if there is so little mutual cooperation the production manager simply cannot function efficiently.[3]

The responsibility of the preparation of editorial material is twofold as I see it. The editorial department is responsible for writing the material and having it ready in time to meet the publication schedules, and it is the production manager's responsibility to have the material put through promptly and proofs returned to the editor quickly to allow ample time to read and correct where necessary.

4. *Preparing Editorial Layouts, Art, Photos, and Cuts.* In this activity, the responsibility is usually that of the editor. Although some organizations employ an art director, he has practically the last word in anything that affects appearance.

In our office, the art and engraving departments are under the supervision of the production manager. We feel justified in this, because the production manager can keep in touch with the work in progress to be sure that all deadlines along the way of preparation are met.

In some organizations, the activity of making editorial page layouts, ordering art, ordering engravings, etc., is made a part of the editorial department's activities, and is under the responsibility of a managing editor. This is satisfactory, providing the managing editor has the constant consideration of closing dates and is religious in adhering to them.

It is our experience, however, that while editors have the best of intentions, they do not always see the over-all operation from the same perspective. They are not as concerned about closing dates as a production manager who has this as a prime responsibility and who should, therefore, be in a position to regulate and speed up every operation that enters into the manufacturing process.

In the ordering of engravings there is another advantage aside from the matter of control that makes it advisable to give this responsibility to the production manager. By concentrating your buying, you probably can get better work, better prices, and better delivery. If you have several

---

[3] In many multiple publishing houses a member of the editorial staff, often the managing editor, handles all editorial production. Sometimes he is assisted by an art director.

people in the organization ordering from the same suppliers, each party interested in their own book, or activity, you are virtually in competition with yourselves. When this ordering of engravings or artwork, for example, is done through a central source, the party doing the ordering can take advantage of volume and may be able to effect better prices and can distribute the work more evenly so that one artist or engraving house does not have too much of your own work at any one time. Furthermore, by segregating this activity you can effect a more orderly system of follow-up for delivery on time and checking on the bills for recharging.

5. *Advertising Copy*. The advertising department sells the space, and it should be the responsibility of every salesman to get his copy in. When a salesman sells a contract, the space is only half sold. It is not until you get the copy, print it, and deliver the magazine to the reader that you can really ring up the sale on the cash register.

We have tried to make advertising copy follow-up the individual responsibility of each salesman and we have tried to have it done by the secretaries in the advertising department. While they have been able to do a fair job in most cases, we find that the most effective job of follow-up is done by handling it in the production department under the immediate supervision of the production manager. Having one person on a book make all the telephone contacts with agencies and advertisers has several advantages.

In the first place we find that there are no promises made to accept copy after our designated closing date. The production people who handle this have a keener interest in getting the copy in on time. In following up on copy they are more careful to ask about color, bleed, and other details that are so important to know before the book is made up. People in the advertising department simply do not have a realization of the importance of such details and often forget to inquire about them.

The practice in following up copy varies with each organization. Our experience has proven that there is a distinct advantage in having the activity regulated, if not supervised, by the production manager. It is only by so doing that we have all the information at hand at the time the book is laid out. And, as we shall learn later, it is the exceptional happening that adds to our production difficulties and production expenses.

6. *Making Up the Book*. This is the customary way of referring to the procedure of planning the book by pages. I suppose everyone realizes that this should be the undisputed function of the production department.

Yet how many times is a production man or make-up man hogtied by some unfortunate special position commitment made by an advertising space salesman, or by an editor's demand for color or added pages?

The practice in some small organizations is to leave the actual make-up to the printer so that he can decide for himself as to the most economical way of arranging the pages in forms. What trust these publishers must have in their printer!

Make-up is a very important part of the whole activity and a production man who is competent in laying out forms can save many times his salary cost in a year on this one activity alone. Leaving the make-up to the responsible head of the production department, who has control of both editorial and advertising, provides the opportunity to concentrate on certain forms and to give more time on others. The printer therefore can get an earlier start on some forms with a later closing on others so as to cut down on the time between closing and issuance date. When this activity is divided, say between advertising and editorial departments, the operation cannot be as efficient.

This, of all functions, calls for coordinated control. The number of advertising pages that are coming in affect the number of editorial pages that should be run. The total should be decided according to a formula left to the production manager to execute. The placing of color advertisements, the watching of preferred positions, the placing of color editorial pages—all can be very costly unless carefully laid out by the production man who is in a position to take into account the requirements of advertising department, editorial department, and printer's press and binding equipment.

7. *Instructing the Printer*. Unless the printer recognizes one individual in an organization that he is responsible to it is very difficult, if not impossible, for a publication to get the best quality and delivery. The fellow who gives the print order, or instructions, should be the man who checks the fulfillment of the print order, and he alone should contact the printer. If you have more than one person calling the printer without knowledge of what the other person is demanding, things could easily get balled up. If the demands on the printer are screened through one individual, he can insist upon those things that are most important and give more time on those which are less important. If this was left up to the printer, he would not be in the position to judge between two requests. All communications with the printer, therefore, should be routed through one production man or production department.

8. *Checking Printer for Quality and Delivery.* When it comes to checking on the results, this job is obviously the production manager's. If he has proper control of all of the activities that have gone into the job, and has been able to deliver the material to the printer as promised, he will be able to insist on the various activities being performed by the printer on time. If he has full knowledge of all the operations, he will not allow any printer to alibi his way out. But I think you can realize how impossible it would be for a production manager to ask or insist on delivery and quality if he has not been familiar with all the circumstances. To the printer, the production manager should represent the magazine. At the same time, he himself should be fully responsible to the printer for the proper execution of activities of the publishing organization on which the printer must depend. When the activities are performed well from his end, he has a right to insist on the printer's performance being done well and on time. If the printer does not perform his part of the work properly, then the production manager should have the right to correct the situation. It is only by a full realization of the responsibility of all departments in the publishing house to cooperate with the printer that an efficient job can be accomplished.

9. *Checking Invoices.* Where the production manager is in control of all operations, there is no one better than he to check the invoices, paper consumption, and other practices. He alone is in the best position to check and stop the costly practices of poor copy preparation, unnecessary office corrections, press delays, and other such items of waste.

Some years ago a friend of mine who was production manager of a technical paper had the responsibility of preparing all the editorial material, ordering the cuts, and okeying the proofs; yet he was never given an opportunity to check the printer's bill. He used to get the usual riding from the publisher about authors' corrections, yet he was unable to do much about it because the publisher, for some reason or other, did not want him to see what he was paying. The checking of the bills was left to some confidential bookkeeper. This is simply shortsightedness. To try to keep rates on operations from a production manager who has the responsibility for the job is just plain silly.

10. *Preparing Wrappers or Envelopes.* This operation is usually a part of the circulation routine, yet in the standard ABP Cost Breakdown, the cost of running off the stencils on the labels as well as the cost of the container is considered a mechanical, or production, expense. How this operation is charged is of little concern here. However, it is another ac-

tivity that the production manager has to be sure is performed on time. If all the other departments supplied the material as per schedule, and the printer completed his binding, and the wrappers, or envelopes, were not ready, he could lose all the good he has accomplished by control up to this point.

So here, too, the production manager should be watchful that wrappers or envelopes are addressed and available on time to meet mailing needs and the material supplied in a way that assures efficient handling at the plant.

11. *Scheduling Operations: Advertising and Editorial Closing Dates.* In my mind, this is one of the most important elements of production. Unless you have someone in authority within your organization who can prepare schedules for all departments and for the printer, and make them adhere to these schedules, you are bound to lose in production efficiency.

Sticking to schedules may be difficult, but it is the only way that I have ever found that you can come out on time. This is a job that must be given to someone in a neutral corner. If we leave it to an advertising man, or to an editorial man, either is bound to be influenced by his own difficulties or advantages. A bonafide schedule should be drawn up which takes into account the obligations of a publication to its subscribers, the requirements of the advertising and editorial departments, and the facilities of the printer. A production man who is capable will weigh all these considerations and prepare a realistic schedule that it is possible to maintain.

To get the advertising manager or managing editor to keep to a schedule is probably the hardest job a production manager has. We all are familiar with the advertising manager (or the publisher) who will hold an issue for days (or a week) to get in one more advertising page plate and that last two hundred dollars. Look at it impartially: such a practice is both unwise and unfair.

First, it is unfair to thousands of subscribers to hold up news information for days or a week. Second, it is unfair to all the other advertisers in the issue who have made your closing date on time with messages they consider vital for your readers. Third, it is unfair to your printer in disrupting his schedule, because you are rarely his only customer. Fourth, it embarrasses your production man who has tried to keep to schedule. He loses face with the printer. Fifth, in delaying an issue, you shorten the reading life of your publication. Sixth, you delay collections to some extent of advertising revenue. Seventh, you probably delay payment of your own bills from suppliers as a result. Eighth, you place yourself at the mercy of advertising agencies who conclude you would not dare close an issue until their copy arrived.

Against this you pick up a couple of extra dollars (which you might have got anyway in the next issue). The gain to your company is not the gross amount of the space. Deduct the agency commission, the sales-

Layout for_____ Date_____

Kind of form_____

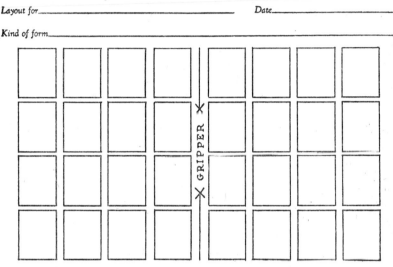

Fig. 2 Printer's imposition sheet is made up by the publication's production manager to show how color is to run. A separate sheet is used for each form.

man's cut, the cash discount, the cost of printing the ad, overhead, and there is not much left. The reasons for holding an issue for the one last ad are small and costly compared to the many reasons for keeping to schedule.

When you play fast and loose with a schedule, it does not take a printer long to realize that the production manager does not have the authority in his own outfit. Then the printer takes little liberties himself with deadlines. Publishers often pay time-and-a-half for overtime to the printer in a desperate attempt to come out on time after accepting advertising copy after deadlines, and the situation grows from bad to worse. To repeat: Getting the book out on time requires the full cooperation of all departments with the production manager so that he can fulfill his pledge to the printer and the publisher's pledge to the reader. Unless this is done, you can never expect deliveries of your publication on time from the printer.

SUMMARY

The production department is in contact with all other departments of a businesspaper publishing house, and requires an unusual amount of cooperation from all departments. Editors must produce a good content so the circulation department can sell it. The circulation department must do its part in selling a good portion of the field, so the advertising department can sell the advertiser. The production department must produce the book in time and in a way to satisfy the reader and the advertiser and the auditor and owner. It requires team play all around.

THE "EFFICIENT JOURNAL VERSUS THE "DISORGANIZED REVIEW"*

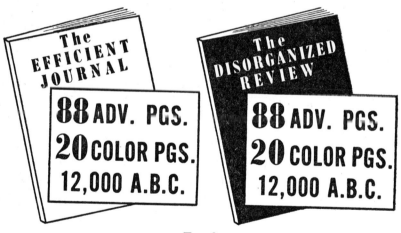

FIG. 3

These two hypothetical trade papers (Fig. 3) are practically alike.

1. Both have the same number of advertising pages—88 in each.
2. Both have the same number of color pages—20 in each.
3. Both have a paid circulation of 12,000.
4. Both are printed on the same weight and grade of paper stock.

Now the most important fact to keep in mind is that the costs of all printing operations have been computed on identical rates in both publishing properties. As a matter of fact, we can assume they are printed in the same shop, under identical conditions. The unit rates we have used in projecting these figures are going rates for printing in a metropolitan area, under today's conditions (1947).

Despite the fact that these two papers are practically identical, the "Efficient Journal" cost $4302 to produce, while the "Disorganized Review" cost $5640, or $1300 more. This is an actual difference in printing cost of 31 per cent. How can two papers with the same advertising, same amount of color, same circulation, same paper, and same printing rates be 31 per cent apart in printing costs? The answer is easy.

It simply represents the difference between coordinated control and cooperation on the one hand and the absence of it on the other.

In the "Disorganized Review" many decisions affecting production were made by others in the production department without consulting the production manager, or made outside the department in disregard of the production manager's suggestions. In the "Efficient Journal" the production manager took an active part in the planning and, as a result the publisher was able to save over $1300 on one month's issue!

Let us analyze the reasons for the 31 per cent difference on the cost of these publications.

In the first place, in the "Efficient Journal" the editorial pages were in control. This publication decided on a ratio of 69 per cent advertising to 31 per cent text. The production manager planned the book with this in mind and the editor was obliged to accommodate his needs within that total. They sold 88 pages of advertising, had 40 pages of text, and ran a total of 128 pages.

The "Disorganized Review" on this point was careless. Here, the editor insisted that he could not get along with so little text. He claimed he simply had to have at least eight more pages. The production manager without authority to refuse had to give in to him. These eight pages, on a base of 128 pages, added more than 6 per cent to its size and approximately the same amount to its cost. So this one detail resulted in an extra expenditure for printing—besides added cost for manuscripts, art, or cuts—of $295.

I am not suggesting that your own publication should allow but 31

* Charles H. Hashagen, Business Manager, *Chain Store Age*, from a lecture, New York University, November 6, 1947.

per cent for text pages. However, that figure is a reasonable one. Many successful business publications keep to that percentage and some good businesspapers use even less. The point I want to emphasize is that the amount of text you provide should be based on a definite formula related to your gross income. This formula should be established for a quarter or for a year's operation, since it is not always possible to keep to an exact percentage in any one month due to the break in the forms. However, by keeping a record of editorial pages over and under the number, you should finish the year within three pages of your allotment.

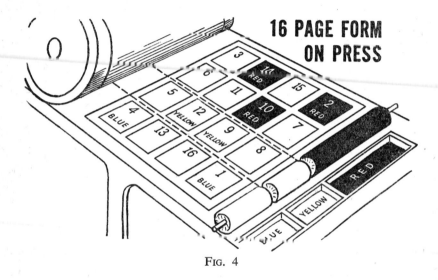

FIG. 4

The second point of difference between these two magazines:

In both cases, the editorial department used three color pages, a spread in color, and a section cover in color.

The difference in the two magazines was that the editor of the "Disorganized Review" insisted that the section cover be a bleed page and run in blue in a certain position among the text pages. This had to be provided despite the protests of the production manager. Because of the extra color and the bleed and particular position, it was necessary to print the form twice, causing an extra impression on the full sheet.

In the "Efficient Journal" the production manager, with the cooperation of the editor, was able to give him a color spread and section cover;

but by changing the color in the editorial spread to pick up an advertiser's color and by redesigning the section cover slightly so as to eliminate the color bleed at the top and bottom of the page, he was able to save an extra color impression on a 16-page run.

Before we go any further into this matter of extra color impressions, it is important that we have a clear understanding as to what this operation entails. I have prepared this simplified picture of a press to illustrate how color pages are handled (Fig. 4). (This is not the form under discussion. This is another we introduced here to explain split rollers.)

As you probably know, most businesspapers are printed in sheets of 16 pages, that is 9×12 pages sixteen at a time. This is the most economical unit for a book of this page size. If we run an 8, the proportionate cost per page would be more, and if we printed it 4 pages, or 2 pages, at a time, the cost would be still more. The more large 16-page forms we use for a job, the more economical it is to print.

When we print 16 pages at a time, 4 across and 4 up and down, the pages are arranged in the printing form in a way that will make them face one another and back up one another in proper sequence when the printed sheet is folded. But the pages laid out on a single sheet do not necessarily come together in a form. In fact in most cases they are apart. This operation of laying out the pages so that they will come in the proper sequence when the sheets are folded is a technical operation known as *imposition* (Fig. 2).

It is the imposition of any form that determines the best place for color pages to run. There are many ways to fold the sheet, depending on the printer's binding equipment, and therefore there are many different types of impositions. A production manager has to be familiar with the various ways a job can be handled in his plant to determine which one is best and most economical on a particular job.

When we come to print color in a large form, we are sometimes able to print several colors at the same time by using a device known as a split roller, or split fountain. By having the printer cut his ink roller and split the fountain, we are able to print 2, 3, or even 4 colors on different pages at one time in one single run through the press (Fig. 4).

In the lower right-hand corner is the ink roller and fountain which you can see has been cut to separate the red, yellow, and blue. At each revolution of the press the ink roller gathers up a certain amount of ink from the ink fountain and rolls over the pages to ink them in preparation for the sheet that is to be printed.

In this example one-half the roller is printing in red, which can take care of the eight pages on the upper half of the form. However, in this case, we are printing red on only three of the eight pages in these two channels. If it were necessary we could have printed red on the five other pages on this half of the form without any additional press cost. One-fourth of this roller is printing in yellow, and we have four pages that can carry yellow, but in this case only two are being printed in yellow. The last quarter of the roller is printing blue, and two of the four pages in that channel are being printed in blue and the other two have no color.

The DISORGANIZED REVIEW

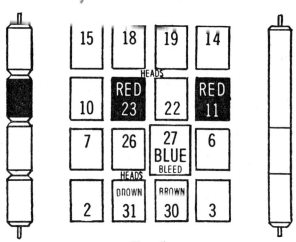

Fig. 5

Now you can see from this that if someone had insisted on running a red ad on page 5, for example, it would have come in the same channel as the yellow ads and necessitated, therefore, printing the 16-page sheet again for just one page. Obviously, we could not print yellow and red in the same channel at the same time. We can print different colors at the same time providing they are in different channels. We could have printed red on pages 3, 15, 6, 11, or 7 without any extra expense, but we could not have printed red in 5, 8, 13, or 16 without incurring an extra rerun of the entire form.

One other detail in this connection. There always has to be one and one-half or two inches between color plates in each channel to allow for a split roller on a press. If they came closer than that it is likely that the two colors would overlap and blend together, producing an off-color reproduction.

Advertising men and editors do not have to worry about this technical detail. This is the job of the production manager. I use this example to illustrate, as simply as possible, just how it is possible to print several colors at one time and on the other hand how impossible it is to print the same color on certain other pages without going into an extra run.

The DISORGANIZED REVIEW

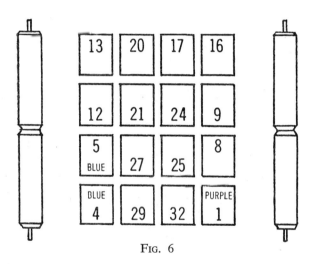

FIG. 6

Now, getting back to our two publications again.

As mentioned before, the second point of difference between these two magazines was in the editorial color pages. The editor on the "Disorganized Review" had planned for a *blue* bleed section cover which he required to be run on page 27. In addition he had a color spread which he insisted be run in brown on pages 30 and 31. Here is the form laid out on the press (Fig. 5). Because of the bleed on the top and bottom of page 27, there was not sufficient room for a split roller so as to print the brown on pages 30 and 31, and the red on 11 and 23 at the same time. It was necessary, therefore, to run an extra impression for this section cover to comply with the editor's demands. We will see in a minute how this situation was improved on the "Efficient Journal."

The advertising department on the "Disorganized Review" caused some extra expense too. They had a commitment of a blue spread to run somewhere in the first 8 pages of the magazine. This had been expected as it had been running for months in this position. But, without knowledge of the production department, the advertising department had accepted an ad in purple, the lower part of which was bleed, promising

The EFFICIENT JOURNAL

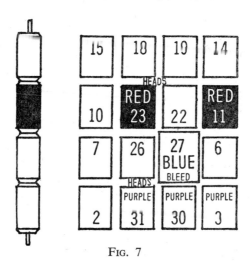

Fig. 7

the advertiser the first page in the book. This was the way the form looked on the press (Fig. 6). You can see from this that because the purple ad on page 1 ran in the same channel with the blue on page 4, it required an extra printing of this sheet. There was no other place to put the blue spread. The other spreads ahead of page 8, the position promised, pages 2 and 3 and 6 and 7, were on the other side of the sheet, which would have required another impression on that side. So, under any circumstances, this position, even though there were only three ads involved, requires three impressions, one black, one purple, and one blue, to accommodate the commitments made by the advertising department.

Now, here is the way the editorial and advertising pages were handled on the "Efficient Journal" through the cooperation between editorial, advertising, and production. Because of the give and take, they were able to print all the editorial pages and advertising pages in one form requiring only one black and one color impression (Fig. 7).

In the first place, the advertising department checked with the production department before committing themselves to page 1 and they found that while the production department could not put the ad on page 1 without extra expenses they could take it on page 3. The advertising department then sold it for page 3. At the same time the production manager prevailed upon the editor to change the color on his color

The EFFICIENT JOURNAL   The DISORGANIZED REVIEW

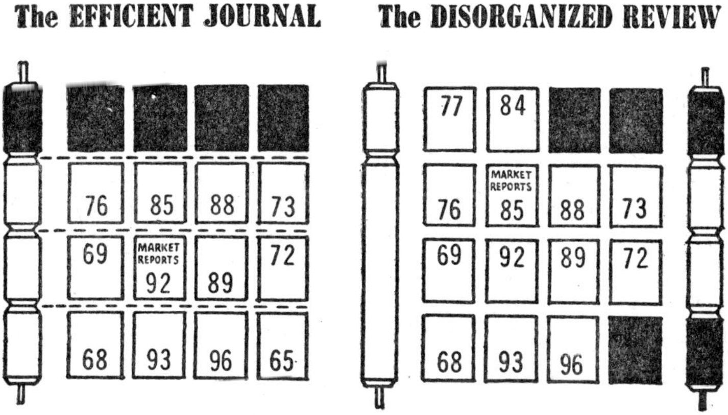

FIG. 8

spread 30 and 31 from brown to purple, inasmuch as the color used on these pages was only background and headline. In addition, the editor consented to change the design of his bleed section cover on page 27 so that there was a bleed in the black form rather than the blue form, thereby permitting the use of a split roller between the blue pages and the purple pages at the bottom and between the blue pages and red pages at the top, thereby printing all these color pages in but one color impression.

The net result of these adjustments on the part of the advertising department and the change of color and modification of design by the editorial department effected a net saving of $450.

Here is the third point of difference between these papers.

In the "Disorganized Review" the advertising department sold an advertiser a position opposite a special feature called "Market Reports" in the back of the book. It was reported that this ad was coming in in red. Going on this information, the production department in laying out the book placed the ad in a certain position on page 84, and the text feature opposite on page 85. Due to careless follow-up on copy, the plates came in late and with them a progressive proof showing that the ad was to be printed in a special orange. Since this page was planned to run in a channel with other red ads, and it was too late to change this page, the production department had no alternative but to print this form twice.

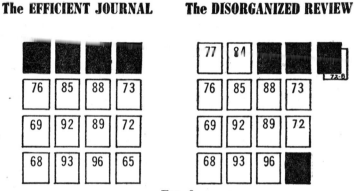

FIG. 9

We see the sheet as it was printed in the "Disorganized Review" (Fig. 8). Note that the page in orange, page 84, comes in the same channel as the red color on pages 80 and 81. There being no time to change the position of the feature, in order to print the ad an extra run on the form was necessary, costing $150.

In the "Efficient Journal" the production department knew in time that the ad was coming in in special orange. It arranged to have the editorial feature "Market Reports" placed on page 92, so that the orange could be run opposite on page 93 in a channel by itself to print at the same time as the red without an additional impression. The form in the left in this case (Fig. 8) shows how this was printed, thereby saving $150.

In these examples you may get the impression that the situations cited are unlikely to happen in one publication. Any production manager knows that each one of these things happen every month on most businesspapers.

Another situation that accounted for part of the difference in cost: I said that both papers finished with a total of 88 pages of advertising. However, in the case of the "Disorganized Review" they only had 87 when they made up the book. After the main book had been released, the advertising department was able to pick up another page in color which the advertising manager insisted should be run in the current issue.

The color form had already been put on the press. It would have been a terrific expense to lift it and reimpose the form. The only alternative was to print a special two-page insert and include it as a separate form. To do this the production manager of the "Disorganized Review" had to supply one blank page to back it up. The cost of the composition, the added paper, the printing, and the binding by hand involved in inserting this two-page form totaled up to $183, which was a considerable portion of the net revenue from this page (Fig. 9).

After deducting sales cost and printing and binding cost, the difference between income and cost was very slight.

In the "Efficient Journal" the salesman on this account was more alert. He followed his account more carefully, got the ad in on time, and made it possible for the production department to include it in one of the existing color forms without the extra run, thereby saving $178 in production cost in this one operation.

WRAPPERS AND ENVELOPES

The business manager of the "Disorganized Review" had a fetish that the only way the publication should be mailed to subscribers was in envelopes. This is very nice; it protects the book, and the magazine arrives flat. But the publication pays more for its envelopes and more for the cost of inserting. Actually, a total of $237 to the cost for the operations and the envelopes.

The "Efficient Journal" on the other hand was not governed by guess in this activity. By conducting a simple survey of its readers it found that, for all practical purposes, wrappers proved just as effective a protection for the magazine and did not affect the condition of the book on its arrival. Therefore they arranged to mail their books in wrappers at a cost of $106 for the material and operation, which saved them $131 (Table 7).

OVERRUNS

The circulation department also may be held responsible for a small part of the loss on the "Disorganized Review." Both publications have a 12,000 ABC circulation. The circulation manager of the "Efficient Journal" watched carefully his overrun, solicitations, free lists, etc. In the case of the "Disorganized Review," the circulation manager ordered 1000 overrun without too much investigation to determine whether he could get along with fewer copies. The "Efficient Journal," by watching the free copies, kept overrun to 500, making the total run 12,500. The difference in the total run was a matter of 4 per cent. Although the cost of extra copies on any run is obviously less per 1000 than the original run, in this case the actual cost of the paper for the extra run, the running time, and the extra binding came to $135, adding that much more to the loss on the publication.

TABLE 7. TOTAL SAVINGS BETWEEN THE TWO PUBLICATIONS THROUGH COOPERATION OF DEPARTMENTS AND COORDINATED CONTROL

Saving eight text pages	$ 295.00
Changing preferred advertising position and adjusting color in text form	450.00
Knowing before closing about special color required on ad sold opposite "Market Reports"	150.00
Getting last color ad early to eliminate separate 2-page form	178.00
Mailing issue in wrappers instead of envelopes	131.00
Saving 500 copies on overrun	135.00
TOTAL	$1,338.00—31%

Table 7 is a tabulation of the savings of the various operations we have reviewed, showing how each operation (seemingly small in itself) added to the others, making the considerable difference of $1338, or 31 per cent, in the printing cost of the two nearly identical publications, for one month's operations.

While these, of course, are hypothetical examples, they are based on actual situations that happen every month in a businesspaper publishing concern.

In these times of high cost it is necessary to review all unit operations of the printer, try to hold down on unit cost, take advantage of the best paper prices, buy the most economical size, etc.; but the real advantage comes in better over-all control of production operations in your own shop. Coordinated control of all production activities, given to some one expert who has the authority to effectively regulate all production operations, is the one best way to perform an efficient production operation.

TABLE 8. SUMMARY OF STATISTICS OF THE HYPOTHETICAL PUBLICATIONS "EFFICIENT JOURNAL" AND "DISORGANIZED REVIEW"

	"Efficient Journal"	"Disorganized Review"
Number of ad pages	88	88
Number of color pages	20	20
ABC subscribers	12,000	12,000
Printing cost at current metropolitan rates	$4,302.00	$5,640.00
Saving between both costs	$1,338.00 (31%)	
Advertising income on an assumed net average of $200 per page	$17,600.00	$17,600.00
Ratio of printing cost to advertising income	24.4%	31.8%

Part Two

Editorial Department

CHAPTER 8

Editorial Problems

FOUR DIMENSIONS OF EDITORIAL SERVICE

The intelligent advertising space buyer never judges a businesspaper by its circulation alone. In deciding which businesspaper to use and which not to use the most important consideration goes to editorial appeal. In every survey I have ever seen on the subject, editorial appeal is placed far ahead of all other considerations.

To an intelligent publisher who wants to make more money this can suggest only one course: constantly improve the quality of the editorial service.

No one ever improved the quality of a product by giving less value, by substituting inferior material, by hiring second-rate people, or by doing nothing.

One of the deans of businesspaper publishing practice, Colonel Chevalier, named four "dimensions" of editorial service at a recent gathering of his colleagues.[1]

He named as the first dimension:

1. ADEQUATE COVERAGE OF THE FIELD

The editors of a businesspaper must have extensive and frequent contact with the leaders and managers in the industry they serve. Their publication must reach an ever larger number of the units in their industry. They must render a more flexible and authoritative service to readers, Colonel Chevalier said.

Today adequate coverage of any field is a big job because of the rapid change taking place   turnover in key men; new and expanding plants; facility conversions; entirely new industries and products; new attitudes.

---

[1] Colonel Willard Chevalier, Executive Vice-President, McGraw-Hill Publishing Co., at the annual meeting of The Associated Business Publications, The Homestead, Hot Springs, Va., May, 1951.

"We will never return to normal," Colonel Chevalier said. "The only normal is the abnormal."

He named as his second dimension:

2. INTERPRETATION AND GUIDANCE

"We must develop sound and temperate judgment of what is happening all around us," Colonel Chevalier said. "Because of the abnormal conditions we work in we cannot afford to be exclusive crusaders for the special field we serve." We must guide our readers in the formation of opinion on broad subjects by supplying the right information.

"The most dangerous thing in a democracy is opinions without understanding," Chevalier said. "We teach the right to know something about the subject on which one has an opinion." Too much editorial opinion is often based on opinions expressed by industrial or trade association leaders with selfish motives and too little facts—not quite willing to stick the editor's neck out. The third dimension:

3. EFFECTIVE PRESENTATION

So many distractions battle for the time and interest of the reader that we must go back to school and learn (a) how to use pictures and type; (b) how to use words; (c) more functional makeup.

The fourth dimension:

4. ECONOMY OF PRODUCTION

Editors and their assistants must be trained in the economics of putting a modern businesspaper together.

The information on production which relates to the editorial manuscript is contained in Part Two, Chapter 12, but should be studied in connection with Chapter 7 on production in Part One.

Editors will find it necessary to understand the operations of all departments in the modern businesspaper publishing house, in order to perform their own functions smoothly and efficiently. By this process they place themselves in line to become tomorrow's businesspaper publishers.

EDITORIAL CONTENT—OR DISCONTENT?*

The question, "Editorial content—or discontent?" is posed for two reasons. First, it affords a chance to impress upon you the importance

* Julien Elfenbein, lecture given at New York University, February 5, 1947, and University of Wisconsin, April, 1947.

in business journalism of word-meanings. For instance, the word "content." With the accent on the last syllable the *Oxford Dictionary* defines it as "satisfied with something." It also defines content, with the accent on the first syllable, as "the amount that a vessel can contain," or "what is contained in a house, or a book, or a mind."

You have here one word with two distinctly different meanings by shifting the accent of your voice. So it is with many words. Many words when printed indicate no accent. You depend on the context. You use a word to describe what you mean. The listener or reader takes it to describe what he means. Do you both mean the same thing? If you do, that is communication. If you do not, that is confusion.[2] In business journalism it is essential first to understand something correctly, then to write so the reader understands exactly what *you* understand.

If editorial content means the amount of information contained between the covers of a businesspaper, exclusive of the advertising messages, I have no fault to find with the word; but if editorial content means a state of satisfaction with things as they are, smug complacency, approval of the *status quo*, or any sort of tranquillity or mental contentment, then I cannot hold with the term "content." I give it back to the Carnation people who use the slogan "Milk from contented cows." The business press readership does not thrive on a milk-toast diet.

There is nothing contented about a successful businesspaper editor because his readership is never contented. In a good editor, on a successful businesspaper, there exists a spiritual discontent which simply reflects the discontent of the thinking minds in the editor's own field; the divine discontent of all creative minds—a discontent which springs from a desire to improve something: a product or service or function, a job, a business, an industry, a businesspaper, an economy, the condition of industrial man.

Here is my reason for raising the point of discontent: The content of a businesspaper must be dynamic, never static. It must produce more than reader interest. It must produce reader action. Readers must do things—buy, sell, display, promote, manage, train, serve, research, design, raise the standards of conduct, the quality of products and performance, the condition of workers, the status of the industry—as a

[2] Some South Americans interpreted the Marshall Plan, when first proposed, as a military program—confusing General Marshall's name with the word *Martial.*

direct result of the inspiration contained in the editorial material between the covers of a businesspaper.

THE "M" FORMULA

There is a formula known as the "M" formula for preparing the editorial "discontent" in a businesspaper to fit the functions of the readers. This "M" formula supplies the kind of information and know-how readers want (or should have) in order to make a better living for themselves and others, and stimulate them to act as well as to read.

I am indebted for the idea of the "M" formula to a distinguished ex-businesspaper editor, Douglas Wolff, for many years editor of *Textile World*. He is the author of *The Business Paper Editor at Work*,[3] a book worth adding to your library. The "M" formula is easy to remember since every word begins with the letter "M." The "M" formula looks simple enough: men, materials, management, maintenance, methods, machines, merchandising, mill engineering, markets, media, money. But then, every formula you understand looks simple enough. The quality of the different ingredients and the proper proportions in a formula are as important for a businesspaper as they are for an aspirin tablet.

DUTY SPECIFICATIONS

The "M" formula may be explained in terms of the duty specifications of editorial staff members:[4]

1. *Regional Representatives or Field Editors.* The larger business-papers have full-time field editors or regional editorial representatives in key cities or in key centers, depending upon the kind of fields they serve. What may be a key center for one sort of businesspaper may be of little use to another. In my own field, for example, concerned with consumer goods, we are not as interested in Tulsa, Oklahoma, as we are in Kansas City. Tulsa, however, is a key center for businesspapers in the oil field. Readers of our businesspapers, for example, buy and sell consumer goods, both durable and nondurable goods. They are manufacturers, wholesalers, jobbers, importers, exporters, and retail merchants. We maintain branch offices in such key cities of consumer goods trading areas as Boston, Chicago, Pittsburgh, St. Louis, Kansas City, San Francisco, Los Angeles, and, because we are interested in foreign trade, in London and Belfast. In normal times, we also have offices on the Euro-

[3] McGraw-Hill Book Co., New York, 1936, p. 9.
[4] The duty specifications of the staff of *Chemical Engineering* has been selected.

pean continent. In our American branch offices, full-time field editors work directly out of the branch offices.

2. *Correspondents.* We are also served by free-lance writers or correspondents who cover the retail fields.

There are several organizations of correspondents who will assign their trained writers in a given territory to do a job for you. Such a service is rendered by International News Service and United Press whose correspondents, stationed all over the world, work chiefly for newspapers but take assignments for businesspapers. Some businesspapers, published daily or weekly like the Fairchild publications, have leased wire services of The Associated Press and the United Press to serve them.[5] Universal Trade Press serves business publications. *Billboard's* editorial center in New York City and printing plant in Cincinnati are connected by remote control tolotype setting equipment.

3. *News Editors.* At headquarters, the news editors select and boil down the news coming from the various regional editors or correspondents or wire services. They also rewrite news from other publications, publicity releases, and they tap other news sources close at hand. (See list of news sources.) They cover assignments looking to the developments a piece of news may suggest.

4. *Assistant Editors.* These staff members have major responsibilities, such as production schedules, the mechanics of lay-out and make-up, and usually departmental responsibilities. On *Chemical Engineering* they cover certain organic industries, study manufacturers' house organs and related publications, and cover the fields of engineering equipment, maintenance and repair, Washington rulings and directives, technical books, and current literature.

Among their contacts, for example, are the American Institute of Chemists, Petroleum Institute, Institute of Chemical Engineers, and such divisions of the industry as manufacture oils and fats, soap and glycerine and dyes; also the transportation, packaging, and shipping end of the chemical and metallurgical industry.

5. *Market Editor.* He is responsible for coverage of the markets for chemicals and allied materials and engineering news.

6. *Associate Editor.* He is concerned with chemical engineering equipment, design and performance, the theory and practice of operations, and heavy chemicals, rayon, textiles, glass and ceramics.

[5] *Women's Wear Daily, Daily News Record, Retailing Daily.*

7. *Consulting Editors or Editorial Consultants.* These are advisors to the editors, usually on topics of technical interest, education, relations with the government, or in connection with certain types of industries.

8. *Managing Editor.* He supervises the actual editorial production schedule and the work of some of the assistants, and has charge of the organization of much of the editorial material. On "Chem" he also has certain major responsibilities; he is concerned with the materials of construction, metals and alloys, plastics, electro-chemicals, pulp and paper, rubber, paint, and varnish. To many of you, these things will be extremely technical, but I bring them out to indicate the tremendous work that a staff of editors has before it on a publication like *Chemical Engineering.*

So you see all these editors, as I described their duties, are following the "M" formula: men, materials, management, maintenance, methods, machines, merchandising, mill engineering, markets, media, money.

9. *Editor-in-Chief.* It would seem that there is very little left for the editor-in-chief to do. However, I have never known an editor-in-chief on a businesspaper to suffer from boredom.

It has been said the value of a man to his employer progresses in three stages. You might call it the "success capsule": *First, you get paid for what you do. Then, you get paid for what you know. Finally, you get paid for whom you know.*

When a man has reached the high estate of editor-in-chief on a national businesspaper, you can be sure it is his close contacts with other leaders who guide the destiny of his industry, as well as the leaders of related fields of management and government, which make him valuable to his publisher, to his readers, to the advertisers, to his industry generally. (He is himself a leader.)

If a chief editor makes a speech or tours a plant, he is performing four functions: (1) an editorial function, (2) a public relations function, (3) an advertising function, and (4) a selling function. An editor may editorialize with the spoken word as well as with the printed word —outside the pages of his publication as well as inside.

The public relations value and advertising value of an editor's speeches and excursions in the field are inestimable to the publisher of his businesspaper. Even if the editor never mentions his publication by name or his company by name, if his speeches are any good, you may be sure people will find out who employs him, seek out the name of his publication, and remember what he said. It will pay off for his publisher, one way or another.

No successful businesspaper editor ever stayed that way who was not constantly selling his paper, his publishing house, his industry, and his profession. When an editor advances the status of his industry by his outside activities, he advances the status of everyone who has a stake in that industry, not the least of whom is the publisher of his businesspaper which is serving that industry and receiving its financial support from that industry.

When an editor gives time to the advancement of his own profession of journalism, he also advances the publisher's interest, in much the same way as a doctor attending meetings of the medical society or spending hours in clinics advances the interest of those who operate hospitals or those who sell medicine and surgical instruments for profit. *The profession of the editor is very important to the business of the publisher.*

WHEN IS IT "TECHNICAL"?

A word about the word "technical": There is no particular part of the business press which is actually "nontechnical." Some papers are considered more technical than others. An advertising agency man who handles a consumer food account, for instance, might consider a story in *Iron Age* technical, if he happened to see it.

But an advertising agency executive handling a stainless steel account might consider a story about dollar-and-cents markup in *Chain Store Age* technical. Every businesspaper is a technical paper—it is concerned with the "technics" or "applied science" of making a living. The words "technics" and "applied science" are sometimes just fancy words used to describe "know-how."

SPOT NEWS

News becomes quickly stale, or new slants develop, or different news items begin to coalesce or merge as we approach deadline. Meanwhile, the significance of certain reported events begins to become apparent to the trained minds of the editors. A relationship between seemingly separate and unrelated news stories may be recognized. Thus, a series of spot news items on the third of the month may indicate an important trend by deadline time on the eighteenth of the month. This may suggest the need for some personal interviews or that the editorial staff should take a quick opinion poll or perhaps begin the preparation of some feature articles on this trend. A personnel change, a merger, or a bankruptcy often starts a chain-reaction.

The dynamics of a field will often influence the frequency of publication. Some fields, like women's apparel, being high fashion or high style operate almost entirely on the basis of spot news. This explains the success of *Women's Wear* which is a daily; also the success of papers like *The Wall Street Journal* or the *Journal of Commerce*. The buyers and sellers who read these publications operate on the same spot news basis in the fast moving fields these business publications cover.

In a business magazine issued once a month spot news becomes less important while judicious interpretation and evaluation of the month's news stream becomes more important. In some fields you will find both a daily and a monthly. The readers depend on the daily for spot news but read the monthly magazine for interpretation, integration, editorial guidance, and the news digest.

In the over-all picture some of my colleagues believe that spot news is becoming less important.[6] Leading daily newspapers have expanded their business news pages. You have news weeklies giving emphasis to business news. Also, news letter services, financial reports, Federal Reserve and U. S. Department of Commerce reports, bank bulletins, and radio and TV broadcasts which include business news, tend to remove the newness from news by the time it reaches a reader via the monthly businesspaper.

I have always believed businessmen are more interested in having businesspaper editors tell them what is going to happen. They have so many means of finding out quickly what has already happened, although they do not always get the real meaning of the events past until the businesspaper's analysis of the month's news reaches them.

I must add one word here about an editorial staff member whose glory is often unsung—the editor's secretary. Beyond question she is the most important person on any editorial staff.

She is the diplomat, the buffer, the alarm clock, the liaison officer, and trouble shooter. She never gets mad, she never gets sick, she never gets drunk.

She is a philosopher, politician, psychologist; custodian of state secrets; official dispenser of aspirin, bicarbonate of soda, and the editor's cab fare.

She sews buttons on his shirt, criticizes his clothes, reminds him when

[6] See discussion by L. C. Morrow in this chapter.

he needs a haircut or has a date with his wife. She holds back the memos or letters he dictates in anger, until he has cooled off. Then she obligingly looks the other way as he drops them in the waste basket.

A businesspaper is the product of three groups of people: First, those who own the businesspaper. Second, those who manufacture the businesspaper. Third, those who read the businesspaper.

The good and bad judgments, prejudices and enthusiasms, selfish and unselfish interests, the good and bad tastes of these three groups check and offset each other and contribute in their own way to make the end product—the businesspaper—what it is: poor, fair, indifferent, or a good businesspaper.

The third of these three groups, the reader, is the final arbiter. He accepts or rejects the final product. He, the reader, really creates the product we call a businesspaper because he makes the news in his field; provides the know-how, which is published in the businesspaper and which *is* the businesspaper. He makes or withholds decisions on what he reads. His decisions advance or retard the status of his field.

The reader puts into action the inspiration and the know-how which the editors pass on to him in words or symbols—or he ignores what you write because it is not any good or because it is not plain enough to understand, or not attractively presented to make him read, or because he did not open the magazine that month or even take it out of its wrapper or envelope.

It was, therefore, neither altruism nor idealism, nor lofty exaltation which prompted the business press association back in 1914 to write this Number 1 "objective" in their code of ethics:

"*To consider first the interests of the subscriber.*" This was plain horse sense.

In his lecture on this platform, J. K. Lasser made a very significant statement in answer to a question from this audience. Mr. Lasser is probably the most competent appraiser of the value of a businesspaper publishing property one could go to. He was asked whether the building of a circulation created an asset for the owner of a businesspaper. His answer was "No."

"The circulation of a businesspaper is not *per se* an asset," Lasser said. "The only asset is the good will of the reader."

Reader confidence and good will in a businesspaper is to a large extent in the hands of the editors. That confidence is created and maintained by continuously serving the reader's best interests, by accurate and faithful reporting of the news of men, materials, machines, mill engineering, markets, methods, management, merchandising and money.

By his honest, fearless interpretation, appraisal, and evaluation of news significance and market trends, the editor manifests editorial leadership.

It is only after the reader's confidence has been won by patient, honest, courageous, and continuous coverage of the news that the reader will be willing to listen to the editor as a guide, mentor, counsellor, or critic. Years must be spent winning the confidence of your readers by honest news reporting and news interpretation before you can hope to offer counsel, advice, or criticism with any assurance that it will be followed. There is no short cut to editorial leadership.

Also, there is no short cut to becoming a good businesspaper editor. A business journalist must have a background in the humanities, in social and natural sciences, in history and literature, in language and communications, in economics, in public relations, in mixing with people and understanding their work. He belongs to a great and honorable profession that is older than most other professions. It is his function to communicate to other members of human society what all of its members feel, what they think, what they do, what they hope. The journalist, therefore, must have the widest range of knowledge and experience, the broadest intelligence of any man, rare judgment and, in addition to trained powers of observation, reasoning, and appraisal, he must have natural instincts and talents. He must have a great curiosity, which is sometime called "a nose for news." And he must have courage.

Teachers cannot give talents to journalists any more than to artists or musicians. But do not let that discourage you. Sometimes publishers do not have the talent to discover that they have a good editor. And sometimes editors do not have the talent to discover they have a good assistant. Often publishers and editors lose these men and women to others who do discover their rare talents, and are not afraid to advertise them and promote them and pay them well.

To the talents and instincts and to the intellectual training, there must be added skills and techniques, correct practices and procedures, the know-how of publishing and editorial practice.

The great and the small private enterprises of our country appreciate what good businesspaper editors have done to improve the intelligence and the know-how of American industry. When they buy twelve pages or twelve half pages of advertising in a businesspaper, they are doing more than paying for white space to place messages which will attract the attention of part of this trained readership to their product or service and their know-how: the advertisers are also underwriting the pioneering work of the independent businesspaper publisher over the many years when he paid out more than he took in.

The advertiser in a businesspaper is underwriting the best insurance policy private competitive enterprise will ever have against state or private monopoly.

Those who sell our advertising space are not only selling markets conditioned by the editorial department; they are selling the ability of their publishers to continue rendering this service to industry; they are selling the ability of their editors to hold this readership; they are selling the ability of their editors to make readers do things, buy and sell more goods, improve their know-how, their research, improve the quality of their products and services, manage better, design better, manufacture better, improve their conduct, their practices, the standards of living and employment for all people, in free and competitive markets everywhere in the world under a private enterprise system.

They are selling the ability of their editors to keep their readers *discontented* with the *status quo*.

NEWS CONTENT OF THE BUSINESSPAPER*

A conviction is held in some quarters that spot news is not nearly so important as it was only a few years ago. The war accentuated the movement. Obviously, what makes spot news of less importance in the business press is the increasing application of radio and television news casts. What a reader knows has happened, because he heard about it over the radio or TV, he does not want to be told again in his business publication. That is, he does not want to be told the mere fact that it has happened. When he is told what that news event *means* in his industry, or to his job, however, that is something else. Interpretation and analysis are his prime news needs.

An example of the interpretative news need is found in the extensive acceptance on the part of industrial readers of the job done by the

* L. C. Morrow, Consulting Editor, *Factory Management and Maintenance;* former president, National Conference of Business Paper Editors; Revised in 1950 by author from a paper read before The Associated Business Publications, Westchester Country Club, Rye, N.Y., May, 1944.

business press in connection with the Controlled Materials Plan when it was introduced by the War Production Board. There was a mass of rules and regulations which, for many companies, called for setting up a CMP department. Someone had to become conversant with all the details of the plan. These people were helped immeasurably by the interpretative work done by the business press. In the case of plants which could not set up men to become experts, the business press alone sufficed to guide the proceedings. It was much simpler for a few businesspaper editors to go to Washington and secure the assistance of WPB in understanding and explaining the plan.

Additional examples of the kinds of subjects lending themselves particularly to interpretative or analytical news reporting were surplus property policies and regulations, veteran rehabilitation, seniority as complicated by law and the return of veterans, synthetic rubber possibilities and practicalities, high octane gas requirements and prospects, availability of food and materials for food containers. It is well to remember these opportunities for service during a defense economy.

PRODUCTION AND EQUIPMENT NEWS STILL IMPORTANT

This new emphasis upon news does not mean that the handling of news as heretofore practiced is obsolete in all respects. There is a very important type of news that the reader of the business press must have and which he will get nowhere else: news of new equipment. In a competitive economy, every new machine or device is of intense interest to the industrial reader because he follows every clue that he can find which would seem to offer some chance to discover ways and means of reducing production or distribution costs. Product news, of course, is the first news demanded in the fields of distribution and merchandising.

PERSONALS IN THE NEWS

Another kind of news that will continue to be acceptable, even though it may not seem important, in the single-industry papers, is personals. It parallels the so-called society news of the country weeklies, which is read with avidity by a large share of the subscribers.

THE BUSINESS PRESS AS INDUSTRY'S PROXY

Not only current material is in demand, but basic material published a good many years ago. On our publications we have had undeniable proof that industry looks to the business press in time of emergency for the technical and managerial help needed to see it through. Of extraordinary value during the war was the ability of the business press to do industry's visiting for it. The press went into the plants as well as into Washington and carried to all units of industry the best practices of the most experienced or the most efficient units. The accentuation of this great proxy service of industry carried over from war to peace, and the business press has a greater obligation in this direction than ever before. The reason is that industry and the business press are parts of a new kind of world, characterized by less monopoly and more competition. Fortunately, business in this country is well aware of the over-all beneficial results from a program of participation in the dissemination of information.

THE BUSINESS PRESS ABROAD

A big job ahead of the business press is going to be the necessity to observe and report news of business progress in foreign countries. Heretofore, in many respects, and with important exceptions—notably research—the publications of the United States have been giving much, receiving little. In the future, conditions are likely to be different. Now all countries are awake to the advantages of industrialization and mass production. Because other countries do not know things cannot be done, they are likely to go ahead and do them.

Must these developments in European and Asiatic countries be watched? They must indeed It may be a long time before we actually are able to cash in on the methods of production and distribution that we learn about in other countries. But all signs point to our having a great deal to do with foreign countries from now on. If our relations are to be on the giving end only for some time to come, we still must know what we are doing and what they are doing. The industry and business of the country must have its observers, analysts, and interpreters on the job. Specific branches of industry and business will be more extensively involved in foreign affairs than others, for example air transportation and the merchant marine, but all will be concerned to some extent. Because of the interpretative need in its news reports, the business press can no longer be satisfied with the Frenchman in France as his representative, the German in Germany, the Englishman in England, and so on.

NEWS SOURCES FOR A BUSINESSPAPER EDITORIAL DEPARTMENT[7]

Your readers
Your market
Showrooms
Your advertising space salesmen
Your subscription salesmen
The morgue
News "releases" from publicity departments
Correspondence files
Index to back issues
Speeches at luncheons, dinners, meetings, clinics, forums
Trade associations and their bulletins
Professional societies and their publications
Public officials, Congress, state commissions
Department of Commerce: publications
Federal Trade Commission
Federal Reserve Banks: reports
Brokerage houses
Government reprints, statistics, reports
Courts
Consulates
Corporation reports
Public records
Stores, plants, factories, laboratories, mines, mills
Libraries
Trade shows
Club and social affairs
Golf tournaments
Openings, cocktail parties, luncheons, dinners, breakfasts

Charitable activities
Press conferences
Prominent people, trade leaders, labor leaders
Small people, taxi drivers, salespeople
Editors and reporters on other publications in your organization
Public relations men
Designers and architects
Letters and phone calls
Surveys of your own readership, opinion polls
Advertisements
Advertising agencies
House organs
Books
Surveys by consumer magazines and newspapers
Other businesspaper editors (See Standard Rate & Data Businesspaper Section)
Research organizations
Your research department
Opinion Poll organizations
Committee for Economic Development
National Association of Manufacturers
Convention bureaus
The Advertising Council
Better Business Bureaus
Chamber of Commerce of U. S.
Investment brokers
Other periodicals[8]
Radio-Television Programs

[7] Julien Elfenbein; from a lecture at City College of New York, 1946.
[8] See "Basic Bookshelf" in Appendix for list of publications that are news sources.

BASIC APPROACH TO EDITORIAL PROBLEMS*

My conception of the function of an editor is that he bears the same relationship to his publishing organization that a production superintendent bears to his sales and research staff in a manufacturing plant. In other words, the editor's job is to produce a product which can be sold to readers and to advertisers. In order to sell it to readers, he has to make the product interesting and attractive, and in addition he has to resort to every artifice of design available to him in order to attract maximum readership.

FRONT COVER

We begin on the assumption that our primary selling tool is the magazine itself. Therefore, we begin by focusing our first attention on the wrapper of the product, that is, the front cover. We realize we are competing with the advertising department for the use of that cover. It is valuable space which could be sold to an advertiser at a premium. If we, as editors, expect to use the cover, we know that we have to make it more valuable as a wrapper or attention-getter than it can be in terms of revenue from an advertiser. So we attempt to design the cover in a manner that will attract the attention of our subscribers, and induce them to look at it. As we see it, that is the first function of a cover. The second function is that, having induced the reader to look at the cover, it should carry something which leads him into the inside of the magazine. To explain what we attempt to do with regard to the second function, I shall have to digress for a moment, and briefly discuss one of our policies.

A THEME FOR EACH ISSUE

We use a theme, or a lead feature, in every issue. Sometimes this theme or lead feature is a short article of two to four pages. Sometimes it is a section of 16 to 32 pages, and other times it is an entire issue with a change of pace to relieve what otherwise would be monotonous adherence to a single phase of this complex building industry. Regardless of the length of the theme or lead feature, we attempt to convey it to the reader by the design of the cover and a descriptive catch phrase.

* Edward Gavin, Editor, *The American Builder,* from an address before the 25th Annual Conference, Associated Business Publications, Inc., May, 1950.

My thought here is that if we have chosen an interesting feature or theme, we lead the reader into the magazine.

APPEARANCE AND FACTUAL WRITING

We realize that just as we compete with the business or advertising department for the use of the front cover, once we get the reader inside we are competing with the advertisers for reader attention. Since the advertising is the product of the most highly skilled copywriters, layout experts, and artists that industry can buy in the form of advertising managers and advertising agencies, we have to style our editorial material so that it gets a fair share of the reader's attention.

To accomplish this end, we strive for two things—appearance and factual writing. The appearance we get is due to the unique talents of our managing editor. With background in art, building construction, and selling, he is able to temper each of these talents or backgrounds with the other two, and come up with a realistic balance between utility and esthetics.

Knowing what the theme of an issue is, and having worked on the accumulation of source material for several months in advance, we begin the editorial design of an issue by selecting material that in our judgment has definite reader interest. We think we know our readers, their problems, and the language which will appeal to them because of the great amount of time spent by all members of the staff in the field. If we do not know these things there is something badly wrong with us, because we have every opportunity in the world to learn.

DESIGN AND ILLUSTRATION

Having selected the material, the managing editor then embarks on the design and layout of each story and each section if the feature is to occupy an entire section of an issue. The design begins with illustrations, both photographs and professionally executed drawings. Meticulous attention is given to the choice of illustrations with a view to choosing the most dramatic and the most pertinent ones available. The illustrations are then assembled to give prominence by both size and position to the ones that most aptly and compellingly describe the story. Knowing something of the pressure under which all business executives work today, we believe that we have to tell the story with the illustrations to enable the busy reader to make an instantaneous decision with respect to whether he wants to go further with the story or not. We think that if we do not give him this instant clue he might not read anything. This might be criticized on the ground that it encourages selective reading, but we feel that we owe the reader an opportunity to select, and thus conserve his time, as an alternative to probably not reading at all.

HEADS AND SUBHEADS

Having told the story to the best of our ability with pictures, we next devote our attention to a headline. This we consider to be all-important, because it can add up the prospective reader's first impression and tell him specifically what the text matter is going to tell him about the illustration he has seen. We consider the headline to be an extremely important part of the story. On the theory that a verb always lends action to a statement, we use one in every main head and try to challenge the reader and lead him in to the subhead. The main head, of course, is not subordinate to the illustration to the extent that it must be looked for or worked at. We want it to stand out. In fact, one of the things that we do not know is whether the reader is attracted first by the illustrations and then by the head, or the reverse. Not knowing the answer to that one, we try to give equal prominence to the head and to the principal attention-getting illustration. A verb is always used in the head regardless of whether the head is a statement or a question.

We consider the subhead to be a bridge between the main head and the text. If we have gotten the reader far enough through the illustrations and the main head to challenge his attention, we want the subhead to elaborate just enough over the main head to make him curious about the text.

THE LEAD SENTENCE

A whole volume could be written about the text, but I am sure that nothing I say will apply to all business magazines. In our particular case we are convinced that our readers want ideas and want them fast. Therefore we never use a trick lead. We always write factually, and begin the story by saying something positively in the first sentence which always, of course, must be short.

RUN-OVERS AND SPLIT MAKE-UP

In laying out the feature stories, after the managing editor has determined upon the illustrations and, in conjunction with the author of the story, determined the main head and the subhead, they have already decided how many pages the story will take. Then it is up to the author of the story, having worked out the relative allotment of space between illustrations and text matters, to write to precisely the allotted space with no run-over into the back of the book. Now this ban on run-overs is not an absolutely inflexible rule. We do find possibly two or three times a year that because of some unusual set of circumstances it becomes necessary to run a story into the fractional pages in the back. We definitely frown on the idea, however, and usually in the allotment of space attempt to give the author of the story a little less than he thinks he needs. This we believe makes for tighter writing. We have found that it is an excellent check on the writer who tends to be wordy.

Like most magazines, we have a split page make-up after our section. This always poses a problem, or at least it has always posed a problem to us. The natural tendency on these split pages, if my experience is any criterion, is to fill them with a relatively unrelated assortment of news items. Up to this point, one of the things we have achieved in tailoring our pages to come out exactly even, is to avoid the costly expense of overset. On our magazine, and I suppose we are not unusual, we never know until a few hours before going to press just how much split page space we are going to have to fill in the back of the book. Here, of course, the easy thing is to go ahead and set up enough editorial material to more than fill any calculated amount of space. This practice, however, again leads to costly overset which we frown upon. To try to offset it and to give some very definite character to these split pages, we take a lot of material which has feature value, but could not be made into a full page or two-page story without an excess of extraneous illustrations or the use of a lot of words merely to fill the space. We therefore tailor these short features to exact column length just as carefully as we tailor the long multi-page features in the front of the book. We believe that by doing this we give the advertiser on the split page as good a reader-attention break as anybody gets any place in the book. Now, I would very much dislike to leave the impression that all of our split pages are filled with very meaty, specially designed short features. That is not the case. What we strive to do is achieve a nice balance between this kind of material and pertinent news items on these pages.

TYPOGRAPHY

On the subject of typography, there have been so many textbooks written that it seems hardly necessary here to discuss the subject other than to say that we, like every editorial staff, attempt to pick a type face that is suitable to our field. This is a more or less nebulous statement, but in a very broad way it simply boils down to this. We want a good, strong, bold, masculine type for the kind of readers we have. Whether we get it or not must always be somewhat a matter of opinion.

NEWS IMPORTANCE

At this point, it is probably appropriate to say that a long time ago we asked ourselves when we really should start to sell the reader on the importance of our editorial content. The answer is simply this. We start our effort, good or bad as it may be, with the preliminary planning of each issue. In the selection of material we always try to keep sharply in mind the question as to why the reader subscribes to the magazine. Does he do it for general news of the industry, for entertainment, for success stories, for human interest stories, or how to be a better businessman, scientist, or technician. We believe that a monthly magazine with a deadline a few days before the close of the second month prior to the date of issue is hardly in a position to be of much use as a news medium. Therefore we make little or no attempt to include spot news. There are, of course, always the usual items of interest about important personages in various segments of the industry, and the interesting and helpful news concerning the activities of the local and national associations to which the readers belong. At any rate we believe, after considerable study and constant attention to the receptivity of association news, that it is important.

As far as entertainment is concerned, we believe that the theater, radio, television, and humor magazines can do a much better job of that than we can, and that our readers do not subscribe to *The American Builder* with the idea of being entertained. About the same thing goes for success stories and human interest stories. We may have a too coldly realistic view of our function as editors, but we think our subscribers stay with us because we give them information about design, building techniques, distribution, advertising, and merchandising that they can use in the conduct of their own operation.

TRAVEL AND FIELD WORK

It seems to me quite possible that I have said nothing at all that is new to any businesspaper editor, and having said it, I think I possibly am in danger of having left the impression that I have recently wakened to a lot of things which I should have known twenty years ago. If that is the impression that has been left, no doubt some of it is justified. The reason is that we keep changing almost from month to month many of our concepts and policies because in our industry, at any rate, change is the order of the day. Nothing stays put. As things stand at the moment, however, what I have said up to now is in brief our basic approach to the business of selling the reader on our product.

That leads to another statement, and one which quite possibly might be challenged. I can remember the day when an editor was supposed to be a man who sat at a desk, pulled some strings, and got action from various members of the editorial staff. He had some pretty fixed ideas and he was quite a man with a blue pencil. I may be terribly wrong, but I believe that that style of business magazine editing is just about as decadent as the era of the horse and buggy. As I see my job today, it must embrace, in addition to the usual supervision of staff activities and production operation, an enormous amount of travel for personal contact with the various categories of readers to whom we direct our appeal, and with many of our advertisers.

NEW PRODUCTS SECTION

In our industry nothing new in home design can happen until a manufacturer produces a new or improved product. At the moment he does, he becomes news and so does his product. We became convinced a long time ago that the so-called new products section of our magazine is far from being a handout of free publicity for an advertiser or a prospect. Numerous reader surveys have convinced us that the new products section is one of the most intensely read that we have because it is one of the most newsy features that we have. We therefore devote a lot of space to the announcement of new and improved products. After those products have been announced, then we must concern ourselves with the chore of determining the best job-site technique for using them and applying them. As a result the advertiser, far from being something to be frowned upon as a source of news, is something we must cultivate as one of our most fruitful sources of vital news to the industry. There are many things which we think we can and should say editorially about a product or a category of products that for numerous reasons the advertiser is unable to say in the space which he pays for. And yet I want to emphasize that no part of our function is to supplement what the advertiser pays for by giving him free space. We simply are convinced that we have to follow the experience and application techniques among distributors and builders with respect to all products, particularly the new and improved ones.

ADVERTISING AND SUBSCRIPTION SALESMEN

That changes another concept which in my early days as a business-paper editor I had quite thoroughly drummed in to me. I was told that the advertising salesmen of our organization were people who must not be consorted with, that if I had much to do with them I would contaminate the sanctity of the editorial prerogative. That likewise, if it ever was true, certainly today is as dead as the horse and buggy era. I find that I have to live very close to our advertising salesmen and to our subscription salesmen, that I have to be just as thoroughly conversant with the problems they have in selling circulation and advertising as I am with the problems of producing the product that they have to sell. Thus, since I conceive my job to be that of producing a product that the circulation department can sell and keep sold so that we get a high renewal percentage, and that the advertising department can sell, there must be close coordination and close cooperation between the editors, the circulation department salesmen, and the advertising department salesmen.

To me an editor, if he ever could afford to do it, certainly cannot today sit on a throne and hand down weighty decisions while he pontificates for the edification of the other departments of the publishing company. If he is going to sell his product, or be a factor in the sale of his product to his readers, he certainly must know every problem there is in connection with the work that confronts the men that have to get names on the dotted line.

PERIODIC READER SURVEYS

While we think we know what is of most importance and value to our readers today, we are also sure that because we are in a period of continuing change we have to make periodic surveys to check our judgment. We have to learn our reader traffic, our reader interest, our reader value, the intensity of our reading through these surveys, and in fact have just concluded an agreement with Roy Eastman in which we did, over a period of two or three years, check all of these items. That contact was a very illuminating one. Mr. Eastman confirmed some of the things that we thought we knew, shocked the daylights out of us in connection with others, and indicated new or different ways to present some other features of the magazine.

THE POLITICAL ECONOMY

It seems to me, too, that in connection with selling, this observation should be made. In our business, at any rate, there usually is a principal editorial function contingent upon some national condition. For instance, during the depths of the depression of the early thirties, the principal function was to try to provide information which at least could keep some builders, manufacturers, and distributors in business on a declining or relatively nonexistent market. Then during the war when we were subject to all sorts of limitations and restrictions with respect to building activity due to the fact that most of the materials ordinarily consumed by home builders and most of the labor ordinarily used by them, had to be diverted to the all-essential purpose of winning the war in as short a time as possible, our principal editorial function became that of interpreting these regulations and providing the builder with the methods necessary to get business under government control. Immediately at the conclusion of the war, the function again very sharply changed. It became one of providing designs for what everyone knew would be an enormous demand for post-war houses. It also became one of attempting to expose some of the gray market practices, to iron them out and get more equitable distribution, and of pointing out ways and techniques of using substitute materials in place of pre-war standard materials in short supply. Then there came a time about the middle of 1948 when in some sections of the country the seriousness of the housing shortage began to disappear. For the first time in ten years it was becoming necessary for manufacturers, distributors, and builders to go back into the business of actually selling their product. That is where we are today as far as *The American Builder* is concerned.

One of our functions therefore, has to be to recognize the principal important subjects in the minds of our readers, and to apprehend as closely as we can when that subject is going to change, to give way to another, and to know what that other one is going to be. While this probably has little to do directly with selling, it nevertheless is a subject which under the conditions confronting business today, it seems to me every editor has to concern himself with and make up his mind.

We knew from certain things which were perfectly obvious about 1943 that at the conclusion of the war there would be a concerted drive to socialize housing in the United States. We therefore began to point out the danger and the need for combating this drift to socialism long before the war was over. That required some finesse, of course, in order not to give the impression that we were more concerned with what might happen after the war than we were with the immediate essential problem of winning the war. Nevertheless, we did make up our minds and take our stand, and we have, under the conviction that government is in business today, made up our minds that we are going to take very definite stands for and against anything proposed by government which in any way affects the industry which we serve. Whether we like it or not, we believe that we have to take definite stands on subjects involving political economy, and keep our readers informed even if we sound politically partisan from time to time.

A LANGUAGE NORM

Back again on the subject of selling the reader, we think that we have to make up our mind with respect to a language norm of the industry. In other words, shall we use highly technical language, semitechnical language, pure English, or some other named or unnamed brand of English. We hope we have the answer to that because of the fact that we maintain a constant and ever-growing broad acquaintance with our readers. Then we think, also, that our job is much more than just reporting. We believe that we must lead, and one of the problems which we do not know the answer to and doubt if we ever will know, is just how far ahead of contemporary thinking we can afford to lead.

We know that if we get too far ahead of the capacity of our readers to comprehend what we are talking about we will lose them and suffer a drop in circulation. We also know that if we do not lead them far enough or rapidly enough they will find us extremely dull because we are simply a reporting medium and drop us in favor of something else. I probably should have put that in the form of a question, because I now would like to ask a few questions, and suggest that if the answers to these questions are not settled in the minds of any of us as editors, we might well afford to devote some time in seminars in attempting to arrive at some criteria.

SOME QUESTIONS

Speech-making. One of the major problems in my life, and I know that it must be in the lives of practically all businesspaper editors, is what to do about invitations to make speeches. In my own case, and I suppose I am not unlike anyone else, I get from 200 to 300 invitations a year.

Obviously, it is physically impossible to accept anything like all of these. I do, however, get myself down to a point of accepting something between 30 and 45 of them a year. The question in my mind is this—how do other editors determine which ones they can afford to accept, or to put it differently, which ones they cannot afford not to accept. Where is the line drawn between using this medium as effective selling to the reader, and being a good-time Charlie? What do you do about the important reader or the important advertiser who suddenly finds himself the program chairman of a local service club or a local or department organization of veterans. He has heard you at a convention, and he thinks the things you have to say would be very interesting to the membership of his organization. While the organization probably wields no purchasing power for your advertisers, or contains relatively no readers or reader prospects, this man nevertheless is important to you. How many of these can you afford to take on, or do you take any of them? Frankly, I have no rule of thumb for determining which ones to take and which ones not to take.

Conventions. Then, what do you do about conventions? In our industry, we have about 300 conventions. They range all the way from local annual county meetings to state and national conclaves. Obviously, we cannot touch them all. Equally obviously, there are some of them that we cannot afford not to attend. And once you get there what do you do? In our case, because there are so many of them, we do not make even a passing attempt to report the proceedings. Even if there were not many of them we still would not make an attempt to report proceedings on the theory that the only people that are interested actually are the people who were there, and that the only fellow interested in reading the contents of the speech usually is the fellow who made it. Maybe we are a thousand miles off base on that one, but nevertheless that is our thinking, and we believe that if we did any extensive coverage of even the two or three important national conventions, we might simply be wasting space which could be used to much better advantage. Really, what we go there for is to contact many of our important readers, to get a lot of leads for stories from various parts of the country, to talk to district sales managers, local salesmen, and some of the top brass among our advertisers. And none of that is to impress any of these factors. It is simply that we can meet a lot more of them and talk to a lot more of them in one place than we can if we had to visit their offices individually. It is an economical way of making a lot of contacts in a short time, and it pays off in keeping us informed of developments of all kinds which we think are editorially interesting and vital.

Preprints of Articles. What do you think is the value of preprints of important articles, that is, perhaps 100, or 200 to 300, pulled off in advance of the issue date and sent out to a number of subscribers and advertisers for their comments? I do not know the answer to that one. I know that it is a practice in some publishing houses.

Contents Page. What do you think of using a part of the contents page to give a brief résumé of the principal features of the next issue? We do it, and we believe that it has some intangible yet very definite value in stimulating interest in readership for the issue to come.

Planning Future Issues. Then, here is an important one: projecting a fixed editorial feature program a year in advance. I realize, of course, all of the dangers inherent in any such activity on the part of an editor. It is very dangerous, and can have exceedingly unpleasant repercussions. We nevertheless for the last several years have chosen to take the risk, and either through good fortune or good sense we have got into no serious trouble thus far. On the other hand, the material thus projected has proved to be of real value to both the subscription and the advertising salesmen.

Reader Contests. Then, what do you think of contests? The kind which the magazine initiates for the dual purpose of stimulating some forward or advanced thinking and obtaining some exclusive editorial material. We have engaged in only one in recent years, but the results indicate that perhaps we should repeat the activity.

Trade Association Memberships. What do you do about associate or active memberships in the trade associations whose members are served by your publication? That is a continuing problem to us. We are active in several of them up to the point of holding executive or administrative offices or heading important committees. We think it is an important and necessary activity for our editors, but we thoroughly realize that such activity can be carried to a point where there is no time left for an editor's primary justification for existing, that is, to edit a magazine.

THE EDITORIAL BUDGET*

When you get around to cost control, you will find that the integration of personalities, team play, working together for mutual understanding

* Norman G. Shidle, Executive Editor, *Society of Automotive Engineers Journal;* from a lecture at New York University, February 19, 1947. Mr. Shidle is the author of *Clear Writing For Easy Reading,* McGraw-Hill Book Company, N.Y., 1951.

of problems is even more important than in the mechanical presentation area. Let us take just a quick look at what you need for editorial cost control.[9]

COST FIGURES

Number 1, you have got to have cost figures.

Number 2, you have got to get them promptly. If you do not get them regularly and you do not get them promptly, you cannot possibly hope to control your costs.

Number 3, you have to have budget control, so that you have some sort of a guide, some sort of a standard, against which to judge the thousands of individual little decisions that have to be made all up and down the line by everybody on the staff.

When you get your cost figures as editor you have got to have figures which are costs on the items that *you* control. If the cost figures that come down to you are all fouled up with overhead and executive salaries and a whole lot of other stuff you cannot do anything about, just send them back and say, "I cannot control costs until you give me figures on the things I control. When I get the figures on what I alone control, then I can be responsible for them."

YOUR BUDGET

Those are some of your necessary tools. But that is all that they are. Even after you have them, you have to have guide-posts, you have to have danger signals, you have to have things as an editor that point out to you the things that need to be done.

No top editor can control costs by himself. Costs actually have to be controlled by concerted action. Costs cannot always be controlled by *not* doing something. You can call in your gang and tell them a lot of things that "from now on we are not going to do." That will help you. That will keep you out of the worst woods. For example, you can say, "We are not going to have any more bleeds. We are going to cut down on silhouettes. We are not going to do this and we are not going to do that." But that will just take a little bite out of it. If it takes too big a bite, standing alone, it may hurt your paper more than the cost control can help it.

So you have got to get participation in cost control on the part of every person on the staff. You have got to get a mutual interest in cost control. That means, You have got to get the staff together and keep

[9] See Chapter 2, Editorial Cost Controls.

them informed (do not give them lectures). You have got to keep them informed about what the problems are, what the costs are, what your budget limits are. Just as you need figures to control your costs, the staff members need figures within their own areas to have some idea of what they are spending and can spend. They have got to be interested in it. Keep them interested and, if you can, keep them informed. Regular editorial conferences are a "must" in a well-run editorial department.

After you have got them informed, still you cannot do a complete job on cost control by the negative method; just not doing something will ruin your publication as well as your disposition—probably the disposition first. The main idea to get across when you are starting to try to control costs or to cut costs is this: Editors expend two things: We expend money and we expend ideas. When the money starts to get scarce, the ideas have got to come faster and better. You can make up for lack of money with abundance of ideas. If you know what costs money in a businesspaper you can go through plenty of papers and you will see that they are spending plenty of money but that there is still not an idea per page. You can go through other publications where you are struck with the ingenuity, you are struck with ideas, you are struck with presentations that came from good ideas, and if you know costs, you will see that these publication perhaps do not cost a great deal of money in spite of their attractiveness.

These two things, money and ideas, are interchangeable and the quicker a staff learns and understands that they are interchangeable, the better chance you have to begin to get some results. Your staff begins to learn that the real job of controlling costs is not just to cut something out; the real job is to get the most out of the editorial dollars that are available. That is the first thing any sensible editor seeks to do when he first goes to work. That is the reason you have to have a budget. The budget tells you how many editorial dollars you have available and if you are a good editor, you tell the publisher: "Well, of course, I will get out for you the best paper there is for X dollars."

Then when you get your staff thinking about that, they begin to think of ideas and you begin to get ideas and the ideas flow in a thousand small ways as you go along. There is no budget on ideas. I cannot give you ideas in a few minutes here, but there are many ways of exchanging money for ideas. You can use more white space to get better and more dramatic effect when you are using a white space instead of a cut. You can figure out more ingenious ways of using type arrangements to get dramatic effects. You might even spend a little money playing up in a large size and very dramatically a couple of photos which give the reader some excitement and thrill so he does not miss the ten cuts that you did not use.

You can work in a better industry contact job. You can learn to write better letters so that you make more friends among your readers by mail and you begin to develop stuff that you bring in by mail and save yourself some traveling expenses or free-lance manuscript fees.

You can do a better job of selling what you have to your sales staff, keep them so busy thinking about new ideas that they have not got time to criticize you about the things you are not doing.

The result is worth all the time, education, trouble, and conferences you need to get it. And there is no substitute for having people who automatically grow or can be trained to work together as a team, for having clean-cut responsibilities with a minimum of red tape and a maximum of general interest in the problems of your paper.

EVERY PAPER HAS A POLICY*

The Wall Street Journal is, of course, a business newspaper. If it were not for the fact that it is such a formidable term, we might say it is an economic newspaper. We are interested in everything that affects the economy—in steel production, in coal supply and demand, in auto prices, in dust storms that affect crops, and in thousands of such things.

What we try to do every day is to gather, write, edit, and print all the business news of national—and to some extent international—importance.

We lay great stress on accuracy. All good newspapers do that, of course, but we think it is particularly important for us. Most people read most newspapers to be informed and entertained. We believe, in fact we know, that *The Wall Street Journal* readers buy our newspaper not only to be informed but to use the information in running their business.

If we make a mistake some of our readers may act on it and they may lose money. We do not like that to happen!

We also feel that we have an obligation to report bad news as well as good news. I mention this only because there are some people who think

* B. H. McCormack, Senior Associate Editor, *The Wall Street Journal;* from a paper read at Temple University Clinic For Industrial Editors, Pocono Manor, Pennsylvania, April 27, 1950.

it is bad business to talk about bad business. But we think we are not fulfilling our obligations to our readers if we write only about uptrends.

The editorial policy for *The Wall Street Journal* could best be summed briefly this way: We believe in freedom—freedom of the individual, the businessman, and the farmer. We think the government has no right to encroach on that freedom, except to see that we all abide by certain moral laws.

The problem, of course, is how you follow such a policy in the light of day-to-day news developments.

Take an example in labor. John L. Lewis has been exercising a monopoly control over the workers in the coal mines. And by doing so he has been able to enjoy monopoly control over coal production. So the coal industry lost its freedom.

I think it is interesting to dig back into history a bit and see what the policy was of Adolph S. Ochs, the man who built *The Times* into the paper it is. In the very first edition of this newspaper published under Ochs' supervision he carried a statement on policy. I'd like to read you part of that:

It will be my earnest aim that *The New York Times* give the news, all the news, in concise and attractive form, in language that is permissible in good society, and give it as early if not earlier, than it can be learned through any other reliable medium; to give the news impartially, without fear or favor, regardless of party, sect or interests involved; to make of the columns of *The New York Times* a forum for consideration of all questions of public importance, and to that end to invite intelligent discussion from all shades of opinion.

There, it seems to me, is a very clear statement of a news policy in a very few words.

FIVE INGREDIENTS OF EDITORIAL ENTERPRISE*

1. The first, and maybe the most important factor in editorial enterprise is *instinct*. A good editor has to do a certain amount of his playing by ear. He has to write the music as he goes along. He must sense changes in reader attitudes and reader needs. And no matter how many guides he has in the way of readership surveys, fan mail, letters of complaint and commendation, the good editor has to continue to lean on instinct.

* C. B. Larrabee, President and Publisher of *Printers' Ink*; from an editorial, "The Importance of Know-How," *Printers' Ink,* February 4, 1949, and an editorial "Balance—Basic Magazine Ingredient," *Printers' Ink*, April 7, 1950.

2. A second important ingredient is the power of *selection*. Putting together each issue of a magazine like *Printers' Ink* is an exercise in selection. Long before some of the articles were even written, some editor picked out of all the day's confusing trends those he felt would be most important on that certain tomorrow when a particular issue was to be published. In many cases his next steps were to select the writer, select the phase of the subject to be studied, and then when the manuscript was prepared, select out of it the vital facts and discard the not vital.

But beyond that, each individual issue is in itself a challenge. The editor must choose out of the vast amount of material at his disposal what he believes will be of most use to the largest number of readers at a particular time. Although he must keep his eye on the whole commonwealth of readers, he also has to select for the minority.

Many times he may discard an article with fairly wide appeal for one of pretty narrow appeal. He does so because he knows that the article he chooses will be appreciated by a small but important group of readers.

3. A third ingredient is *courage*. There are various types of editorial courage, all necessary for a good editor. First, and most obvious of course, is the courage to take up an unpopular cause and make it popular. But there are other kinds equally important. There is the courage to tell the reader, by implication at least, that sometimes the reader can be wrong in thinking he knows what he needs. It is this kind of fortitude that sometimes gets the editor ahead of his readers. Then there is the courage to fight the box office. Often by being courageous the editor does the box office more good than he would if he followed the easier course of not stirring up the animals.

4. Another ingredient is *timing*. A paragraph back I mentioned the danger of getting ahead of his readers. It is always better to be ahead of them than behind them. And a good editor always realizes that good timing may consist both of being ahead and then being on the job when the reader catches up.

I think every good editor has developed the qualities I have mentioned to a high degree. I believe that is true of all editors here at P.I.

But, by and large, as I look back over the achievements of our editors during recent years I find myself frequently amazed at the accuracy with which they have called the turn on developing trends, at their ability to uncover the types of authors who understand the most about trends, and at their ability to be out ahead of the marketing parade, but not so far ahead that they lose touch with those behind them.

5. Perhaps the most difficult job that faces an editor is to give the reader a properly balanced editorial program. He starts out with one strike on him. He knows that it is almost impossible for him to build a magazine that even one reader will read from cover to cover. He knows that if he could build an issue which a dozen readers would read from cover to cover, it probably would be for the general run of readers the least helpful and interesting issue he had built that year. Realizing this basic handicap, he proceeds to build his magazine issue by issue using a combination of judgment, intuition, common sense, and gambler's hunch—backed by a careful and continuous study of reader interest indicators.

He knows that for every magazine there is a certain audience with enough common interest to be served by the kind of magazine he publishes. He knows he cannot please every reader all of the time. He knows that he loses the reader who is displeased or indifferent too much of the time.

Happily, the editors of *Printers' Ink* serve an audience that does not hesitate to praise or blame. It does not take us long to find out when a particular feature or article is good. For instance, right now we know that for many years we have not put in a feature which has had quite such enthusiastic reader reception as the weekly feature, Which Ad Pulled Best? We know that certain other features are liked by a minority of our readers—but that that same minority like those features so well that they would complain bitterly and loudly if we dropped them.

Our editors have more indicators of reader interest than almost any other editors in either the businesspaper or consumer magazine fields. But, no matter how many indicators they have, eventually they have to fall back on experience, judgment, common sense.

The rewards are many. There is the old renewal percentage on the ABC report, which shows what percentage of readers back our editors' judgment with their own reader dollars. There are your comments given to field workers of The Eastman Research Organization. There are your fan letters, hundreds of them every year. And there are your inquiries to the Readers' Service Department.

CHAPTER 9

Pressures on Editors

"Never lunch alone . . . if you're not lunching with a client always try to lunch with a newspaper or magazine writer or editor, preferably an editor. Staff members should never lunch together. It is career suicide."
—Benjamin Sonnenberg.[1]

PROPAGANDA AND IMPROPERGANDA*

Nineteen kinds of pressure groups try to exert influence on editors of businesspapers for the very obvious reason that the editors are opinion-moulders—advising and guiding decision-makers and policy-makers in particular fields in which these pressure groups have an interest. Editors also influence purchasing of supplies—art, photography, engraving, paper, printing, other things in their own field—and every thing from A to Z in Industry.

Here are some of these pressure groups:

TYPES OF PRESSURE GROUPS

1. Advertisers
2. Nonadvertisers
3. Advertising agencies
4. Public relations people
5. Trade associations and professional groups
6. Government bureaus, local, state, federal, U.N.
7. Agents of other countries, embassies, consulates, bureaus
8. The readers of your publication
9. Other departments of your own organization
10. Labor organizations
11. Political organizations
12. Educational groups
13. Religious groups
14. Philanthropic groups
15. Sources of supply

---

[1] Benjamin Sonnenberg's advice to his staff, in "Reputation by Sonnenberg," an article by Croswell Bowen, *Harpers' Magazine*, February, 1950, page 47. Mr. Sonnenberg's New York public relations firm is called "Publicity Consultants." Several well-known authors and magazine writers are on his staff.

* Julien Elfenbein; from a lecture at New York University, February 5, 1947.

16. Other media: consumer maga- 17. Racketeers
    zines, newspapers, radio and 18. Subversive groups
    television broadcasters, book 19. Crackpots
    publishers, house organs

I do not use the term "pressure group" in any derogatory sense. We must remember that our own publishing organizations are pressure groups. Our businesspapers are pressure groups. Our advertising and our circulation salesmen are pressure groups, trying to "manufacture favorable attitudes" for our publications with certain other groups in the above list. An association of businesspapers or of any other units of business or society, becomes a pressure group, under this definition. Nor do I use the term "propaganda" in a derogatory sense.

Propaganda is defined as a device or technique for influencing human action, inaction, or reaction. It is as old as communications. It is done by manipulating spoken, written, pictorial, musical, or physical symbols or representations for the purpose of attacking or promoting a cause, interest, product, service, person, project, group, or institution in the eyes, ears, or minds of the general public or some segment of the public.

It can be done by flourishing a pistol, using a dagger, or tossing a bomb. The assassination of a political leader is propaganda by deed. You have also heard of character assassination accomplished with words, especially during political campaigns.

The National Association of Manufacturers describes its own public relations program as "policy-forming activities."

"Through this program," it says, "the policies and viewpoints evolved by NAM are interpreted to the general public (and to key segments of the public) in the everyday language of America, through the use of every effective public relations medium—advertising, radio, pamphlets, movies, contacts with opinion moulders, etc.—to enlist public support for them."[2]

---

[2] The annual budget of NAM for "public relations" is between three and four million dollars. The Special House Committee on Lobbying Activities in Washington on October 21, 1950, said 152 corporations spent $31,124,800 between January 1, 1947, and June 1, 1950, on "activities relating to attempts to influence legislation." Chairman Frank Buchanan (Democrat, Pennsylvania) said the report covered the activity of only a small part of the country's 500,000 corporations. The information on expenditures came from 152 corporations that replied to a questionnaire sent by the committee to 173 corporations. Sixty-five reported spending $2 million on publications and 31 reported spending $2 million on advertising dealing with public issues. *New York Times,* October 22, 1950, p. 1.

The art of the propagandist, as I have said, is the art of manufacturing attitudes, the art of "engineering mass consent" for something. When it is good propaganda, it is sometimes called public relations. When it is bad propaganda, it is a very slippery, insidious, or even criminal thing which we will call *improperganda*—a word coined years ago by Herbert Bayard Swope when he was editor of the old *New York World*.

"A successful journalist," according to the distinguished columnist Marquis Childs, "must be able to smell lying propaganda." The editors on a businesspaper certainly must have a keen sense of judgment in order to separate proper from improperganda. It is the "nose for news" developed to an even greater degree of sensitivity.

Because some propaganda may have news value or educational value, members of the editorial staff must scan and examine every clip sheet and press release that comes in, even though much of it goes eventually into the cylindrical file.

Let us consider two of the pressure groups in our list, the advertisers and nonadvertisers (prospects).

The advertiser is not always trying to get editorial space just because he bought some advertising space. There may really be news value in his publicity releases. And no salesman of advertising space promises an advertiser space in the editorial columns, in return for a contract, unless he is an utter fool. He is much smarter if he promises nothing. All good editors are cooperative. Why not? If the editor of a businesspaper was not willing to cooperate with people, he would not be an editor very long. The publishers lay down a policy. If what the editors publish does not conform to that policy, does not produce reader interest and desired reader action, then the editors should be brought into line.

By the same token no advertising space salesman will threaten an incurable nonadvertiser with exclusion from the editorial columns, even by innuendo, if he is in his right mind. Advertiser or nonadvertiser—if a firm has a story the editors judge to be of interest to the reader—it should be published, and it usually will be published, regardless of whether an advertising space contract is involved.

All legitimate pressure groups realize that whatever propaganda they manufacture to change the attitudes of a reader or to influence a reader, that material must stand this editorial test:

Is it news? Has it the timeliness, the scope, and consequence to deserve the reader's attention?

HOW TO DEAL WITH EDITORIAL PRESSURES*

Editorial pressure may be defined as the force used to influence editorial action. It may range all the way from a direct order to a mild request or suggestion either to publish or to refrain from publishing.

Editorial pressure by order or edict may come lawfully from only two sources: (1) the government; and (2) the owner of the publication. It might come unlawfully in the form of coercion or blackmail from individuals or groups powerful enough to presume to interfere with the "freedom of the press."

Of course, even the government has no right to order a businesspaper to print or refrain from printing anything except when martial law prevails; although in time of war or other national emergency, the government may request the press to do what it could not order it to do, and the press would almost invariably comply.

But the editorial pressure which comes in a peremptory form can come normally only from the owner of a publication. It may come by way of "the business office," but it might come through any department provided it had the sanction of the owner.

Only the owner has a legal right to direct the editor of a businesspaper to depart from the paper's established editorial policies or principles, or to change them. Of course that right does not necessarily imply the wisdom of such a course.

The practical question which would confront an editor who could not conscientiously go along with a departure from policy ordered by the owner or a change of policy would be to decide whether he wanted to continue to work for such a publisher. When the owner tells an editor to follow certain lines, or resign, the self-respecting editor will resign rather than follow a course which he cannot conscientiously accept.

This does not mean, of course, that the editor of a businesspaper has the right, as against the owner, to frame the paper's policies. It means only that once such policies have been established, he should abide by them until they are duly changed. He should accept orders from no one

* Godfrey M. Lebhar, Chief Editor of *Chain Store Age;* President, Lebhar-Friedman Publications. Mr. Lebhar, a graduate of New York University Law School, practiced law in New York City from 1904 to 1909. He was on the editorial staff of the *New York American* (1909-1918); established and edited *Underwear & Hosiery Review;* author of *Chain Store, Boon or Bane?* and other books. A lecture given before Mr. Elfenbein's class in Business Journalism, New York University, November 22, 1948.

—not even the owner—to depart from them for reasons of expediency or whim or just plain orneriness.

So much for direct orders.

By far the greatest category of editorial pressures embraces those which come in the shape of requests.

Such requests may come from the outside—from advertisers or non-advertisers—or they may come from inside your own organization—from the advertising department, the circulation department, the production department, or any other department or individual.

Such requests in the majority of cases relate to desired "write-ups" from or in behalf of advertisers or prospective advertisers. They may come direct from the individual or company involved, or indirectly from your own advertising department working presumably in the interest of the advertiser or prospect.

More rarely in the case of businespapers will the request involve the suppression of news or features in the interest of someone who might be embarrassed or harmed by their publication. In the case of newspapers, however, the pressure not to publish is met more frequently.

Included in these requests for space are, of course, the whole body of releases from press agents, publicity departments, and other representatives of individuals, companies, or groups with special axes to grind.

Whether such requests come from or in behalf of advertisers or non-advertisers, their treatment should be governed by the same principles. The acid test which most businesspaper editors use is threefold:

1. Is the stuff in line with your established editorial policies?

2. If it is, is it worth printing from the standpoint of your readers?

3. Have you room for it—which means does it deserve priority over other material which it would displace?

Of course, if the item in question falls right in line with your policies and needs, it does not involve any editorial pressure at all. On the contrary, it takes the form of an editorial service. You not only accept it but thank those who supply it. The question of pressure does not really arise except in cases where you find it necessary to reject the proffered item, or the outside suggestion. If you do not resist, you have no pressure—just movement. The item moves right in. But if you do find it necessary or desirable to resist, you at once suffer pressure, the force of which will, however, vary with the circumstances.

The third type of pressure is of the mildest kind. It comes by way of suggestion. The suggestion may come from either outside or inside your organization. Such suggestions should be treated in the same way as requests. If the suggestion is one you can use, you are naturally thankful for it. For that reason, it does not pay to discourage suggestions from any source. If the suggestion is one you cannot use or do not want, you just do not use it. If repeated often enough, so that it develops into nagging, a suggestion can become very troublesome and annoying, but never let it wear you down.

Editors are frequently confronted with a choice of direction. One may involve little or no problem, the other may bring all kinds of new problems in the form of resentment on the part of those who do not like the new direction.

For instance, you may decide that certain trends or practices in your industry are not for its best long-pull interests. If you do nothing about it, you may save yourself a lot of headaches. But if your editorial conscience suggests that you might to take the matter up editorially, you probably will not sleep easy of nights until you have done what your conscience dictates. It may stir up a hornet's nest in your field. Some of your best advertisers or readers may not like it, but what can you do other than follow your own best judgment?

There is a case of editorial pressure which you *bring upon yourself* by taking a course which you know in advance will run you smack into resistance. In other words, in such a case, you will be supplying the movement and someone else the resistance. But the end result is the same— you suffer editorial pressure, and whether you yield to it or overcome it will depend upon what kind of editor you are and the backing you get from your own organization.

One word of caution may be added. No editor should go around with a chip on his shoulder—ready to throw up his job everytime he finds he cannot have his own way. Do not forget that it is the owner's privilege to set the policies for his paper, editorial as well as business policies. If you cannot live with the editorial policies established, you may have a case where your only course is to resign. But if the issue involved is not all-important even though it involves a deviation from what you would consider a better policy, you may not be justified, from the standpoint of your own best interest, in throwing up your job.

Finally, sticking to editorial policies means, as a general proposition, hewing pretty straight to the line. It means ignoring all arguments based on such points as:

1. "This is the *first* time, I've ever asked you to do it." The very *worst* time to depart from a policy is the *first* time.

2. "This is a special case—very important to one of our biggest cus-

tomers, etc." Never fail to point out that doing something to please a friend in the trade may mean displeasing twenty of his competitors, who are also friends of your paper.

3. "Other trade papers are using the item—we'll be the only one that won't carry it." Either your policy in not carrying such items is sound or unsound. If it is unsound, scrap it—not for the sake of carrying the item offered at the moment but with the idea of carrying all such items in future. If your policy is sound, do not worry about what other papers may do with the item.

4. "The item is harmless. It won't hurt anybody and will please the person offering it." If your policy to exclude such items is a good one, stick to it. If it is not, change it. If, for instance, people in your field have been marrying, having babies, divorcing, dying without ever a line in your paper about such events, because you just do not carry them, do not listen to anyone who wants you to do him a favor just because the chairman of the board of your most important advertiser has just decided to get married.

One thing I have learned in my 41 years of newspaper and business-paper editorial experience is this: in following a straight-line editorial policy you will occasionally run into some bumpy going, but you will get more satisfaction in the long run than if you try short-cuts and detours everytime you hit a trouble spot.

PUBLICISTS GIVE THE PITCH

On May 11, 1950, publicists were guests of the New York Business Paper Editors at their monthly luncheon in the Advertising Club of New York. The panel discussion on publicity releases was unrehearsed and extemporaneous. The preliminary statements of two of the speakers and the answers by one of the editors were wire-recorded and are included here to show the attitudes that exist between businesspaper editors and publicity men.

1. OUR TROUBLE IS WITH CLIENTS—NOT EDITORS*

Our trouble really is not from editors or with trade publications. Our trouble is with clients. I think the main job we do (and maybe we do not

---

* Ray Josephs, member of Publicity Associates (Benjamin Sonnenberg), before New York Businesspaper Editors, May 11, 1950. Mr. Josephs is author of *Argentine Diary, Latin American Diary* (1944), *Spies and Saboteurs in Argentina* (1943), Random House, N.Y., and magazine articles; foreign correspondent and lecturer.

always do it as completely well as we should) is to try to serve as intermediary between client and editor. Now, please note how we go about
it from our end. Much of this may be familiar, but I think it may present
the publicity or public relations man's point of view a little clearer and
explain why he sometimes has troubles with you.

We have a new client who is going to introduce a new, and we think
a rather startling, product. Last week I went out to Chicago with two of
my assistants. We sat down with all the executives of the company. These
were the men who were going to tell us what this product was about and
what to do about it.

Generally, the client first wants to tell you all about his plan, and how
he makes his "Wheaties." He will bore you for a week, take you all
through the plant, show you how many units of this he makes, and so on.
You know darn well the story you have to tell the editor is going to be
an entirely different one.

We think we have solved it, by bringing the weight of our past experience to bear on the client. For a good many years I have been a magazine
writer whose job has been to write pieces that I could *sell* to magazines,
not give away. In selling pieces to *Colliers,* the *Digest*, the *Post* and so
on, even though I have written a couple of books, nobody would buy
any of my stories (or the books or the lectures or anything else) unless
the editor was sold that it was a good story.

This time in Chicago, having a general idea of the fields in which this
client's product might be sold, we sat these executives down and we said
"We don't want to hear speeches from you—just answers to our questions." I set up one of these new small dictaphones, and we said "First,
here are the fields we think might be of interest on this particular
product. For example, farm papers, general consumer publications, financial papers, etc." We had them give us the answers, not on the basis
of what they wanted to tell us, but why this particular product would
appeal for example to farmers. We came up with the answers in specific
terms of what the pitch might be in each field.

As we went through the questioning our clients got limper and limper,
because the thing started at eight in the morning and went on until eight
at night with only sandwiches in between. Then we turned to the next
field. What we were attempting to do in between was this. Instead of
finding out what their story was and then worrying, we were going to sell
it to you. We said, "The editors in this field are interested in such and
such a thing. If it is for the department stores, what is it going to do for

the department store, instead of the fabulous story of what produced it, or about how Jones designed it." By putting it that way we emerged at the end of that session with four or five rolls of dictated material that was approved and agreed upon right then and there.

I know now if I go out to you, if it is in your field, paint, or drygoods or whatever it will be, I will have a basic story that will interest you because it is pitched in your own direction. The problem we have is that very few clients are willing to do this. As a matter of fact, battling through as we did, hour after hour with these people in Chicago, revealed that these manufacturers did not have all the facts. Somebody would have to go out and get them. Actually I feel if we are to be most successful, we must simply serve as leg men, in a sense, to dig out the very angles you want and then bring them to you in almost such a form as you would say "That's a good story, I can use it almost as is." Or you would say, "Now our own man can go out and look over this story himself.

Essentially that has been the big problem we have faced so far as publicity is concerned. The one weakness we find with businesspaper editors is that you do not ask us enough questions, or demand specific things, so that we can go out and try to get the answers for you. I would say that in many cases the ideas (at least in our own organization) originated with us, and then we tried to go out and place them with you. We would like you to say: "Dig up this for me on this angle or that angle" or "give us some other subject." Frequently, in our own experience, we will get a call from an editor on Thursday morning that he wants the story in by Friday afternoon. Perhaps the client is not around or he has to clear it with a couple of vice presidents. We try to set up with our own clients a direct pipeline to the president or the chairman of the board of the company. As soon as we get tied up with vice presidents or assistants, it will take us a month before we can get anything cleared. If we know specifically what you want and we get it in sufficient time, we can also do a better job. I know that you are interested in getting your own story because you are anxious to serve your readers your way.

Sometimes a client will say, well why should we bother to dig all that up for such-and-such journal? They do not use my name, or they leave us out of it entirely, or they will twist it around. It may mean putting a vice president back to work for a week in order to dig out just the kind of thing you editors want. We try to sell them the idea that such-and-such journal is the greatest paper in its field. That it covers every buyer, every manufacturer. But sometimes the client is a little hard to convince and he says, "Why don't you get me the front cover on *Life* instead? I don't want to get in a trade paper."

I want to say that we publicity people do a selling job for the trade press. If *Linen & Domestics* runs a story of ours, for example, we tell our client that this is worth all the time and expense involved for it is going to reach the most important people that he wants to reach. And though he may not think so, it is as important as getting in *Life*.

To sum up. First I think our own relationship should be a little closer. You ought to try us on some more things and at least give us a chance to see whether we cannot get these things up for you. Second, we ought to try if possible to get a little longer advance notice of what you are anxious to get. For example if we could find out, as we frequently try to do in our own contacts, that you want production stories or you want personality stories, or whatever it would be, I think the editors with whom we work would agree that we get them a pretty good result on the stuff that they want as quickly as we can.

If you do not get what you want, it is not because we have not tried. As I said before, our chief problem is with the client. We do not have any real troubles with you; we know what you want. We speak your language. Gradually we hope to educate our clients, and when that time comes then I think we will be a lot happier.

2. PUBLICITY MEN HAVE GRIPES, TOO*

I contacted our membership and I asked them if they had any gripes or beefs or if they had any accolades for the businesspaper editors. Some of their gripes follow:

One member questions the frequent distortion of facts in a story sent in to a businesspaper, after it is rewritten. He feels, from a point of accuracy, it might be wise when a story is rewritten, to contact the publicist so that he can be sure when it comes out in print there will be no room for a beef. I do not think that is asking too much, do you?

Some of the boys and girls in our group seem to have the feeling that the businespasper editor is influenced too much by the advertising department or the potential advertisers, in the publication of stories. Your own conscience I suppose can answer this one. Then there is the question, must there be personal contact with businesspaper editors? One

* Henry Schapper, Henry Schapper Associates, Public Relations Counsel; Mr. Schapper is secretary of the New York Publicity Club.

publicist feels that releases to businesspapers should be handled for the most part through the mails as he handles them with the daily newspapers.

Here is something else: When exclusive copy is given to a specific businesspaper, the publicist would like to know if and when the stuff is going to be used, before it gets too old and cannot be used elsewhere. I wonder if some of the businesspapers say, "yes, we'll take an exclusive," and then hold it simply because they do not want the competition to get that story?

One of our members made this statement: "The publicists themselves are too lax." This confirms what Mr. Josephs was saying. The publicists *are* too lax; they do not go out and dig up the facts. Some of them are lazy. They will send out a release which is general to everybody and it ends up in the waste basket. Too few of them recognize, I believe, that the job of the publicist who is working for the business press is almost a specialist's job, with special treatment in each area.

This one I have to read to you: This man happens to be vice president of a very large agency in charge of public relations. He writes: "Too often they (meaning the businesspaper editors) kill legitimate news, if it is about a nonadvertiser. Too often they are too lazy to do rewrites of a release, too often they have lower standards of good journalism than good publicists have."

3. AN EDITOR'S ATTITUDE*

Most all the speeches here today were concerned with publicity releases, but on our publication we consider we ought to *beat* you people to the news. That is what we are in business for. We are not in business to sit back and get a publicity release from you people. If our district men are awake (and I think they are awake) we ought to be able to get the story if we know what is going on in our field. We do not particularly suffer from editors getting a shine on the seat of their pants. However, once we do get on the trail of something, we like to talk to publicity people like you to get some of the details we do not have. But in doing that we are cautious—we do not think a good public relations man will protect the private talk he has with an editor when the editor has dug out his own story. We are afraid he will call up our competition five

---

* Tom Campbell, Chief Editor, *Iron Age*. Wire-recorded. Mr. Campbell was not on the panel but spoke from the floor. He is a member of the executive committee, New York Business Paper Editors.

minutes afterward. When the publicist or public relations man who digs up the story says to us—"you can't print that," "this is wrong," or "you can't say that about us," we laugh because after all we are in the business of getting and printing news.

The editor who is on his toes is going to get the story. So if his enterprising reporter does not get the story, he is going to get fired. Any trade paper editor who will sit at his desk and have you publicity men do his work for him, as you say you are willing to do, should not be called a trade paper editor!"

Now I want to answer one point, the question over which you were extremely worried, where the editors ditched your publicity material. You say the question is asked by editors when they get a piece of publicity material: Is he an advertiser or is he not? If he is a nonadvertiser you suggest the editor might throw it in the wastepaper basket. That is just the opposite to what the editor does or ought to do. If the editor is any good and thinks about the business part of his paper, a story from a nonadvertiser is a story from a *potential* advertiser. But it should be weighed on its *news* basis alone."

What I mean is that if it was a good news item and if the fellow was not an advertiser, I think anybody ought to figure it was good business to publish it because you have got to have a paper published with news in it in order for it to pay the publisher. But the thought I want to leave is that if a stranger came into this room and he did not know too much about the publicists or the businesspaper publishers, he would assume that all the information published in these trade papers was furnished by you publicists.

The percentage of material appearing in our papers which emanates from publicity releases or material of that type is this: about half of the new products news comes from publicity releases, and very little, if any, of the feature material.

There is one thing for publicity people to bear in mind. We seldom ask presidents or vice presidents to look at galleys after the story is set up. We often let them see the manuscript before we run it, only for facts, but in the first five minutes they will begin to say "we didn't say this," or "what do you want to say that for?" So if we can possibly avoid it we do not show galleys or manuscripts to any outsider. We work on the formula that it is our story.

One thing more about releases: Any public relations man who puts out a release which is a bid to get something in the paper or magazine, must of necessity take the gamble as to what happens to it. We put out a release to daily newspapers once a week ourselves for *Iron Age*. We may feel like calling some newspaper up and saying they took the wrong interpretation out of it, but we never have. We abide by the fact that we gave the newspaper services or the wire services a hand out, which is what it is. You have taken the gamble; it is out of your hands. If you squawk, as we know from being on both sides of the fence, it will do you no good.

You ought to be accurate and clear enough in your release so there is not much chance to complain about misinterpretation.

CHAPTER 10

Writing and Headlines

"The written word
Should be clean as a bone
Clear as light,
Firm as stone.
Two words are not as good as one." Anon.

WRITING FOR THE BUSINESS PRESS

An associate professor of English at Princeton University called on me to apply for a job on the editorial staff of one of our businesspapers. He was on the last lap for his Ph.D. degree and had been promised a full professorship after he received it. When I asked him why he was willing to give up his career as a college professor, he replied that the cook in his boarding house made more money than he could hope for as an English professor at Princeton.

The professor had come to the right place for better wages, but he had overlooked one essential. He was not qualified to write for the business press. He had only a vague, academic concept of the business process, no knowledge of any of its specialized fields, no practical experience or training in business or in journalism.

To those interested in writing for businesspapers, I recommend a book edited by Arthur Wimer,[1] containing contributions by a score or more of businesspaper editors and publishers. It is not a text on writing but a volume of essays which tells writers what editors in different fields of business journalism expect of their writers.

For texts on writing for the business press[2] I suggest the works of Dr.

[1] *Writing for the Business Press,* Arthur Wimer, chairman, Department of Journalism, San Diego State College, William C. Brown Co., Dubuque, Iowa, 1950.

[2] See Julien Elfenbein, *Business Journalism*, Harper & Brothers, N. Y., 1945, ch. 11.

283

Rudolf Flesch,[3] Dr. S. I. Hayakawa, and Dr. Bernard De Voto. These men are experts on readability. The style guides of *Tide* and *Printers' Ink* are helpful for practical points on interviewing and writing. A portion of the *Guide to Tide* is included in this chapter. Also analyze the feature articles in any specialized business publication.

Nothing produces a good businesspaper writer like the daily discipline of the writing job itself. There is no substitute for apprenticeship, months of it, years of it, to produce a good businesspaper writer.

If I had to describe the language of the business press in one short sentence I would say this: It is the language used in everyday talk by people who know what they are talking about. Short words. Short sentences. Examples. Idiom. Some slang.

It is my good fortune to have a secretary who takes it right on the typewriter as I talk. I say whatever I want to say to an audience I can see as palinly as if they were in a hall before me.

When I finish, the sheet is pulled out and handed to me. I begin to read my copy aloud to myself. I edit as I read. I may cut, switch sentences or paragraphs, insert, or leave it as is. Usually the editorial or article will go through the machine three or four times before it satisfies me. I want to be sure everything I said was worth saying. But I also want it to be interesting.

Philip Swain, chief editor of *Power* and *Power Maintenance,* has to man his staff with engineers. His problem, he says, is to get graduate engineers who are also articulate engineers—as skilled in the language of words as they are in the language of mathematics.

James G. Lyne, chief editor of *Railway Age,* has the same problem. He says:

"Wherever some phase of the younger editor's background is observed to be deficient, we encourage him to correct this deficiency by outside study.

"The principal difficulty, of course, comes in the writing of good, clear English—a handicap suffered more by our editors with technical training than by those with other educational backgrounds.

"I do not believe that, in the business press generally, we have even scratched the surface in the improvement which we might attain if we would set about seriously to improve the quality of work done by our editors—and particularly our younger editors, who, of course, are more

[3] See "Shirt Sleeve English in One Easy Lesson," by Rudolf Flesch, *Printers' Ink,* June 30, 1950.

teachable than most of us old fellows are. We have all seen the tremendous success and acclaim visited on such men as Laurence of the *Times*, who have learned how to report scientific developments in language which is both interesting and understandable. Undoubtedly, similar success and renown awaits the businesspaper editors who will master the art of reporting the technological accomplishments of specific industries with similar clarity and interest-value."[4]

Other materials relating to writing will be found in Chapter 8 and in the Dusenbury notes in Chapter 11. Dusenbury's studies on headlines, lead sentences, and captions supplement the materials in this chapter.

THE BUSINESSPAPER ARTICLE*

Perhaps the most important part of any story is the lead—the first paragraph or the first two or three paragraphs. Leads should make the reader want to continue with the story; ideally, they should make him feel that he must continue. For those reasons, you should be particularly careful in selecting opening material. For example, you should try not to start with facts that everyone knows. Paragraphs which lead off with obvious knowledge—e.g., "For nearly a hundred years Brazil has been the world's biggest coffee supplier and the U. S. its biggest coffe cup" —are so dull probably no one will read beyond them. If you absolutely cannot avoid such a construction, at least temper it with something like this: "For nearly a hundred years, as everyone knows, Brazil has been . . . etc."

Another lead to avoid is the one which employs a bromide, outworn adage or phrase that is not naturally related to what follows. Do not ever start stories with anything like the following: "Everybody talks about the weather but no one ever does anything about it. Last week, however, the XYZ Thermometer Co. brought out a new product that may help to improve . . . etc." Similarly, unless you can be thoroughly skillful, do not try to manufacture a synthetic lead; in writing about a pay-as-you-go tax, do not say anything like this: "All over the country last week, shiny new silver jingled in the jeans of war workers who thought they were

[4] From an address before the Eastern Editorial Clinic, ABP, Savoy Plaza Hotel, New York, Jan. 9, 1951; Mr. Lyne is former board chairman of ABP. He is president of Simmons-Boardman Pub. Co.

* From *Guide to Tide*, a style book containing instructions to editorial staff members and correspondents, published in mimeograph form in 1943; revised in 1951. *Tide* started in 1927 as an external house organ for *Time* Magazine; it became an independent business magazine of the advertising industry in 1931.

riding high. But according to the Gallup Poll, they won't have enough to meet the tax collector next month."

The most important thing to remember about a lead is to pick a specific one; general leads, no matter how well written, almost never come off as well. Really, too, if your story does not have enough meat in it or something interesting enough to put right up front, it probably does not belong in the book and should be dropped at once. If you are thoroughly hard-pressed for a lead, always consider starting it with a quote, or with an interesting paragraph about the person responsible for the news you are reporting.

TRANSITIONS

Most newspaper stories are built like an inverted pyramid, with the base at the top. (In the first paragraph is the news lead—the "who, what, when, why and where" of the story—with the facts diminishing in importance as the story grows longer, so that the final paragraphs can be cut out or not as the case requires.) *Tide* stories are built more like a solid column, which may collapse if any part of it is missing. For that reason, the last paragraph should be, if not as important as the first, at least as necessary—and so should all the paragraphs in between.

This tends to make *Tide* stories closely knit—paragraph by paragraph and even sentence by sentence—and it makes unity and transitions important problems. You should plan the story so that the facts run in a natural and normal sequence, of course, and you should develop certain techniques which link the paragraphs closely and establish clear and logical transitions. The use at or near the beginning of paragraphs of such words as "meanwhile," "likewise," "also," "additionally," "moreover," "however" and the like all may help tie the paragraphs together; you should be careful, though, not to overdo these tricks and, if you can get along without them, do so.

LENGTH OF PARAGRAPHS

Because of *Tide*'s make-up and the nature of its stories, it is wise to follow a rather definite pattern on the length of paragraphs, breaking up stories with short paragraphs, etc. Generally, no paragraph should run more than six typewritten lines on copy paper (or 12 lines of type). Many times paragraphs have to and should run longer than that, but that is nevertheless a good yardstick to follow. Another desirable policy, particularly for medium and long stories, is to include one very short paragraph (of one or two typewritten lines) between several normal paragraphs. This helps break the monotony of the story, gives you a chance to sum up what you have said, to prepare the reader for a change in thought or developments or to give the story a punch that will help lead the reader through the next paragraph.

ASTERISKS AND PARENTHESES

From time to time, writers at *Tide* have used asterisks and parentheses with great carelessness—unforgivable because it is so unnecessary. To avoid this, you should never use an asterisk in the middle of a sentence, and never in the middle of a paragraph if you can help it. If you cannot figure a way to put it at the end of a sentence, rewrite the sentence until you can. And never use an asterisk in the lead paragraph.

Somewhat the same rule should follow for parentheses. The worst (and most common) example of how not to use a parenthesis is something like the following: "Last week (via BBD&O) a new campaign started in newspapers, magazines and radio for Swan soap sponsored by Lever Bros." Say instead: "Last week, Lever Bros. started a new campaign (via BBD&O) for Swan soap in newspapers, magazines and radio. Put the parenthesis where it belongs—which means after the names or facts on which it depends.

The difference between footnotes and parenthetical phrases is one you should know thoroughly. Footnotes are used when you want to add something germane to the story, though it may not necessarily explain the next thing you are going to say; parenthetical phrases are used when you want to add something germane which will help explain what immediately follows. Do not use too many of either of them. Except in rare cases, one footnote to the average story should be the ceiling, and when you can get along without any, do so.

SIMILES AND METAPHORS

Various figures of speech—similes, metaphors, and other such devices —are desirable in almost any story and they help make your writing more imaginative, colorful and, in some cases, more exact. But they should be used with extreme care and, unless you are positive that what you are saying makes sense, you should avoid them. In any case, do not mix up figures of speech, and once you start with one figure, stick with it. Never indulge in such nonsense as the following: "A new element entered the scene of the network-FCC fight last week, determined to buck the current tide and to prevent the government agency from delivering a knockout blow." There are at least three mixed figures in the sentence, but it is no more ridiculous than several that have turned up on occasion in *Tide* copy.

Another type of figure to avoid is the one that does not quite jibe with the rest of the sentence or paragraph or that gives the facts an incorrect or strange implication. For example, do not use one like this: "As familiar as an old wives' tale is the current fight between the networks and the FCC." Old wives' tales are apocryphal; they do not exist but people believe they do, and that is what makes them old wives' tales. The fight between the networks and the FCC is not apocryphal; it exists in fact. Connecting it with such a figure of speech suggests that the fight is apocryphal, or that we believe it is. That may seem like a fine point, but good writing is built on fine points.

INFINITIVES AND PARTICIPLES

Despite their growing general use, split infinitives and dangling participles are strictly tabu at *Tide*. They are not necessary, the same thing can be said just as easily in the correct form and, until someone demonstrates some useful purpose for them, they definitely are out. Do not say: "Jones claimed that the campaign was planned to partially cure the company's distribution troubles." Do say: "Jones claimed that the campaign was planned partially to cure the company's. . . ." Also do not say: "Planning to use 47 newspapers and 6 national magazines, the copy will show what the company is doing in the war." Do say: "Planning to use 47 newspapers and 6 national magazines, the company will show what it is doing in the war."

PERSONALITIES AND WRITING

Tide has always proposed to tell the news in terms of personalities and, with certain reservations, will continue doing so. Always remember that, in our sphere at least, things never happen; people do things to make them happen. Therefore, you should include the people who did the things as well as the things themselves, if you are to tell a complete and interesting story. Include the people whenever you can, providing they seem to belong there—but never include them if you have to drag them in by the heels.

ACCURACY

Not enough can ever be said on the importance of accuracy to a newspaper, a magazine, or anything else for that matter. You may write a perfectly good story, with everything checked and double checked; it may have everything the best *Tide* story ever had, and then some; but if you misspell one word, get an agency wrong, or mix up someone's name or position, the whole piece suffers—and rightly so.

The one cardinal rule on accuracy is to check with everyone that you can reach who is involved in any story you may be doing. Even trying to reach someone is a mitigating circumstance in the event anything goes wrong. (That is one reason why it is so important to leave your name and a request to be called back whenever you call anyone and find him out.) This is particularly important on controversial stories, or those where there is even a slight difference of opinion. A person may be displeased that a fight is on, he may think it unwise to publish anything about it, he may not want to talk, but if he is at all reasonable, he will be grateful to you for checking with him —and you should stress this point on occasion.

Here are a few hints on accuracy:

Check names of companies, agencies, people, or groups in the source books. Always double check to make sure you get the proper advertising agency for each product and further that you get the proper agency for that portion of the product's advertising. Be positive that it is the Senate Committee on Banking & Currency, not the House Committee on Currency & Banking. Find out for sure that it is Coordinator of Inter-American Affairs Nelson Rockefeller, not Inter-American Coordinator Nelson Rockefeller. Make sure which office of the agency is handling the account, or where the radio station is located; say: BBD&O (Manhattan), or WBBM (Chicago).

Identify unfamiliar organizations with their location: "Olian Advertising Co. (St. Louis)," or "Seidman & Seidman, Manhattan public accountants . . . ," etc.

BROMIDES AND CLICHÉS

By all means avoid every word or phrase that smacks of being trite, commonplace, overworked, or provincial. Never use such bromides as John Citizen, Joe Doakes, George Spelvin, John Q. Public, or John Doe. If you mean the people, the taxpayer, the voter, the client, the consumer, say so. Make up names only on the rarest occasions, and only when you are certain you can be skillful enough to get away with it naturally and smoothly.

Beware, too, of someone else's once-fresh phrase that has become outworn. Expressions like bowed in, lion's share, tout, boast, spawn, copy-cat should be used sparingly if at all.

The right word is important, but do not go to extreme lengths to avoid repetition; if there is no good synonym for certain words, no one will expect you to find one. In any case, remember that today's soldiers may be doughboys or fighting men (only when absolutely necessary) but they are never gladiators or warriors. Pretentious words like yesteryear should disappear from your vocabulary at once. Do not say war effort and do not say defense job or defense plant. These expressions are stilted, do not mean much and should not appear again in print; they crop up from time to time in publications everywhere, but you can help make *Tide* a better magazine by not using them.

CHOICES OF WORDS

There are other choices of words that can improve *Tide's* style. Use the word *ad*, for example, with great caution. You may use it in a story, if you do not overdo it, providing you have first mentioned the word *advertisement* or *advertising*. But never use it in certain combinations, like ad campaign, ad manager, ad agency. And used alone, it has a rather strange ring. "The firm ran its ads" is not as good as "The firm ran its copy." Words like agencyman, agent, or adman are all right, but they should be used carefully. The best rule for choosing words is simply to use good taste, always.

Be cautious, too, about crediting "the trade" with your information. Maybe it really is the "consensus of the trade," and in those instances the expression is satisfactory. But often the trade is used when you really mean "one element in the trade," "a few in the trade," or "some in the trade."

Additionally, too, be careful not to inject your own opinions or to use constructions, phrases, or words that make you even seem to be editorializing. If opinions are necessary, cite your source for them and pin them definitely on him; if you cannot use his name, you can at least say: "one person in the trade" or perhaps "one element (or faction) in the trade." But whatever you do, do not burden the reader with your own opinions. Be careful with adjectives. Do not say: "P&G's practical approach to this tough problem was as follows." Do say: "P&G solved the problem, which had stumped many other companies, by the following means."

Companies, agencies, associations, and similar groups are all inanimate, and you should therefore always say: "the company which," never "the company who." Similarly, "The company ran its copy," never "the company ran their copy." Both points hold, too, whether you use the word *company*, or its proper name: Lever Bros., General Electric or Columbia Broadcasting. People are always *of* a company, seldom *at*, *with* or *for* it. Always say: "John Jones, research director of Lever Bros.," never "John Jones, research director at (or *with* or *for*) Lever Bros."

STANDARDS FOR HEADLINE WRITING*

I believe there are two basic reasons why we are always in hot water about heads.

First, part of our trouble stems from the fact that we have not recognized headlines for what they really are: a highly specialized type of writing. The writing of good heads requires a sharp sense of editorial values, a feeling for rhythm and movement and color, and a rich and extensive vocabulary. It also requires a great deal of practice.

Second, part of our learning and teaching troubles is traceable to a lack of clear recognition of the fact that the headlines we write for our own papers must really meet three different sets of standards:

1. They must meet the standards that, in general, govern the writing of all good heads—standards that pretty well apply across the board.

2. They must meet a second set of standards dictated by the character of your specific audience and the nature of your publication. (Yours is a weekly; mine is a semimonthly; yours is technical; mine is nontechnical, etc.)

3. They must meet a third set of standards that are dictated by the character of the material offered and the context in which it appears.

If you go along with me this far, we now must admit the necessity for buckling down to the job of writing the specifications for our own heads in our own papers. We have been waiting for someone to put something in a can. Yet when we analyze the situation as we have done here, we know full well no one can do this for us.

We have been largely writing heads by ear. Most of us have had no formal training in headline writing. There are few books that will give us any substantial help. The idea I am advancing is this: we have got to quit doing it by ear. We must set down in writing a set of standards to use

---

* A. R. Hahn, Managing Editor of *Sales Management*. New York Business Paper Editors Panel, March 18, 1947. Miss Hahn is a former chairman of the New York Business Paper Editors.

as a base. Then we can measure our own heads against the standards to see where we are weak.

I say "set down in writing" because not until you are forced to commit your thoughts to black and white will you think through to learn what your standards really are, or what they should be. If they are not in writing, they are probably too nebulous to use.

I believe, as I have said, that there are actually three sets of standards required. The members of this panel cannot do anything for you on the second and third sets—those you will have to custom build for yourselves.

But we did discuss, the other day, some of the principles we felt applied to all heads. I am going to list eight of them. We give them to you as thought-starters. They by no means exhaust the subject. Here they are:

1. A good headline sells the story.
2. A headline is not any good unless it is truthful. It must not oversell the story, or undersell the story—or distort the facts in the story.
3. Short heads are, in general, preferable to long heads.
4. A good headline is in tune with the article.
5. A good headline is specific rather than general.
6. A good headline has unity—it does not try to do too many things at once.
7. A good headline has life, or lift, or movement, or whatever you may choose to call it. You may think of it merely as "attention value." If you will use active voice, for example, in writing heads, they will have a quality of life they never will achieve if you write them in passive voice.
8. A good headline has individuality as compared with other headlines in the same issue.

You may add to this list as you choose—or quarrel with it as you choose. But you do need to draft a set of principles which will provide criteria by which you can judge whether your heads are good or bad or mediocre—and why. I have one word of caution to throw in here: as you develop your statements of principle, please distinguish between matters of *principle*, and matters of *technique*.

Let me take a minute to make this clear.

When we say a good headline tells the story, we are stating a principle. But when we note that fights and forecasts make good headline material, we are talking about matters of technique. When we say a good headline has liveliness or spontaneity, we are stating a principle. But when we point out that we can achieve this effect by the use of such language tools as analogy, and alliteration, or balanced or contrasting pairs of words, we are again talking about techniques.

How can you go about developing headline standards? I would suggest the conference method. Make use of the best ideas of your entire editorial staff. It would be fine if we could all engage in some kind of scientific research on headline response, but we cannot. (Anyway, I doubt if there is a satisfactory technique for doing it.) The next best thing is to trust the combined judgment of the people who have had experience in your field and on your publication. I think you will find that judgment quite sound. I am not talking entirely through my hat on this score, because I have had some experience with it. That is the way we developed our standards for heads on *Sales Management*. They are far from perfect, but they are a thousand per cent better than no standards at all.

HEADLINES FOR THE BUSINESS NEWSPAPER*

News headlines pose different problems from headlines for magazine stories or for advertisements. News headlines *sell* the reader the story usually by telling him the guts of it.

In effect, the news headline says: This is the story. This is the who, what, when, where of it—and often the how and the why. The editor assumes that the main facts of the event, as told in the banner or the head and amplified a bit in the lead paragraph, are interesting enough to pull the reader into the whole story.

For years researchers have studied readership of editorial and advertising content—including headlines—of various kinds of publications. But Dr. Daniel Starch tells me that, to his knowledge, no one ever had studied readership of news headlines as such.

The Continuing Study of Newspaper Reading, conducted by the Advertising Research Foundation, finds the proportions of people who read headlines and stories, page by page. But the Foundation has no evidence to show that *this* headline would be better than *that* on the same story.

* Lawrence M. Hughes, *Sales Management*. Mr. Hughes was Executive Editor of *Advertising Age* in 1947 when he appeared on this Businesspaper Editors panel at Hotel Sheraton, New York City. That paper uses a newspaper format.

Some paper ought to test it on important heads in a split run.

Because a news headline is simply the gist of the story, it might seem easy to write. But even old hands at it sometimes feel like the man who wrote the Lord's Prayer on the head of a pin.

Brevity, of course, means nothing without clarity. The tell-the-story headline has been developed, chiefly since World War I, to *sell papers*. It still sells papers—especially the on-the-street bulldog or predate editions.

Only after you have made the headline brief and clear can you make it vigorous and compelling.

Most straight news stories require the direct declarative head, because most news—in businesspapers as in newspapers—concerns straight-faced problems.

But the head must fit the spirit of the story. If the event is funny, the head should be funny. If serious, the head should be serious. But most newspapers at one time or another appropriately can use heads that question, tease, or even rhyme.

There may be room for more emotion in businesspapers. But we do not have to go tabloid to develop it. We seldom have occasion, for example, to write:

"Jealous wife slays banker in love nest."

Maybe we are in the wrong field. But even most newspapers would not put the story that strongly. The *New York Times*—carrying the story only because of what it calls its interest in sociology—probably would skip the jealousy and the love nest and say: "Wife's Bullet Proves Fatal to Financier."

Many papers ban adjectives from heads—as they do, by and large, from stories.

Instead they develop vigor mostly from the verbs. They use active verbs—preferably three- or four-letter Anglo-Saxon. Verbs such as rid, hit, nip, rap, woo, bow, halt, curb, leap, gird, cut, sap. Verbs such as slug, balk, urge, defy, deny. Verbs such as go and do.

The verb's meaning in heads may not always conform to Webster, but readers know what they are *intended* to mean. I do not think many readers of *Advertising Age* got the wrong idea when I wrote, a couple of months ago: "Robert R. Young *woos* 1,000,000 railroad stockholders."

It is still possible, however, to stretch the mother tongue too far. A headline in *Variety*, "Stix nix hix pix" stumped even some *showbiz* people. Subject, predicate, object, and adjective all ended in *X*. What

Variety was saying was that rural America wanted no corn on the screen.

But readers like liveliness. Ruth Hahn tells me of a headline a couple of years back on the Spirit of Notre Dame: "Wild Irish rose in fourth quarter." "Man bites dog" itself is a head. *PM* carried one on England's floods today: "Waves rule Britain."

Some editors gripe about straight-jacket headline requirements. To get balance in make-up—and presumably eye-appeal—many papers rest heavily on unit count. A head cannot be too wide. Or too narrow. Or each line must be the same length. Or the head must be flush to the column rules. Or an inverted pyramid.

Such effects can be strained. We are dealing not with geometrical patterns but with living words and events.

On the other hand, there are papers which seem to go out of their way to *jumble* their heads and make-up.

Most papers follow the rule of not repeating a key word—prepositions and conjunctions excepted—in the head *and* in its decks or banks. Truman can be Truman only once. After that he is President or Executive. Head-writers get around this, however, by starting the banks with verbs telling what Truman says or does.

One word of caution. Your readers cannot grasp many abbreviations or initials. How many war agencies can you recall, besides OPA? Most of us know U.S., and U.S.S.R. But how many know that P.Q. stands for Province of Quebec?

One thing I fuss about. Sid Bernstein, my editor, does not agree with me, but I regard a headline as a sentence and try to make each line of it a phrase. I think that dangling adverbs and prepositions and conjunctions confuse the reader. Note the difference between

Steel Orders Slump *as*
Mills Increase Prices
and
Steel Demand *Slackens*
as Mills Boost Prices

Let us carry this further:

Morticians Plan *to*
Fight Penicillin *as*
Means to Longevity

Surely this would be clearer and stronger:

> Morticians *Mobilize*
> to Fight *Penicillin*
> as Aid to *Longevity*

I write the headline *before* I write the story. It clarifies the story in my mind. It puts the five W's—the Who, What, When, Where, and Why —into place right off the bat.

A simple headline says merely *who* is doing *what* about *what*:

> "Truman Urges $5 Billion Cut in U. S. Budget"

In news headlines the *when* usually goes without saying. It was today or yesterday. But sometimes the *when* is vital—and dramatic:

> "Young Diva Dies *as Curtain Rises on Opera Debut*"

Because news is largely a matter of nearness—and a child breaking his arm on your block may affect you more than the death of thousands in a flood in China—*where* breaks into many headlines. Consider this one: The late Fred Bonfils of the *Denver Post* used to say: "A dog fight on Champa St. is more important than a revolution in Europe." Consider this one:

> "Five-Alarm Blaze
> Traps Business Editors
> At Hotel Sheraton"

(Maybe you should not have come!)

I will just let the *how* and the *why* take care of themselves. I think you get what I am driving at.

But just one more thought:

Every writer can learn to say a lot in a little space by writing heads. It is like sending a cable to a stranger in Shanghai—on your own money:

You have got to make every word *count*.

CHAPTER 11

Techniques of Editorial Presentation

"There is a new contemporary art: the art of fusing words-and-pictures into an integrated whole."—From a piece of promotional material sent out by *Life* magazine.

THE ARCHITECTURE OF A BUSINESS MAGAZINE

Business managers, operating executives, and other technicians when they open their favorite business magazines do not expect to see circus make-up—or a picture book. They do expect news information to be transmitted to them quickly and professionally by word, symbol, and picture, each doing a good job.

I am not so sure businesspaper readers are in the same *hurry* as readers of other media. Too much blue-pencil surgery can harm a technical manuscript. Even the best pictures need captions. To paraphrase the excellent Chinese: *a few good words are worth a thousand poor pictures.*

The business press, criticized some years ago by *Fortune* for being "stodgy" (heavy, indigestible, overstuffed with facts) has become aware of the competition for everyman's time; it shows up in the low subscription renewal percentage. They are alert to new techniques in everything else—why not in editorial presentation?

We are indebted to George Dusenbury who has given so much of his know-how to improve the architecture of businesspapers. At the Dusenbury Clinics editors and publishers have attended critical examinations of consumer magazines dating from 1900, noting the main trends in editorial presentation: style, size, format, handling of art, pictures, captions, charts, tables, headlines, story, typography, layout, fast writing, etc. By means of before-and-after slides we have noted the extent to which business publications in many fields have taken advantage of these new trends. It has been a rewarding experience for all editors and for many advertising and sales promotion managers who attended Dusenbury sessions in New York and Chicago under the sponsorship of the National Conference of Business Paper Editors. I am grateful for permission to include in this chapter the rather telegraphic notes I took of his lectures. It is difficult to convey the full meanings in words, as he used slides and diagrams to make his points.

Similarly I must mention my indebtedness to Peter Davis for his know-how on photography and to Cortland G. Smith for the lucid description and diagram of the steps in putting the magazine to bed.

The integration of pictures and running commentary has caused a revolution in magazine journalism, stimulated by the research and pioneering of *Life* and *Look*,[1] but in business journalism, to repeat, pictures are not likely to replace the detailed know-how which words, charts, and tables can convey. But charts and tables can be improved, and words simplified.

There are four fundamental uses of the picture (1) to illustrate the text; (2) the picture-text combination, or story telling by related pictures and captions, the sequence, or the pictorial chronology; (3) the pure picture story without text, which is rare; (4) picture story continuity within a text story, to make an article more appetizing and increase reading time.

NOTES ON THE DUSENBURY FINDINGS[2]

Aside from editorial quality, the remarkable success of the picture magazines, *Life* and *Look*, is based upon scientific studies of visual presentation, especially by the use of the "Eye Camera" and the "One-way Mirror."

EYE CAMERA

A contact lens with a mirrored surface is inserted over the pupil in one eye of the reader. A directed beam of light striking this mirrored

---

[1] A practical guide to the production of visual articles is *The Technique of the Picture Story* by Daniel Mich and Edwin Eberman of *Look* (McGraw-Hill Book Co.), which contains, in the back, an excellent article entitled "Writing the Picture Story."

[2] Notes made by the editor during editorial clinics in the Advertising Club of New York, June 14-15, 1950, and November 8, 1951, conducted by George A. Dusenbury. Mr. Dusenbury was formerly in charge of publishing activities for Allis Chalmers; formerly in charge of Plymouth dealer publications, Chrysler Corporation; former director of visual presentation, *Look* magazine; former consultant, McGraw-Hill Publishing Company. These clinics were held under the auspices of ABP and the National Conference of Business Paper Editors. They were repeated in Chicago for the Chicago Business Paper Editors. The notes are published with Mr. Dusenbury's permission.—Editor.

surface is reflected to the exact spot which the uncovered eye is looking at. As the reader glances at the editorial pages of a businesspaper, or at the advertisements, a time-exposure of the course traveled by the eye is photographed by a still camera and recorded on motion picture film.[3]

The eye tends to explore a magazine page in a clockwise manner. It spends more time in the left side of the field. The eye muscles controlling the movement of the eyes from left to right (or sideways) are stronger than the muscles controlling the up and down movement.

Years of reading lines of type cause the eye to have an automatic return to the left like a typewriter. In a right-handed person the left side of the brain is the busiest. The theory is that most people are right handed, so the left-hand side of the field is the most important.

Eye camera tests changed previous thinking of artists, layout men, and visualizers as follows:

The left-hand page is the hot page. The left-hand page gets the most readership.

A spread is preferable to a right-hand page for a feature article.

The eye looks before it reads. So key or lead pictures should be shown *above* the headline, not beneath.

Bodoni is Number One type for readability.

The new order in page layout is as follows: (1) picture, (2) headline, (3) deck.

In a spread, more of the reader's total time is spent on a left-hand page. The line of eye drifts. As the eye comes away from the picture it drifts to the right and downward.

ONE-WAY MIRROR

To test how people read, not by asking them but by spying on them, *Look* used the one-way mirror in the reading rooms of Boston, New York, and Los Angeles public libraries. This was regarded as a more unbiased type of research. Instead of asking a person what he read, the researcher observed what he read through a mirror on the wall which was transparent on the back side of the wall where the watcher stood.

Among other things, *Look* discovered that men spend more time looking at pictures of men than pictures of women.

[3] Called the Ophthalmograph, the eye camera apparatus was developed by Dr. Herman Brandt, Drake University Visual Research Laboratory; The Taylor brothers (Educational Laboratories, Brownwood, Texas) are the inventors. See *Controlled Reading*, by E. A. Taylor, University of Chicago Press, Chicago, 1937, a treatise on eye movement photography. See also *Tide*, October 15, 1939.

BACK OF THE BOOK

About 25 per cent of the readers, it was observed through the one-way mirror, began at the back and read the magazine in reverse. As a result the architecture of *Look* was changed: two *opening* sections were introduced—one in the back for one-fourth of the readers.

The contents of departments are generally undersold in a business magazine. Departments are valuable to sell for subscription renewals. The department should be merchandised to the reader and prospective reader. *Look* magazine put its most expensive feature articles and spreads near the back of the book where the readership is lowest and the cost is highest. It also brought certain departments from the back of the book up to the front and exposed them to more readers. Later, when these departments were moved to the back of the book, they pulled all their new readers with them. Periodically *Look* moves many of its big departments back and forth for better focus. (*Life* is said to have paid a million dollars to the Duke of Windsor for "A King's Story." After being widely advertised, the issue carrying the first installment placed it in the *back* of the magazine.

CHANGE OF PACE

Do not run a group of long articles or double spreads one after the other. Change the pace. Use some shorts, six or seven, and then another spread. Laziness is the reason for so many long articles. Careful editing would produce six or eight short units to one double spread at a saving of six pages.

When you throw a lot of stuff at the reader, break it down by numbers, 1, 2, 3, 4, etc.

THE LEAD

The reader today goes through a piece of reading matter at a terrific clip. The competition for his time is great: TV, radio, movies, newspapers, books, family, business, etc.

Hit the reader with everything you can on your opening. If your magazine runs a lot of advertisements up front it is a good idea on the first major editorial page to tell the reader the name of your magazine by showing the logotype. In other words, to say to the reader *You are now out of the ad section.*

Open your editorial section with the story that reaches the largest number possible of readers.

Should a businesspaper look like a general magazine? That depends on the connotation of your magazine. If you want to be fancy, be fancy. Few readers of business magazines want it anything but straight. Fancy does not go.

Editors are not good people to make tests on. They read differently from the average reader. They are skilled to quickly take in a lot of material.

HEADS

The headline should always work with the pictures. The total impact on the reader is greater when picture and headline tell the same story. Observe good billboard posters. To achieve the poster effect have only a one-line caption under pictures. More than one line insulates the impact.

Headlines interpret what the eye sees in a picture. We are becoming a nation of photographers and caption writers. The trend to visual communication is rapid. "Every major magazine success of the past 20 years was based on making it easier for the reader to read," Mike Cowles, publisher of *Look*, declares.

Avoid irritating the reader by failing to give a clear meaning.

The "tense" of a magazine is important. The more present and future tense you have in your headlines, the better.

Ten seconds is a long time to hold the reader before he is gone to the next spread.

Do not use caps in headlines. People are not used to reading caps. Anything difficult to read takes away from the willingness or pleasure in reading.

People are reluctant to read more than a line or two of italics.

Serifs are easier to read than sans serifs. When you change to sans serif you lose a lot of recognition factors.

THE "HOW TO" HEADLINE

Three magic words in headlines are you, now, and new. Avoid headlines that suggest academic consideration of an old subject. The headline should suggest urgency, something different, timeliness, new developments, benefit to the reader. The "How to" headline is dynamic—it always follows up with "do something."

Use words and phrases like *new*, "It's *time* for you to do this," "This year *don't miss* such and such"; use the "overlooked" technique, the word "*next*": on your *next* window, promotion, sale, experiment, etc. "*New* view on such and such," "*Fresh* point of view," "*New* approach," "Before you do something . . . *do this*," "*Now* is the time to . . . ," "What stores are doing *Today*," "Why *new* widget plants will be different," "Simplify *your* department this year," "What will your operation be *tomorrow*?" "What's *new* in window display?" Emphasize today's situation. Note how pix magazines play up the words *this* and *here*.

In department headlines the trend is away from static, say-nothing heads. Do not say "Court Decisions," say "New Court Decisions," and play up the unusual ones in a feature. The working headline should not be lost beneath the standing head.

The first ten seconds is the critical time in the life of a businesspaper article—when the hesitating reader is about to pass on to the next page. Reflect benefits to the reader in the headline. Note high incidence in business journalism of the words Who, What, Why, When, Where, and How (the news formula).

Since the eye is first attracted to the picture and then to the caption under the picture, the lead in the text should presume that the reader has already read the caption.

PIX

The eye camera and the one-way mirror prove that pix (pictures) grouped together have more interest than pix scattered through an article.

Do not scale down pix where they cannot be seen. If it is not worth showing large enough to see, it is not worth showing.

Lapping pix is unfortunate and should be avoided.

The assumption that the text can control pix is wrong. You cannot lead the reader by the ear from the text back to the picture.

Cropping pix is a gift. Some cropping gives a close-up effect.

Pix should be cropped with a T-square to be vertical or horizontal. It is unnerving to look at pictures that lean.

When you jazz up the editorial pages they get confused with the ads.

"Reader in a Hurry" describes most readers. Watch the commuter thumb through a magazine on the train. Use pix for maximum impact to stop the reader.

In assembling pix for a feature try to find at least one to use as the headline picture, a picture that will work faster with the headline.

Continuity of pix and captions are the most popular with readers. Pictorial journalism frequently employs the numbered caption and the picture sequence.

Years ago magazine editors employed the trick layout for pictures and test. Today they know readers want to see the pictures, not the layout.

Human interest "keyhole" or candid pictures are the best and a series of pictures or a sequence (numbered) always gets the highest readership.

CAPTIONS

Looking occurs before reading. The reader always reads the captions before the text. It is bad for the captions to be larger type than the text type, which forces the reader to focus down on the text.

Pictures without captions do not get reader interest. They simply advertise the fact that the editor had nothing to say about them.

SCHEMATIC DIAGRAM

Like an engineer's schematic drawing, this helps to advance the final construction. It is the important step before the layout. Usually the editor makes it.

The editor is never an expert layout man (unless he was trained that way) and the layout man is never an editor. It is folly, therefore, to drop a pile of copy and photos in the lap of an art director or layout man and expect him to come up with the right visual presentation. It is the editor's business to provide the managing editor or the art director a schematic diagram telling how he sees the story, how he sees the layout, and the pictures. The art director should ask the question, "What's the story?" and the editor should give him the answer before he begins work.

The editor, not the art director, should indicate which are the most important pictures in a group. The editor should suggest the proper grouping of pictures to bring out the points in the story.

A story falls into two parts: (1) Glance-level material such as the picture, the caption, the headline, and the deck, and (2) the text.

LAYOUT

The trend in layout today in the best publications is to square up. The modular arrangement is the simplest and most effective. The module is the two-dimensional unit of design. A large departmental heading weakens your headline. Screen it down.

Trick layouts are no good. The reader should see the content of the pix, not the layout. Bring the pix into a meaningful relationship.

Clean reading line and layout clarity are essential. Editors and layout men must give more study to the material they have at hand which makes up a feature article and to the simplest, most direct, clear way it can be presented to the reader to avoid confusion in the reader's mind or to prevent losing the reader altogether by having him flip over to the next page.

Changing the patterns or design or layout is not as important as good new pix and new information. Consider the movie house. The pattern remains the same. Entrance, aisles, seats, screen. But the pix are always different. Similarly, the design of your TV set remains the same or much the same.

Use the glance level to sell more people to read the text.

Weave into the headline, the deck, and caption as many benefits to the reader as you can. Many good stories sum up the benefits to the reader near the end of the story. Use the summary of the benefits up front in your article, in a box—or dramatize it some other way.

REPETITION

Avoid in magazine articles the repetition which occurs in a daily newspaper article where the lead sentence repeats the information contained in the head and deck. In a magazine article if the reader reads the head for certain information and is thus led to the subhead or deck for additional information, he may be thrown right into the body of the story. The lead sentence of the article should be still more new information rather than a repetition of what he read in the head and deck. If you repeat the head and deck you may lose your reader.

FAST WRITING

Short sentences, the big idea first, and boiled-down information are essential in this age of speed. Remove all optional reading from your feature articles so that the main body of the text is fast reading and the reader may then elect to read background material or biographical sketch of the author or other optional material if he wishes.

FEATURE ARTICLES

Because they are *news* or contain news, people read feature articles. It is a mistake, therefore, to label some other section of the magazine as "News." Shorten articles. Use more of them. Avoid carryover if possible. Use bullets, arrows, or fists to emphasize the points in an article or in a summary.

Editors do not give enough time to analyzing the articles contributed. It is better to play up one good article on three pages than to publish three mediocre one-page articles.

Why do readers read? Because they are looking for bread and butter ideas to make more money or improve their techniques.

Serialized text is dangerous. Important qualities in an article are timeliness, immediacy, urgency. No feature should run longer than two or three issues.

POLLS

Round-ups and opinion polls are a familiar and acceptable editorial device for getting fairly authentic "dope" for readers in a hurry. The results should be reported in a breezy style.

Some editors use a "Ten Man Advisory Board" set up for polls—key readers who can provide a quick sample of current opinion on any issue.

KIPLINGER-TYPE PAGE

It is doubtful if a page up front in a monthly magazine in typewriter type or on colored stock in telegraphic style impresses readers as being last-minute, hot news because it is in typewriter type. No particular free ride can be taken on the Kiplinger-type letter because not enough people subscribe to it to have ever seen it.

Avoid the Kiplinger-type letter if you have a monthly magazine. Except for last-minute information, the use of typewriter type is a bit tricky, even fraudulent because there is a lapse of days between deadline and closing dates and mail delivery of a monthly magazine. No news in it could be last minute. The novelty of typewriter type is wearing off.

TABLE OF CONTENTS PAGE

Let the titles pop instead of the categories. On most contents pages all you see is the departments or categories which are always the same so that the contents pages always look the same. Mr. Dusenbury said it was a shock to him after years and years as an art director to find out how much he was doing wrong. He says the shelter, clothes, and service magazines try to look stylish and smart. They overlook the things *Look* and *Life* have learned which build circulation.

Some editors have changed the title to "In This Issue." Everything in an issue is not of equal importance so it should not be listed that way on the contents page. Have one line of selling copy under some titles and three lines under more important ones. The title of the article can be shortened for convenience on the contents page. Some editors put check marks after or before key articles. "Avoid the murderous monotony of equal rows of titles," says Dusenbury. Dress up contents page with pictures.

BYLINES

Authors' names are important in how-to articles. Do not operate on the theory that everyone knows an authority. State the author's qualifications in a box. Use his picture and a thumbnail biographical sketch. Candid shots of authors add human interest. Do not put the author's byline between the headline and the subhead unless the author himself has written the subhead.

LETTERS TO THE EDITOR

Several such letters should appear in each issue—concrete proof of reader interest. Put this column up front as indication of high reader participation. Many letters means your magazine pulls.

At the top of the "Letters to the Editor" column should be a box inviting letters and giving the address of the editor. On the contents page or mastheads of many magazines the address of the printer appears. Many readers find it difficult or impossible to locate the address of the editorial department of a publication and give up. Make it easy for readers to write. Agree to leave off their signature if they wish to remain anonymous. Send advance proofs of articles to certain readers inviting their reaction. Use a box on controversial articles with this question: What is your attitude on this subject?

SOME TRENDS

White space between columns is increasing. Use more features in the back of the magazine. Get away from carryovers. Use fresh new material all through the book to impel the reader to read all through. Advertising is just as good in back as in front of a magazine. There is a strong tendency to sell the next issue in a box on the contents page or on the Index to Advertisers page in the back.

Body type faces should be 9 to 10 point optimum. Over 10 point is hard to read and so is 8 point. Caps have few recognition factors. Sans serif is hard to read. Lower case serif type is best for heads or body. Serious talking headlines should use serious looking type faces. Use boldface if the message is a bold one. Type is like a salesman: if he looks serious, talks seriously, dresses seriously, you will accept his message as a sincere one. Italics were not designed for headlines. A printed page has a load limit—just like a floor. A pile-up of type variations breaks right through.

It is most important that the reader become aware that each succeeding issue is a new magazine. He must recognize a new issue. This is achieved by the change of subject matter on the *cover*—by changing the color and by changing the scale of the photograph or changing the scene.

Dress up the back of the book with *cartoons*.

We live in a color world. Everything we see is in color but what we see in color is four-color or eight-color process. Color should only be used if you can use a four-color process. Use of a second color to jazz up a page simply destroys the value of black and white. It makes the black and white halftone look dingy and dull. The use of colored stock has the same effect on halftones, destroying the sharp contrasts of black and white since the colored stock eliminates the white. Putting headlines in color is nonprofessional and robs the headline of its eye value. Color, however, may be used to dramatize charts or diagrams.

Observe that nearly every feature in *Life* opens on a *spread*.

Personal journalism is replacing what Dusenbury calls the "IBM type of journalism." (He refers evidently to the cold impersonality of the IBM precision business machine, and not to the journalism, for example, of IBM's famous house organ called *Think*.) The first person singular content of newspaper "Columns" has outstripped the "We" editorials of newspapers in popularity because people react favorably to warm, personal journalism. Popularity of *Reader's Digest* is attributed to the number of "I" stories in anecdotal, easy-reading, narrative style. "But," pleads Dusenbury, "avoid the Voice-of-God style."

AN EYE FOR BETTER PIX*

WHAT IS A GOOD PHOTOGRAPH?

A good photograph is many things. It has form. It has composition. It makes you stop and look twice, and perhaps say to yourself: "Isn't

* Peter Davis, from a brochure designed and prepared for *Business Week* correspondents, McGraw-Hill Publishing Co., Inc., 1949.

that a swell shot?" It stresses the details that the photographer wished to stress. And, above all, a good photograph is alive.

A good photographer can figure out a variety of ways to give dramatic interest to even the most commonplace subject—a figure dramatically placed, objects taken from an angle that creates an interesting pattern. If you are working with a photographer whose ability you have no reason to doubt, leave him alone to compose as he wishes. On the other hand, no amount of prodding could ever turn a bad photographer into a good one. So the only solution to getting a good photograph is: Pick your photographers well, then make diplomatic suggestions.

LIGHTING

One of the most important aspects of good picture-making is lighting. And it is right here that most newspaper photographers fail badly. They are so used to taking pictures with a single flashbulb on the camera, and thereby producing a flat uninteresting picture, that they forget there are other ways to make more exciting shots.

When you get a photographer to take an indoors picture, the first thing you want to ask him is: "Do you have flash extension equipment?" If he does not, find a photographer that has. If he has, tell him to use it.

Actually, a good photographer can get variety into his shots by using many different sources. Natural lighting, when it is possible to use it, cannot be beaten. Then, of course, there are floodlights, spotlights, or the diffused light of a flashbulb reflected from a ceiling or wall.

COVER PORTRAITS

These are always a problem. A photograph which will be used as a cover, or as the basis for a cover painting, must be a good sharp shot, with plenty of detail. And it must not be retouched. If Mr. Big has wrinkles, he has wrinkles; his wife knows it; his associates know it. He will come in for a lot more congratulations if his picture looks like him than if it is all prettied up to make him look ten years younger.

As in the case of all photographs, portraits must be on glossy paper. Matte paper does not reproduce well, and has a tendency to soften out the picture when it is engraved. Also, be sure your photographer uses fine-grain film wherever possible.

As for posing, we want easy informal shots—not pictures of an executive sitting at his desk looking as if he could not stand the photographer's presence another minute. If the photographer has any imagination, he should be able to work something into the shot representative of the profession the man is in. Other than this, backgrounds must be simple and uncrowded. Never send in a portrait taken against a flowered wall paper—or any background that detracts from the subject.

INSIDE-THE-BOOK PORTRAITS

In general, the same rules hold for a small portrait inside the book as for a cover portrait. But even more informality should be the rule, and the picture should be proportioned so that it is taller than it is wide. That is because most portraits inside the book are one column wide.

Above all, the subject should look like a human being.

GROUP SHOTS

One of the most boring clichés in photography is the stock shot of three or four men lined up as if they were facing a firing squad. When people are lined up in this position their facial expressions become frozen. They become frightened—and so do the readers who have to look at the pictures.

Group shots should be easy and informal, with the subjects arranged so that all the faces are not on one level. Get the subjects talking among themselves, then shoot. The people should also be grouped closely enough together so that there are no blank spaces between them. Good lighting is especially important in group shots. The only thing worse than one face washed out by a single flash is three faces washed out.

And again: keep the backgrounds simple.

NEW PRODUCTS

When a company has spent a lot of time and money developing a new product, it would naturally like to see the item illustrated. Unfortunately, most handout pictures of new products reach new lows in pictorial quality. Their backgrounds are air-brushed away. They are empty of people. And they lack anything eye-catching.

Pictures of new products, like all other pictures we want, should be informal and attractive, and should contain some human form to give the product a reference point with reality. It does not have to be much; often just the outline of a hand will do the trick.

BUILDINGS

In architectural photography, composition is all-important. A photographer who works in this field must be painstaking and meticulous. He must case a building he is planning to photograph from different angles, noting overhanging trees, arches, columns, or nearby structures that may add to the framing effects. He must watch the play of light and shade, often waiting hours for the sun to come into a position which will give him the best effect. To get darkness into the sky, he must use a yellow or red filter over his lens.

Air views of vast expanses of factories are no solution to the problem of showing hugeness. More often than not, one plant picture from the air can hardly be told from another.

BUSINESS IS PEOPLE

What is a store without customers? A restaurant without diners? A factory without workers?

Could you imagine spending an evening at a theater performance in which there were no actors—only sets? Of course not. Drama comes out of human relations. It is the same with pictures. You have to have people in pictures to make them exciting, to make them dramatic, to tie them in with the reader's personal experience.

So, when you send in, for example, a picture of a production line, be sure that there are workers in the picture. What is more, get them in poses which make them look as if they are really at work—not just standing around staring or mugging at the camera.

THE PICTURE STORY

Of course you go to the movies. Have you ever really considered how much a movie camera roves around? How scenes shift from long shots to closeups? You may not be consciously aware of it; it is a trick of a good cameraman to keep you from getting bored. But if you have ever seen a revival of a pioneer movie, you will notice how static the scenes are. That is because in those days the camera stayed in the same spot for a whole scene. It took moviemen years to learn the trick of coming in for a closeup.

Good still cameramen have learned the same trick. In laying out a story—say, of an assembly line—we like to have long shots as well as closeups. So if you are showing a step-by-step sequence of how an assembly line works, do not have all the pictures taken from the same spot.

Normally, a good picture story takes much planning and research. And before a photographer is sent out to shoot the story he should get a complete shooting script, outlining the shots expected from him. The specialized knowledge of planning and producing a picture story is not something we expect you to have; we will help you with it.

IN SUMMARY

Do not call in a photographer just because he is handy; look around for one that has good qualifications, one whose work you are sure of.

See that pictures you submit of buildings and plants have people in them. This adds life to pictures, relates them to human experience.

Do not accept pictures that have been washed out by poor lighting. Look for interesting highlights, sidelights, etc.

Strive to submit photographs that are striking, dramatic, and interesting picture-wise as well as subject-wise.

Do not send in pictures of groups of individuals who look like they are standing before a firing squad. Get them arranged informally.

Make sure that photographs of new products which you submit have some form of human interest—even if it is just an arm or a hand.

Do not try to let aerial views take the place of good ground-level views of large, extensive plants.

Look for portraits that are easy and informal—not stiff, formal studio-type shots.

Do not write on the backs of pictures—it shows through. Captions should be typed out on separate sheets of paper and attached to the edge of the photograph with scotch tape or rubber cement, so they can be easily pulled off. Also do not put arrows or X's on the picture itself to indicate some particular object. If you want to point out specific points in the photograph make an overlay of onionskin paper and write on that.

Number each picture in picture sequences carefully.

Mail pictures carefully, and make sure that you have enough heavy cardboard stiffening to thwart the most muscular postal clerk.

CHAPTER 12

*Putting the Magazine to Bed**

No matter how much thought and care have gone into the planning and preparation of the material for an issue of any publication, the final product will not be good unless the same painstaking care is exercised in following through each step in its production.

The most perfectly laid-out page can be spoiled by careless page make-up and the most perfect copy ruined by typographical errors, bad spacing, or transpositions. And from a cost standpoint, the author's alteration charges have a nasty habit of piling up if there is sloppy work in the dummying of pages that must be straightened out on the page proof.

Assume we have carried through the getting and editing of the manuscript, we have become familiar with the page itself, and have carefully planned the art work and the copy so they fit and hang together. We have the layouts made and have marked and sent the copy to the printer. The art work has gone to the engraver and we are ready now to start the closing-up process known as "putting the 'book' to bed."

The steps in the closing and printing of magazine pages that must be done by editor and printer are: dummy and composition, break of magazines, okay of pages to close forms, imposition and line-up on stone, make-ready and printing, folding, gathering, binding, trimming, mailing. Offset printing may sometimes be used for special sections (in which case insertion orders are required) or for entire issues.

No matter by which process the type has been set, it is placed on long, narrow, shallow trays, called galleys. Proofs are pulled and proof-

* Cortland G. Smith, from "The Mechanics of Magazine Publishing," *Magazine World*, Jan.–June, 1945, Business Magazines, Inc., N.Y. Mr. Smith was formerly in charge of editorial art direction and production at the McGraw-Hill organization on ten of the company's publications.

read. Corrections are made and the galleys are re-proved, proofread, and sent to the editors. One proof (usually on colored paper) has the number and letter of the galley written by hand all over it so that no matter what part is used the type can be located in the rack. This is the proof which is used for dummying.

When the galley proofs reach the make-up desk of the editorial department they are checked for completeness and accuracy. If errors are found, the proof may be sent back for revision. The colored proof is trimmed and placed in a manuscript envelope previously prepared for that article. When all type proofs and cut proofs have been received the article is ready to be dummied, either according to a previously made layout, or in any desired manner consistent with the rules of good make-up.

Dummying a page consists of pasting the proofs of each type or engraving element as nearly as possible in the position on the page where it is desired to have the printer put the actual type and cuts. To facilitate this operation, most magazines have dummy forms on which are guide lines for trim edges, fold, type-page size, and columns.

A few simple rules must be observed:

1. Do not have widows (fractional lines at paragraph ends) at top of columns.

2. Do not permit the last line on a *right-hand* page to be a sentence ending unless it is also the end of the article.

3. Learn the style of your magazine in the matter of spacing around headlines, authors, subheads, above and below pictures, around department headings and titles of articles in departments. Be as consistent as possible in spacing. Use a guide to insure accuracy of spacing.

4. When sending dummy pages to the printer be certain that they are clearly labeled with the name of the publication, date of issue, page number. Be sure cuts are sent with dummies.

5. If copy is attached to fill, be sure it, too, is identified as copy A (or B or C) for page (69), (June) issue of (*Power*) magazine, and the place where it is to go is marked "copy attached A (or B)."

Not all publications follow the practice of dummying both type proofs and engraving proofs to show the printer how the page is to be made up. Some dummy only the art work and indicate by lines how type is to be set around the art. Others send layout and manuscript to the printer to get back page proofs. To be practical, both of these methods require carefully typed manuscripts with lines calculated exactly to measure.

Such preparation is costly in time and labor. Because dummying permits some flexibility and is not wasteful of preliminary preparation time and effort, it is standard practice.

Page make-up by the printer consists of locating the type on the galley from the handwritten number on the proofs, getting the cuts from the

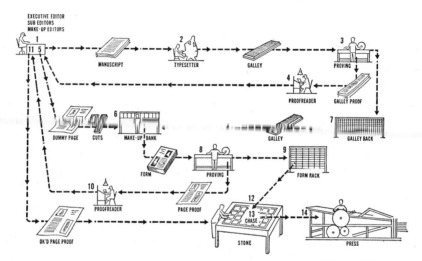

Fig. 10   Fourteen steps in putting the magazine to bed. Editor (1) sends manuscript to printer. Type is set (2), placed on galley, and galley proofs are pulled (3). Proof goes to printer's proofreader (4). Galley is placed in rack (7). Corrected galley proof goes to editor (5), who pastes up dummy of page. Dummy is sent to printer for page composition (6). Galley is drawn from rack (7) and cuts (sent to printer with dummy) are picked up from cut bank. Type and cuts are assembled with furniture to form pattern corresponding to dummy. Page proofs are pulled (8). Type and cut assembly goes into rack (9). Proofs are read (10) and sent to editor (11), who marks corrections and gives okay. Okayed proof is returned to printer and goes to stone (12). Type assembly is drawn from rack (9) and placed in chase (13) with type assemblies for other pages in form. When properly imposed, aligned, and corrected, type is locked in chase and sent to press (14) to be printed.

cut rack where they have been received and held waiting, and assembling them in a pattern corresponding to the dummy. All areas that are shown as space in the finished page must be filled with furniture (wood or metal pieces that are too low to print) so that no holes and no looseness exist in the assembly.

The assembled type is bound round with string, proved, and proof-read. Again an identifying number (board number) is handwritten at the bottom of the proof to show location of the type in the rack. Proofs are sent to the editors and the type is placed in a rack.

Page proofs should be carefully inspected by the editors (1) for over-all appearance, spacing, adherence to the style of the publication, (2) correct location of cuts and captions, references, figure numbers, etc., (3) final proofreading of all copy, and (4) correct folio and issue date.

When all corrections, if any, have been neatly and clearly noted in the margins of the page proof, it is stamped "Okay" or "Okay with Corrections" and returned to the printer. Pages requiring extensive changes should be marked "Revised." This requires the printer to make the changes and submit a new set of proofs for "Okay."

BREAKING UP THE "BOOK"

At this stage in the process of "putting the magazine to bed" (earlier if feasible) the "break of the book" should be determined. That is, the pages between front and back covers should be separated into printable units called forms.

There are two binding methods (sidewire and saddle-wire stitching) that influence the selection of forms.

In saddle-wire binding, the stitches are driven through the cover and through all inside pages, bending over at the center spread. For this type of binding it is necessary to know the total number of pages and to separate this total into printing units of 4, 8, 12, or 16 pages. Because it takes about as long and costs nearly as much to print a 4-page form as it does a 16-page unit, the largest forms possible should be used in order to keep down the number of forms to be printed. Unless other considerations interfere, a 72-page magazine (not counting covers) breaks up into four 16-page and one 8-page form. The first 16-page form (for saddle-wire binding) consists of pages 1–8 and 65–72. The next 16, pages 9–16 and 57–64. If there are four 2-color advertisements and these are to appear immediately ahead of the editorial section, these 2-color pages are placed in the 8-page form (17–20 and 53–56). The two center 16's would then be the editorial pages. They would break up thus: 21–28 and 45–52; 29–44.

In a sidewire or flat binding magazine it is not necessary to know the total number of pages before starting the break up. This is so because each form contains consecutively numbered pages and when gathered for binding, the forms are assembled like books on a bookshelf. The staples are driven, about ¼ inch from the folding edge, from page 1 through all the pages and bending over at the last page. The cover is then added and glued to the folded edges of the stapled forms.

In flat binding the folded edges are slotted to allow glue to penetrate through and hold all pages. Staples are omitted. Forms are imposed and gathered the same as for sidewire stitching.

Permissible forms for sidewire stitching or perfect binding include 2- and 6-page units in addition to the 4-, 8-, 12-, and 16-page units used in saddle-wire binding. Either binding will permit 32-page forms if size of magazine and the printer's equipment will allow their use. Frequently 32-page forms are printed, then cut into two 16's for folding and binding.

Generally, saddle-wire binding is preferable for publications not more than ¼ inch thick. Thicker magazines are usually sidewire stitched or glued.

When the "break" has been determined and the printer has his copy of the break-up sheet, a schedule of closing is agreed upon. A general schedule has probably been set. The specific schedule for a known number of forms is now fixed. It must be rigidly adhered to. Idle presses are costly. If your forms are not closed on schedule, the printer may either charge you for press waiting time or put other work on the press and let your publication come out late.

The order in which forms are closed does not matter. You may be able to send through and give okays on a form in the middle of the book much earlier than you can close the opening pages. The important thing about closing is that *all the pages in a form* must be okayed in order to close the form and enable it to go to press. Therefore, concentrate on closing all the pages in one form, then tackle the next.

When the printer has received okayed proofs on all the pages for a form he is ready to lock up. On a large table, called a "stone" an iron frame (chase) is placed. Within it are gathered from their respective racks the type assemblies corresponding to the page proofs for the form being locked up. These "pages" are grouped inside the chase according to an imposition pattern.

On the stone all final corrections are made, pages are carefully aligned and justified (made compact and tight). The whole is then locked solidly, so that no pieces will fall out when the frame is lifted, and is carted away to the printing press.

The form, locked in the chase, is placed on the bed of a press and make-ready is started. The press (flat-bed, cylinder) consists of a type-carrying table that is alternately run under inking rolls then reversed to run under a cylinder that causes the paper sheet to be forcibly pressed against the inked type. Make-ready involves the adjustment of ink flow and printing pressure to produce a good printing result. The first trial proof is usually far from acceptable. Adjustment and test proofing continue, often for hours, before the required degree of printing perfection is accomplished and the press is ready to begin turning out its normal 1000 to 1500 sheets per hour.

If the press happens to be a two-color unit, there is a problem of register to be battled out as well as the problems of ink distribution and printing pressure.

Rotary presses, printing from curved electros that have been molded from the locked-up form, operate at considerably higher speeds than do flat-bed presses. They print continuously instead of intermittently, deliver folded units instead of flat sheets, are more practical for long runs (over 50,000) than for short runs.

The printed sheets (from flat-bed presses) go to a folding machine and, when folded, are put into the proper compartments of a gathering (collating) machine where they are assembled in correct page order, stapled, glued, and have covers added. Trimming to final size is the last operation. The magazine is now ready to be mailed by the printer to the subscribers' list supplied by the circulation department of the publication, or sent to distributors.

Folding Inserts. Occasionally there are to be published pictures, tables, or diagrams that cannot sensibly be compressed into a page, yet must be presented as unbroken units. To do this, folding inserts of 4, 6, or more pages can be used. These may be either loosely inserted or bound in. If loosely inserted they should not require to be placed between any specific pages. Post office restrictions also apply. It is wise to check your plans with the postal authorities before becoming too deeply involved with any folding insert.

Paper. Magazines that are printed by letterpress usually use either a coated stock (60 to 80 lb.) or a supercalendered stock (40 to 60 lb.). Coated stock is used for fine printing of halftone cuts; "super" for less quality and lower cost. When no halftones are used, the stock may be English finish, book, or bond. Either offset stock or bond is suitable for offset printing and some coated stocks will print well by offset.

Halftone screens suitable for various stocks are:

Coated	120 or 133
Machine coated	100 or 110
Supercalendered	100
Machine finish, smooth bonds	85
English finish, antique, newsprint	65

Part Three

Public Responsibility

CHAPTER 13

Editorial Responsibility

INTRODUCTION

The lecture to Journalism seniors at Rutgers University which opens Chapter 13 expresses my views on the public responsibilities assumed by a journalist when he becomes a businesspaper's chief editor. The elder McGraw when he had completed nearly half a century of business journalism stated a truth which all publishers sooner or later must recognize:

"While the business of publishing is a commercial enterprise, at its core it is professional. If the commercial should dominate, the enterprise would lose public confidence. Always we must conduct it with an eye single to the interests of the reader. We must keep convenant with him."[1]

I have listened to endless discussions on whether journalism is a profession. The matter remains academic. The important thing is for journalists to conduct themselves *as if* it were a profession.

To look upon one's own publication not as a property but as an instrument for public service may be difficult for some publishers. The McGraw-Hill skyscraper on forty-second street in New York City is an eloquent testimonial that the elder McGraw's publishing philosophy paid off.

The editor of an independent businesspaper is a trustee of the free enterprise system. He must have the courage and competence to recognize its faults and criticize them. Not all business, as editor Ralph Paine points out in his paper in this chapter, is operated with a sense of trusteeship and public service. That is why Mr. Paine believes the modern corporation needs a critical business press.

---

[1] *Teacher of Business*, the publishing philosophy of James H. McGraw, edited by G. D. Crain, Jr., Advertising Publications, Inc., Chicago, 1944. Mr. McGraw made this statement in a lecture at Princeton, May 14, 1929.

EDITOR'S RESPONSIBILITY IS PRIVATE ENTERPRISE*

An American business journalist derives his living from the free enterprise system. So does every other kind of journalist.

But no journalist is so *close* to the free enterprise system as the business journalist.

If our free, competitive system of enterprise is ever taken over by a handful of men—and I do not care what they call it: socialism, communism, collectivism, statism, fascism, private monopoly capitalism, or autocratic labor monopoly—in any case you and I are out of luck. Uncontrolled monopoly, whatever its form, private or public, has no *use* for a business press. Indeed, its first act is to *suppress* the publication of news and know-how.

Independent businesspapers like *Iron Age, Railway Age,* or *Printers' Ink* and great corporation magazines like *G-E News, The Lamp,* and *Dun's Review* would fold up in twenty-four hours. Who needs businesspapers in a monopoly system of enterprise? The purpose of disseminating technical know-how or any business news information is to encourage competition, more production, greater exchanges of goods and ideas in free markets of the whole world.

Who wants nosey, prying, curious house organ editors, or trade paper editors, digging around in a monopoly economy, asking a lot of questions, explaining things, making suggestions for improvement, or possibly criticizing? The purpose of monopoly is to discourage competition, liquidate competitors, practice scarcity, sequester or cartellize the free markets—"tell 'em nothing"—"no comment."

No—in any monopoly or totalitarian system of enterprise we are dead ducks as journalists. The future of free, competitive enterprise and the future of dynamic business journalism are the same future.

The business journalist, being closest to the business enterprise picture, should see this picture quite clearly. What does he see? He sees the American free enterprise system each year become a tougher proposition to sell in the political marketplace. You cannot sell this free enterprise package anywhere outside the borders of the United States. Less and less buyers for it in England and even Canada.

Nowhere else in the world, in any industrial country, is there a market

* Julien Elfenbein; a lecture delivered before senior members of the School of Journalism, Rutgers University, and the New Jersey Industrial Editors Association, at a luncheon conference. Hotel Roger Smith, New Brunswick, New Jersey, December 8, 1948.

at all for our free enterprise system. Nobody will buy it in Russia or anywhere in Asia or Europe or South America or Africa.

It is not easy to sell free competitive enterprise even to Americans in the United States, where they actually profit from it, see its abundant fruits, and constantly hear its praises sung. The American voter shows an increasing willingness to give up individual initiative, personal liberty, and freedom of enterprise for the promise of economic security. People do not seem to want freedom; they want protection from people who have too much freedom.

Opinion polls are in disfavor at the moment but there have been too many opinion polls on this point for anyone to misinterpret them except one who is blind or stupid. *Fortune* magazine polls for several years show that about 30 to 40 per cent of all Americans favor government monopoly of steel, coal, oil, and other basic industries, while another 40 to 50 per cent favor free private enterprise. About 10 to 15 per cent are undecided, and these 10 to 15 per cent hold the balance of power. If they swing to the left, free enterprise may be out of luck.

I am suggesting, therefore, that the free competitive enterprise system is the chief editorial responsibility of American business journalists. But I am not suggesting that journalists use the formula some top-drawer management executives in the free enterprise system use and which some business journalists have also used to try to sell the system, or to try and save it. You know—the friends and chief beneficiaries of a system sometimes can be its worst enemies.

That becomes obvious in a study of the formula used in the past by the National Association of Manufacturers, the U. S. Chamber of Commerce, and other groups, to sell free enterprise.[2] That sort of formula has failed to sell free enterprise to new prospects and is not likely to save the system. Perhaps we have missed a point.

Freedom of enterprise is not the core of creative democracy. The freedom is secondary and derivative. The core of creative democracy is the common objectives, common opportunities, common purposes, and common interests—the commonalty. The common objective is the bond which holds our corporate society together. This objective is not reached by uttering a formula at a convention of the U. S. C. of C., or by pub-

---

[2] Some readers may be interested in a survey in *Fortune* magazine for September, 1950, page 77: "Is Anybody Listening?" which contains the unfavorable opinion of top executives on the free enterprise campaign waged by NAM (National Association of Manufacturers).

lishing a formula in full-page newspaper advertisements signed by NAM.
People speak loosely of their "rights."

Some people think the Bill of Rights was something we inherited from
nature. They call them "natural rights." Actually, the Bill of Rights is
something our forefathers fought for, something their descendants are
still fighting for. The so-called "rights" are privileges extended to members of organized society who are in good standing If men can deprive
one man of his "rights" they can deprive every other man of them.

Let us seek a proper definition of our system. A good way to start is
by reminding our readers and our employers what the American free
enterprise system is *not*.

The free enterprise system is not, never has been, never should be, a system of complete *laissez faire* (let well enough alone, *status quo*, every-man-
for-himself, dog-eat-dog).

It is not freedom to seek profit by any and all means
—not the right to profit at the expense of the welfare of the community.
—not the freedom of any man to exploit any other
—not the freedom to waste the natural resources of the country; (pollute
waters and air, destroy top soil and timber)
—not the right to monopolize (which impedes or prevents the establishment
of new business, creates scarcity, and imperils the spirit of enterprise)
—not opposition to necessary and appropriate government regulation or
operation

The free enterprise system is a system of production, investment and consumption under which private individuals and business firms, largely by their
own initiative and responsibility, combine the community's labor skills,
community's managerial skills, and community's capital to produce the
bulk of the goods and services men want.

Its [private enterprise] most characteristic features as compared with
other economic systems are the following:

1. Maximum dependence upon competition and the free play of prices to
determine who shall produce what.

2. Maximum dependence on profit as an incentive rather than on compul-
sion or prestige.

3. Maximum emphasis on free personal choice among the economic opportunities—be they goods or jobs—that are available to men.

I did not write this definition. This definition was formulated, while
we were still at war, by the trustees of the Committee for Economic
Development. It was published in *Fortune* magazine as "A Declaration

of American Business Policy," over the signature of William Benton.[3]

Let me read the names of some of the other trustees who approved this definition: U. S. Senator Ralph Flanders of Vermont, who is president of Jones & Lamson Corp., a director of the Federal Reserve Bank of Boston; Eric Johnston,[4] former head U. S. C. of C.; Clarence Francis, head of General Foods; Philip Reed, head of General Electric; Dr. Charles Kettering of General Motors; Charles Hook, president of the American Rolling Mill; Raymond Rubicam, founder of Young & Rubicam, advertising agency; John Collier, president, Goodrich; John D. Biggers, president, Libbey-Owens-Ford; Beardsley Ruml, chairman of the Board, Macy's.

Not a long-haired dreamer among them. Not one communist or ex-communist—not even a parlor pink or left-winger. All rich men. All corporation heads. All successful, prominent American business leaders, themselves products of the free enterprise system.

Perhaps this definition of free enterprise these rich men wrote, this entire "Declaration of American Business Policy" ought to be published under the masthead of every businesspaper and every house magazine in America, for in it are the canons of responsible business journalism.

The way to answer the critics of a people's capitalism which is what our private competitive enterprise system is—or should be—is not by a repetitious and monotonous recital of its accomplishments *ad nauseam,* but by a dynamic plan of action, by a plan which will create more opportunities for more people to improve their condition of life, give more people a sense of human dignity that comes from feeling their work is useful to society, create a climate for more people to be treated like human beings and not just numbers on some corporation's payroll—a sense of participation. Explain to more people what makes the wheels go around.

These are the common objectives in our corporate society.

The validity of the principle that the common good—the public interest—is superior to the economic interest of any private group goes unchallenged in time of war.

[3] "The Economics of a Free Society," by William Benton, *Fortune* magazine, October, 1944. Mr. Benton at the time was chairman of the Board of Trustees, CED, former head of Benton & Bowles advertising agency, former Assistant Secretary of State, former vice-president of the University of Chicago, former chairman of the board of the *Encyclopedia Britannica*; now trustee of the Ford Foundation and U. S. Senator.

[4] Eric Johnston in 1951 was Economic Stabilization Director of the U.S.

I think it has become our editorial responsibility to establish the validity of the public interest in time of peace, in all enterprise, public or private, as superior to the economic interests of any private group.

The businesspaper editor and the industrial magazine editor, however, also have a responsibility to their employers. You may ask, does it transcend the editor's responsibility to the public interest? This is my answer:

If an editor regards journalism as a profession and himself, therefore, as a professional, he is in the same position as the lawyer, doctor, public accountant, banker, advertising agent, or public relations counsellor.

The professional editor's first concern must be the public interest—and that should be the publisher's first concern.

THE CORPORATION NEEDS A CRITICAL BUSINESS PRESS*

For the man who only has to worry about maximizing his profits and minimizing his losses, the critical business press has little interest. With some justification he can say to us, "My business is none of your business." But not the modern corporation as it is now evolving; that is everybody's business, and the management needs a freely critical press in the same sense that government needs a freely critical political press.

Let us look at this kind of press. What about the modern corporation and the press? First let us set aside as no particular problem all that part of the business press which might be called Service, the communication of information. This in sheer quantity is by far the largest element. In our magazine it is the straight reporting of information which we think would interest our readers. No important critical judgments are involved. Of course all reporting involves judgment in some degree—what facts to select, what facts to leave out, whether to report the story at all. But what concerns you most and what concerns me most is *critical* business journalism; that is, the analysis and evaluation of information or news, and coming to some sort of conclusion, some net judgment on it.

To repeat, the modern corporation needs the free—that is, free to be critical—press just as much as government does; it needs it as one of the fundamental checks and balances of a free enterprise economy.

* Ralph D. Paine, Jr., Managing Editor, *Fortune* magazine; from an address before the Seventh National Conference of Business Public Relations Executives, New York, May 5, 1950. In granting permission to publish, Mr. Paine made the point that his approach was "informal" and that "credit goes to Berle, Drucker, Barnard, Mayo, and many others who did the seminal work."

But some very interesting differences appear when you attempt to carry over the principles of a freely critical press into business journalism.

Now political journalism depends in very large measure on an elementary fact of political life: it is almost always to somebody's interest to spill the inside stuff, to talk, to let the cat out of the bag. That "authoritative source" quoted in Washington dispatches may be merely peaching on his boss. Higher than "authoritative sources" are—by a curious trick of language—"unimpeachable sources," which no doubt means that some top brass is spilling perhaps because he thinks it is in the national interest to do so.

Business journalism is unique, I believe, in that it is seldom to *anybody's* interest to let the cat out of the bag. Bad news is exceedingly hard to come by while it is still fresh, particularly corporation news. Even competitors clam up when bad news is in the wind. One has to deal with a conspiracy of silence, a sort of we-are-all-in-the-same-club attitude.

I find this attitude hard to understand. If businessmen are all in the same club, then the club is surely suspect, for there are some pretty unattractive, if not dangerous, characters playing poker upstairs. Business got in the doghouse originally as a result of the actions of a few particular rascals, not because of the actions of businessmen in general. But do good businessmen, even anonymously, speak out against bad businessmen? No. Why not? I do not know. But if business is going in for club life, ordinary prudence, it seems to me, would dictate at least *two* clubs —a respectable club and one for the rascals.

Let me say again—the problem is bad news, not just *news*. You gentlemen have made it increasingly easy to get good news. Usually it is referred to as "legitimate" news; "legitimate" news might be defined as good news plus any bad news the law compels you to reveal. Do not misunderstand; this is no blanket indictment for attempting to obstruct the search for truth. I am merely suggesting that there is such a thing as the bad news problem.

It is your problem as well as mine. It is your problem because it is greatly to your interest, and thus to the interest of American business economy, to have a press that the people believe. The credibility of the press as it affects business is of the utmost importance. No small part of the popular revulsion against business in the 1930's was the result of the false impressions created by so much silly, uncritical puffery that passed for business journalism in the twenties.

We can study the lessons of the twenties, to our profit, for as we all know, the vast majority of businessmen were not guilty of fraud, misrepresentation, malfeasance, or peculation. Yet when the deluge came, the public was ill-equipped to distinguish between the Insulls, the Kreugers, the Musicas, the Hopsons, and the rest of American Business whose behavior was largely honorable if not always wise.

Business is no saintly order. There are all kinds of businessmen, good and bad, great and bold, timid and indifferent. There are not many real villains, not many real heroes. Nor is all business operated with a sense of trusteeship and public service. And even well and honestly run companies have skeletons in the closet.

The picture we should strive to imprint upon the public is the picture of the American business economy as it really is, a true picture—like everything in life, *partly* good, *partly* bad, on balance *much* more good than bad, but certainly the best that man has yet devised for solving the age-old problem of making a living.

The American temperament being what it is, normally optimistic and energetic, but extremely volatile, it is dangerous to overplay good news, to overemphasize the success story, to mistake the spectacular for solid achievement. Certainly, the business press has been guilty of all these, *Fortune* not excepted.

There has been entirely too much pressagentry both in business and in the business press. It has impaired the credibility of the press and it has done business more harm than good. To sum up, there has been too much pressagentry, not enough public relations.

Do not get me wrong; I am not indicting pressagentry. It is as old as history, it is legitimate and frequently a lot of fun. But the free press will lose some of its franchise if it cannot cope with it.

What I do bespeak most seriously is the cooperation of the public relations men of business in a joint effort to understand the modern corporation and its place in American society. If we could succeed first in understanding the modern corporation ourselves, and then in getting it understood by others, then perhaps American business might have a hundred years of political peace.

CHAPTER 14

Public Relations

WHO IS THE PUBLIC?

The businesspaper is a working organization of ideas.

It prospers by the distribution and execution of workable ideas.

Its task is to see that as many as possible of the ideas which members of our industrial society produce are quickly available for examination and application by other members.

Like every other business organization a businesspaper publishing house has many publics: Its readers and advertisers, actual or potential, employees and potential employees, stockholders, the advertising agencies, the graphic arts industries, trade associations, scientific and professional bodies, libraries, schools and colleges, research organizations, UN, federal and state governments, agriculture, labor, its own community, and, of course, the public relations counsellors themselves.

Public Relations News has defined public relations:

. . . the management function which evaluates public attitudes, identifies the policies and procedures of an individual or an organization with the public interest, and executes a program of action to earn public understanding and acceptance.

The present chapter contains a summary of the kinds of public relations activity businesspapers are currently engaged in. The reader is referred to Chapter 5 on Research which describes the industry's program for continuing readership study and other programs which bring the businesspaper into closer relationship with its many publics. From these studies will evolve, we believe, the program of action which the business press will some day promote to earn a better public appreciation of the role it plays in preserving free, competitive private incentive enterprise.[1]

[1] See essay by Bernays in Chapter 17.

PUBLIC RELATIONS AND THE BUSINESS PRESS*

Now that Public Relations has been isolated and identified as a distinct force for progress, all individuals and organizations who seek to use it advantageously must not fail to recognize the primary position of business publications in achieving their aims.

Marketing experts are agreed that a product should have attained adequate distribution before its promotion to the ultimate consumer is undertaken. The advertising world has learned over and over again that without prior and adequate product distribution, the advertising appropriation can be dissipated in the "glamorous" and expensive consumer media without establishing a market.

Likewise, the public relations world must learn that the primary lever for moving public opinion in any field is the medium that reaches the leaders of that field—those who influence the habits and the thinking of the thousands and the millions. Much effort, energy, and money can be expended by going "over the heads" of these moulders of industrial thought and opinion, but such expenditures will never yield dollar-for-dollar value. By the same token, greater things may be set in motion with less effort, energy, and money by starting with the primary and "wholesale" vehicle of education and influence—the business press.

There are many reasons why the business press holds this primary position. A study of the development of the many industries that were begun in our own time and have grown to be giants will reveal that in each one there was a virile industry press (or perhaps a lone business-paper) fighting side by side with its leaders for coordination of its highest interests.

In many cases the editors and publishers were the "architects" of their industries—technical or trade experts, whose judgment and experience were constantly called upon to guide, define, and integrate the service of the industry.

Hundreds of examples point to the service of business publications in older industries that are more static and fully integrated. In the merchandising field there are publications that are literally the spokesmen of their entire industries. Trade magazines have been influential in chang-

---

* Andrew J. Haire, Sr., President, the Haire Publishing Company; former President and board chairman, Associated Business Publications, Inc.; former President, Advertising Club of New York; creator of the Advertising Hall of Fame; from *Public Relations Directory and Year Book,* vol. I, p. 223, the Longacre Press, N.Y., 1945.

ing many of the aspects of retailing through the years. They have coordinated, enlarged, and brought greater profits to the respective departments in department stores and specialty shops throughout the country. Their editors have been crusaders for better promotion, more efficient buying, adequate sales training, and smoother relations between buyer and manufacturer.

In many cases the editors of these magazines are the prime movers in their respective industries for every forward step, on every issue, that may affect manufacturers and retailers. They have organized local and national clubs, round tables for discussions of mutual problems, and have represented the interests of all in the matter of government rulings and legislation.

Trade and industrial associations and institutions particularly have found their trade magazines adequate vehicles for unity and articulate expression of their plans and aspirations. In cases where the editors are not actually officers or organizers of these trade associations, they are active members and either have special departments in their magazines or otherwise give adequate coverage to the news, in addition to appropriate editorial support. This is a prime service of every trade publication worth its salt: to be the spokesman for every forward looking group and movement affecting the welfare of the entire industry.

Aside from the intimacy and influence of the editors in their trades, live businesspaper publishers have research departments and reader services that make them indispensable to manufacturers, advertising agencies, and the retail trades they serve. These departments often have vital facts about their industries that are not obtainable anywhere else.

For the public relations fraternity all this means that the business press is a ready, willing, and experienced ally in every legitimate undertaking that will prove beneficial to the respective industries in which they operate. Advertising agencies, advertising managers, public relations counsellors must, in fact, rediscover the business press in all its importance as a prime lever for industrial influence and economic action.

A SURVEY OF PUBLIC RELATIONS ACTIVITIES OF BUSINESSPAPERS*

The good will enjoyed by a businesspaper is measured primarily by the merit of the paper itself. If it covers its particular field adequately,

* From the report, "Public Relations for Your Paper," spring, 1948, conference, Associated Business Publications, by the ABP Public Relations Committee, Godfrey M. Lebhar, Chairman.

it does what it is ordinarily expected to do and commands the prestige and respect to which that kind of a job entitles it.

But very few businesspapers confine their activities to the publishing of the paper itself. In fact, it is practically impossible for the typical businesspaper to cover its field adequately without participating actively in the events affecting its field.

The typical businesspaper aspires to leadership in its field. Only to a limited extent can that be achieved through the medium of the publication itself. Thus it becomes necessary for businesspaper publishers and editors not only to publish a good magazine but to engage in, if not to initiate, whatever outside activities the needs of the field may demand.

The opportunities for serving its field which are open to businesspapers are so many and cover such a wide range that no paper can hope to take advantage of them all. Most papers, however, go as far as they can in that direction because they realize that their good will depends largely upon such activities.

Because most fields served by businesspapers are served also by trade, industrial, or professional associations, a businesspaper must decide to what extent it will work with the associations in its field.

For more or less obvious reasons, most papers decide to work just as closely with their associations as conditions permit. This is essential in most cases if for no other reason than to keep abreast of what is happening in the field, but in addition to the news sources which such contacts provide, the prestige of the paper may very well depend in large measure upon the contribution it makes to its field through its participation in association activities.

In many cases, businesspapers have been entirely responsible or at least active in the organization of associations in their fields. Under such favorable conditions, the paper and the association have worked hand in hand for many years in some cases. Businesspaper publishers value such relationships very highly.

Wherever the need for a new association exists, the businesspaper which takes the initiative in organizing it builds for itself an asset of untold possibilities. The importance which most businesspapers put on the benefits they have obtained from such projects suggest that it might be worthwhile for all businesspapers to explore the possibilities in their respective fields. Even though in most cases no additional associations may be needed, yet in those few instances in which a new organization might serve a useful purpose outside of the scope of any existing organization, why should not a businesspaper in the field undertake to found it?

1. COOPERATING WITH ASSOCIATIONS

With very few exceptions, businesspapers cooperate with their associations to the fullest extent possible. Such cooperation obviously takes many forms, ranging all the way from mere membership to active direction of the association's affairs.

A brief description of some of the things businesspapers have done to help their associations may be even more useful than a list of affiliations.

Conventions in Print. *Railway Age*, during the depression and also during the war, when conventions were either impractical or banned, backed up its associations by "conventions in print" which were literally "reports" of conventions which were not held but which would no doubt have produced copy of the same kind if they had been. *Chain Store Age* published a "Stay-at-home Convention" issue, which was complete not only with "speeches" which might have been delivered had the convention been held, but discussions of the papers in question by other members, and to cap the climax, a typical after-dinner speech written in humorous vein such as might have been delivered at the annual banquet had there been one.

Registration Lists. Many businesspapers assume the responsibility of printing and distributing the registration list at the annual meetings or conventions of their associations. Publishers who have never undertaken such a project will find it to their interest to offer such cooperation wherever possible. Publishers who have had experience in that connection are unanimous in expressing their satisfaction with it as a good will builder.

Convention Dailies. Many businesspapers not only publish the registration lists at conventions, but get out daily papers covering the activities.

Preparing the Program. More important than reporting the proceedings of association meetings is the part businesspapers play in arranging them. One unique way in which one businesspaper helps associations prepare their programs is reported by *Printers' Ink*:

We offer bibliographies of articles which have appeared in *Printers' Ink* to the officers of the associations in our field and these bibliographies are put to work in planning programs for the meetings of those associations. Consequently it is hard to attend a convention or meeting of almost any sort in our field at which you won't hear *Printers' Ink* referred to.

A particularly well-organized program-building technique is reported by the *American Lumberman* in connection with the meetings held annually by thirty-two regional associations of the National Retail Lumber Dealers Association: "One of our services to the national organization is an annual report covering suggestions for the 32 dealer conventions which they hold each year."

Membership Committees. Because of their many intimate and constant contacts with the field, through both their editorial and advertising departments, businesspapers are ideally equipped to cooperate with their associations in the frequently vital matter of extending the membership. Many businesspapers render such service, not only through the medium of their own publications by extolling the advantages of membership but by serving on the membership committees of such organizations.

Association Promotion Material. Some businesspapers have rendered valuable service to their associations by providing them with printed material of various kinds which, as publications, they are better equipped to produce than the associations themselves.

Supplying associations with reprints of articles or reports which have appeared in businesspapers covering the activities of such associations or pointing out the advantages of affiliation with them is a service of obvious value. The businesspaper can speak for an association much more effectively and disinterestedly than the association can speak for itself. Businesspapers which give due credit to the achievements of their associations earn a lot of good will for themselves at the same time. A check-up of the actual editorial support given to your trade associations during the past year, or any other period, might be worthwhile.

2. GRANTING OF AWARDS

One of the obvious ways in which a businesspaper can demonstrate its interest in the progress of its field is by establishing an award for meritorious achievement by individuals, companies, or groups. Such awards may not directly inspire the kind of achievements they hope to encourage but they undoubtedly have that effect indirectly. By honoring those who have rendered unusual service in a particular field or in the public interest, such awards serve to publicize achievements which might otherwise be known to a relative few. They honor not only the recipient of the award but also the field whose progress he has advanced. Thus, the businesspaper which sets up such an award makes a valuable contribution to its field and undoubtedly adds to its own good will at the same time.

Many such awards have been established by businesspapers.[2]

3. SPONSORSHIP OF CLINICS, PANELS, FORUMS, SEMINARS, ROUND TABLES

Many businesspapers find it desirable from time to time to sponsor meetings of leaders in the industry or the field covered in connection with current problems which call for united action.

One publication arranges a one-day meeting every year for the leaders in its field, and after the day's sessions are over entertains the group at dinner. The editor takes advantage of the occasion to deliver a report on the state of the industry and its outlook.

Restaurant Management sponsored thirty six forums for its field to consider the various problems which the repeal of prohibition created in the restaurant field. The meetings were held in the publication's conference room.

4. SUPPLEMENTARY PUBLICATIONS

The publication of *Trade Directories* as an adjunct to the publication of businesspapers must be included in any compilation of the services which businesspapers render.

From the standpoint of public relations, the important thing to note is that if a directory would serve a useful purpose in any field, the businesspaper which publishes it, either as a separate issue or as part of one of its regular issues, is rendering an additional service to its field.

[2] Three awards are worthy of special note: The Industrial Marketing Award for Editorial Achievement, the annual ABP Advertising Competitions, and the Putman Awards.

The Industrial Marketing Award, founded by C. D. Crain, Jr., publisher of *Industrial Marketing,* gives placques and citations to editors and businesspapers for distinguished editorial service, published research, and the best graphic presentations. The juries are advertising managers, advertising agency executives, typographical experts, and typical readers.

The Putman Awards, founded by Russell L. Putman, president of the Putman Publishing Co., are given "to demonstrate that industrial advertising is an integral part of effective selling to industry." Awards consist of cash honorariums of $5000 and certificates.

Both the Industrial Marketing and Putnam Awards are generally given at conventions of the National Industrial Advertisers' Association.

Every year since 1942 the Associated Business Publications' juries judge advertising campaigns submitted by advertisers and advertising agencies for the most effective use of businesspapers as a "strategic sales tool."

5. READER'S SERVICE

Most businesspapers operate a reference department. It would be almost impossible to publish a periodical without the help of such a department.

What public relations goal could businesspapers set for themselves that would be more rewarding than to secure universal acceptance of the idea that "when you want information on any phase of business, the place to go for it is your businesspaper?"

Obviously it is not enough to have the information available for the paper's own use or to confine its use to subscribers or advertisers, if it is to serve as a builder of good will. The information collected should be made available to everybody who is seriously interested in it; it should be so maintained that it can be supplied with a minimum of delay to such inquirers; and once the department is set up so that it is equipped to function efficiently, its availability might well be publicized.

6. LEGISLATION

Many businesspapers take a position editorially for or against proposed legislation affecting their respective fields. Some go farther and support or oppose such measures by personal appearances, before committees or other legislative bodies, direct mail, public addresses, debates, etc. They all make their columns available to their readers.

A common way of exercising the paper's influence in behalf of or against proposed legislation is to circulate reprints of editorials or stories where they will do the most good.

When an industry is threatened with complete elimination through the medium of discriminatory taxes leveled against it, the businesspaper in the field has little choice but to take an aggressive position against such legislation not only within its own pages, where it could achieve only a minimum of results, but outside of its pages as well. That was the position in which *Chain Store Age* found itself almost from its inception in 1925. Within the next few years, state after state took up the question of imposing special taxes against chain stores to check their growth or eliminate them altogether.

The editor of *Chain Store Age* found himself engaged in public debates, appearances before legislative committees, public addresses wherever the opportunity presented itself to arouse public opinion against the threatened taxes, and preparing printed material for distribution wherever it would be most effective. *Chain Store Age* reports that such outside activities probably earned more enduring good will for the paper in its own field than anything it could have done in the paper itself.

On the constructive side of legislative activity, *Printers' Ink*'s success in getting its "model statute" on fair advertising enacted in 43 of the 48 states must stand out as a shining example of what businesspapers can do in this area. It has recently revised the model statute and the revision has already been put before several state legislatures.[3]

7. SURVEYS

Businesspapers make all kinds of surveys for editorial use or for use in promoting their own publications, but sometimes a paper makes a survey solely for the betterment of its field.

Such a survey was undertaken by *Railway Age* in 1946 when it retained the Opinion Research Corporation to make a study of "What Employes Think About the Railroad Industry." While this survey "was expensive," according to the publication, "it was very greatly appreciated."

Similar surveys of the field itself or outside the field have been made by other businesspapers.

It is quite obvious that any businesspaper which takes the initiative and shoulders the expense of a survey designed to promote the welfare of the field it serves is bound to earn considerable good will.

8. EDUCATION AND RESEARCH

Businesspapers in many fields have used their "know-how" and the technical ability of their editors to produce manuals and textbooks to be used in schools and colleges and to promote the efficiency of men already engaged in the various fields covered. Many editorial staffs include a sales training director who prepares manuals for retail store sales clerks.

In highly technical fields such as engineering, it is only natural that the editors of the businesspapers should be men of the highest possible professional standing and that such men should be the authors of the leading textbooks and scientific treatises.[4]

[3] See Chapter 16.

[4] Businesspaper editors are authors of numerous technical handbooks and manuals which were used by the armed services and by industrial war plants in World Wars I and II. Many such books are described in a booklet called "The Story of Forty Years Growth," published by the McGraw-Hill Book Co.

Scholarships and prizes in colleges and schools to promote interest in special fields are reported by a number of businesspapers. Many more, however, could undoubtedly follow the same course to their own benefit. Contributing even in a small way to the education of those who will one day be leaders in their respective fields should commend itself to businesspapers as one of the most logical ways to develop their prestige and good will.

9. PUBLIC SPEAKING[5]

Editors and other executives of businesspapers frequently appear as public speakers before all kinds of audiences. The benefits to be gained by such activities in one's own field are more or less obvious, provided, of course, that the speaker can be relied upon always to do a good job.

But some businesspaper editors go further than that and take advantage of frequent opportunities to speak before audiences far removed from their own specific fields.

The editors and other staff members of a number of businesspapers are members of such organizations as the American Marketing Association and are frequently active participants in the programs of the various chapters of that organization as well as of the national body.

10. HOUSE ORGANS AND NEWS LETTERS

House organs or news letters for the staff are common features in the employee relations programs of businesspapers. They provide a logical medium through which all employees could be taught, or reminded of, the ethics of businesspaper publishing and, at the same time, what it means for a businesspaper to be a member of ABP. Here is a concrete suggestion which most of us might adopt to advantage.

11. PUBLICITY

In conclusion,[6] it should be pointed out that no public relations program is complete unless it provides not only for doing things that make for greater good will but also for publicizing them. The biblical warning against hiding one's light "under a bushel" has direct application to this phase of public relations.

[5] More than fifty colleges are on the ABP speaker's bureau list for lectures every year by editors and publishers.

[6] Although the purpose of this study was primarily to describe certain activities of businesspapers outside of their printed pages, it should not be overlooked that many of the greatest services which a businesspaper can render its field originate in the publication itself.

HOW TO HANDLE INQUIRIES FROM READERS*

Some publications use the term "reader service" as a glorified name for the circulation department. In other cases reader service consists almost wholly of transmitting free literature requests from readers to advertisers or prospects—or of filling requests for reprints offered in the editorial pages.

Of course, if you want to stretch the term you can call the whole editorial function "reader service." But what it means to most of us is the handling of unsolicited inquiries from readers—requests for help in solving problems, for sources of supply, requests for clippings, and so on.

You often hear an editor say, "I spent the whole morning answering inquiries. Haven't had a chance to do any real work." If inquiries are regarded as unproductive effort, the person on whom they are saddled is bound to become sorry for himself.

Unanswered inquiries prey on editors' minds. They are the commonest source of editorial stomach ulcers.

INQUIRIES AS A MEASURE OF INFLUENCE

The cure for this condition begins with a change in attitude. The change should start at the top—preferably with the publisher's recognition of the fact that the volume of unsolicited inquiries a publication gets is an excellent index of its influence in its field, and that inquiries have a cash value.

Let us assume, therefore, that the publisher comes back from a meeting where he ran across another publisher who bragged at the volume of inquiries his paper received. Word comes from on high that inquiries are to be switched from the nuisance column to the asset side of the ledger —that the forbidding scowl or forced grin that means "we are here to serve you but for God's sake don't overdo it," is to give way to the best Grade A Rotary Club 26-tooth smile of welcome.

Then what?

ROUTE INQUIRIES THROUGH ONE PERSON

The first step is to designate some individual in the editorial, circulation, or another department as inquiry specialist. This person should preferably be of the eager beaver type with a supercharged Boy Scout

* Arthur Dix, Director of Research, Conover Mast Corporation; from a talk before the New York Business Paper Editors, April 19, 1945.

complex for doing dozens of good deeds daily. All inquiries should channel through him or her.

Your centralized inquiry staff may be as little as 25 per cent of one person, up to one or more—depending on your field.

Of course, your inquiry specialist may not personally answer all the inquiries. He may handle most of them but will route certain ones to staff authorities on the particular subject. But the inquiry specialist will keep a check on whether they are answered.

DATA FILE IS INQUIRY SPECIALIST'S CHIEF RELIANCE

Your inquiry specialist's chief reliance is an information file—which can be simply a drawerful of correspondence folders, classified by subject. Let us see how this works. Before you have an inquiry specialist, you get a complaint from your Chicago advertising representative who has just called on Herman Vogel in Milwaukee. Herman is on the point of cancelling his advertising because an inquiry he sent in a month ago on what to do when hops turn moldy was not answered. The advertising manager gets nasty about it.

You recall with a sickly smile that the letter is at the bottom of your little pile of unanswered inquiries you have been intending to get at one of these days.

You put it hurriedly at the top and ask Miss Schultz to dig up that moldy hops letter you sent about a year and a half ago to the Fagleheimer Brewery in St. Louis. Miss Schultz reports that your answer got into the general file and the whole file was thrown out at the first of the year. So you have to do it all over again.

But under your perfect inquiry-answering system, your inquiry specialist flicks a careless finger over some folders until he comes to "hops, comma, moldy," pulls out the carbon of the letter you wrote to Fagleheimer, sends the same letter to Herman Vogel in Milwaukee. Herman marvels at the extent of your knowledge, the speed of your reply, and doubles his advertising.

INQUIRY REPLIES USED IN EDITORIAL SPACE

But that is only the first of the many ways in which your inquiry file can be used. If moldy hops are bothering several brewers the condition may be common in the industry, so you may expand the answer into an article.

Or in the absence of an article, you can run the queries as letters to the editor, along with a reply. If you feel that it would be indelicate to reveal Vogel's moldy hops trouble to the whole field, you can use his initials.

INQUIRIES USED AS AN EDITORIAL FEATURE

At least one publication regularly takes all its inquiries and runs the cream of them, along with answers, in a Letter to the Editor page in every issue. A page of this kind has interesting possibilities. In the first place readers are frequently more interested in what other readers write than what editors write. The page is a vitamin injection for reader responsiveness. It quickens reader interest. And it is not a bad way at all to plug a given feature and advertise what has appeared in past issues.

INQUIRIES ARE A CONTINUING SURVEY OF READER INTEREST

Inquiries are a continuing reader interest survey. If a pet project of yours, in which you have invested your heart's blood, meets with deadly silence, you are within your rights in suspecting that your editorial omniscience has blown a temporary gasket.

Or if a certain Cinderella section that you privately thought was tripe starts to pull like everything you can get on the bandwagon while there is still time—and thereby keep your reputation for knowing exactly what the reader wants.

INQUIRIES SELL ADVERTISING

After you have wrung every last ounce of editorial value out of inquiries, you can put them to mercenary use. If your advertising salesmen have to present proof that your paper is actually read—and what advertising salesmen docs not?—there is no more convincing evidence than a stock of unsolicited letters beginning, "On page . . . of your April issue I noticed a . . ." and so on.

A fat inquiry file is one of the finest space-selling aids that any advertising salesman can possibly have. It is incontrovertible evidence that your book is read.

INQUIRIES SELL YOUR ADVERTISERS' GOODS

You can cash in on inquiries in still another way. Many of them ask "where can we buy so-and-so?" On these your inquiry specialist confers with the advertising department. Of course, he withholds the lead from the Blatz Tank Co., which never placed any space with us, and gives it to our good friends (and advertisers) the Glutz Tank Co.

INQUIRIES SELL SUBSCRIPTIONS

Another important use of inquiries—in temporary hibernation—is in selling subscriptions. Never answer an inquiry without checking against your subscription list. Inquiries furnish leads that sell subscriptions.

INQUIRIES RAISE THE SUBSCRIPTION RENEWAL RATE

Of course, one of the most important fruits of efficient handling of inquiries is the elevating effect it has on the renewal rate. The subscriber for whom you have done a favor turns a deaf ear to the circulation salesman of a competitive paper. He is yours for a long time.

So important is the effect of inquiry-handling on renewal rate that in one or more letters of their subscription renewal series, some publications invite the reader to send in inquiries. And some publications direct their field representatives to offer the publication's information service freely to subscribers.

It builds good will, and means a higher renewal percentage.

DO NOT ANSWER ALL INQUIRIES

I have enumerated the advantages of actually seeking inquiries from readers, and handling them promptly. These advantages are to be weighted against the effort and expense involved in handling more inquiries.

First, the effort is reduced considerably by letting all inquiries channel through one source. Your inquiry specialist has a well indexed information file, reference books, etc. The inquiry specialist will acquire a delicate sense of what inquiries should be answered in full, which should get Grade B treatment, and which should be ignored. You might, for example, ignore inquiries from intermediate organizations that simply use you to build themselves up. Among these are certain banks, retail reporting services, and so-called "National" research organizations. These are Sinbad the Sailors that ride on editors' shoulders. They send out an endless stream of inquiries, but do not tell you for whom they want the information. You do the work, they get the credit. As you handle inquiries for ultimate profit—not for fun—you ignore their requests or at least use a polite form asking them to give you the inquirer's name so that you may reply direct. They never respond to this because they want the credit.

Or there is the Wall St. firm that would like you to spend a couple of days building up a prospectus on a new process. Or the young lady attending the Cheyenne College for Women who would like you to write her thesis on the impact of synthetic rubber on tooth brush buying among Dutch East Indians.

If you can handle these inquiries with a clipping, you do so. Otherwise, you coldly weigh the time required against what you would get out of it, resisting the temptation to do good where the prospect of a return to you is slight or absent.

USE GREAT CARE IN SELECTING INQUIRIES TO BE IGNORED

Of course, you use great care in selecting the inquiries to be given absent or once-over-lightly treatment. The young lady who is preparing her thesis, and wants you to do it for her, may be the daughter of a 12-page-in-color advertiser.

But if you have a well-stocked data file you may be able to satisfy her with little effort on your part.

CLIPPINGS AND PHOTOSTATS

A considerable proportion of inquiries are easily answered. Many merely call for a clipping of an article. The inquiry specialist maintains a cut copy file. If he runs out of clippings of a certain article that hit the jackpot, he can decide whether to order reprints—and whether or not to charge for them. In the absence of clippings he will be able to mention the name of a back-number dealer, or a library that can furnish photostats, or he may have a photostat machine.

He may avail himself of a little printed memo, such as Ruth Hahn of *Sales Management* uses, simply checking the appropriate paragraph in answering the inquiry.

INQUIRY FILE IS BOON TO EDITORS

The ease with which the inquiry specialist answers inquiries will be in proportion to how well stocked his information file is. This file will become one of the most useful tools in the editorial department. If you have to write an article on a given subject, you are off to a flying start when you have the data folder on that subject tucked under your arm.

CARDS OR CLIPPINGS

There is a violent difference of opinion as to how the information file should be maintained. *Printers' Ink* uses and advocates cards rather than actual clippings.

But *Printers' Ink* is the B-29 of reader service, and most of us are still in the Piper Cub stage. We may find that correspondence folders into which clippings, pamphlets, etc., can be filed, will do very well. My concluding suggestion is that you include clippings from competing publications, for if your publication is the leader in its field, six months after the article has appeared elsewhere the reader will swear he read it in your paper regardless of where it appeared.

In summary, it pays to encourage readers to send in inquiries—and the best way to handle them is to funnel them through one person.

CLERICAL PROCEDURE IN READERS' SERVICE*

The switch from ledgers to a card indexing system was necessary because it proved impossible to index the editorial content of *Printers' Ink* properly in alphabetized ledgers. A comprehensive study of indexing systems was made and the present plan, based on the Dewey Decimal System, was built to embrace all the important subjects of advertising, merchandising, marketing, selling, and distribution.

Every article and news item published in *Printers' Ink* pages is carefully cross-indexed under each of the important topics covered. One article might necessitate the typing and filing of anywhere from 15 to 20 index cards on different subjects. Altogether, we have over 1200 numerical, subject, and commodity headings under which our articles are indexed.

Each of the cards we make out bears the index number or subject heading, together with an appropriate subtitle pertaining to that heading, the title of the article, the name of the author, and the date of issue and page number where the article appears.

Before our index cards are prepared, one copy of each *Printers' Ink* issue is indexed, with the proper index numbers, subject headings, and appropriate subtitles written in at the top and along the margins of each article. When writing out the various subtitles, each of which is a digest of an indexable part of an article, it is important to incorporate in the subtitle those words which are necessary for properly recording that portion of the article in the subject file. In other words, while some subtitles that are written in along the margin of an article are accompanied by numerical headings under which that particular subtitle is filed, others are not accompanied by numbers, but are written for the purpose of recording that portion of the article in the subject file.

* From "A Brief Picture of the *Printers' Ink* Readers' Service Department," a pamphlet published by *Printers' Ink*.

Each year we use a different color index card in order that the cards in each file classification can be conveniently separated by years. When you are familiar with the various colors, it is a great deal easier to re-file cards by years, using the colors as your guide, than it would be to have to file cards of the same color, according to the date on each.

During the course of a year, we prepare and file over 35,000 card references to our articles. That means an average of over 700 cards per issue. Our files extend back over 40 years and include over 850,000 index cards.

When indexing news items, the entire item is pasted on the index card, with the appropriate numerical or subject heading. Of course, if a news item is too long to fit on a card, it is treated the same as a regular article.

In addition to the numerical and subject files, we also maintain a general file, where articles are filed according to the names of persons or companies about which or by whom the articles were written.

To round out the facilities of the Readers' Service Department, we have a library of close to 3000 books on advertising and related subjects, as well as numerous standard reference works containing various media and market data, plus information on a host of subjects not normally covered in the pages of *Printers' Ink*. We also maintain a file of several hundred house organs; a record of over 5000 house organ titles, and a slogan file comprising over 9000 phrases.

The Readers' Service Department provides working space for visitors who wish to avail themselves of our complete bound volume files of every *Printers' Ink* issue ever published and the references to their contents.

The entire department facilities are at your disposal. We invite you to make use of them whenever and as often as you feel we can be of assistance to you on any advertising, merchandising, or sales subject.

MECHANICS OF AN INFORMATION FILE*

A subject file is one where the papers or information are arranged by subject or descriptive feature.

It is one of the most difficult methods of filing for both the clerk and file user, because no two people think exactly alike about any one topic.

I am aware of the fact that you will not be personally setting up this

* Ann McDonald, librarian, Lennen & Mitchell Advertising Agency; a paper read before the New York Business Paper Editors, November, 1949.

file, but that the job will be done by one of your assistants, who will probably be in need of guidance from you.

If you are starting out to set up a new information file, or revise an existing one, there are certain definite steps that should be taken, whether you are preparing to establish one drawer of material or one hundred drawers of material, in order to insure its success.

SUBJECT AUTHORITY LIST

The first and most important step should be the development of a subject authority list. That is a list of your main subject headings with their divisions and subdivisions. The development of such a list requires close and detailed study of your organization, material filed, and nature of reference.

A good subject heading must express the topic as exactly and concisely as possible. A single word is best chosen to describe the contents of the paper, and that word a noun. Plural form should be used, unless usage calls for the singular.

There are many printed aids to help you in the selection of subject headings covering almost any and every industry. Most of the information pertaining to these lists may be obtained through the Special Libraries Association, if your librarian is a member, or the H. W. Wilson & Co.

There are two or three courses being offered at this time on subject filing, or the classification of subject matter, which anyone faced with this task of setting up an information file would find most helpful.

If you have a particularly difficult problem it might be best for you to seek the services of a filing consultant. All of the large equipment houses maintain staffs of analysts and there are several excellent independent consultants here in town.

As an example I have such a list here that contains the titles of some 400 subject classifications dealing with everything from Accounting to Zoology. There are several other sources for such lists.

If anyone is interested in obtaining such a list for their particular field, I will be glad to check further into it and direct you to the source for obtaining one.

I have never found it possible to use in its entirety any classification scheme developed for any industry, without considerable alterations. However, a study of these lists will save a great deal of work which has already been done by somebody else.

METHOD OF ARRANGEMENT

Once you have developed your subject authority list, or in the beginning a skeleton of it, it is well to consider the method of arrangement you are going to adopt. In the absence of a well-trained staff, keep it as simple as possible. There are several standard methods of arranging subject material. I will outline these briefly:

1. *Alphabetically by dictionary method,* that is, the subjects are filed in strict alphabetic order, with no logical connection between subjects filed next to each other.

2. *Alphabetically by Encyclopedic method,* where the subjects are filed alphabetically by main subject breakdowns and the subdivisions of this subject filed together. This is the most widely used method of arrangement for subject files

3. There is the *Duplex-numeric system*, where numbers are assigned to principal main subject headings and subdivided as the subject grows.

4. Some files are based on the *Sequential numbering plan* with the next number in rotation assigned to each new subject.

5. Or there is the decimal system based on the *Dewey Decimal*, which is used mostly in public libraries and highly specialized businesses.

No matter which type of arrangement is used, in order to be a good file it must be simple to understand, have its divisions and subdivisions well defined, be as inexpensive as possible to operate in time, labor, and equipment, and be flexible in allowing for expansion.

CROSS-REFERENCES

In an information file adequate cross-referencing is imperative if the file is to fully serve its purpose.

Cross-references are used where there is a choice of terms and *See also* references are used to refer you to one or more places where allied material thought to be valuable in connection with this same subject may be found.

There are many methods of handling this: on a standard cross-reference sheet which can be purchased at any stationary store or filing equipment house; a tabbed half of a regular correspondence for permanent cross-reference, on regular 3 x 5 index cards filed in standard index card cabinets; the Wheeldex Cub which is not much larger than your telephone and holds one thousand cards; or on flex-o-line strips which range from ⅛ to ⅓ inch in width. These strips are excellent for single-line enteries.

INDEX

Every subject file, no matter how small, should have an index. This applies even to the alphabetic subject files to which reference may be made directly.

An index is an alphabetically arranged list of subject headings and subdivisions plus all cross-references.

The value of an index lies in the fact that it gives a quick review of the contents of a subject file when choosing new headings and that it acts as an aid in identifying material asked for under unusual headings.

There are certain requirements for any good index: it should be standardized in that specific headings under which material shall be filed should be drawn up before the file is started; it must be flexible enough to allow for the absorption of entirely new material; it must be understandable to others than the indexer.

The index may be made up on loose-leaf sheets in a binder, or on cards, wheeldex, or strips; the cards or strips are usually used as they allow for expansion without retyping.

Color in an index leads to quick identification—one color card for headings, another for cross-reference, or any other situation you wish to signal by the use of color.

So important is the index that it is practically impossible for a subject file to function satisfactorily without one.

EQUIPMENT

Very often after much time and thought has been put into the development of a subject classification we fail to give enough thought to the physical setup of this material or to take advantage of the many new equipment developments to aid in faster filing and finding.

The problem of the best arrangement for a subject file has been given much thought by the filing analysts and the equipment manufacturers. It is interesting to note that they have all come up with the same answers —with slight variations.

RETENTION AND DESTRUCTION PLAN

An information file is not transferred at regular intervals. Very often material on a subject becomes more valuable as it accumulates over a period of years. Old material that has been superseded should be discarded. The file should be gone through every two or three years in order to keep the material in file fairly permanent. From the index should be removed all cards, main entry, and cross-references which refer to the material descarded.

MANUAL OF PROCEDURE

Every file should have a written manual of procedure. This is especially important in a small, one-person file where the system is likely to become personalized. It should explain your subject classification system, routines, and even the typing and pasting of labels. Such a manual serves as an excellent textbook for training new clerks, as the assistant is assured of clear instructions. It can be studied as often as desired and it relieves the new clerk of constant questioning and the supervisor of repetitious answers. It can be as simple or elaborate as you care to make it.

To sum it all up in capsule form:
Develop your subject authority list
Decide on your method of arrangement
Cross-reference thoroughly
Maintain an up-to-date index
Choose the correct equipment and supplies
Have some sort of a retention and destruction plan
Have a written manual of procedure

If all of this sounds like a bore, call in a consultant and let him worry about it.

CHAPTER 15

Personnel

LABORATORY OF HUMAN RELATIONSHIPS

No private enterprise in our economy is more vitally concerned with the high performance of human talent than a businesspaper publishing organization.

The modern businesspaper has become, in one sense, a laboratory of human relationships. As we have seen in the preceding chapters the editorial and research staffs, and even the sales staffs, conduct an unending investigation of ways and means to increase human efficiency as well as mechanical efficiency. Indeed, one complements the other.

All the problems of human relationships in every other type of organization become the problems of the editorial staffs of businesspapers. It is not enough to simply report such problems and the attempts to solve them. The businesspaper must join in the search for solutions and even conduct its own experiments.

Since the businesspaper is a dispenser of know-how for improving human relationships in industry it follows that its own policies, methods, and attitudes regarding the human talent gathered in its own shop must be exemplary.

A large field of opportunity faces the business press in personnel administration and should become a major project for future study.

For example, it is only in recent years that the majority of businesspaper publishers have begun to sense the value of top editorial talent in order to gain a top position in their field.

Colonel Chevalier's paper in this chapter scans the various stages of personnel administration in a businesspaper publishing house: recruitment, supervisory training, and job evaluation as it applies to administrative, advertising, and editorial personnel. Some of the practices he discusses, based on his experience as administrator in a modern multi-publishing house, may appear to be of doubtful interest to single-paper publishers. On second reading it will be discovered that in the principles set out lies the secret of consistent growth from single-paper publishing into multi-publishing or from a weak, small paper to a large strong leader in the industry served.

The administrative agency that coordinates all the separate groups in a businesspaper publishing house cannot function smoothly so long as it fails to make certain decisions on personnel administration. One of these decisions must be to appoint a competent personnel director if the size of the company warrants it, or to assign the functions of such office to a competent, qualified person to discharge with his other duties.

In theory, this personnel officer is as important as the sales manager to the healthy growth of the company.

Once the employees of a businesspaper publishing organization know that there is a chance to improve their position and that their chance is equal with every other employee—once they know their efforts are impartially and scientifically assessed periodically, a "peace of mind" descends upon the entire organization. This feeling naturally increases the sense of loyalty and the incentive to better individual and cooperative performance. The next step is benefit plans and the future security of employees.

Security involves either a profit-sharing or a pension plan and Mr. David Chase, whose firm are consultants to the business press, describes the comparative advantages and disadvantages of these two plans for publishers and employees, at the end of this chapter.

PERSONNEL ADMINISTRATION*

Quite generally, publishers have come to the realization that it pays them to expend as much care, time, and money in maintaining a well satisfied and efficient work force as does a manufacturer in selecting, maintaining, and improving his plant and equipment. To a greater extent than in most industries, people form the backbone of businesspaper publishing. It follows, therefore, that personnel administration should be regarded as an activity of prime importance requiring the close attention of executives, publishers, editors, and other managerial personnel right down to the first-line supervisor.

Those charged with responsibility for getting out the businesspaper

* Willard Chevalier, Executive Vice-President, McGraw-Hill Publishing Company; written specially for this volume.

have a corresponding responsibility for the maintenance of good human relationships within their respective groups. This concept of personnel administration as a major function of the line organization holds true in publishing as it does in other industries.

However, since consistency of treatment of the individual is basic to the smooth functioning of any personnel program, it is essential that provision be made for a coordinating agency. That is where the personnel officer comes into the picture. It matters little whether he be the head of an integrated personnel department in a large multi-publication concern or the publisher of a small single-paper operation who acts as a personnel specialist along with his other duties. In either case, his functions will be similar, varying only in complexity rather than in scope.

PRIMARY FUNCTIONS OF PERSONNEL OFFICER

In his position as coordinator of the personnel program the personnel officer acts in a staff capacity and in so far as over-all policy matters are concerned, his primary functions involve developing, proposing, reviewing, and analyzing. The personnel director of a large company would probably operate through a policy-making committee comprised of top executives. It is his responsibility to recommend the adoption of new personnel policies and the revision of existing ones. Having cleared a proposed policy with the top committee, he should then arrange to have it circulated among all members of the management group for their comments, criticisms, and suggestions. This procedure is particularly important in businesspaper publishing where the team is made up of various sharply defined elements, all working toward a common goal but from different angles and with diverse points of view. The personnel officer in a businesspaper publishing house soon senses the difficulty of finding a common denominator of policy that will be acceptable to the statistical-minded and hard-headed circulation man, the rather easygoing editor who typifies the creative type, and the space salesman who prides himself on his rugged individualism and who bridles at the mere mention of restraints.

To reconcile these varying points of view requires personal contacts, patience, perseverance, and persuasion. Once a policy has been cleared with all management people concerned, it is the function of the personnel officer to redraft it giving effect to opinions expressed by those who will be called upon to administer the policy. He then submits the revised draft to the top policy committee, and after that body has given its blessing, the policy is released over the signature of the chief executive.

The above procedure which admittedly is time consuming can be streamlined in single-paper operations, but the publisher who acts as his own personnel officer would be making a mistake if he followed the practice of establishing policy by fiat. His key people, upon whom he must rely for the application and enforcement of policy, should have a voice in their formulation. In his capacity as publisher he undoubtedly has the authority to issue directives, but when he puts on the personnel officer's hat, the consultative approach is more likely to achieve the desired results.

With the establishment of policies, the work of a personnel officer of a business publication has barely begun. He then faces the task of developing procedures by which the policies may be implemented, and when that has been completed, there is the ever-present problem of interpretation. Perhaps it is because of the nature of the business with its recurring deadlines, or perhaps it is because of the temperament which is characteristic of creative genius, that editorial people seem to regard personnel administration as an extra-curricular activity that need not be engaged in regularly. To overcome this tendency in specific instances the personnel officer must once more resort to frequent personal contacts, which not only serve to resolve particular situations but also act as a training device when continued over an extended period of time.

Because the personnel officer lacks the power to command (except with respect to his immediate staff) it is extremely important that he be identified with and have the wholehearted support of top management. Unless he holds such a position and has such support, his efforts to advise, guide, explain, and recommend would come to nought. This is particularly true where the personnel officer acts strictly as a specialist in personnel matters. Where a publisher or chief editor handles personnel as a sideline, his position is secure.

SCOPE OF PROGRAM

So far as the fundamentals of human relationships are concerned, businesspaper publishing is no different from any other business, and publishers should not arbitrarily exclude from consideration any of the elements that go to make up a well-rounded personnel program. Which aspects of personnel relations are to be emphasized and which are to be sidetracked will depend in large measure upon the size, nature, and circumstances of each particular company, with financial considerations playing the most important part in making the determination. The more important items that comprise a balanced personnel program will be touched upon briefly further along in this chapter. Space does not permit detailed consideration of all of them, but there is one which deserves special mention because of the nature of the business and because of the inherent characteristics of the people who choose publishing as a career.

SUPERVISORY TRAINING

Supervisory training is an activity which has been sadly neglected in many publishing houses, yet it is one of the most effective means of improving relations with employees. A company may have the most progressive set of policies in existence, but if they are not properly administered, they might just as well never have been written.

In all business establishments, the introduction and maintenance of training programs present a problem. Even in industry, where in most cases the wage earners greatly outnumber the salaried personnel, there is resistance to "going to school." In publishing, where there are no "machine operators" in the common sense of the term, and where the level of intelligence is well above that found in other organizations of comparable size, training must frequently be introduced through the back door as a by-product of some other activity.

Salesmen, it is true, have no hesitancy in taking a course in public speaking or any other subject that will aid them in making sales, but sales managers who pride themselves on their knowledge of business psychology usually can see no need for training in the techniques of handling people. Erudite editors also are inclined to balk at the suggestion that their supervisory skills might be improved upon. In the circulation and production departments where the atmosphere is apt to be less free and easy, training programs usually have smoother sailing, but in the areas where it is needed most, supervisory training is hard to sell.

The personnel officer who recognizes that the success of his program depends upon the skill with which it is administered, must push relentlessly for supervisory training in one form or another. The approach must be a subtle one and high pressure will get him nowhere, but as he gains the confidence of the members of the management group, methods will suggest themselves to him. For the most part, supervisory training programs in businesspaper publishing must be custom made and more likely than not will be conducted informally. It is a waste of time, for example, to insist upon the conference method approach with a publisher or editor who is "too busy to hold meetings." It may be possible, however, to sell him the idea of dumping his problems into the lap of the personnel officer. If the latter is smart, he will hand them right back accompanied by a solution rather than handling them himself. The next time that particular problem arises, the publisher or editor will·know what to do about it.

Because of the personalities with whom he must deal, the personnel officer in a businesspaper publishing house must "play it by ear" to a much greater extent than his confrères in industry. But the time and energy which such an approach demands is compensated for to a great extent by the fact that he is dealing with an intelligent, well-educated, and highly interesting group of people.

He has little difficulty in explaining, for example, that sound employment practices call for the personnel department to act as a screening agency, with responsibility for the final selection of candidates resting with the respective supervisor under whose jurisdiction the new employee will work. Likewise the importance of two-way communications with employees is readily understood by people who are themselves engaged in communicating through the printed word and who need not be sold on the idea that an informed group is an interested group.

Being in close touch with a large segment of industry, regardless of what field their publications may serve, businesspaper publishers cannot help but be aware of the important part which benefit plans play in any personnel program. Thus the personnel officer has had the groundwork laid for him when he advocates the adoption of group insurance, hospitalization, and pension or profit-sharing plans. His difficulty will arise in attempting to reconcile his concept of adequate benefits with the company's willingness to finance such protection. The astute personnel officer will, of course, recognize the necessity of cutting the pattern to fit the cloth, and will not recommend benefits that are beyond his company's means.

Most publishers would probably admit that job evaluation is so much Greek so far as they are concerned. Nevertheless, the personnel officer who senses the need for a scientific method of comparing jobs in his particular organization would probably have no difficulty in explaining what is involved and in getting the publishers, editors, and others in management circles to go along with the idea. The same holds true in the development of a medical program, a workable grievance procedure, sound accident prevention practices, and the countless other items that are today encompassed in the term personnel relations.

Quite aside from his staff functions as an advisor to management, the personnel officer carries line authority in the administration of his own department. Here the circumstance of his being in businesspaper publishing has little effect upon his method of operation. In a large organization, the personnel department will probably be organized along functional lines with one section having primary responsibility for recruiting and employment, another salary administration, another training and safety, and another communications. Responsibility for the administration of benefit plans, social and recreational activities, research, and other minor activities of the personnel department is usually assigned as best fits the circumstances of each particular case, with the work load and personalities as major determinants. The medical department is usually set up as a separate unit headed by a doctor or medical director who reports administratively to the personnel officer.

In small, single-paper operations, where no personnel staff is justified, the personnel officer must possess great versatility and perform many of the functions himself. The requirements of the job, however, are not so complex as in larger organizations, and in all cases there must be adequate clerical help to process the paper work and to maintain the complete records which are so vital to effective personnel administration.

JOB EVALUATION

Job evaluation is the method by which a company decides how much individual jobs are worth in relation to other jobs. The other jobs may be within the company, the community, or the industry. All three categories may be involved.

The method of evaluating jobs may be quite informal—for example, a comparison by department heads of the job duties and salaries of their employees. Or it may be formal, making use of fairly elaborate systems, such as those adopted by the National Metal Trades Association, by which values are determined on a system of point ratings.

Within the individual company, job descriptions can be compared with each other. If the organization is quite small, there may be only one job of a kind, in which case it will be advisable to compare it with similar jobs outside the company as well as with different jobs within the company. If there are two or more jobs of a kind, internal comparison should be made, but comparison with outside jobs probably will give additional worthwhile information.

The individual company knows that it must pay at least $X to secure passable quality on a job of a given description. Therefore, $X is the minimum rate for that job. The company is willing to pay up to $X plus Y as the quality increases. The range, therefore, becomes $X to $X plus Y.

For the individual company to be able to compare its job descriptions and rates with those of other companies, it is necessary that the individual companies furnish job descriptions and salary ranges for their jobs to some agency on a confidential basis. The agency then makes tabulations of salary ranges and job descriptions, against which the individual companies can compare their own data.

Merit rating frequently is an adjunct of job evaluation. It is used to determine the position within the salary range which a given employee's salary should occupy.

By the methods described, uniformity in titles on mastheads is not necessary. At the same time, the individual company is able to classify employees by job descriptions within definite salary ranges.

RECRUITING OF SALES PERSONNEL

The selection of sales trainees is a three-part procedure: screening, checking, and testing.

Screening. The applicant is interviewed first by the director of sales training, who gives him a careful preliminary screening. Successful here, he next goes before a six-man screening committee. The screening committee is made up of men who have had many years of sales experience. With their knowledge of salesmen, and guided additionally by a carefully compiled rating sheet, they are able to evaluate each applicant well.

Checking. Having survived the screening committee, the applicant's references are checked and the Retail Credit Company is retained to make a complete report on the applicant's past history. With all of his background brought to light, the applicant at this point is ready for testing.

Testing. The applicant is given a battery of tests which reveal his dominance, extroversion, mental ability, social intelligence, and his sales aptitudes. At this point a few of the applicants strike out, although the preceding care in screening and checking keeps this number to a minimum. If the decision is made to hire the man, he is given a physical examination before he takes his first training position.

Training. This takes the form of on-the-job training, and the first spot is in the research department. Here the sales trainee learns something about the markets he will be serving as well as a good deal about the magazines that reach those markets. In this department he becomes familiar in other words with both his market and his product. The information he gets here will be of real value to him when he goes out to sell.

After two months in research, though the time is flexible, he is moved to the circulation department. A month here will give him the fundamentals of circulation practice and further build his product and market knowledge.

Next comes a period in the production department, where he will pick up vocabulary and working knowledge on the mechanics of putting a magazine together. While he will not become an expert in graphic arts, he will be expected to learn enough to understand problems on printing, plates, etc. This again comes under the heading of product knowledge.

Next spot would be the publication's promotion manager, where he can become familiar with magazine promotion, sales kit material, etc.

Then he will also talk with editors, their make-up man, and others, and learn something about meeting deadlines and editorial and advertising policy.

While the first selling job can be one as a junior on a magazine, more often the new man will start on classified advertising or direct mail or directory. It is expected that he will spend about two years in this activity, working under the careful supervision of the senior in the territory, the department head, and the district manager. In addition, he will report to the director of sales training who will watch his progress, getting regular reports from his supervisors.

By the end of two years he should be ready for greater sales responsibilities, and at this time he is moved to a sales territory on a publication. His learning continues under his publication sales manager. While the director of sales training has less contact from here on, his progress is watched as he works his way into major sales status.

EVALUATION OF ADVERTISING PERSONNEL

This takes several forms: discussions with sales and district managers, observation of sales control reports, reading of call reports, meetings, and periodical personal discussion with every man. With this close contact, it is possible to watch growth and to make note of those who are likely to become management material. Beyond personal evaluation, psychological testing is occasionally resorted to for objective verification of a man's potential.

EVALUATION OF ADMINISTRATIVE PERSONNEL

At this level, it is necessary to watch and stimulate the administrative leadership which in turn will be carried on down to the salesmen. An outline of the duties of sales managers is put into operation and is followed by sales managers. Meetings are held frequently to sustain interest and to exchange information on methods, techniques, etc.

The above structure of activities proves efficient in hiring, training, and supervising salesmen. Inherent in the above, but not stated, is the fact that salesmen should never be allowed to forget the basic principles of selling. To guard against this, at frequent intervals a refresher course in salesmanship is advisable in any sales organization. This course should be made available to both sales managers and salesmen. Obviously, then, sales training is a never-ending job if sales ability, sales enthusiasm, and success are to be maintained.

RECRUITMENT OF EDITORIAL PERSONNEL

A businesspaper publisher wants, if he can get them, editorial job candidates who have some background in the theory and practice of the kind of business for which he is publishing. Sources of such talent are:

1. Colleges that give courses providing such background. He can keep heads of appropriate departments and of job-finding agencies of such colleges aware of his interest, invite them to refer graduating class members or post-graduates to him. Since he is likely to have few jobs open at any one time, he may want to confine this invitation to institutions in his own publishing area, thus avoiding any obligation to defray expenses of men coming to see him. Letters of invitation should be very precise as to his frequency of job openings and as to the qualifications he is looking for.

College faculties in institutions whose curricula touch on the field of business covered by the publisher should be regularly contacted by the publisher or members of his editorial staff for the purpose of spotting likely candidates for editorial job openings. Younger teachers at the "instructor" level frequently have the temperament and background that pay out in editorial work, particularly if their professional activities have brought them into close relationships with industry. But, like industry men and association men, they must be caught young, while their powers of observation and appraisal are unjaded and before they have acquired the kind of academic habits that show up in editorial offices as arrogance and dilettantism.

2. Industry men in his field of readership, men encountered by his editors in the course of industrial coverage who show promise of easy conversion to editorial jobs. The cream of this crop is likely to be found among men who have been drawn on as contributors to his publication, who have already been, in a sense, part-time or avocational editors. Best prospects for conversion to editorial work are probably those with good records in their jobs who have been in those jobs less than ten, or even five years. Care must be taken not to pick up unstable characters whose principal interest in changing jobs is in changing jobs, or monastic characters who see the editorial chair as a refuge from the hurly-burly of practical affairs.

Correspondents on their own full-time jobs in industry or journalism and working for him in the field on a part-time basis. Good men in such part-time field positions, schooled in a publication's editorial requirements by practical reporting experience, frequently become prime candidates for consideration for full-time staff jobs, particularly jobs that simply transfer to a broader field the reporting activities that they have already undertaken in a single city or region. But in selecting such men for headquarter jobs, the publisher must make sure that he is not confusing the ability to do a good reporting job on the basis of a carefully outlined assignment with a capacity for the kind of creative work that was demanded of the man who outlined the assignment in the first place; that he is not confusing a talent for working well on a lone-wolf basis with the variety of talents needed for work within a staff—or on top of a staff.

3. Associations in the field whose activities and proceedings reveal men with an interest in, and talent for, appraisal and teaching of the techniques of the field in which the associations—and the publisher— exist. These will be, preferably, industry men spotted through association activities, rather than professional association personnel, though the latter should also come under the publishers' scrutiny, particularly if they are under 40.

4. Other magazines in competing or allied fields, whose editors can be encountered in meetings of publishing and industrial organizations and whose work can be watched by following it in their magazines. No

intelligent publisher should need a formulation of the cautionary rules governing the acquisition of editors brought up in other "schools" of publishing or identified with competitive enterprises.

5. Government offices in federal agencies that work in the same field as the publisher, whose employees are often in the line of background, temperament, and talent needed for editorial work. But, in almost every case, such men must be "caught young" before they have succumbed to the habits and frustrations common to government work.

6. Anywhere, if the publisher is filling an editorial job at the bottom of the ladder, that he can spot a well-educated youngster who can express himself in written language and who has an abnormally high I.Q., indicating a superior ability to handle himself in social relations and a superior learning capacity.

TRAINING EDITORIAL PERSONNEL

Philosophy, economics, and specialized routines of publishing in general and in terms of the particular publisher's operations can best be taught—and probably can only be taught—by having the publisher or one or more senior members of his staff make a point of holding frequent luncheon and other sessions with the new employee during his first six to twelve months of employment and drawing him into solo- or group-discussions of these subjects. This is an obligation which too few publishers and chief editors take the time to discharge. Where operations are highly departmentalized, actual schedules should be set up under which new employees will meet for such discussions periodically with department heads during their initial months of employment. In a very large operation, this can be done on a group basis or department heads can put on actual class-presentations of their activities and problems at intervals.

Business Milieu of the Publishing Operation. This is probably best taught by seeing that a new employee, during the initial months of work, makes field trips under chaperonage of an experienced editorial staff member. The chief editor should also require a new employee to read back issues of his magazine—and possibly even write a report on impression of objectives and techniques of the magazine on the basis of such reading, relating these to the character and problems of the magazine's field as sized up from such reading. Such a report could be made the occasion of a formal discussion with the new employee by the publisher and/or other appropriate executives.

Business Writing Per Se. During the initial months of a new employee's work, some superior editor must turn himself into a teacher, taking time to discuss at length all editing changes made in the neophyte's copy. He should also encourage the latter to read books on writing. If the publisher's operation is large enough, he can hire teaching talent and set up classes in writing.

Magazine Making. A great weakness among editors is that they read too few magazines for instruction in presentation. So far as I know, the complex job of manipulating such presentation elements as headings, illustration, break-up, and point-up devices to key publishing to reading psychology is not formally taught anywhere—except by such trained and relatively expensive specialists as George Dusenbury.[1] However, American magazine publishing is an open laboratory of experimentation in new ideas for anyone who will take the trouble to see it in that guise. Even a small staff could split up a number of business and general magazines for regular reading by staff members and hold periodical bull sessions at which readers would report on what they had seen and promote discussions as to the applicability of other publications' ideas and techniques to work in hand.

HUMAN RELATIONS ON THE EDITORIAL STAFF

Editors, like other employees, place a high value on money. However, they probably also place a higher value than normal on professional recognition and on a principal's interest in and willingness to discuss the techniques and problems of editorial work. The "happiest" publishing house is one that operates like a golf club in which the nonplaying hours are largely devoted to talking about everyone's game. Too few publishers fully appreciate the average editor's capacity for self-analysis—or "proneness to self-analysis, whatever his actual capacity"—and his inclination toward lush articulateness about his job, its satisfactions, and its worries. The smart publisher, who spares the time and takes the pains to learn to "speak the editor's language," can turn these editorial characteristics to great account for his paper. However, if he essays Socrates' role without Socrates' interest in it, he will probably end up as a gripe-collector and crying-shoulder, rather than as a participant in staff-stimulation.

Editors also probably place a higher valuation than most other types of publishing employees on "working conditions." I know of no study that proves anything about how an editorial office can best be set up to

[1] See Chapter 12.

promote the highest working efficiency, but I suspect that something as simple as an L-shaped desk, in place of the standard office desk, would step up editorial production—and publishers would probably save money by spending more on dictating equipment, secretarial help, messenger service, air conditioning, etc.

VACATIONS FOR EDITORS

Editors—and all creative workers in a creative business such as publishing—must work at a high mental pitch. They burn up energy at a rate that, in the publisher's own interest, demands that they get a longer-than-normal amount of vacation-recuperative time, and it would probably be better if it were split into two vacation periods per year. Publishers will have to (and must) take the cost of organizing their operations and manpower setup to permit it as part of the price they pay for doing business in ideas and quasi-literary expression: a business requiring an abnormal degree of concentration and an abnormal amount of absorption of information. No school (and an editor is going to school all the time) could get results on a two-week-vacation-a-year policy. No artist or craftsman—and an editor is his distant cousin—could gear his production to a clerical time-schedule.

PENSIONS AND PROFIT-SHARING*

The current popularity of profit-sharing and pension plans stems, in a limited sense, from the interest aroused during the recent process of amending the Social Security Law. In a greater measure, however, it is the result of a combination of circumstances, similar to those that prevailed during World War II. Then, as now, individual and corporate federal income tax rates were in ascendancy; a corporate excess profits tax law was in effect; and compensation levels had been frozen by wage and salary controls.

There is one important difference. Previously, under the freeze orders, the employer's contribution to a newly created employee plan did not constitute an increase in the compensation of the employees. Today it does, and if that brings the employee compensation to a point above a fixed percentage of the base period level, the new plan requires the blessing of the wage and salary stabilization authorities. This does not apply to plans put into effect before the inception of the present freeze orders.

* David B. Chase, C.P.A., member of the firm of J. K. Lasser & Company, consultants to the business press; prepared specially for this volume.

The advantages of profit-sharing and pension plans are many, particularly where the plans conform with Section 165 (a) of the Internal Revenue Code. They promote employee efficiency, reduce labor turnover, and give employees peace of mind as to the future, which in turn is reflected in increased loyalty. They have an even more practical side for both the employer and employee.

The employer's contributions to the plan are deductible on his income tax return. Because of high tax rates, this means that only a small part of each dollar paid is actually an out-of-pocket expense for the employer. The government would get the balance anyway in the form of additional taxes, if the employer had not contributed to the plan and procured a deduction thereby. In this way, the employer is able to contribute substantial sums for the benefit of his employees at a small net cost to himself.

The employee too, is entitled to special tax treatment. His share of the employer's contribution is not taxable until it is distributed to him. This may not be for a great many years and foreseeably tax rates will be less in the future. If it is paid to the employee on retirement or other severance of employment, or to his nominees on death, and this payment is made in one taxable year, he is taxed at long-term capital gain rates (presently at a maximum of 25 per cent). If it is paid over a longer period or for other reasons, the distribution is subject to the same tax rate as regular compensation. Where the distribution takes the form of the retirement annuity contract, the employee does not have any tax liability until he surrenders the contract. Then he has ordinary income based upon the cash surrender value received. On the other hand if, instead of surrendering the contract, he holds on to it he is taxed on each annuity payment when received.

Most of the employers who established plans during World War II are still continuing them. Those employers who have no plans are now giving serious consideration to the creation of one. There are various types of employees' plans. Here we are concerned only with pension and profit-sharing plans that meet the requirements of the Internal Revenue Code. Many of these provide for a trust to which the employer's contributions are paid and through which the plan is administered.

PENSION PLAN

The major portion of pension plans in existence today are of the insured type, that is, the plan requires the purchase of insurance. The contract may be of the group type without the use of a trust, as in the case of group annuity and group permanent plans where only a master contract is written. Such plans are available only where large groups of employees are involved. The group annuity contract provides only for retirement benefit, while the group permanent has life insurance and other features as well. Some pension plans call for the purchase of an individual insurance contract for each participant. Here a trust is almost always used. This type of plan is more expensive than the group plan and is most frequently adopted by smaller companies. The contract benefits are limited only by the size of the premiums the employer desires to pay. Finally there is the self-administered pension plan, where insurance contracts are usually not involved. The employer, with the aid of an actuary, actuarially computes the annual contribution required from the employer to provide the benefits set out in the plan. The employer's contributions are paid into the trust. The benefits payable by the trust in such a plan, in addition to retirement benefits, depend completely upon the ingenuity of the trust draftsmen and the desires of the employer.

PROFIT-SHARING PLAN

Profit-sharing plans are always administered through a trust. These plans are not keyed to retirement necessarily. Distribution to employees may be made under a variety of circumstances. Insurance contracts are rarely used in profit-sharing plans, except sometimes as a trust investment.

The employer, once convinced that he needs an employees' plan, must then decide whether it ought to be a pension or a profit-sharing plan.

Where the business of the employer is such that over an extended period of years he can look forward to continuous profit, without too much fluctuation between the high and the low, a pension plan might well be in order. On the other hand, if that financial constancy is not historically true, and there is no promise of such for the future, a profit-sharing plan will more completely fill the bill for most trade magazine publishers. Additional important considerations in arriving at the eventual decision, particularly if it is to be a pension plan, are the extent of normal labor turnover and the ages of the employees to be covered.

An employer's contributions to a profit-sharing plan are dependent upon the employer's operations producing a profit, and the extent of the contributions is dependent upon the contribution provisions he incorporated in the plan. The typical contribution formula is keyed to a fixed percentage of net profits, in excess of a stated amount, the net profits being computed before federal income and excess profits taxes. Thus, if the employer's net profits are nonexistent or less than the stipulated amount, no contribution is required. The age of the employees or the frequency of the labor turnover are not reflected in the employer's contributions. However, the total compensation otherwise paid to the participating employees may be. The reason is that, under the code, the maximum amount deductible by the employer on account of each year's contribution is limited to 15 per cent of such compensation. Therefore most contribution formulas contain this limitation.

With pension plans it is different. The plan promises to the retired employee a definite amount every so often. In order for that promise to be fulfilled, the employer's contribution to a self-insured pension plan, or the premium payments on an insured pension plan, cannot be dependent on the existence or the size of the employer's annual profits. (If current profits are not available, then there should be an adequate surplus to take up the slack.) The net amount of the employer's contribution or payments to a pension plan bear a direct relationship to the age of the employees covered by the plan and the extent of the labor turnover.

Because of these important differences, trade magazine publishers, who have adopted employee plans, have for the most part initiated profit-sharing rather than pension plans.

Experience with employees of trade magazine publishers has shown that by and large they prefer profit participation to a promise of an annuity many years hence. The probable reason is that essentially they are a white-collar group, whose earnings are measured by their individual abilities in contradistinction to factory help, whose pay is usually fixed by labor-management negotiations on a group basis.

Since, from both the employer's and employees' point of views, the profit-sharing plan is preferred, all further discussion will be limited to typical provisions of such a plan.

The plan must not discriminate in favor of stockholders or highly paid employees. That does not mean that every employee must be made a participant. Part-time employees, employees with less than a certain number of years of continuous employment with the employer, and employees in certain departments may be disqualified. If that does not result in discrimination, according to tests laid down by the commissioner, the plan will be approved by him.

The employer's annual contribution usually is prorated in the ratio of each participant's annual compensation to the total compensation of all of the participants. Under prescribed circumstances, length of service may be an additional factor in the division of the employer's contributions. Whichever basis is used, from time to time to the employee's share is added his share of the trust's profits and income, and those amounts are held for him until his distribution date.

Distribution dates vary with plans and with the reasons which give rise to the distribution. Frequently, severance of employment, retirement at retirement age (usually 65 years), permanent disability, death, or participation for a fixed number of years entitles an employee or his heirs to distribution—this, in the case of death, retirement, or disability being a total distribution of the trust credits within one taxable year. On other forms of severance of employment, or after participation for a fixed number of years, there is a great deal of variation. In the former instance, distribution may be over a period of years, often about five. As to the latter, the distribution starts mostly after 10 years of participation, with the rate of annual distribution being 1/10th of the participant's credit balance as constituted at the end of each year.

CHAPTER 16

Laws, Codes, and Regulations

THE RULES OF CONDUCT

In a quarter-century of business journalism it has never been my misfortune to involve my publishers in litigation. I have published corrections and written apologies when they were justified; equally, my publishers have always backed me up when, in the face of threatening letters from lawyers, we were sure of our ground and our facts. At the Law School of the University of Texas where I received some of my formal education I learned two things of value to any journalist: (1) how to dig up facts on both sides of an issue; (2) not to be afraid of lawyers. In choosing journalism as a career instead of law practice (as in my case) one does not actually "forsake" the law, for the law is the warp of the fabric of business. (Occasionally it is the woof.)

The young man who enters the practice of businesspaper publishing, no matter in what department, should be grounded in the laws, regulations, and codes governing business journalism and business enterprise. A journalist operates under three sets of laws: (1) An unwritten code of honor and decency based on morals and precepts learned at home, in church, in school, and on the fields of sport; (2) rules of self-government set up as standards of practice or as codes of ethics by trade and semi-professional associations, and by professional societies; and (3) the law of the press, based on the English Common Law, the Law Merchant, the Bill of Rights, the Constitution of the United States, federal and state statutory laws, and legal decisions.

Professor Thayer[1] classifies the law of the press this way:

[1] Frank Thayer, M.A., J.D., *Legal Control of the Press*, Chicago, The Foundation Press, Inc., 1944, Chap. 1, p. 5. (Revised Edition, 1950.) Dr. Thayer, a member of the Illinois Bar, is a lecturer in the Law of Journalism, University of Wisconsin. He also has courses in business journalism. See also "Shifting Concepts in Laws Affecting the Press," by Dr. Thayer, *Journalism Quarterly*. Vol. 28, No. 1. Winter, 1951, p. 24.

Torts:	Libel, privacy, and unfair competition
Criminal Law:	Libel and contempt
Personal Property:	Copyright and trade mark
Constitutional Law:	Rights, guaranties of freedom of press, guaranty that liberty will not be deprived without due process of law
Administrative Law:	Regulation of advertising through Federal Trade Commission, Securities and Exchange Commission, Post Office Department, Library of Congress, and Patent Office
	Regulation of circulation through Post Office Department
	Regulation of communications through Federal Communications Commission
Procedure:	Enforcement of substantive rights, determination of damages, and injunctive relief where there is no full, complete, and adequate remedy at law

By 1900, for example, fraudulent circulation statements, non-uniform advertising rates, subsidized editorial columns, and misleading advertising were the chief problems of the various trade and technical press associations. Their solution was attempted by the formation of such organizations as the Federation of Trade Press Associations (1913), Audit Bureau of Circulations (1914), Associated Advertising Clubs of the World (incorporated into Advertising Federation of America) and by the formulation of certain rules of self-government, codes of professional ethics, and standards of fair practice.

Space does not permit the inclusion in this chapter of the codes of the two principal businesspaper publishing associations and the two national businesspaper editorial societies. See the Appendix to find out where to get them; also the *Printers' Ink* model statute, the standards of practice of the advertising profession, and a proposed standard of professional practice for market research. Recommended for study are the rules laid down by the Interstate Commerce Commission, Federal Trade Commission, Securities Exchange Commission, Federal Communications Commission, Better Business Bureaus, the Anti-Trust Laws, and the Commercial Arbitration Standards for the conduct of business enterprise. Every businesspaper editor should also be familiar with recent Supreme Court decisions on "Fair Trade" Acts.

Someone once pointed out that codes of ethics, like the Decalogue, do not insure saintliness in either publishers or editors. However, the desire to establish a code of honor, or the mere majority vote of approval of a code of fair practice published for all the world to see, may be taken at least as a sign of intention.

For those who believe in the press, [declared the Curator of the Neiman Fellowships[2]] and its potential to pull its weight with the other great institutions men must live by, these standards are what we have to hold to. They are essential to our faith in the worth of the profession we claim. They give whatever distinction attaches to the Fourth Estate in our time.

The businesspaper is neither a private enterprise nor a public utility. It is a little of both.

It is a private enterprise to this extent: (1) Its business managers may carry or refuse to carry the advertising of any concern or group; may sell or refuse to sell copies of the publication to any individuals or groups; (2) Its editors may publish or refuse to publish certain news stories or opinion; (3) the publishers may continue to publish or suspend publication; may make changes in their service or rates at will. The owners of the businesspaper are free to contract or deal with whomever they choose.

On the other hand, the businesspaper is a quasi-public utility to the extent that it is affected with a public interest in the continuity of its communication service. Moreover it enjoys special mailing privileges which amount to a government subsidy. It is guaranteed certain rights and privileges denied to others.[3] It cannot be forced to reveal the sources of its information. It may criticize with a certain amount of impunity. It may publish without censorship (except in time of war).

Railroads, power, water, telephone, and telegraph companies are public utilities. In the public interest they are often permitted to operate as monopolies by public franchise. Public commissions regulate their services, rates, and the conduct of such enterprises. No businesspaper enjoys a publishing monopoly.

The businesspaper that deserves to exist must nevertheless regard itself

[2] Louis M. Lyons, from a talk, "The Individual Standards of Journalism," given to the National Conference of Editorial Writers, Des Moines, Iowa, November 18, 1950. The paper appeared in *Nieman Reports,* Jan., 1951, Vol. V, No. 1, p. 15, Cambridge, Mass.

[3] Guaranty of freedom of the press found in the First Amendment to the Federal Constitution adopted in 1791.

as a quasi-public institution—holding a trusteeship for private enterprise and its own field.[4]

The granting of certain rights, privileges, and subsidies to the American press under our Constitution imposes certain limitations and controls on businesspaper publishers and journalists. The controls, as much as the rights and privileges, tend to keep our press the kind of free press which will be always operated in the public interest.

Every business journalist should know (1) the history of the struggle of society for press freedom; (2) the legal controls of the press; (3) postal laws and regulations;[5] (4) codes of ethics of his own and related professions; (5) rules of fair practice of the industry he serves.

By applying to any of the associations listed in Appendix 1 one may obtain a copy of their code or rules. Like the tenets of all the popular religions these will be found similar in ideals and objectives.

In the canons of business journalism subscribed to by the editorial societies and businesspaper publishers' associations public interest is placed above group interest, truth and honor are paramount, venality is shunned.

The NCBPE, oldest society of business journalists, declares "it is the duty of a businesspaper to publish significant ideas *contrary to its own*" and "to provide a forum within its columns for the exchange of ideas, opinions, facts, comment and *criticism* in the interest of the readership." (Italics are mine.)

All groups agree that the sources of news information should be checked for accuracy and identified; and to refuse to publish paid write-ups or any editorial material as a consideration for an advertising contract. They agree to refuse advertising copy known to be untrue or which disparages the goods or services of anyone else. Everyone subscribes to "accepted standards" of good taste and decency. Everyone is against deception and fraud, agrees to charge uniform rates, avoid all favoritism, place quality above price.

The organized research groups have proposed (but not adopted) these standards: Every report of a survey should explain these points: (1) purpose, (2) for who and by whom conducted, (3) description of the

---

[4] See "Special Responsibility of the Business Journalist," p. 285, in *Business Journalism,* Harper & Brothers, New York, 1945; see also Chapter XI, "Future of the Business Press," in this volume.

[5] See Appendix 2 for an analysis of Postal Laws and Regulations by John R. Pearson.

universe covered, (4) size and nature of sample and description of weighting methods, (5) the time the field work was done, (6) whether personal or mail interviews, (7) description of field staff and control methods. Also, every survey report should contain questionnaire and findings, bases of percentages, and distribution of interviews.[6]

LEGAL ASPECTS OF THE BUSINESSPAPER EDITORIAL DEPARTMENT*

My purpose is to attempt to give you a few pointers which might be of assistance in enabling you to avoid some of the legal pitfalls in businesspaper publishing.

I urge that you observe carefully these four points in order to avoid legal difficulties and keep down costs:

1. Recognize the probability of trouble at all times. This simply means that you should orient your thinking in your daily work so as to have in mind that legal pitfalls are one of your important responsibilities.

2. Be alert in sensing the existence of a legal problem. If, for instance, your immediate work happens to be the review of a manuscript which, we will say, is based upon a report of a proceeding to revoke a transport pilot's license for violation of some of the air rules, that should immediately suggest a legal problem and you should immediately be on your toes to take proper steps to avoid difficulties.

3. Use care in applying proper measures to avoid difficulties. In the case of the manuscript that I have mentioned, that would mean that you should study the manuscript carefully, discuss it with whoever prepared it, get more information, make sure it is accurate and, above all, since we are talking about a report of a proceeding, make sure that it is not a biased or one-sided statement of the proceeding.

4. Use care in handling a difficulty when it arises. This is where your judgment comes into play.

Now, merely because you get a complaint in the form of a letter does not make it necessary to seek legal advice immediately. That may involve an unnecessary expense. However, if you are at all doubtful about the matter, then the safe thing to do is to employ an attorney, because so often I have found that laymen in handling a problem say or do things

[6] Approved by the Market Research Council and submitted to the American Marketing Association in May, 1948.

* Joseph A. Gerardi, Attorney and Secretary, McGraw-Hill Publishing Co.; a lecture at New York University, February 19, 1947.

which make the defense of a case later very difficult. If the communication is from an attorney, you should almost invariably follow the practice of seeking legal advice. By communication, I mean the complaint.

Coming to some of the common legal problems which arise from time to time in editing businesspapers: Of course, the usual one is libel. Libel has been defined in the courts many times and very few of the definitions are alike. I think for your purpose a rather broad definition would aid you more in detecting libel than even a more accurate one. So I would say for your purpose, any false disparagement may be a libel.

In reviewing a manuscript for libel, particularly if it appears to be libelous, if you are certain from a discussion with the person who prepared the article, or from investigation, that it is a truthful statement beyond any question of doubt, you are safe in publishing the statement. If, on the other hand, you cannot be certain of the truth—and bear in mind that in libel actions the truth is a very elusive thing—in that case you are far better off to change or exclude the statement. In my experience I have found that the exclusion of libelous statements in businesspapers, or statements which appear to be libelous, rarely does any damage or harm to the article.

Bear in mind that quoting from newspapers or other printed sources or from verbal statements is no defense in the libel action. You are just as much responsible as the originator of the libelous statement. It is a peculiar thing that many editors have the impression that the way to avoid libel is to preface their otherwise libelous statements by some remarks such as "It is said" or "It is reported." That just is not so.

When trouble occurs your judgment again comes into play. You can often tell from the source of the communication you get or from the tone of the communication whether or not you have a serious matter before you. If it is not serious in your judgment, you may proceed yourself to handle the matter, because quite often keeping a matter of that kind at the editorial level, which is to me a friendly level, is far better than getting the matter into the hands of an attorney. Bear in mind that I say you can do that if the statement or the communication does not appear to raise a serious question.

Now, one or two words on the subject of retraction. It is a fact that I have perhaps written hundreds of what you might call retractions but, as a matter of fact, very few of them are in reality retractions. A retraction in law is an admission of error coupled with some sort of apology or expression of regret. I never find it wise to admit error because it may put the publisher in a rather embarrassing situation later on. What we try to do is to interpret the statement or to show that it did not have the meaning attributed to it by the party claiming the libel. Or in some cases, within reasonable bounds, we allow the claimant to make his own statement—any device to avoid an outright admission of error.

Coming now to the subject of copyrights, that is, your own copyrights: A copyright is a federal grant giving you the exclusive right to reproduce your literary work. In the businesspaper field your copyright covers both your editorial material and your advertising material. In order to secure the copyright, the first step is to print the magazine with the notice of copyright. That notice should contain the name of the copyright owner and the actual date of publication. By actual publication I mean not your date of issue of the publication because that is often different from the date of mailing, but the actual date you put the publication in the mails.

The next step, of course, is to mail the publication and then file your application for registration with the Registrar of Copyrights.

Reprints need not be separately copyrighted but if you intend to retain your rights to the material in reprints, you should put the same copyright notice on the reprint as you have in the magazine from which it is taken.

Of course, it goes without saying that if you value your copyrights, you should protest against any unauthorized use. You can, if you wish— and most people do—allow reasonable extracting and quotation by newspapers and others under the doctrine of fair use.

I recently noticed quite a few new so-called digest services. These people take articles published in businesspapers, digest them, compile them in pamphlet form, and sell them as a service for a price far in excess of what magazine publishers get as their subscription price. They do no original work, because the entire document is copied. As a matter of fact, they are in competition with businesspapers. Here again, if you expect to retain your copyrights, you should protest against digesting in that manner.

Your magazine titles are, under the law, what are known as trade marks. But it is surprising to hear many experienced publishers call them "copyrights." In order to acquire trade mark rights, that is, rights to the exclusive use of your magazine title, you need only use the title. It is not necessary to register the title. Registration has certain advantages, however, and should not be overlooked. It is a peculiar thing that businesspaper publishers, in their desire to call their publication by names which best describe the field or function of the paper, adopt titles which are very difficult to protect, because in law purely descriptive titles, particularly in recent court decisions, are very difficult to protect. Descriptive titles consisting of combinations of words such as *Iron Age, Engineering News Record,* and so on are easier to protect than one-word titles. We cannot go into the reasons; it is a long story. But take my word for it, that is the trend of late decisions.

On the subject of postal requirements, get a copy of the Postal Laws and Regulations from the Government Printing Office.[7] It will answer about 90 per cent of your postal questions. I have been asked literally hundreds of postal questions and they are all in the book. When you are in doubt, when your postal laws and regulations do not answer your questions, all you need to do is to telephone the Classification Division of the Post Office, or go over there and they will cooperate with you one hundred per cent.

HOW MUCH COPYRIGHTED MATERIAL CAN BE QUOTED

In March and April of 1949, Joseph Gerardi, McGraw-Hill's counsel, and Edward L. Merrigan of the well-known New York law firm of Weil, Gotshal & Manges, were asked for a legal opinion on quoting copyrighted material in the *Consumer Reports.* These reports, while declared to be "confidential for members only," are widely distributed in magazine form. Our publishing firm holds a membership in Consumers Union. It was to see if the law gave C.U. any privileges other than those given to any publication of copyrighted material that the lawyers were consulted. Their replies follow.

YOU MAY CRITICIZE AND "QUOTE SPARINGLY"*

I cannot agree that the publication of the findings of the Consumers Union in a widely circulated magazine makes those findings public property which may be freely reproduced or used by others. I am assuming, of course, that the magazine in which the findings are published is a copyrighted magazine.

I think it might be in order to critically analyze their findings, particularly if you are writing an article which takes issue with them in some particulars and, in that connection, to quote sparingly from their report, but this is not greatly different from the right of a newspaper critic to

[7] See Appendix 2 for a brief review of Postal Laws and Regulations.
* Joseph Gerardi.

criticize a published book and, in doing so, to present some of the material from the book.

CONTENTS OF A PUBLICATION ARE NOT "PUBLIC PROPERTY"*

We have investigated the *Consumer Reports,* published by the Consumers Union of U.S., Inc. and we have found that said reports are fully copyrighted.

You stated that it was your desire to write articles commenting upon or criticizing certain matters contained in said *Consumer Reports.* You also indicated a desire to use direct quotations from the reports in the course of your comments or criticisms.

The law with regard to your ability to criticize or comment upon copyrighted matter is well stated in Hill *vs.* Whalen & Martell, Inc., 200 Fed. 359, wherein the United States District Court, Southern District of New York, held:

A copyrighted work is subject to fair criticism, serious or humorous. So far as is necessary to that end, quotations may be made from it, and it may be described by words, representations, pictures or suggestions. It is not always easy to say where the line should be drawn between the use which for such purposes is permitted and that which is forbidden.

One test which, when applicable, would seem to be ordinarily decisive, is whether or not so much as has been re-produced will materially reduce the demand for the original. If it has, the rights of the owner of the copyright have been injuriously affected. A word of explanation will be here necessary. The reduction in demand, to be a ground of complaint, must result from the partial satisfaction of that demand by the alleged infringing production. A criticism of the original work, which lessened its money value by showing that it was not worth seeing or hearing, could not give any right of action for infringement of copyright.

This matter is also discussed in *Corpus Juris Secundum,* Vol. 18, Sec. 105, p. 224, as follows:

Thus, it is not necessarily piracy for a reviewer or commentator to make use of extracts or quotations from a copyrighted work for the purpose of fair exposition or reasonable criticism, and considerable license is allowed in such cases, but it is illegitimate to publish extracts to such an extent that the publication may serve as a more or less complete substitute for the work from which they are borrowed, as excessive quotation is an infringement. If so much be taken that the value of the original is sensibly diminished, or

* Edward L. Merrigan.

the labors of the author are substantially or to an injurious extent appropriated, that is sufficient in law to constitute a piracy.

It would therefore seem proper for you to write comments or criticisms of articles contained in *Consumer Reports,* and in so doing, you may use quotations from and references to such articles in your write-ups. However, it is advisable that you limit yourself in this respect, and only use quotations and references where they are absolutely necessary to the meaning of your comments or criticisms.

None of the foregoing of course is intended to mean that, simply because the Consumers Union publishes its reports in a widely circulated magazine, they become public property and can be copied by anyone. Rather, we mean to imply that parts of the reports can be used by persons commenting upon or criticizing the reports in good faith.

CHAPTER 17

Agenda for the Future

For this final chapter, I have selected some critical essays designed to broaden the vision of the working business press, educators, and those who are thinking of making a career of some phase of business journalism.

These appraisals of the business press with suggestions for its advancement are by distinguished spokesmen from the fields of journalism, advertising, public relations, and business.

There are many problems in business journalism implicit in the need by businessmen for better understanding of our dynamic business process as a whole. It has been said by many, with deep conviction, that the business press will secure its greatest dividends by "selling private enterprise" to the public in our country and in other countries. My own feeling is that private competitive enterprise will be *bought* by more people not so much by propagandizing the system as by perfecting it. The full potential of our businesspaper publishing know-how is directed toward this objective: making the private competitive enterprise system work better for more people; making every man understand it in terms of his own job, his productivity, his essentiality.

No one can deny that the continued existence of the private competitive enterprise system is threatened. If we wish to protect it we must perfect it and pass on the know-how to other countries as a reproducible experiment. So far we have passed on to other countries only some of the vast wealth our own system produces and some of its machines, especially weapons, but little if any of its principles and standards of practice and know-how.

We have built a big inventory of specialized know-how about machines and methods. It now becomes necessary to know more about the human personality which Bernays in his essay calls "the most important unexplored market we have today."

WHAT DOES THE FUTURE HOLD FOR THE BUSINESS PRESS?*

The future of businesspaper publishing and its influence on industrial and commercial enterprise will depend on: (1) the continuing and increasing need for such a service by those who administer and manage the American business organizations, and (2) the ability of the business press to meet this challenge with still more efficient service.

The first point, as to the need for service in coming years, can be covered by a brief analysis and forecast. The second point, as to how business publishing will meet the future demand for service, depends on such elements as editorial planning, improvements in physical presentation, circulation and manufacturing problems, competition, and the maintenance of advertising revenues.

Three widely recognized conditions form the basis for an unqualified prediction that industry will require increasing service from the business press during coming years:

1. The accelerating rate of technological developments with corresponding needs for greater exchange of factual information
2. The increasing need for the highest managerial efficiency in planning, production, distribution, and every other phase of business to secure a reasonable margin of return to investors between the restrictive limits of high taxes and higher labor costs
3. The increasing awareness of businessmen and leaders of industry that economic, social, and political influences exert a direct effect on their daily and long-range operations, with a resulting need for authoritative data and interpretation on these subjects

The business press has a responsibility to become the accepted means of bringing this vital information to industry through a combination of the printed word and the instructive illustration.

Considering first the march of technical progress, it is obvious that the next few years will be a period of intense business and industrial activity. Competition will take its toll of those organizations which are not alert, flexible, and fast-moving enough to adopt new techniques all the way from planning the original design of the product to the selling of the plant output. This situation will present an increasing obligation to the

---

* James H. McGraw, Jr., former President, McGraw-Hill Publishing Co., excerpts from a paper read by Col. Willard Chevalier, Executive Vice-President, at New York University, April 9, 1947, and at Northwestern University in 1948.

business press to record and analyze technical progress and, at the same time, provide a corresponding opportunity to exert greater influence on the efficiency of industry.

Second, paralleling the service to be rendered on these phases of technical progress, is the corresponding responsibility to discuss and evaluate developments in plant and office management, distribution and selling all the way from the end of the production line to the point-of-sale, financing, servicing, and maintenance. Every department of modern business enterprise will be called upon, during the next few years, to operate at levels of increasing efficiency to survive between the millstones of taxes and rising costs. Those businesspapers which deal with these special elements of commercial activity have an opportunity for service never approached in pre-war years.

The third demand on business publishers results from the awakened awareness of American business to the less technical but equally essential factors in business management which are conveniently listed under the headings of economic, social, and political. The technical problems of how to build a machine or produce a chemical now are paralleled, if not overshadowed, by questions involved in the relation between industrial management and its workers, its public, and its government. More than ever before, management recognizes that its profit and survival will depend upon its constructive service to all the people rather than upon its shrewdness in exploiting the people and the resources of the nation.

There is no lack of published material on these general subjects. But the men who must direct and manage individual business operations need this information properly condensed and currently interpreted for application to immediate problems such as producing steel, refining petroleum, or selling shoes. Herein lies a challenge for the business press to render a major service on subjects that have represented, in too many cases, only a minor editorial phase of this type of publishing in past years.

The combination of technical information, managerial practice, and public policy will result in magazines of greater breadth of editorial treatment and corresponding potential value to a larger cross-section of the technicians and operating executives in any business or industrial organization.

RESPONSIBILITY TO THE AMERICAN SYSTEM OF BUSINESS

The great opportunity and the great responsibility of the business press during the years ahead lie in the fact that the survival of the present economic system will depend upon maintaining the highest possible productivity per man-hour of employment. This will maintain and, if possible, raise the living standard to carry the huge debt burden left by the war.

This productivity can be maintained only by putting into the hands of technicians and managers the most complete information that technical research and experience make available. Productivity is the answer to keeping the largest possible number of workers steadily employed without the wastes and interruptions that result from depression, financial dislocation, and industrial strife.

These vital missions of business management during these critical years ahead will need a business press of the highest standard. It is a privilege to try and meet this challenge.

REFINEMENT OF EDITORIAL CONCEPT

As always, the editor is the key to the businesspaper of the future. The tempo of industry and commercial activity, its complexity, and its demand for other-than-technical information require the successful editor of the future to be a leader in his field. No longer can he be a mere "reporter" and a recorder of industrial or business history.

If he is to be a wise counselor for those in this field of enterprise, its able defender against unwarranted attacks, and its candid critic when faults deserve analysis, he must be an educated and judicial student, a courageous spokesman, and a tireless worker. Nothing less than an accepted leader in his profession or industry will mark the stature of tomorrow's businesspaper editor.

In trying to serve the diversified needs of their readers throughout all the fields and functions of business, the editors of the business press will be confronted by an exacting problem. The swift march of technical progress in all of the industrial processes points clearly to the need for higher specialization. This applies particularly in the case of technicians and operating men. When, on the other hand, they are writing to those men of management who are responsible for the formulation of sound economic and public policies, the editors must cover the broad fields of human affairs.

Here is a dilemma that must tax the resourcefulness of the editor and his staff; for somehow they must reconcile the breadth of scope required in matters of policy with the depth of practical penetration that is required in operating matters, if their publication is to meet the urgent needs of tomorrow.

On the one hand, the businesspaper editor is in danger of diluting the specialized information that is essential to one part of his field and, on the other, he is in danger of narrowing the horizons of those who must have, at all times, a hilltop view of business operations.

NEWS AND ITS SIGNIFICANCE

It is frequently stated that the business publication of the future must deal more largely with news than did its forebears. There is a large measure of truth in that statement. But, as so often happens, some careful defining is necessary.

"News," when applied to the business press, does not mean mere gossip concerning people and events. Neither does it mean the sort of spot news that constitutes the bulk of the average newspaper's content. News in a business publication may be the news of scientific research, the news of technical development, the news of modern merchandising and distribution practice, the news of new developments in organization and new policies of management.

It nearly always requires more than mere reporting of facts and events, and calls for the kind of selection and interpretation that will enable the business reader to understand the special significance of current developments with respect to what has gone before and what may come after. Moreover, such interpretation in a business publication should be pointed as precisely as may be possible toward the special concerns of the selected reader group.

As a result it is possible that some business publications which do not get credit for a good "news" job are, in fact, doing an excellent news job in the true sense of "news" in business journalism.

In reporting such news, with its interpretation, the competent businesspaper editor will use discretion in the matter of presentation. This is where the news concept of the business journal differs from that of the daily newspaper, which must be edited for the average layman. The businesspaper editor, on the other hand, is dealing with a selected audience and his standards of adequate treatment for a given story may be very different from those of the newspaper editor's.

In formulating an editorial policy and carrying it into practice, the competent editor and his publisher will distinguish always between the reporting of authentic and usable knowledge on the one hand and editorial interpretation on the other. This distinction will be particularly important during the years just ahead now that so many people have become suspicious of propaganda in all its forms. The business press will not meet the challenge of its present opportunity if it permits its reporting of fact and information to be colored by editorial judgments, however honest or worthy the latter may be. He will be a wise and competent editor who will so conduct his columns that his readers can identify and respect his objective reporting, even though they may differ with his editorial opinion and interpretation.

KNOWING THE READER AND HIS PROBLEMS

It will be more necessary than ever for the business journalist to live with the problems of his readers and if he is to do that he must spend a large part of his life with them. There will be no room in the business press of tomorrow for the stuffed shirt in the editorial pulpit. The men of management—executives, technicians, adminstrators—will need help and sound counsel. They will not be in the market for rhetoric, platitudes, and generalities into which they cannot sink their teeth and find real nourishment.

During the competitive and controversial times through which this generation of business journalists must live in which they must achieve their successes, it will be more necessary than ever to have journalistic courage. A business publication should be a spokesman for the industry it serves. But it should never become a *mouthpiece* for that industry or for any special group within the industry.

THE INTERNATIONAL EDITORIAL HORIZON

Many business publications will be faced in the near future by the need for broadening their horizons to world-wide rather than merely nation-wide scope. It may be a long time before the nations of the world will have reestablished workable patterns for their peacetime relationships, but whether that day be soon or distant, it is certain that the part this country must play will be far more important than it ever has been in the past. This means that American business and industrial management also must have a better first-hand knowledge of what is going on the world over and a clearer understanding of what may be the impact of world events upon its policies and operations.

BUSINESSPAPER PUBLISHING IS A BUSINESS

Coordinating and unifying the basic publishing functions (editorial, circulation, and advertising sales) is the businesspaper publisher's task. To provide the editorial service expected by readers of tomorrow's businesspaper, and develop the necessary volume of selected circulation within the financial limits of resulting advertising revenue in the face of mounting manufacturing costs, will require business acumen never before demanded of the publisher.

In much of the foregoing emphasis has been placed on the journalistic job that the businesspaper publisher must do in order to retain his franchise. But he never can forget that, if he is going to stay in business and continue to do that job, he must also be a businessman. As business journalism is a profession, businesspaper publishing is a business.

PUBLISHING STATESMANSHIP

Another quality that will mark the successful businesspaper of tomorrow is that of courage in calling its shots as its publishers and editors see them. The publication must be willing to stick its neck out when necessary to anticipate situations. It must be ahead of the thinking of its readers, for once the readers get ahead of the paper, the paper will be lost; it then will have lost its position of leadership. The quality of courage must be applied both within and outside the reader-group served by the paper. Obviously, this cannot be done if a businesspaper suffers from domination by the box-office in matters of industry policy. The publisher must be willing to sell business statesmanship to readers so that more and more of those in the ranks of management will be able to see the welfare of the country as well as the prosperity of their own enterprises.

One of the essential contributions that can be made by an adequate business press is that of preserving the competitive spirit among individuals and business organizations. Freedom of scientific and technological progress is essential to freedom of commercial enterprise and that is, in turn, essential to political freedom. A free business press that is on its job will make it possible for the largest number of people to share in the latest lessons of technology and management experience and thereby foster the individual opportunity that is our national heritage.

THE CHALLENGE TO BUSINESSPAPER EDITING*

I can give you many reasons for my personal belief in businesspapers, but there is one that impresses me increasingly. It is a very basic reason that I have never seen developed in a presentation.

* Allen L. Billingsley, President, Fuller & Smith & Ross, Inc.; former President, American Association of Advertising Agencies; from an address before a general conference of the Associated Business Publications, Hotel Biltmore, November 29, 1949.

Students of social affairs tell us that one thing wrong with mankind today is that he has been torn loose from his time-honored moorings. He used to feel he belonged to society—through the strengths of the ties to his family, his clan, his village, his church, his nation, his race. Under present conditions such ties have weakened.

Man has one tie, however, which is gaining in strength, and that is the tie he has to the members of his vocation.

This fact gives the good businesspaper a social significance as well as an economic one. It is a challenge to businesspaper editing that has perhaps not been fully recognized. It has solid meaning for the advertiser—solid because it is not created, but arises from within the human being himself.

To fully meet this challenge will require from businesspapers an advanced kind of editing—imaginative, daring, penetrating. It will be great editing, as journalists use the term. And it will be costly editing. But it will surely come if many businesspapers are to capitalize fully the potentialities that are spread before them.

Men are more than economic mechanisms; they are men—men in their vocations. Through their daily work they desire to express their aspirations as citizens and responsible human beings. The vocational channel is the only clear channel that many see before them.

Too much of the thinking and writing expressive of this interest does *not* appear in businesspapers. It appears in other media. The result is that the businesspapers drive many readers to other media for the satisfaction of many of their basic interests.

It should not be that way, and when it is otherwise businesspapers will have real stature and significance—real and recognized, not merely by readers but, very importantly, by advertisers as well.

THE CAUSES OF EDITORIAL ANEMIA*

Taken as a whole, the trade, technical, scientific, and professional press has reached a dangerously comfortable plateau in its development. It is a period that sooner or later must be faced by every important industry and by every useful individual business concern. Perhaps you may call it the menopause of business. In any event, it is usually accom-

---

* W. A. Marsteller, former President, National Industrial Advertisers Association (1948); Vice-President, Rockwell Manufacturing Co.; Vice-President, Edward Valves, Inc.; from an address before the National Business Publications, the Greenbrier, White Sulphur Springs, West Va., May 18, 1950.

panied by a variety of complexes—fear, complacency, loss of lust, personal withdrawal, resignation to circumstances, and dimming of objectives. It is characterized by the noon siesta, the shushing of children, the complete regularity of habits, and avoidance of mirrors.

Certain of our great industries have reached this point and slipped backward. The coal industry is one. The building industry is in it now and its fate—decadence or a new higher peak of efficiency and service—is yet undetermined. Individual business likewise must face this problem. Ford has done so successfully. In each of your fields, you can name companies which have failed to do so. Our associations in trade and professional fields, our educational institutions, our political organizations all come to these periods.

I think that a large share of the business press is on or nearing that plateau of decision right now.

Let me give you an example of what I mean.

A couple of years ago, a leading businesspaper publisher jacked up his page rates and the arbitrary manner in which he did it so irritated me that I wrote him a letter of objection. To document my complaints, I looked over his last twelve issues, and then went back to the files and got a couple of issues of twenty years before.

First, I found that his editorial content was essentially unchanged in twenty years, in so far as physical appearance was concerned, though the appearance of the advertising pages had undergone a great transformation. The advertising pages made much greater use of color, bleed, illustrations, the headlines were sharper and so on. We have learned quite a bit in the last twenty years about businesspaper advertising, perhaps because we have had so much to learn, and most of our learning has been subsidized in one form or another by the publishers.

The editorial pages of this magazine, however, were using the same body and headline types as twenty years before. There was no color used on the editorial pages then or now. In the twelve more recent issues I examined, there were only two instances of any art work obviously prepared especially for the article. The only articles illustrated with any profusion were obviously making use of cuts provided by the companies being described. Finally, most of the headlines had all the sales appeal of a water-soaked baking powder biscuit.

Then, we looked at his circulation and were startled to realize that it had increased only 17 per cent from 1933 to 1948, while during the same period the output of the industry this magazine served had doubled and the manufacturing units in the industry were up about 60 per cent. All of this we called to his attention. His reply started the first of a series of readership studies our company had made—paid for and done within our own organization.

He told us we did not know his readers, but he did. He had been putting out a magazine for them for nearly forty years, he said. Of course, we had been selling them goods for that long, too, but I began to wonder if we were wrong in our sales approach, because he said that his readers were engineers; that they were suspicious of trick layouts; that subject matter of articles was necessarily so technical that it could not be boiled down much more; that his readers were so interested in their business that all a headline needed to do was state the general subject matter, not sell readership; that while his circulation had not gone up much it was ever so much more selective now; that in general we should quit worrying about the editorial pages; and that there would be no charge, other than the new higher rates, for this lesson in publishing he had just given us.

So we called on our market research department. A great deal of market research, you know, is undertaken just to prove that someone else is crazy. First, they made a study of a whole series of businesspapers we used, just sitting in the office. Here are a few of their conclusions:

1. Many magazines used color on editorial pages only when they were on the same forms as an ad, so that the advertiser paid the freight, and usually the use of color did not contribute anything. If we added color to our ads only for decoration and not to build readership, the Copy Chasers would jump down our throat.

2. Headlines were usually written to fill a space, not sell a story.

3. Illustrations, when used, often had dim relationship to the story matter. A story about a new refining process, for instance, would be illustrated by a night view of an already existing refinery.

4. Catalogue items often ran unchanged through a half-dozen issues.

5. There was very little timeliness about the editorial matter, even in the weeklies.

Then our market research department went out into the field and talked to our customers in this industry. Since that time we have confirmed our general findings with several other similar studies in other industries. Our results were not always the same as Roy Eastman's, but we did not always ask the same questions. Some of the principal points these studies have highlighted are:

1. The best read editorial matter is usually not only basically important or appealing material, but is also best presented graphically.

2. When the same story is covered by several magazines in each field, the one which is best read in relation to the readership of the other stories in the same magazine is the one which is best headed, illustrated, or merchandised.

3. The best read editorial material usually matches our previous evaluation of the sales appeal of the headlines.

4. The correlation of color and interest in editorial matter is at least as great as on advertising pages.

5. There are essentially no completely thorough readers of businesspapers.

6. Technical and professional readers are still people and are motivated by appealing physical presentations as much as by subject matter.

Up to the present I have dwelt on the weak circulation and poor physical make-up of businesspapers. The criticisms I have made, if they are valid, are easily corrected because the causes are, after all, superficial.

EDITORIAL ANEMIA

I believe, however, that the business press is on the edge of a much more serious editorial anemia, a dissipation of red corpuscles which, if it persists, can result in a creeping death. Here are several causes for that editorial anemia:

1. *Special Issues.* As advertising has started to slip off, the number of special-issue promotions has increased as a hedge against declining revenues. That is no long-range solution and is, instead, a factor which will speed up the spread of the disease. Rarely; very rarely; very, very, very rarely, I think, are special issues justified. And when they result in 7- and 13-page rate structures for monthly magazines, or the equivalent on other time cycles, they are blatant rackets. Even a special-regular issue—that is, a regular issue given over to a single subject—is objectionable to me. All too often, these are the results:

They shoot the wad of the editorial and advertising sales staffs to the extent that the issues preceding and following the special issue suffer.

They detract from timeliness of editorial material by pushing back current material to later issues.

They take reading emphasis away from regular features.

Because they usually carry more advertising they can support more editorial, and consequently more often become so big that readership falls off and, while business leaders write testimonial promotion letters praising the issue, the issue gets less average reading than a regular issue.

2. *People.* There is a great tendency to forget the "who" in business-paper editing. Businesspapers tend to become "what" magazines. They are concerned with ideas or developments, but not much with people, except buried in personal columns in the back. We should not forget that it is people who make the news—that the man who developed a new drug, a new process, or a new theory may be much more interesting than the drug, process, or theory he developed.

We in the advertising business avidly read our excellent periodicals like *Advertising Age, Printer's Ink,* and *Tide,* especially the complete news columns of stories and pictures of people, and then go on editing and advertising as if we were trying to establish forever the principle that the machine is more important than the man who designs, builds, or runs it—or finances it.

3. *Voice-of-God.* Many businesspapers try to be all things to all people and wind up becoming nothing to anyone. Some of the so-called "bibles of the industry" have slipped into this. They have become so obsessed with their god-given mission to speak for the industry that actually they have become a hodge-podge of superficiality.

4. *Technology.* Many other businesspapers are conversely too narrow editorially. Many of our new books are in this category, apparently going to the extremes of specialization as a protest against the catch-all practices of some of their longer entrenched competitors. They have become concerned only with technology—often a segment of technology —rather than the broad problem of operating in a given industry under today's problems. In the chemical field, for instance, they tell only of the methods of or the results of research, rather than how much should be spent for it; case histories of company research operations or how business can profitably support it. These magazines—most magazines—fail miserably when it comes to teaching the place of their special field in the total industry or the economic relation of one industry to another. They leave the interpretation of the free enterprise system to the National Association of Manufacturers or other associations, but miss the opportunity—no, responsibility—of teaching free enterprise in action, as it applies to his job, to the research chemist, the doctor, the machinist, the chain-store manager, or the corset clerk. And that leads finally to the fifth manifestation of editorial anemia.

5. *Controversy.* As a whole, our businesspapers are afraid to be

controversial. They are lacking in editorial objectives. They have no platform for their industry. Walking the fence, afraid to offend any part of their industry or profession, they have closed their eyes to all problems within their industry, except those upon which there can be no rebuttal. They are overlooking the clear lesson in the newspaper field where the colorless and gutless papers have died, but the controversial ones, loved or hated, prosper and exert influence.

YOUR HIDDEN MARKETS IN THE HUMAN PERSONALITY*

America's 1600 businesspapers perform many vital services for American business enterprises of every kind. Among other things, they carry advertisements and sales messages addressed to specific markets or segments of industry, and articles on selling and salesmanship.

It is natural for businesspapers to give so much attention to selling. One of the main functions of all business is to sell goods, commodities, or services. Today America leads the world in the many varied aspects of direct and indirect selling. Our business enterprises have developed selling techniques brilliant in their effectiveness and without counterpart in any other country. Businesspapers play an active part in this steady growth of American salesmanship in all its forms.

In the many years in which I have been practicing public relations, I have, however, been struck by one basic lack in the prevailing approaches in American distribution. There is insufficient realization that human personality is the most important unexplored market we have today. Not enough attention is given to *the hidden markets in the human personality*.

Selling is moving a product from producer to consumer. The word "consumer," however, is only an abstraction. We sell goods to *people*. We attempt to persuade men and women—human beings—to buy our goods or services.

To do this successfully, we must have the clearest idea of how people function. And to understand people, we must know not only how the body works, but why we think and feel as we do. Our whole personality plays a part in this. Our family background, childhood experiences, and culture pattern enter into the decisions we make at the counter. All kinds

* Edward L. Bernays, Counsel on Public Relations, New York; written expressly for this volume. *Time* magazine described Mr. Bernays as "America's No. 1 Public Relations Man"; lecturer at New York University and University of Hawaii; author of *Crystallizing Public Opinion* (1924), *Propaganda* (1928), *Speak Up for Democracy* (1940), *Take Your Place at the Peace Table* (1945), etc.

of pressures, subconscious and unconscious, condition our actions. These invisible factors of human personality must be understood and mastered if we are really going to deal with our trade paper readers or markets effectively.

You do only three things in attempting to persuade people to a course of action: (1) You can intensify an existing favorable attitude; (2) you can convert an unfavorable attitude into a favorable one; (3) you can negate an unfavorable attitude. All three approaches deal with *attitudes*. They must therefore be based on a realistic understanding of human nature and conduct.

A good deal of your salesmanship today is still based on the antiquated myth that, when it comes to business, everybody can be neatly pigeon-holed as the Economic Man, with a neat additional classification of a few instincts—sex, self-preservation, desire for food, shelter, clothing. But we know from everyday experience, and science knows from patient investigation and experiment, that there is no such creature. The human personality is far too complex to be pinned down to any simple formula. We all have hidden urges, anxieties, insecurities, inferiorities, resentments which play a part in our desire to respond favorably or not to a trade paper.

Though these are hidden, they can be charted. But to take advantage of your hidden markets in the human personality, attitude polls or so-called market surveys are not enough. To know why we behave as we do, we need to go to the social scientists. It is they who have identified such behavior as rationalization, projection, sublimation, and compensation.

Because the physical sciences are three centuries old, and because their results—from the spinning jenny to the atom bomb—are so spectacular, we are all familiar with their importance. The social sciences are only half a century old, but their findings are already of the utmost importance. It would be to our advantage to make greater use of them in our sales efforts.

Thirty thousand social scientists all over the United States are making discoveries about man which are important for America and the world, but which also have practical bearing on the hidden markets in the human personality. Psychologists are discovering more and more how the mind works. Sociologists are giving us greater and greater insight into the way various social groups function in this country. Social psychologists have expert knowledge on how groups react, as distinguished from the way individuals react. Political economists investigate and test how economic and political groups act and react under varying circumstances.

All these social scientists, working day and night in our great universities, in field expeditions, and through their nation-wide scientific organizations, are making studies and findings of the utmost importance to business. Yet many businessmen scarcely know they exist and fail to take advantage of their vital knowledge.

In 1948, budget-conscious business interests spent some $27,000,000 in putting social science methods to work in market research on production, personnel relations, purchasing, financing, and consumer preference. This was an increase of $17,000,000 over 1938.

In 1948, social science services cost the government $52,000,000, or three times more than in 1938. And last year the military establishment spent $7,000,000 for social science studies of human resources, personnel selection, morale factors, leadership, fatigue, and so on. The armed forces also employed the social sciences widely in World War II.

It seems to me it is important for American business to take advantage of the knowledge and skills of our social sciences in order to integrate business processes even more fully with the dynamics of American society.

I know this is easier said than done, but I also know how much American business can do once it makes up its mind. I should therefore like to suggest the following four-point program which might aid American business and businesspapers to take advantage of the techniques and findings of the social sciences which specialize in understanding the human personality and human society.

1. Add a leading educator to your board of directors; this will give you continuous, direct contact with the scientific groups engaged in studying our society;
2. Go to specific fields of education and add to your board of directors one or more social scientists—a great sociologist like Professor Robert M. MacIver of Columbia University, or a leading psychologist like Professor Gardner Murphy of the College of the City of New York; these will give you direct working contact with all the social sciences and the men and women who are making studies of specific interest to you;
3. Keep up to date a social science library in your office; the books,

magazines, monographs, and bibliographies published by various universities, scientific bodies, and individual scientists will give you and your staff valuable knowledge which you can transform for your own practical purposes;

4. To facilitate this work, assign one or more members of your staff to read, analyze, and abstract the social sciences publications that come to your office, and to feed you memos about them, so that you can conveniently keep in touch with developments in the field.

At the level of statistics, market research, and attitude polls American business already avails itself of the findings of the social scientist with considerable profit to itself and the country. Businessmen and business-papers can now take this process a step further and tap the hidden markets in the human personality by integrating their sales techniques with the discoveries which our 30,000 social scientists have made and are making about man and society.

THE DECISION-MAKERS*

American businesspaper editors see the world as one inseparable community; no part of the world can progress alone anymore than a single field can prosper without all industry prospering.

The destiny of our world community is in the hands of the decision-makers—less than 5 per cent of the population—who hold in trust the mass direction of men, materials, money, methods, markets, and the media of transportation and communication. These decision-makers must make the decisions which order and influence the lives of two billion people on this planet.

Who are these decision-makers? They are the readers of the technical and professional press of the world—those continuous textbooks of adult education, those publications that transmit the know-how, the know-what, and the know-when: the *intelligence* for making the correct top policy and operating decisions at the correct time, in all fields of human endeavor: industry, agriculture, finance, education, religion, science, medicine, communications, government.

The decision-makers are the managers of human enterprise, the exceptional men and women with creative abilities, with extraordinary

* Julien Elfenbein; a message sent, as President of the National Conference of Business Paper Editors, to the delegates to the Tenth International Congress of the Technical and Periodical Press in Paris, May 9, 1950.

talents for organization and administration. Today they are directly charged with the delivery of standards of living which will satisfy ordinary men and women with ordinary talents, who outnumber them 95 to 5.

The 95 per cent who work with their hands also make decisions: their decisions about our products and services are rung up on the cash registers in thousands of stores and shops. Their decisions on our policies and plans are registered in ballot boxes.

To make this next point, I address myself to editors as distinguished from publishers. If the press is to remain free and an important independent force, there must always be a sharp distinction between the *business* of the publisher and the *profession* of the editor, just as there must be a sharp distinction between the business of a corporation and the profession of its counsellors.

Who are the counsellors of business? They are lawyers, economists, bankers, public accountants, advertising and public relations men, insurance men, engineers, technical experts, designers, businesspaper editors, and the various managers of business organizations.

These counsellors and managers are *trustees,* in a sense, with obligations to the owners and stockholders, to the employees, to the government, and to the public.

The fortunes and destinies of the public, indeed the peace of the world, depend on the understanding and intelligent decisions of the managers of human enterprise, the readers of our technical and professional publications.

It is my fervent hope that close collaboration and exchange of ideas and technics may be accomplished between the publishers and editors of the American business press and the European business press as a means of bettering mutual economic understanding between masses of people.

Appendix

1. ALPHABET OF THE BUSINESSPAPER PUBLISHING INDUSTRY

AAAA	American Association of Advertising Agencies
ABC	Audit Bureau of Circulations
ABP	Associated Business Publications
AFA	Advertising Federation of America
AMA	American Marketing Association
ANA	Association of National Advertisers
ANPA	American Newspaper Publishers' Association
BBB	Better Business Bureau
BPEA	Business Paper Editors Association (Canada)
BNAC	Business Newspaper Association of Canada
CBPA	Chicago Business Paper Association
CCA	Controlled Circulation Audit
CED	Committee for Economic Development
FTC	Federal Trade Commission
ICIE	International Council of Industrial Editors
NAM	National Association of Manufacturers
NAMP	National Association of Magazine Publishers
NBP	National Business Publications
NCBPE	National Conference of Business Paper Editors
NYBPE	New York Business Paper Editors
NIAA	National Industrial Advertisers Association
PIB	Publishers Information Bureau
PPA	Periodical Publishers' Association
SBME	Society of Business Magazine Editors
SRDS	Standard Rate & Data Service

2. POSTAL LAWS AND REGULATIONS*

Postal Laws and Regulations divides mailable matter into four classes:

FIRST: Written matter
SECOND: Periodical publications
THIRD: Miscellaneous printed matter and other matter (weighing less than eight ounces) not in the first, second, or fourth class.

* John R. Pearson, Production Department, McGraw-Hill Publishing Co.; prepared especially for this volume in April, 1951.

FOURTH: Merchandise and other mailable matter weighing more than eight ounces and not in any other class.

Here we are concerned only with second-class matter and with the several sections of the regulations which govern the admissibility of such matter to the mails.

Postal Laws and Regulations state that "except as otherwise provided by law, the conditions upon which a publication shall be admitted to the Second-class are as follows:

1. It must be issued at stated intervals, as frequently as four times a year, and bear a date of issue, and be numbered consecutively.
2. It must be issued from a known office of publication.
3. It must be formed of printed paper sheets, without board, cloth, leather, or other substantial binding, such as distinguish printed books for preservation from periodical publications.
4. It must be originated and published for the dissemination of information of a public character, or devoted to literature, the sciences, arts, or some special industry, and having a legitimate list of subscribers."

The benefit which a periodical receives by being accepted as second-class mail matter is a much lower postage rate per pound than is enjoyed by mail matter of the other classes. In return, publications enjoying the second-class privilege must give up some freedom of action and abide by certain regulations which have been established to make sure that only periodicals which meet the four conditions outlined above are accepted as second-class matter by the post office.

Different rates of postages apply to the editorial and to the advertising portions of second-class publications. In order that the correct postage may be computed, such publications are required to file with the Postmaster of the office where the periodicals are regularly mailed a copy of each issue that has been marked or stamped to show the "Advertising" and the "Other than Advertising" pages or fractional pages.

In complying with this requirement, there is little difficulty in identifying as "Advertising" those pages which are occupied either by paid display or classified advertisements, or by filler ads, or by house display or classified space. To quote *Postal Laws and Regulations,* those are "obvious in character."

However, uncertainty more easily arises when it comes to marking editorial pages, some of which, given certain text or layout treatment, may be classed as "Advertising." The section of *Postal Laws and Regulations* which causes most of the trouble is Section 34.46, Paragraph C, in Title IV, 1948 Edition. This defines advertising as "display, classified, and all other forms of advertisements and all editorial or other reading matter for the publication of which money or other valuable consideration is paid, accepted, or promised . . ." and then goes on to state:

"... when a newspaper or periodical *advertises its own services* or issues, or any other business of the publisher, in the form of either display advertisements, or *editorial* or reading matter, this is advertising within the meaning of the law and shall be charged the advertising mailing rate therefor" (our italics).

Some editorial activities of a reader-promotional character must be classified as "Advertising" and so stamped in the marked copies. For example:

1. Whenever it is stated, in connection with listings of manufacturers' literature, catalogs, bulletins, etc., that the publication will send to readers upon request further information regarding the catalogs, etc., or that the publication will ask manufacturers to mail copies of their literature to readers when requested, the Post Office Department in Washington has ruled that all pages or columns occupied by such listings must be marked "Advertising." This is based on the opinion that since the announcements made to readers regarding the service offered always contain a reference to the listings, all the editorial text in Manufacturers' Literature Section is part of the announcement and is also promoting, i.e., advertising, a "service of the publisher" to the reader. *Reference:* Letter dated February 11, 1946 from Third Assistant Postmaster General, Washington, D.C., to Postmaster, Albany, N.Y. This letter reads:

"... The matter concerning the catalog service of the publishers including the 54 items thereunder on the six pages with the names of the manufacturers, dealers, etc., of the equipment described therein, from whom catalogs, bulletins, booklets, etc., on these items will be obtained by the publishers and sent to the persons requesting same, must be regarded as advertising a service of the publishers, and therefore, such matter in its entirety comes within the postal classification of advertising."

It is not that the items may be serially numbered, or that they include the names of the manufacturers, or even mention prices, which makes them "Advertising." It is solely the cross-reference to the items in a service-to-readers "advertisement."

2. Any endeavor to advise readers that reprints of feature articles are available may lead to difficulty with the post office. It has been found that the greatest response from readers comes when announcements that reprints are available are run with feature articles and refer to them specifically by title. In January, 1950 it was ruled by a postmaster, and later confirmed by the Third Assistant Postmaster General in Washington, that whenever such notices are an integral part of the article, even though they may be enclosed in printers' boxes, or separated from the balance of the text by heavy rules, the entire article must be regarded as part of the publication's promotional effort to dispose of reprints and therefore all the pages the text occupies must be considered "Advertising" and the higher advertising postage rate applied to them. If reference is made to the article, the same interpretation governs, even though the reprint notice is run elsewhere in the same issue.

This latest ruling should be noted particularly because prior to January, 1950, it had been understood that if a notice that reprints were available was placed within a box, that is, separated by heavy rules from the article to which it referred, only the area so set off was to be considered "Advertising." The January, 1950, ruling may be an indication that the Post Office is drawing the line betwen advertising and editorial more rigidly, although in a sense it is a logical extension of the 1946 ruling with respect to manufacturers' literature, referred to under 1 above. Publications, therefore, must be extremely careful not to offer reprints either for sale or free of charge and refer by title to an article in the same issue unless they are willing to pay the extra postage charge.

3. The wording of editorial announcements of annual awards, prize contests open to readers, offers of compensation for Letters to the Editor, or for solutions to operating problems sent in by readers, must be carefully scrutinized to prevent the Post Office from ruling these editorial sections to be "Advertising" in their entirety. For example, the main part of an announcement of an Annual Award should be written, if possible, without including any direct solicitation to readers to send in entries for the current "contest." The direct solicitation can then be concentrated in a few paragraphs which can be completely enclosed within a box, but must not refer to the accompanying text. Editors will probably remark that this is "a good trick if you can do it." To date there has been no indication that the Post Office would not accept classification of the material in such a panel as "Advertising" (it promotes a service of the publisher) and the remainder as "Other than Advertising."

Similarly, when prizes are offered for the best Letter to the Editor on a specific subject, or for the best answer to another reader's operating problem, the closing date of the contest and other conditions may be set up in a printer's box, and thus be separated from the announcement of the winner of the previous month's contest (if any) and from the printed text of entries received in connection thereof. If no reference is made within the panel to the printed letters and if nothing is said in the letters themselves which might make them adjudged to be solicitations to other readers to enter the contest, then only the announcement within the panel is held to be "Advertising," and the remainder of the department is accepted as "Other than Advertising." *Reference:* Letters from the Third Assistant Postmaster General, dated February 11, 1946, to Postmaster, Albany, N.Y. A paragraph from this letter reads:

"Letters written by contestants, announcements of prize winners, titles, etc., are regarded as other than advertising within the contemplation of the law when wholly free from solicitation for participation in the contest and not connected or tied up with the advertising with respect thereto, nor in the nature of a testimonial or boost of the publication itself or its services."

Note, however, that all text matter outlining the conditions of prize contests (that contained in advertising plates or copy as well as that written by editors) should be submitted to the Post Office for approval and checking to see that the contest rules conform with other sections of the *Postal Laws and Regulations* governing prize contests, etc. It is important to have Post Office prior approval of prize contests because if the terms of the contest are adjudged illegal after the magazine is printed and bound, the pages containing the rules of the contest will have to be torn out or the issue will be banned from the mails.

4. *Book Reviews:* The following is quoted from a letter written by the Third Assistant Postmaster General in April, 1946:

> "As a general rule book reviews are not regarded as advertising even when the prices of the books and the names and addresses of the publishers or the distributors of the books are given, unless the publishers of the publication in which the reviews appear . . . offer to furnish any books reviewed upon receipt of the list price, in which event the reviews are regarded as advertising and subject to postage at the advertising mailing rates. . . ."

MISCELLANEOUS

The following are other regulations which must be kept in mind:

Section 34.31 Indicia on Second-Class Matter: "The following indicia shall be conspicuously printed on one or more of the first five pages, preferably on the first page, of each copy of publications entered as second-class matter:

1. The name of the publication
2. Date of issue
3. Frequency of issue
4. Serial number
5. Known office of publication
6. Subscription price, if required by law
7. Notice of entry readings as follows: 'Entered as second-class matter at the post office at ————.' "

Note that 4 refers to the Volume and Issue number or to any other serial number, if any. No. 5 does not mean the publication's office address but that of the printer of the issue. It may be followed but not preceded by "Editorial" and "Executive Offices, . . ."

Section 34.53. Supplements to second-class matter:
"Publishers of matter of the second class may without subjecting it to extra postage, fold within their regular issues a supplement; but in all cases the added matter must be germane to the publication which it supplements, that is to say, matter supplied in order to complete that to which it is added or supplemented, but omitted from the regular

issue for want of space, time, or greater convenience, which supplement must in every case be issued with the publication."

Section 34.54. Acceptability as supplements:
"(a) Supplements shall in all cases bear the full name of the publication with which they are folded, preceded by the words 'Supplement to,' and also the date corresponding to the regular issue.
"(b) Supplements shall be folded with the regular issue they purpose to supplement. If mailed otherwise, postage shall be prepaid at the third- or fourth-class rates, according to their physical characteristics.
"(c) . . . proceedings of public or deliberative assemblies, boards, or conventions . . . may be mailed as supplemental matter.
"(d) Maps, diagrams, illustrations, or similar inserts which form a necessary part of a publication shall be admitted, either loose or attached, as part of the publication itself, with the words 'Supplement to _____.' "

Note that the foregoing paragraphs refer only to editorial matter. All advertising must be permanently bound in issue (see below).

Section 34.55. Parts and sections of second-class publications:
"(a) The regular pages of publications may be prepared in parts or sections. When so prepared, each part or section shall show the same title and date of issue, and bear appropriate designation such as "Part I or Section I, and Part II or Section II, and a statement shall be printed on the first page of the first part or section showing the number of parts or sections in which the issue is published." (*Note:* the word "Edition" should not be used to designate special sections or special issues.)

Section 35.56. Additions to and inclosures with second-class publications:
"(a) Mailable matter of the second-class shall contain no writing, print, or sign thereon or therein in addition to the original print, except as herein provided, to wit: the name and address of the person to whom the matter shall be sent, index figures of subscription book, either printed or written, the printed title of the publication and the place of its publication, the printed or written name and address without addition of the publisher or sender, or both, and written or printed words or figures, or both, indicating the date on which the subscription to such matter will end, the correction of any typographical error, a mark except by written or printed words, to designate a word or passage to which it is desired to call attention; the words Sample copy when the matter is sent as such, the words Marked copy when the matter contains a marked item or article, and publishers or news agents may inclose in their publications bills, receipts, and orders for subscriptions thereto, but the same shall be in such form as to convey no other information other than the name, place of publication, subscription price of the publication to which they refer and the subscription due thereon.

"(b) Coupons, order forms, and other matter intended for detachment and subsequent use may be included in permanently attached advertisements, or elsewhere in . . . periodicals, provided they constitute only an incidental feature of such publications . . . coupons . . . consisting of not more than one-half of one page shall be regarded as an incidental feature."

Split-run: Up to 1948, the Post Office did not permit split runs except in newspapers that normally issue several editions under the same date line for which changing text and layout have been the usual procedure for years. In early 1949, the Third Assistant Postmaster General's Office permitted testing advertisements in single edition second-class publications, provided the advertisement remained the same size so that no change in the percentage of advertising in any copies of the issues resulted. The acceptable changes may include copy, color, bleed, and even shifting the advertisement from the front to the back of the book, or vice versa.

Fold-Out Inserts: These must carry the Title and Date of Issue of publication in which bound, according to a notice appearing in the *Postal Bulletin.*

Stock and Type: Section 34.20 of *Postal Laws and Regulations* lists the following among conditions for admission as second-class matter:

Paragraph 3. "[Publication] must be formed of printed paper sheets, without board, leather, or other substantial binding, such as distinguish printed books for preservation from periodical publications: Provided that publications produced by the stencil, mimeograph, or hectograph process, or in imitation of typewriting shall not be regarded as printed within the meaning of this clause."

"Cover stock cannot be heavier than Government postcard stock otherwise it would be classed as not being 'formed of printed paper sheets' of which second-class publications are required to be." This means no stock heavier than 200 lb. can be used.

3. BUSINESSPAPER EDITOR'S BASIC BOOKSHELF

Adverb Finder (J. I. Rodale) Rodale Press, Emmaus, Pa.

A New Dictionary of Quotations on Historical Principles from Ancient and Modern Sources (H. L. Mencken)

Anthology of World Poetry (Mark van Doren, Editor)

Bible and Concordance

Business Executive's Handbook

Business Journalism (Julien Elfenbein, contains a style manual and glossary)

Constitution of the United States

Constitutions of Trade Associations (standards of practice, codes of ethics in your field)

Familiar Quotations (John Bartlett)

The Encyclopedia of Practical Quotations (J. K. Hoyt)

The Home Book of Quotations Classical and Modern (Burton Stevenson)

Directories and Year Books:
Advertising and Publishing Production Year Book
American Newspaper Publishers Association List of Advertising Agencies
American Women (Durward Howes, Editor American Publications, Inc., Los Angeles, 1940)
N. W. Ayer & Son Directory of Newspapers and Periodicals
Broadcasting-Telecasting Yearbook
Congressional Directory, official, of most recent sessions, U. S. Congress
Editor & Publisher International Year Book
Industrial Marketing Annual Market Data and Directory Number
International Circulation Managers Association Year Book (*Tulsa World,* Tulsa, Okla.)
McKittrick Directory of Advertisers
National Scholastic Press Association Manual and Scorebook (Fred L. Kildow, University of Minnesota, Department of Journalism)
Poor's Register of Directors
Public Relations Handbook
Standard Advertising Register
Standard Rate and Data Service (business publication section)
Statesman's Year Book
Telephone Directory (Local)
The Red Book (Local)
Ullrich's Periodical Directory
U. S. Camera Annual
The World Almanac and Book of Facts (New York *World-Telegram and Sun*)
Who Knows—And What
Who's Who in Advertising
Who's Who in America
Who's Who in Commerce and Industry
World Who's Who

Dictionaries:
Dictionary of Slang and Unconventional English
Authors and Printers Dictionary (Oxford University Press)
Crowell's Dictionary of English and Handbook of American Usage
Crowell's Handbook for Readers and Writers
Dictionary of American History
Dictionary of Modern English Usage (Fowler)
Dictionary of Religion and Ethics (Mathews and Smith)
Collegiate Dictionary (Webster)
New International Dictionary of the English Language (Webster)
Thorndike Century Senior Dictionary
Comprehensive Desk Dictionary (Thorndike-Barnhart)
Law Dictionary (Black)

Encyclopedias:
  Encyclopedia Britannica Atlas
  Encyclopedia of World History
  Columbia Encyclopedia

Handbooks:
  Handbook of Composition (Wooley)
  Legal Control of the Press (Thayer)
  Library of Essential Information (Lincoln)
  Secretary's Handbook (Taintor and Monroe)

Indices:
  Journalism Quarterly Index
  Fortune Magazine Index
  Agriculture Index

Miscellaneous:
  History of the Business Man (Beard, Miriam)
  Mythology (Bulfinch)
  Magna Carta
  Principles of Rhetoric (Hill)
  Printing Papers, Comprehensive Sample Book of
  Printing Ink Color Book
  Romance of Business (Selfridge)
  Shakespeare
  Standard Industrial Classification Manual; Exec. Office of President
  Style Manual (U. S. Government Printing Office)
  Style Manuals of *Tide* and *Printers' Ink*
  Style Manual (your own)
  Manual of Style Containing Typographical Rules Governing the Publications of the University of (Chicago)
  Thesaurus of the English Language (Roget)
  Type Speciman Book (your printer)
  Typographer's Desk Manual (De Lopatecki)
  Technics and Civilization (Lewis Mumford, contains a list of inventions)
  United Nations Charter
  Your publication, with indices, in bound copies
  Your own idea book—tear sheets, layouts, headlines
  Your own instructions to correspondents
  Your own duty specifications of staff members
  Your own directory of trade association officials and key people in your field
  Your own file of facts about your company, your field (annual reports, booklets, brochures, etc.)
  Your own calendar of seasonal events

4. PUBLISHER'S BOOKSHELF

MONOGRAPHS, BOOKLETS, PAMPHLETS

CCA 1951. (8-page pamphlet)
Defines controlled circulation and describes how CCA operates. Published by Controlled Circulation Audit, Inc. Contains list of publication members.

CCA Member's Guide. (16-page pamphlet)
New and amended rules adopted March 22, 1951, relating to the Audit Form and Report Form.

ABP Checklist to Aid Control of Businesspaper Publishing Costs. (24-pages, mimeographed for members) prepared by ABP
Cost Control Committee (N. O. Wynkoop, Chairman).

Audit Bureau of Circulations, W. H. Boyenton
Published by ABC, Chicago. History of Verified Circulation. Rules and Regulations of ABC.

Proposed Code of Professional Practices for Market Research. The American Marketing Association, New York, N. Y.

Printers' Ink Model Statute. Printers' Ink Pub. Co., New York, N. Y.

Code of Ethics. National Conference of Businesspaper Editors, New York, N. Y.

Code of Ethics. Society of Business Magazine Editors, National Press Building, Washington, D. C.

Principles of Practice. National Business Publications, New York, N. Y.

Advertising Principles. Advertising Federation of America, New York, N. Y.

ABP's Code of Ethics and Standards of Practice. (pocket-sized folder)
The principles believed in and practiced by ABP member-publications in their endeavor to continually improve their service to readers and increase their effectiveness to advertisers. Redesigned format, prepared in 1950. Associated Business Publications Inc., New York, N. Y.

"What's in it . . . for Us?" (32-page booklet)
Complete presentation on ABP's program and how it serves advertisers and agencies, the business press, and the people in the many departments of the organization's member-publications. Introduced at the Annual Conference, Hot Springs, Va., May, 1951.

Copy That Clicks. (48-page booklet)
Published in July, 1948, this booklet uses case histories to show how the fundamentals of effective businesspaper advertising may be put to work under a wide variety of conditions. Partial list of contents includes: When to go after inquiries and when not to . . . Long copy versus short copy . . . How to advertise when "you have nothing to sell" . . . What your dealers want to know. Published by ABP.

Hit the Road. (52-page booklet)
Fourth printing, August, 1951. This is still one of the most helpful

booklets ABP publishes. It shows how "to give the needle" to business-paper advertising by interviewing the users of a product. Tells whom to see . . . how to do it . . . where . . . how many calls to make, etc.

Specialized Advertising. (12-page booklet)
Emphasizes the importance of businesspaper advertising by championing the idea: "the right tool for the right job." Written by ABP's first Managing Director, Jesse H. Neal, in 1920, and reprinted in 1951 because the principles it sets forth are as timely and applicable today as they were over thirty years ago.

Guide to Effective Wartime Advertising. (60-page booklet)
1950 revision of ABP's famous *Guide* from World War II. Case histories which become a record of the kind of problems met and handled by businesspaper editors and advertisers in a mobilized economy.

20 Points—A Checklist of Factors That Make Business Paper Advertising Good
The yardsticks by which the judges have measured the success of advertisements that have been entered in ABP's annual competitions. Covers twenty basic rules governing objectives, coherence, illustrations, typography, copy, use of color, presentation of product uses, and cor-relation.

Winning Entries in the Second Annual Competition for Advertising in Merchandising Publications (1951).
"Why ABP Sponsors the Contest," "Reflections of the Judges," by Raymond S. Reed, Chairman of the contest judges; and illustrations of one advertisement from each of the 28 winning campaigns make up this 40-page booklet.

Winning Entries in the First Annual Competition for Advertising in Merchandising Publications (1950).
56-page booklet illustrated with advertisements from winning cam-paigns in the 1950 contest, and "Reflections" by Chairman Floyd L. Triggs. Published by ABP.

Winning Entries in the Ninth Annual Competition for Advertising in Industrial Institutional and Professional Publications (1951).
Covers the same ground as "merchandising awards" booklets: why the competition is sponsored, "Reflections" by Ernest T. Giles (Ketchum, MacLeod & Grove, Pittsburgh) Chairman of the judges, and illustra-tions of one advertisement from each of the 24 ABP campaigns.

The Place of Advertising and Promotion in Selling to Industry.
A complete report on the study of the influence of industrial advertising which Du Pont, in collaboration with Batten, Barton, Durstore, and Osborne and eight business publications made in 1949. Financed and produced by McGraw-Hill, *Oil and Gas Journal,* and Chilton, copies are available at 75¢ each.

Put Your Whole First Team on the Field. (12-page pamphlet)
Sydney H. Giellerup, advertising agency executive, Marschalk and Pratt

Company, shows the false economy of giving businesspaper advertising the Cinderella treatment, points out that businesspaper advertising deserves the best in planning and creative talent, and how advertisers gain when they make it possible for their agencies to give businesspaper advertising full play. Published by ABP.

A Page of Advertising Is a Page of Advertising. (8-page pamphlet)
Cameron Hawley, director of advertising and sales promotion for the Armstrong Cork Company, tells how he gets the most out of his businesspaper advertising. Published by ABP.

How General Electric Uses Business Papers. (8-page pamphlet)
In spotlighting the importance of advertising in business publications, J. Stanford Smith one of G. E.'s top advertising and promotion executives, gives the "why" and cites examples of "how communication and persuasion (by means of businesspapers) can increase the productivity of a sales staff." Published by ABP.

Intensive Advertising. (28-page booklet)
Practical help in the form of excerpts from a book written by John E. Kennedy, the man who first defined advertising as "Salesmanship in Print." Tells how advertisers and agencies can get a greater return on money invested in businesspaper space. Published by ABP.

How I Hamstrung My Advertising Agency. (16-page booklet)
In a "true confession," an ex-advertising manager writes about the raw deal he gave his advertising agency until he "saw the light," righted the wrong, and got immediate results. Good case history of advertiser-agency relationship. Published by ABP.

Mr. President: Meet Your Advertising Manager. (16-page booklet)
Introduces Mr. Ad. Manager to Mr. President. Tells what kind of chap the advertising manager is, what he knows and does, what he needs in order to do a good job, how to get the most out of him, why he should be regarded as one of the most important members of the team.

How Much Does No Advertising Cost? (8-page pamphlet)
Facts and reasoning behind the answers to the executive who orders "Cut out the advertising." Published by ABP.

Twenty-Five Areas in Which Publishing Practice and Rate Card Terminology Vary. (73-page report.) Pubilshed by ABP.
A study of 528 businesspapers by Robert Marshall and A. R. Venezian for ABP, May, 1951.

What Do Your Dealers Want to Know About the Products and Promotions You Are Trying to Sell? (4-page folder)
The high rating which 355 dealers, in all sections of the country, give merchandising papers is disclosed in this report of a survey which Dun and Bradstreet made for ABP's Merchandising Publications.

Research Data Prepared by Member Merchandising Papers. (4-page mimeographed list)
The titles of more than 100 Sales Training Aids, Opinion Surveys, Studies and Maps on Markets, Calendars, and Manuals which are

made available to advertisers and agencies by ABP's member merchandising papers, through headquarters. Separate pieces on the list provided background material for the preparation of more effective advertising for wholesalers, manufacturers, retailers, and distributors.

ABP Advertisements. (reprints)

These are reprints of the advertisements ABP runs in advertising and sales papers.

Businesspaper Journalism. (7-page mimeographed presentation)

Basic facts on the editorial and advertising services provided by business publications. Published by ABP.

Beneath the Surface in the "Paid-Free Battle." (reprint of an article in *The Advertising Agency*)

To create a better understanding of the subject, Fred Kendall, *The Advertising Agency's* senior editor, gives us a look at this controversial issue. Published by ABP.

A Comparison of Paid and Controlled Circulations. Paper read before Eastern Industrial Advertisers Association, Chicago, Dec. 1, 1951, by Russell L. Putman.

How to Buy Better Circulation Values, Putnam Publishing Co.

Are Readership Studies Valid Guides in Selecting Industrial Advertising Media? Paper read to St. Louis Chapter, NIAA, Dec. 6, 1951, by Russell L. Putnam, President, N.B.P.

MISCELLANEOUS PAMPHLETS

Standards for Commercial Arbitration. (12-page pamphlet)

Prepared by The American Arbitration Association, New York, N. Y.

Talk About Industrial Advertising, Published by NIAA.

Your Career in Printing.

Guidance booklet published by New York Employing Printers Association, Inc., New York, N. Y.

The Language of Pictures by George Dusenbury.

A manual published by McGraw-Hill Publishing Company.

Bibliography of Business Journalism (in preparation), ABP.

Business Paper Promotion Handbook, Chicago, SRDS.

Survey of Advertiser and Agency Buying Practices, Chicago, SRDS.

5. PROOFREADERS' MARKS

Marginal Marks.	Corresponding mark in proof.	Meaning.
ℰ	He made his mar¢k	*take out*
◡	He ma͡de his mark	*close up*
℘	He me̯de his mark	*invert*
⊏	⊏ He made his mark	*bring to mark*
tr	He his͟ made mark	*transpose*
stet	He made ~~his~~ mark	*let stand*
(t.?) (Qy)	He made ‸his mark	*query to author*
¶	Therefore, be it ‸Resolved	*make paragraph*
⊓	‸He made his mark	*indent em-quad*
w.f.	He ma̱de his mark	*wrong font letter*
l.c.	He made his Mark	*lower case letter*
sm.c.	He̱ made his mark	*small capital*
caps	He made his̱ mark	*capitals*
italic	He made his̳ mark	*put in italic*
roman	He made *his* mark	*put in roman*
⊙	He made his mark‸	*period*
⌄	He made Johns‸ mark	*apostrophe*
" "	He made his ‸mark‸	*quotation marks*
/=/	This is a trade‸mark	*hyphen*
#	He made his‸mark	*space*
∨ ∧	He∨made‸his mark	*even spacing*
⊍	He■made his mark	*push down space*
×	He ṃade his mark	*broken letter*
b.f.	He made his mark͜	*bold face*
‸	He made‸mark	*insert*
( ) parens	‸He made his mark‸	*put in parenthesis*
⌊ ⌋	‸He made his mark‸	*put in brackets*
○	He made ⑩marks	*spell out numbers or vice versa*

○ Circle around proof correction means change from original copy.

INDEX

Date Due